Presidential Spirits

Dan Coonan

Goose River Press
Waldoboro, Maine

Library of Congress Card Number: 2020936401

ISBN: 978-1-59713-212-1

First Printing, 2020

Cover art by James Slate.

Published by
Goose River Press
3400 Friendship Road
Waldoboro ME 04572
e-mail: gooseriverpress@gmail.com
www.gooseriverpress.com

To my parents, Tom and Kay, who instilled in all of us Coonans a deep appreciation for history and an abiding love of this country – so much of which I saw from my favorite spot in the back of our Chevy station wagon on three epic cross-country summer vacations.

And to Donna - for signing on with me to make a little history of our own. I'm loving the journey...

"President Washington had no political base to pander to, no election to raise money for, no party to place above the interests of his country, no fear of not being reelected to cloud his judgment, and no list of donors to pay back. We need more like him. Or even one like him—that would be a great start."

—Danny McFadden,
45th president of the United States

Table of Contents

Table of Contents

Table of Contents

Chapter One

Friday, January 20, 2017—4:35 p.m.
Satch

Eugene "Satch" Davis, White House chief usher for four decades of presidents, led us down the walkway of the West Wing colonnade, which linked our new residence with the Oval Office. I was still in a bit of a mental daze, and I'm certain that showed. Satch had been chatting with Denyse, leaving me alone with my thoughts. Leaving me alone with my thoughts, by the way, is never a good thing. It's always an adventure. That will become much more clear as we go along.

Denyse could talk to anybody, but Satch was particularly easy to talk with. These two instant friends could go all day. He looked over at me.

"Powerful speech today, Mr. President."

"Thank you so much, sir," I replied. "I appreciate that. I'm glad to have it over with, to be honest. With my background, I'm not really accustomed to speaking in front of the entire planet."

"Well, I think you'd best get used to it, Mr. President. And please call me Satch. Every first family does."

"Alright then."

"And you can call us Danny and Denyse," Denyse added.

"Oh yeah?" he responded, rather startled. "I don't suspect I'll be doing that anytime soon, but thank you just the same."

I like most people. Love most people actually. But I knew I was really going to enjoy Satch. He was a grizzled veteran of the White House and it showed—in the warmth of his smile, the ease of his conversation, his grace, and his confidence. He was a proud African American southern gentleman who looked to be in his mid-sixties, but I'm notoriously bad at judging someone's age. He was tall and lanky with a full head of short gray hair and leathery, weather-beaten skin. But it all worked. He was very distinguished-looking with an obvious ability to put anyone at ease that Denyse and I found quite charming. He was so well cast in his role—reminded me of an old high school football coach of mine. I thought immediately that not all could be bad about this government if it included any more like him.

"I have to ask," I said, looking over at Satch, "How did you get the nickname? Do you play the trumpet or belt out tunes in a gravelly voice?"

"No, but I like that guess," he replied. "I played ball what seems like a whole lifetime ago, and I pitched. I had an old coach who played in the Negro Leagues with the great Satchel Page. I guess I reminded him of Ol' Satch."

"Wow! That's even better! I love it! You must have had *some* game, baby, to earn that nickname."

"Oh, I threw pretty hard. Trouble is they didn't always go exactly where I intended them to." He paused for effect, then smiled right at me, and added, "But that certainly made it exciting."

"You're gonna love our Brett," Denyse chimed in. "He's a catcher."

"Well how 'bout that!" He was genuinely excited to hear it. "Some of my best friends are catchers—got me out of many a jam in life. Both on the field and off!"

Denyse lit up, "Oh, I can't wait to tell him about you!"

Satch turned his head, revealing a smattering of tiny scars on the side of his face, neck, and ear, quite unlike any birthmarks I'd ever seen. I couldn't ask him about them, of course, as much as I wanted to know the story. There had to be a story.

I pointed to the South Lawn on our left, "When's the last time anybody ever played catch out there?"

"Happens a lot more than you think, sir. Presidents are always asked to throw out the first pitches at ball games. With their egos, they aren't inclined to go in cold. And of course the Bushes were baseball people. They hosted T-ball games here. That was special. Reagan loved baseball too. He hosted a pony league game and the commissioner showed up—so did Roger Maris and Stan Musial."

"Alright, babe," I said looking at Denyse. "Let's add that to the to-do list. Maybe we'll get to meet Koufax."

Just then my new press secretary, Jed Rose, caught up to us. "Mr. President," he barked out, "I am sorry to bother you, but there appears to be an emerging focus by the press on the size of the inauguration crowd. They seem fixated on pointing out that Obama's crowd was much bigger than yours. I'm happy to challenge that for you, if you'd like."

"Listen," I responded, realizing that he needed some direction on the tone we were going to set. "The crowd was huge. I'm not troubled if it wasn't as large as Obama's or anyone else's. We'll be judged in the end by a much more pertinent set of metrics."

Then after a brief pause, I added, "*Was* it really smaller than Obama's?"

"Yes. The photos seem to make that pretty clear." Jed seemed almost apologetic about saying it.

"Believe me, my ego isn't so fragile that I need to have the largest inaugural crowd in history. I would have been as shocked as anyone if we did!"

"Thank you, sir," he replied, looking a bit relieved.

It really didn't bother me. Obama's inauguration was a monumental moment in our nation's history. Mine was more of an accident. I just kind of woke up one day to find out I had been elected. That might not be entirely true, but as you'll soon learn, it's pretty close.

A few moments later, Satch paused in front of the east entrance to the Oval Office. He looked back at Denyse and me as he opened the door. My heart skipped a beat as I took my first glance inside. Somehow this thing was more real at this particular moment than it ever had been before—more than the election night that lasted a lifetime, more than the day Denyse and I spent with the Obamas at Camp David in December, more than all the intelligence briefings I'd been receiving since November, more than all the hits I'd been taking from both the right and the left declaring I'm in way over my head.

Perhaps the most telling indicator of what a political novice I was at this point was the fact that I had not been in the Oval Office before. I thought of Kennedy agonizing over the fate of the world during the Cuban Missile Crisis, of Carter hosting Sadat and Begin to broker their historic Egypt–Israel peace accord, of Truman and his "The Buck Stops Here" sign, of Reagan insisting on wearing a coat and tie each time he entered this hollowed space, and, briefly, as much as I disliked thinking about it, of Clinton and his Oval Office escapades. You can't help it, unfortunately.

Denyse and I walked in wide-eyed as Satch held the door.

"They say this is the power center of the universe. You're going to accomplish great things from this office, sir."

"We'd better. There's certainly no shortage of daunting challenges ahead. The country is so hopelessly divided."

"I have great faith in you, Mr. President. I'll let you two check out your new digs."

Before closing the door and leaving us alone, he added, "By the way, I applaud your selection of photos and portraits."

"We only have a minute," Denyse cautioned as we entered. "You promised you'd give me plenty of time to get ready for tonight."

As we looked around, I saw everything I had asked the decorators to put up. Over the fireplace hung a classic painting of General Washington on horseback leaping over an old wooden fence following two of his dogs in mid-stride on a hunt. Positioned to the right of the fireplace was an iconic portrait of Lincoln deep in thought, seated and leaning forward with his right hand on his chin. On the left hung a photo of American soldiers pouring out of a landing craft storming Normandy Beach on their way to save the world. Photos of Frederick Douglass and Teddy Roosevelt hung to the left of the windows. And next to the door hung a photo of my parents on their very first date standing outside Notre Dame Stadium in 1954, about to attend a USC–Notre Dame football game.

A large framed photo of Jackie Robinson stealing home hung to the right of the windows—not the more famous one with Yogi Berra from the World Series, but the one from Wrigley Field. Jackie has been a hero of mine ever since I was a young kid hearing my dad tell me stories of seeing Jackie play in his youth. When I was in third grade, I attended a Catholic school and wanted to play flag football, but the school didn't have a team. So my dad convinced the public school to let me play on their third- and fourth-grade team. When I came home from my first day of practice with that public school team, my dad asked me how it went. I told him they treated me so poorly that I felt like Jackie Robinson. He was very proud that at my tender age I not only knew who Jackie was but also understood something of his plight, even if I couldn't fully grasp that my comparison was a bit shy of what Jackie had endured.

I looked over at Denyse. "They hung everything I asked them to."

"What do you say, Mr. President?" Denyse asked, doing her most sultry Marilyn Monroe imitation and wrapping her arms around me from behind as I looked out upon the Rose Garden.

"I'm as terrified as I am awestruck," I responded as honestly as any statement I had ever uttered.

"I am so unbelievably proud of you, and you are going to crush this!" Then she added with a smile, "Your next wife would have surely given you a lot more than a hug right there, but for this marriage, you'll have to wait until after the last of the balls tonight."

In what was quite possibly my single greatest lapse of judgment ever, a while back I had joked to Denyse about what my next wife would be like—completely kidding of course—but I'm afraid I hit a nerve of sorts and would not be hearing the end of it anytime soon. I now have no real choice but to just go with it whenever she brings it up, which, it turns out, is rather often. A bit too often.

"You're not kidding," I responded. "She will be absolutely insatiable. Her whole existence for living will be singularly focused on just keeping me happy—"

"Good luck to her on that one!"

"—at all times. That is, when she's not baking for me . . . or teaching her aerobics classes."

"That is some mighty powerful fantasy world you've created for yourself in that head of yours, McFadden. I don't even want to know what other fantasies you may have swirling around in there."

She paused a second before adding, "Oh, and Satch—I think we'll keep him!"

"You're damn right we're keeping him! Please God let all the decisions I have to make in this office be that easy."

We got to this place in a rather unorthodox manner...

Chapter Two

Thirteen Months Earlier—December 12, 2015
Just a Seat-filler

It all started with my rather unlikely "seat-filler" appointment to serve the remainder of Dianne Feinstein's vacant senate seat following her abrupt resignation to help care for her ailing husband. A remarkable turn of events, but hardly the sort of thing that one would look at as a launching pad to the White House. However, without this first serendipitous step, none of what followed would have occurred.

LOS ANGELES TIMES

GOVERNOR TAPS SILICON VALLEY EXEC TO FILL FEINSTEIN SEAT

by Melanie Mason

December 12, 2015. Sacramento—California Governor Jerry Brown has named Silicon Valley executive and philanthropist Danny McFadden to fill the U.S. Senate seat vacated by California's Senior Senator Dianne Feinstein in October. The governor announced the selection in a ceremony in Sacramento this afternoon. The move was somewhat unexpected as McFadden has never held public office. However, he has been a major contributor to political and charitable causes close to his heart and is well thought of in political and philanthropic circles throughout the state. Some Democrats privately questioned the selection, openly speculating about the choice of a relative unknown to fill the role rather than a stalwart Democrat with a proven progressive voting record. However, sources close to Brown suggest the move enables him to avoid having to choose between Lieutenant Governor Gavin Newsom and former Los Angeles Mayor Antonio Villaraigosa. Rising Democratic star Kamala Harris is widely expected to win California's other senate seat in the election next fall to replace Barbara Boxer, who is retiring.

Chapter Three

March 17, 2016
St. Patty's Day Rant

Then, just a few months later, this happened. Some might say I snapped. I was just doing what I thought any rational, reasonable person would do when thrown into the hyperpartisan, dysfunctional maelstrom that we've somehow allowed our political system to morph into. But again, this hardly seemed to be an event that would later prove to be an integral step on the fast track to the White House.

Transcript of Senator Danny McFadden's (D-CA) Speech on the Senate Floor, March 17, 2016

Mr. President:

Sometimes it takes the clear-eyed, fresh perspective of an outsider to fully comprehend just how far afield we are from what our system was designed to be.

I was thrilled and honored when Governor Brown appointed me to fill Senator Feinstein's seat for the state that I love so dearly. I wasn't naive to politics when I accepted this role. I helped run a congressional race twenty years ago, which was an eye-opener. And Denyse and I have been politically active all our lives, contributing to Democrats and Republicans alike. But it's fair to say after these past few months as senator that I didn't know the half of it.

Our present two-party system is no longer working and is

doing a dramatic disservice to our nation. 45 percent of Americans now consider themselves neither Democrat nor Republican. That's an all-time high. That is staggering. What is that telling us? And is anyone listening? Let me tell you what I have seen so far inside the "political industrial complex"— to borrow and slightly update a term coined by President Eisenhower.

During my first week in office, we were hit with dozens and dozens of communications from lobbyists, PACs, and special interest groups with implicit or not-so-implicit assurances of funding for my campaign for reelection if I would simply make a written commitment staking out positions consistent with theirs. The political consultants the party lined up for me counseled me to view fundraising, campaigning for reelection, and toeing the party line as my three primary goals. Needless to say, I fired these consultants.

How and why did we get here as a country? Someone should not have to campaign for two and half years in order to be elected president, and anyone willing to put themselves through such an absurd process should be disqualified as a candidate. George Washington raised no money and spent no time campaigning in either of his elections, and he received 100 percent of the Electoral College vote. Heck—he didn't even *want* to be president! Maybe that was his most endearing quality—and one we should think about as we select our presidents, governors, and other elected officials.

Do we really want to elect people who are willing to devote years of their lives to campaigning around the country, pandering nonstop to every conceivable special interest group and begging for money? Not to mention the requirement that they must belittle their opponents each day in their talking points and distort their opponents' records with nasty attack ads.

I do worry about this country. I worry about it deeply. Each party appears on the verge of producing a woefully inadequate choice to the American public. The promises each Democratic or Republican candidate must make during the primary to secure the election necessarily renders them unacceptable to the 45 percent of Americans who consider themselves politically independent. For the best evidence of this, look no further than John McCain—the one politician most closely associated with crossing party lines at meaningful moments. Even he felt the need to compromise his principles during his presidential campaign to conform to the party in both his selection of a vice president and the reversal of his principled stance on the use of torture. Shameful, but that's what our system spits out.

The truth is that after years of watching all this nastiness, corruption, pandering for money, and placing party squarely above country, I reached a point long ago where I was proud I was not a Republican and ashamed I was a Democrat. I now stand firmly with that 45 percent that considers both parties unpalatable.

I will continue going about my business in the Senate voting for and crafting legislation consistent with what I believe to be in the best interests of California and the country. I don't want to raise money and be beholden to any group, party, or special interest. I will be beholden only to the truth and to the merits of those causes and ideas that make our state and our country better. As such, I am reregistering as an Independent as of today and will no longer be a Democrat. I will caucus with any group that wishes my input and viewpoint.

I realize that this in all likelihood renders me unelectable in our present two-party system with all its built-in self-perpetuating structures. So be it. I can't see a way to proceed effectively in this system without compromising my principles, contorting my values, and shredding my integrity. I won't make that Faustian bargain that seems to be a requirement in today's political landscape.

I would have loved to play a role in fixing this. These structures, however, appear to be too powerful for me to tackle. I'll leave that to others—to the politicians. They've created a self-perpetuating system that preserves their power but does little else. Confronting that reality and bringing about meaningful and wholesale change will necessitate a skill set that I don't believe I possess and a massive grassroots desire for change that I'm not sure exists. I lack the charisma, the oratorical skills, the grassroots following, and perhaps most of all, the tolerance for the frustration necessary to pull this off. This will undoubtedly be a long and arduous struggle with fierce opposition and many, many setbacks. I'll leave that fight for a finer man—or woman—than myself.

I'll be fine and so will Denyse and the kids. We'll go back to our wonderful life in Los Gatos. I'll happily plug back into Silicon Valley with my tech firm, and Denyse and I will reengage with our homelessness fight. We'll be more than fine. We have been incredibly blessed in life, and I thank God for that every day.

Meanwhile, I look forward to working tirelessly on behalf of this great state through the end of my term.

Thank you, fellow senators. God bless. Mr. President, I yield the floor.

Chapter Four

March 27, 2016
Overnight Sensation

So, evidently, my St. Patty's Day rant turned me into something of an overnight cult hero. While I was somewhat uncomfortable with all the media attention and the inevitable hits from both the right and the left for "grandstanding," I was tremendously encouraged to see that this independent message resonated with so many. They were now making their voices heard. At this point, I figured perhaps my method of exiting the stage would do more for the cause than I could ever do from the inside. Therefore, I certainly did not regret it because it gave me a platform from which to effectively convey my message of civility, bipartisanship, and country over party—a message people were not getting from any other sources.

Interview Between Senator Danny McFadden and Talk Show Host Michael Smerconish of Sirius XM Radio's POTUS Channel, March 27, 2016

Michael Smerconish: Welcome back to the *Michael Smerconish Program.* I'm very excited to talk to the guest we have in the on-deck circle. If you've been paying any attention to the political discourse this week—whether on this show or any others—you have undoubtedly heard about Danny McFadden, the relatively new senator from California who created quite a buzz about ten days ago when he very publicly announced his intention to leave the Democratic Party and register as an Independent. I believe his lengthy speech on the senate floor that justified his decision is equally significant. He spoke of a broken political system that seems to exist primarily to further the interests of the parties and the special interests.

McFadden certainly seems to have struck a chord not only with so many of you folks in my audience but also with independents and others throughout the country. If our daily online polls of the audience this week have told us anything, it's that this message resonates with much of the population.

Joining me now by telephone from Washington is Senator McFadden. Thank you so much for agreeing to spend a few minutes with us this morning, Senator.

Senator McFadden: My pleasure, Michael. Thanks for having me.

Smerconish: Let me ask you, Senator, are you familiar with the movie *Jerry Maguire*?

McFadden (laughing): Yes, of course, I am. I love that movie!

Smerconish: Many in my audience are calling your recent decision and your speech justifying it a "Jerry Maguire moment"—where one speaks truth to power and takes a principled stance that may not be in his or her best interests.

McFadden: Ha ha! First of all, I love that analogy. However, when Jerry took his public stand, at least he had Renée Zellweger walking out the door with him.

Smerconish: And the fish.

McFadden: Yes—can't forget the fish! By contrast, I'm rather out there on an island with this, which is part of my point.

Smerconish: Oh sir, with all due respect, that's where I think you are wrong. As you know, your very raw, heartfelt diatribe went viral and made you a social media sensation and the new public face of the independents in this country, who are fed up with the present state of two parties.

Let me ask you this, what did you hope to achieve with your decision and your supporting statement?

McFadden: That's a great question. To be honest, I wasn't fishing for this sort of reaction or to start a movement. Frankly, I didn't think this type of reaction was possible. My reasons were perhaps far less ambitious. I wanted to fully explain to my constituents why I was not consistently voting the party line, so they could adjust their expectations of me about everything: my positions, my voting record, and even whether or not I'll seek reelection. Additionally, I obviously wanted to call attention to the sad state of affairs politically in the country as I see it and attempt to motivate others who follow and others more capable than me to take up that cause.

Smerconish: Leon Panetta, perhaps one of the most respected elder statesmen in the country—and certainly one with a reputation for crossing party lines and putting the country first—penned an editorial for the *LA Times* that got picked up everywhere. Panetta's Op-Ed referenced your statement and encouraged the country to heed your call. Other respected voices have even suggested you as an alternative to what they view as, shall we say, our "less than worthy" slate of presidential candidates. Have you reevaluated your ambitions with respect to this cause?

McFadden: I guess I'm flattered that you think I might be able to impact this. However, I'm afraid it's a much bigger problem than one first-term, fill-in senator can tackle.

Smerconish: Let's take a step back for a second. For the benefit of those who may not be aware of your statement, please give us the CliffsNotes version of the point you are making.

McFadden: Sure thing. So, these days, our two parties exist primarily for the purpose of remaining in power and defeating the opposing party—a goal that is often at odds with the best interests of the country. We don't have any more George Washingtons—phenomenal leaders whose primary allegiance is to the country. The way we select presidents in this country—and governors and members of Congress for that matter—is deeply flawed. Forty-five percent of the country is neither Democrat nor Republican, which means that in many states, those folks have little or no say in who gets on the ballot. As the political middle flees the parties, the parties are left with the extremists at both ends, who, therefore, produce candidates at the ideological fringes who can't work together and have no interest in doing so.

Smerconish: So how did we get to this point?

McFadden: I believe we have several contributing causes. First, generations of gerrymandering has created extremely partisan districts. With the advent of partisan cable television and talk radio, we now have a billion-dollar industry that profits immensely from fueling the great partisan divide and creates an echo chamber and a partisan lens by which people only get exposed to their own viewpoints. And don't even get me started on the money. There's far too much money in politics, which hopelessly corrupts both the system and the politicians themselves.

If you read Washington's Farewell Address, he predicted many of the cancers we see in the system today. It's telling that both Hamilton and Jefferson—two fierce rivals from opposing parties—felt compelled to come together to convince Washington to serve a second term for the benefit of the country. We could all learn some lessons from those three gentlemen.

Smerconish: Would you care to comment on the current presidential race?

McFadden: Only to say that our choices make my point for me. I'm afraid that this election could provide us with the most telling example of how two parties are producing for us candidates who have no legitimate chance of uniting the country and bringing us forward as a nation.

Smerconish: I'm sure you've seen the reports of a group of well-funded and well-organized independents exploring the idea of getting your name on the ballot in all fifty states in time for November.

McFadden (laughing)**:** I'm very flattered, indeed. I'm thrilled my little rant provided a spark that's leading independents and others to rise up and say "Enough is enough!" and acknowledge that we are much better than this as a nation.

Smerconish: If they are able to get your name on the ballot, will you run?

McFadden: I think the ballot access issue for an independent candidate is, at best, a tall order—precisely because of the hold on it the two parties have.

Smerconish: You haven't answered my question.

McFadden: I think it's highly unrealistic.

Smerconish: I'm not hearing you say no.

McFadden: OK. I won't give you a General Sherman answer. I do believe deeply in this cause. If they have no other logical leaders as the face of this movement, and I can help, then yes, I'd lend my name. I don't think I stand a realistic chance of actually being elected, but perhaps the seeds of other victories could be planted.

Smerconish: If my audience is any indication, even that, I suspect, will be music to this nation's ears.

Thank you for your time, Senator. Will you come on again as this movement gains steam, as I'm predicting it will?

McFadden: I highly doubt that it will, but I would gladly come back.

Smerconish: Alright, sir. I will hold you to that.

(after a commercial break)

Smerconish: You heard it, ladies and gentlemen. I think that's what many of you were hoping for. Please call me to offer your thoughts on the interview and what, if any, chance you think there is that this movement could continue to gain steam. You can also tweet me or post on my Facebook page. What do you think?

I'll tell you one thing, if ever there was a chance for a viable independent, this is the year. Each of the likely candidates from the major parties—Hillary, Bernie, Cruz, and Trump—have high negatives. McFadden has almost no political experience, but perhaps this the year the county is ready for that as well.

TC Scornavacchi: Michael, before you take a call please explain the General Sherman reference. You may have lost some people with that.

Smerconish: Yes, of course. It was General William Tecumseh Sherman, of Civil War fame, who first said about running for president and I'm paraphrasing: "If nominated, I will not run; if elected, I will not serve." By the way, I believe he also said something to the effect that he'd rather serve time in a penitentiary than the White House.

So, what I'm hearing from McFadden is the opposite—

that while he may not aggressively campaign, he would nonetheless run if nominated and would serve if elected.

TC: I agree that this election provides an opening for an independent. Have we ever come close to electing an independent?

Smerconish: Ross Perot got about 20 million votes as an independent in 1992. Many think that helped get Bill Clinton elected, although Nate Silver has disputed this claim. One thing McFadden may have going for him now is the Internet and social media. It is so much easier today to get the word out and acquire that name recognition and a national following. If the last ten days are any indicator, I'd say it's at least possible.

Alright, folks. Call me and chime in on the political phenomenon that is Danny McFadden.

Chapter Five

October 8, 2016—8:20 p.m.
Access Hollywood

October 8, 2016 and the release of the Trump–Billy Bush *Access Hollywood* video was a game changer. By then, various independent political groups across the nation had already organized to get me on the ballot in all fifty states. The Trump–Billy Bush video sent that effort into overdrive. Overnight, the country's attitude about me as an independent candidate went from "Ooh, isn't that cute—there's an independent candidate" to "Holy cow! There's a viable alternative on the ballot to these two unpalatable candidates." This was pretty heady stuff. I had the great fortune of being in the right place at the right time. However, even with this seemingly disqualifying Trump video and the record-high negatives Hillary Clinton was polling at, my makeshift, involuntary candidacy was, at best, still a long shot. I was neither campaigning nor raising money. But meanwhile, both of these other two campaigns were imploding.

CNN's *Anderson Cooper 360°*

Anderson Cooper: Good evening. Tonight we are addressing the fallout over the release yesterday of an explosive *Access Hollywood* video shot in 2005 that shows a conversation between Donald Trump and *Access Hollywood* host Billy Bush. In the video, Trump is seen and heard using vulgar language to describe actions he suggests he often takes with women he just met that some tonight are saying can reasonably be described as sexual assault. The release of this incredibly damaging video is only the latest twist in what has to be one of the most remarkable presidential campaigns of our time.

Trump is not the only one struggling. This presidential race is the first in history where both of the major party candidates entered the race with negative favorability rating numbers that exceed their positives. Hillary Clinton has been unable to move past her e-mail scandal or change the national narrative about her in any way. Worse yet, with one month left until the election, 68 percent of likely voters consider her to be dishonest and untrustworthy. Both candidates of the major parties seem to be floundering, which sets the table for our discussion tonight.

We are joined tonight by Chief Political Analyst Gloria Borger, Democrat Political Strategist Paul Begala, CNN Chief Legal Analyst Jeffrey Toobin, Editor of the *Weekly Standard* and CNN Contributor Bill Krystol, and CNN Senior Policy Analyst David Gergen, who has served many presidents.

Gloria, independents and others who support Senator Danny McFadden have been emboldened by these recent events. Even a few short weeks ago, it would've seemed crazy to even suggest this, but do you see a potential path for him to victory?

Gloria Borger: I certainly do, Anderson. Recent polls estimate that as much as 46 percent of the country identify with neither of the two major parties. Only roughly 29 percent identify as Democrats and 25 percent as Republicans. How telling is that? I would suggest that the number-one reason independents don't vote for an independent candidate in presidential elections is that they don't believe the independent is capable of winning. As McFadden, who has a tremendous favorability rating, gains steam and the other two implode, I think it is possible. These campaign mishaps and the high negatives of both Trump and Clinton help independents make the case that he can win.

Jeffrey Toobin: Are you saying he would win a majority of the electoral college, Gloria? That McFadden could win enough states to get a majority of the Electoral College? In order to get elected, he would have to because the more likely scenario might be that he would take away just enough votes from the other two, ensuring that no candidate receives a majority of the votes in the Electoral College. In that case, the House of Representatives would vote to elect the president from the top three vote getters.

Cooper: In that case, with a Republican–controlled House, Trump would be elected.

Toobin: Yes, most likely—although each state delegation is only permitted to cast one vote. However, I do believe that would be the result—unless the House of Representatives felt Donald Trump was simply not fit. The bottom line is that it's terribly hard for an independent candidate to win if the election is decided in the House of Representatives.

Cooper: Bill, can you any see Republicans voting for McFadden?

Bill Kristol: After that video, yes. I think it's disqualifying for Trump, and it should be. When you couple that with his mocking of a disabled reporter, he is disastrous for the Republican brand. He is not a traditional conservative in the first place, and it's difficult, if not dangerous, to attempt to predict what he will stand for once in office. McFadden won some Republican hearts when he publicly abandoned the Democrats. But clearly the best thing about him for Republicans is that he's not Hillary. The Republicans will take an Independent in the office and political gridlock over more of the Clintons any day.

Cooper: Paul, can he pull this off? He has some significant Silicon Valley financial support and an enormous

21

grassroots effort led by multiple independent organizations nationwide who managed to get him on the ballot in all fifty states.

Paul Begala: I would not count Hillary out. If McFadden weren't in the race, this *Access Hollywood* video would make this a slam dunk for Hillary. The last president from outside of the two traditional parties was Millard Fillmore way back in 1850. Think about that! And the last independent president was George Washington. McFadden is the new shiny object, but he's completely untested. Let's face it, the most popular player on most NFL teams is usually the backup quarterback—until they finally call his number and he comes in and throws a pick-six on the first snap.

David Gergen: Anderson, as hard as it might be to believe, I like McFadden's chances. Both Clinton and Trump have been victims of their own self-induced October surprises. What we've seen here recently in this truly remarkable campaign is a sort of parting of the Red Sea. There is now a clear path for McFadden to lead his army of independents with his rod or staff all the way to the White House.

Chapter Six

November 8–9, 2016
Election Night

As unlikely as all the leadup to this point had been—and each new step had been more improbable than the last—none of that came close to matching election night for pure, unadulterated, mind-blowing, shock.

ABC Election Night Coverage

November 9, 2018—2:10 a.m.

George Stephanopoulos: Welcome back to ABC's election night coverage. It is just past 2:00 a.m. in New York, and what a historic and memorable night this has been. Matthew, this is really something! We have witnessed one of the biggest upsets in American history.

Matthew Dowd: This is without question the biggest and most historic political upset news story in a hundred years—in at least a hundred years! Danny McFadden—who didn't even enter a single primary, who never actively campaigned or aggressively sought money, and didn't even clearly select a running mate—has been carried into office by a grassroots and social media wave that swept the country with astonishing speed.

Cokie Roberts: George, the American people have spoken tonight! They have rejected the two major parties that have dominated our political system since before the Civil War.

Stephanopoulos: I believe you have to go all the way back to Millard Fillmore in 1850 to find a president who was neither a Democrat nor a Republican.

Roberts: That's right. Fillmore was the last president from outside the two major parties—unless you count Lincoln in 1864 who technically ran with the newly-formed National Union party together with Southern Democrat Vice President Andrew Johnson.

Stephanopoulos: And McFadden wasn't even directly involved in politics a year ago.

Roberts: Yes. And although he does have very high favorables and a message that resonates, a lot of what we saw today, by looking at the exit polls, seemed to be more of a rejection of the other two candidates than an acceptance of McFadden or his plans for the country. He appears to be seen by the voters as an adequate alternative to two really unpopular candidates.

Jonathan Karl: The exit polling also shows that the electorate clearly felt they just simply could not trust either Trump or Clinton. No candidate has ever won the presidency with untrustworthy numbers as high as either of theirs.

Stephanopoulos: What else do you see in those polls, Jonathan? What kind of coalition did McFadden cobble together to pull this off?

Karl: Well, George, to get 46 percent of the popular vote, he swept the independent vote with 86 percent of all those who didn't identify as either Democrat or Republican. He also drew from both parties. Trump still carried white males and blue-collar voters without college degrees. McFadden and Clinton essentially split the minority vote. Hillary won New York, New England, and DC. Trump took several states out West and in the South, but with the exception of New York, McFadden dominated nearly all of the more densely populated states: California, Florida, Illinois, Michigan, Ohio, Pennsylvania, and Texas. *ABC News* now projects he'll win 287 votes in the Electoral College. Trump appears likely to get 187 and Clinton 64.

Roberts: What is really significant here, George, is that McFadden carried the female vote, and he got 71 percent of voters under age thirty-five. He also did really well with Catholics.

Stephanopoulos: Again, what do you make of the fact that he's only really been involved in politics for a year?

Dowd: I really think that helped him, George. Congress has even higher negatives than Trump and Clinton, and as a relative outsider, particularly an Independent, he's not really tainted by that.

Karl: Well, let's face it, guys, he's barely had time to take a position on anything. I'd be a lot more popular, too, if I never had to take a side. And he never went negative in the campaign because he never had to—Hillary was bashing Trump while he was absolutely crushing her. That enabled McFadden to stay above the fray.

Stephanopoulos: Cokie, it's been a long time since we've elected someone with so little political experience.

Roberts: Yes, George, it has. And McFadden has technically never been elected to public office—heck he's never even run for office—and he hasn't even served a year in the Senate. Of course, Ike had no political experience either, but he was a famous war hero. Before that, you'd have to go back to Woodrow Wilson in 1912, who had only been governor of New Jersey for two years before winning the presidency. Herbert Hoover had never run for any office prior to the presidency, but he had served in the Cabinet under previous administrations.

Stephanopoulos: McFadden's victory, of course, now raises a fascinating legal and constitutional issue pertaining to the vice presidency. Dan Eggen of the *Washington Post* has been writing about this at length. The nationwide effort to get McFadden on the ballots of each state was not particularly well coordinated. And he didn't help matters by not even formally naming a running mate. So, although the various independent organizations across the country managed to successfully get him placed on the top of the ticket on every state ballot, what resulted was a hodge-podge of different running mates on state ballots, and, in a few states, no running mate at all.

Roberts: George, as crazy as it sounds, it may have been calculated on the part of some of his backers. Whether that's true or not, I don't know, but it certainly seems to have helped him. Had he actually chosen a running mate, that decision would have defined him. And to Jonathan's point, it would have been a decision—one of the only decisions—by which he could've been evaluated. McCain's selection of Palin hurt him in '08. If McFadden had chosen a Democrat, he may have lost the right-of-center independents, and vice versa. Chances are slim he could've chosen an independent that would've helped him an all regions. Those who appeared on the ballot with him in the various regions tended to appeal to independents in those areas.

Stephanopoulos: So what happens when the Electoral College casts its votes on December 19?

Dowd: There are a few possibilities. McFadden's electors are pledged to vote for the candidates that appeared on the ballots of their state. If they all vote as pledged, McFadden wins the presidency, but no candidate would obtain the required 50 percent of the votes necessary to be elected vice president. In that case, the Senate would select the vice president. That likely means Mike Pence will serve with McFadden.

The *Post* has suggested that perhaps McFadden could name a candidate now and encourage all of his electors to vote for that person, in which case perhaps his candidate may, in fact, get more than half of the electoral votes for vice president. However, that would require electors to ignore their pledge requirements.

Stephanopoulos: Is that possible, legally speaking?

Roberts: There have been more than 150 instances of so-called "faithless electors" in history. Over the years, most states have attempted to curtail this by enacting fines or penalties or simply attempting to compel the electors to vote as pledged. Each state's laws are different in that regard, however, and many have no laws of any kind to restrict it. If electors do choose to defy their state laws, it could create a huge legal mess—one that would have to be sorted out state by state.

Stephanopoulos: Has there ever been a president elected with a majority in the Electoral College whose vice president failed to get a majority?

Roberts: Actually, George, there has. In 1836, Martin Van Buren won the Electoral College, but the South Carolina electors abstained from voting for his running mate, Richard Johnson. As a result, no vice presidential candidate got 50 percent of the electoral vote, so the Senate was called upon to elect a vice president. In the end, the Senate did select Johnson. I think this Republican Senate would relish the prospect of selecting one of their GOP colleagues to serve with McFadden.

Chapter Seven

November 22, 2016
The Vice Presidential Sweepstakes

Since no one really anticipated that I could win, no one really focused on the consequences for the selection of my vice president. I know that Dan Eggen of the *Washington Post* and a few others who deal in the weeds of these elections had spelled it out, but that never really rose to the nation's radar screen. With different names on the ballot with me in different states, no one VP candidate would get a majority of the vote in the Electoral College. Republicans controlled the Senate, and, therefore, the selection of the VP. Consequently, we needed to reach some sort of backroom deal with the Republicans or else we'd be looking at four years with Mike Pence.

The VP position, of course, doesn't have to play a critical role in an administration. If we didn't like the VP selection, we could freeze the VP out—it's happened many times before. However, I desperately wanted to see if the Republicans would be willing to try to work something out.

WASHINGTON POST

MCFADDEN SEEKS SENATE DEAL ON COMPROMISE VP CANDIDATE

by Leonard Martin

November 22, 2016—President-elect McFadden's top congressional adviser, Christina Murphy, met on Capitol Hill today for over three hours with senate Republican leaders seeking a compromise candidate for vice president that would be acceptable to both the new administration and Republicans. This comes in advance of next month's electoral college vote. If all electoral college votes are cast according to their pledges, no vice presidential candidate will attain a majority of the votes necessary. McFadden won 287 presidential electoral votes with Trump winning 187 and Clinton 64. However, the vice presidential nominee appearing on the ticket with McFadden differed from state to state. Consequently, none of those candidates will receive enough votes necessary to win. If electors vote according to pledge, Tim Kaine and Mike Pence will emerge as the top two vote getters. The Senate will then be called upon to choose a vice president from those two candidates. Christina Murphy is seeking to come to some sort of deal with senate leaders on a compromise candidate. The new administration hopes such a deal with the Senate will avoid a long and drawn-out legal quagmire that could be triggered if McFadden directs his electoral college voters to unite behind one particular vice presidential candidate, which is in violation of many of the states' laws requiring them to vote in favor of the candidate who appeared on their ballots and won the race in their particular states. Several sources speaking on the condition of anonymity have stated that Republican leaders have not warmed to the possibility of such a deal.

Chapter Eight

November 29, 2016
A Major Decision at CordeValle

By the time I entered the large executive boardroom in the main building at the CordeValle Resort, the room looked quite lived-in. Empty coffee cups were strewn everywhere, notes were scribbled on whiteboards adorning the walls, and laptops and tablets crowded the long conference table amidst scattered papers. This distinguished collection of bright minds was certainly doing its damnedest to look busy. I had no doubt that the group had been working feverishly. The sight of this dream team assembled for this cause invigorated me.

CordeValle is a gorgeous, rather secluded resort tucked away in the foothills of the Santa Cruz Mountains south of San Jose. On this spectacular November day in Northern California, an impressive group of advisers and experts had come together to brainstorm and evaluate options and craft a legal or political solution to avoid the Electoral College or the Senate serving up Mike Pence or Tim Kaine as my vice president. The gently rolling hills dotted with live oaks and sycamores amidst rows of grapevines offered up a serene cinematography that contrasted sharply with the terribly vexing dilemma in our lap.

However, I felt the we had the proper team to take this on. Leon Panetta—former head of the CIA, defense secretary, White House chief of staff, and Democratic congressman—had come over from his home in nearby Monterey. He had a reputation for getting beyond politics and party, serving both Democratic and Republican presidents. I met him years ago at a conference we both participated in at his alma mater Santa Clara University, and we had kept in touch. He was happy to help my cause, although I knew it would be a tall order to get him to return to DC.

Next up we had David Gergen, who had similarly served both Democratic and Republican presidents and also enjoyed a decidedly nonpartisan reputation. He had also agreed to serve in my administration as a senior adviser, albeit on a largely part-time basis. With my utter lack of experience, I was willing to accept any bit of assistance from him I could get.

In addition to providing first-rate advice, these two gentlemen fit nicely within the unique "brand" that defined my entire political existence—placing country way over politics and party.

We also had Harold Ford, a former congressman from Tennessee, who came from a prominent political family. He had agreed to work full-time as a senior policy adviser in my administration, and I looked forward to working with him.

Terri Drake, my new chief of staff, was also with us. I'd served on several boards with her in Silicon Valley, and I was absolutely thrilled to have her agree to go to DC with me. A Stanford grad with a Wharton MBA, she'd worked for Governor Schwarzenegger and as a VP at Google running one of its "moonshot" projects. She was eminently capable and so incredibly well connected—I needed her desperately. And no woman had ever before served as a White House Chief of Staff.

Harvard Law Professor Laurence Tribe also agreed to join us for this roundtable discussion. I was vaguely familiar with his reputation as one of the brightest constitutional lawyers in the country, and many people I had consulted regarding this challenge pointed me in his direction.

Rounding out the team that day was Karen Nevarez, a UC Berkeley and Boalt Hall law grad who had worked for Gavin Newsom. She agreed to join us in DC as a senior policy adviser. We also had Christina Murphy ("Murph"), a longtime Capitol Hill behind-the-scenes staffer who'd spent ten years as John McCain's chief of staff. She came on as my top congressional advisor.

Needless to say, this was an extremely distinguished group. I felt an enormous sense of gratitude just to have them devoting their time and talent to my effort. And just being in their company inspired the heck out of me. Each of them was eminently more qualified to tackle the task at hand than I was. That realization filled me with a deep sense of both humility and gratitude.

They stood up and applauded as I entered the room. This was my first postelection interaction with so many of them. I meandered around the room amidst a sea of high fives, handshakes, and bro hugs.

I addressed the group. "First of all, I am so incredibly grateful for your time, effort, and counsel devoted to this cause. The task in front of us is enormous—not just on this particular issue, but on everything we are about to confront in the next few years. We've clearly tapped into something, but the resistance we are about to face from the two parties will be fierce. I love what each of you stands for—that is precisely what I am after, and, more importantly, what the majority of this country clearly wants at this moment in time. Over many generations, a fairly powerful dynamic has built up, and it's designed to work against us. That whole Washington political infrastructure must now be reshaped to better suit the interests of this country and its citizens. But I wouldn't be here if I didn't think we could pull it off, and I don't think you would be, either. However, some causes are well worth the fight regardless of the likelihood of success. Some hills are worth dying on. This is clearly one of them."

The room applauded again, even more vigorously than before. "Put me in, Coach!" yelled Terri Drake. She chose those words aptly, playing to my passion for baseball. The rest of the room fed off her enthusiasm. So did I. She'd clearly passed her first test as chief of staff. I knew I would need a whole lot more of that from her in the years to come if we were going to inspire the troops and really pull this thing off.

The commotion died down after a few moments and everyone took their seats. I took the empty chair they had left for me in the middle of the long conference table. One by one, the group instinctively thanked me for the opportunity to serve and spoke passionately about their firm belief in the cause we were embarking upon.

Terri Drake stood up at the head of the table and looked over at me. "Mr. President-elect," she said with a smile, "we worked late into the night really peeling back the onion on this VP issue. Additionally, we've connected with dozens of colleagues by phone or videoconference. Professor Tribe engaged us all with a deep dive into the complicated legal landscape. Secretary Panetta, Professor Gergen, and Mr. Ford have walked us through the weeds of the political options and the likely consequences of each. Murph has been feverishly working the phones taking the temperature of Congress, particularly among the Republican Congressional leaders."

Terri paused for a second, maybe just to get visual confirmation from me that she was on the right track. After all, we were still new to each other.

"That's terrific!" I responded. "Let me ask you this . . . Do you think we have a plausible shot at engineering a creative solution here?"

"May I, Terri?" Panetta asked.

"Be my guest," she responded.

Panetta continued, "If we do nothing in a proactive sense and let it all play out naturally, the Electoral College will split many ways on the VP selection with all the electors voting as pledged. And if that happens, no one gets the requisite majority. That, of course, kicks this selection into the Senate, and they can only choose from the top two vote getters in the electoral vote, meaning Pence and Kaine. None of the many VP running mates who appeared on the various state ballots will get any meaningful percentage. So given a choice between Mike Pence and Tim Kaine, the senate Republicans will obviously choose Pence."

Gergen jumped in, "In that scenario, really everybody loses. You wouldn't want him as your VP, and he likely wouldn't want the job. Perhaps some Republicans would want him there trying to undermine you, but if he did so, he'd very quickly be cut out of anything substantive."

Nevarez added, "The only real benefits to the Republicans would be succession in the event of your death or resignation and the ability to break ties in the Senate. However, that might be enough to convince Mike Pence that he needs to do this for the Republicans."

"We talked at length last night about the many scenarios," explained Panetta. As he spoke, Terri Drake displayed a slide labeled "Faithless VP Elector Scenario" on the video screen. "We discussed a plan to convince all the electors in states you won to write in one particular candidate of your choosing rather than voting for the candidate they are bound to."

"This scenario is fraught with legal complications," Professor Tribe added. "It invites litigation in numerous states, each with disparate laws and regulations, in addition to posing complicated constitutional issues of first impression for the federal courts to feast upon."

"This scenario also poses terribly challenging logistical issues," David Gergen said. "At the end of the day, we cannot even begin to gauge how likely it may be to organize this group and convince them to fall in line. My guess is not very."

"These are not longtime loyal followers of yours, sir," stated Ford. "We have no real sense of the extent of their commitment to you, so this could be like herding cats. And the risks of failure are terrifying. It could really cost you if people saw you attempting to skirt the rules of the system, no matter how flawed they view that system. You may not recover from the resulting damage to your brand."

"Alright," I responded. "You've convinced me. I'm hoping you folks have a Plan B in that PowerPoint presentation."

Panetta continued, "We examined the merits of working a deal with senate Republican leaders—if we could agree on a candidate palatable to both us and them—and convincing them to vote for that person rather than Pence or Kaine. However, this scenario poses perhaps even more serious constitutional hurdles. We don't believe the senators are even allowed to vote for anyone other than the top two finishers in the electoral vote."

"OK," I said, getting more pessimistic by the moment. "I can understand that. Please proceed to the next scenario."

"Here's where we've made some headway, sir," Terri announced.

Gergen jumped in and took the lead, "We had some conversations last week with people close to Mike Pence, sir, and then this morning I spoke with him directly. He has no interest in serving as vice president merely to break ties in the Senate and attend funerals on your behalf. However, he *would* be willing to allow the process to play out, and then once he's elected, he'd step down, permitting you to choose a replacement. His only condition is that you choose someone in advance and that person must be acceptable to both Mitch McConnell and Paul Ryan."

Tribe piggybacked onto Gergen's comment, "Additionally, Section 2 of the Twenty-fifth Amendment requires that the appointment be confirmed by a majority of both houses of Congress."

"Alright," I said with a very measured tone. "At least we have a structure for how to achieve something here. So to summarize, we need a Republican acceptable to the Republican leadership, whom they wouldn't mind vacating his or her current office for this assignment and whom we would like to have on our team. By the way, does that person have to give up his or her seat to become VP?"

"Great question, sir," Panetta responded. "We discussed that as well. I'll defer to our esteemed Harvard constitutional law professor for his analysis on that issue."

"The Constitution seems to address that," Professor Tribe began. "The

Incompatible Offices Clause states that no person holding any office under the United States shall be a member of either house of Congress. While a few have argued that this may not be binding upon the president or vice president, I believe it would, in fact, prevent someone from doing both."

"OK," I replied, "so we'll need to fold that in as well. Someone the Republicans endorse, who they wouldn't mind vacating a seat perhaps, who wants the job, and by the way, who also fits our mold of serving country over party with a reputation for reaching across the aisle. And that last part is the most important part. But that whole thing is a mouthful. I can't imagine there is anyone out there who possibly fits the bill?"

I paused and looked around the room. After a few moments, their blank poker faces started to morph into smiles.

"Come on guys. Quit messing with me here. What have you got?"

"We had a rather interesting conference call this morning with Mitch McConnell and someone who I think you'll approve of for this assignment who is happy to do it, and the Republicans would be happy to have vacate his senate seat."

"A current Republican senator? One I'd be happy with and they'd be OK parting with? Alright, already. Spill it," I implored of them.

"Murph's old boss."

"Of course! McCain. That's genius."

Chapter Nine

December 2, 2016
O'Reilly

The reviews of our vice presidential backroom deal ran the whole
gamut. Bill O'Reilly offered a very interesting take on it, which was as
entertaining as it was predictable.

FOX News *The O'Reilly Factor*

> Hi, I'm Bill O'Reilly. Thanks for watching us tonight.
> "McFadden Chooses McCain and Republicans Win,"
> that's my headline tonight and the subject of this evening's
> Talking Points Memo.
> Word out of Washington today is that President-elect
> Danny McFadden has reached a deal with Mitch
> McConnell, Paul Ryan, Mike Pence, and John McCain for
> Pence to step down immediately after the Electoral
> College formally elects him vice president, at which time
> McFadden will appoint McCain to the office. McCain
> would then need to be approved by a majority vote of both
> houses of Congress. I see this deal as a total victory for the
> Republicans.
> And by the way, Talking Points does not intend to
> trash John McCain—as many conservatives would like to
> do—but to praise him. He is indeed a war hero, despite
> Donald Trump's misguided comments on the campaign
> trail. And Senator McCain has served honorably for three
> decades, earning himself the nickname "The Maverick."
> He has, however, confounded conservatives at times. His
> critics would say he seeks the limelight and is prone to

drama, and when push comes to shove, he often abandons the conservative cause—usually in front of the cameras with great fanfare.

For these reasons, he continues to be the darling of the left-leaning national media, which relishes his "Maverick" moments because it suits their political agenda to discredit the right. The false news media will praise McFadden for this move and gush about his new-style politics. But, ladies and gentlemen, this is the GOP's dream.

This deal allows Arizona Governor Doug Ducey the opportunity to choose a true conservative who will consistently back the Republican agenda. Now more than ever, we need to hold firm against the radical left, and McCain all too frequently abandoned us when it counted. Moreover, it certainly doesn't hurt to have McCain join the McFadden administration. If he can have any influence on that group—which I still contend is just an extension of Obama's left-wing politics wrapped up in a moderate bow for show—then this deal will benefit conservatives within the executive branch as well. We expect that McCain won't abandon his long-held conservative principles on important issues such as military funding, foreign policy, and controlling federal spending.

Make no mistake about it, though, the conservatives won today. Score one for McConnell, ladies and gentlemen. McFadden hasn't even taken office yet, and he's already trailing Mitch one to nothing. You won't find any headlines declaring that, but you won't be in need of any. You heard it here.

And that's the Memo.

Chapter Ten

January 20, 2017—6:05 p.m., White House Residence
This Fella Is Gonna Be Really Unpredictable

As Denyse and I got ready for the inaugural balls, I made the mistake of flipping on the television to channel surf a bit and gauge the reaction to my speech. It had been my finest possible attempt to articulate in the most lofty prose imaginable my vision of a country rising above all the partisan politics and uniting to reassert itself on the world stage. While I'm sure Kennedy's position as the gold standard of inaugural addresses is secure, I nonetheless felt I had delivered a powerful address.

I started with FOX News to get a sense of how it was playing with my friends on the right:

> "I'm afraid that all his painful contorting to ensure that he pleases everyone will, in actuality, only guarantee that he pleases no one. To me, it demonstrates an absence of any underlying core belief or philosophy. He claims to be a moderate, but I fear he'll be another tax-and-spend liberal. And I worry most about how he intends to shape the Supreme Court."

OK, I thought to myself. *Not exactly the reception I was hoping for there.* I wasn't even sure who the commentator was. Hoping the reviews from the other side of the aisle were more favorable, I flipped over to MSNBC where Chris Matthews was reporting:

> "I'm not sure he'll stand up to the NRA. Also, he's a Notre Dame Catholic, so I'm just not convinced he'll aggressively protect a woman's right to choose. Does anyone know how he really feels about that? I'm concerned about

it. What kind of judges will he appoint? And all his talk today about fiscal responsibility makes me fearful that social programs might be in his crosshairs. He talks of entitlement reform—that scares me too. This fella is gonna be really unpredictable in this office . . . and dangerous."

I flipped to ESPN. I couldn't hit the remote fast enough, actually. On ESPN, Stephen A. Smith was ranting about something with a full head of steam behind him, but it didn't involve politics or my administration, so that was just fine with me. I think it was about the Knicks, for what it's worth.

Denyse came out of her bathroom and saw the look on my face. "What's the matter, babe?"

"I made the fatal mistake of sampling the reviews on cable news."

"Not exactly what you were hoping for?" tilting her head as she tried to fasten an earring.

"Looks like I'm getting ripped by both FOX and MSNBC."

"Good. Wear that like a badge of honor. Given all you stand for, I'd be concerned if either of those two started raving about you."

"You're right. Of course, you are. But each of those operations are so influential with so many people. I need to figure out a way to reach both of their audiences."

"Perhaps, but you certainly don't need to do it tonight. You've been president all of what, fifteen minutes now and my God, you haven't united the country yet? Shameful!"

"Thank you for keeping me grounded." Denyse had both the political and psychiatric skills that I desperately needed right then, the latter even more than the former. But the sheer weight of this political challenge in front of me was becoming clearer by the minute. It was quite overwhelming.

Seeking a respite from this bout of anxiety, I turned away from the television and looked out the window. My nerves calmed immediately as I stared directly at the Washington Monument off in the distance. *How perfect,* I thought. If I was really going to heal this great divide, I needed to channel George Washington. If I couldn't consult him personally as I confronted this daunting political challenge ahead of me, at least I had this impressive structure built in his memory to gaze upon each night for inspiration.

Chapter Eleven

January 20, 2017—7:15 p.m.
A President Can Dream, Right?

After what had already been a long and mentally exhausting day, our evening started at 7:15 p.m. with the Youth Inaugural Ball at the DC Armory. With a sea of kids in tuxes and formal gowns, it looked very much like an overcrowded high school prom, but Denyse and I loved their energy. The musical selections were quite unlike my prom thirty years ago and, for that matter, quite unlike any of the other balls we attended that night. All this unfamiliar music, however, seemed to scream messages of hope and love and tolerance. I don't know if that's truly representative of the music of this newest generation, but we left with a sense that no matter how much hate and divisiveness was presently pervading our elected officials—and the country in general—the future nonetheless was in good hands and looked incredibly bright.

Next came the Liberty and Freedom Inaugural Balls at the Walter E. Washington Convention Center. These were packed affairs as well. At these two galas, our every movement had been carefully timed and choreographed. I could not get over the sheer logistics of this colossal security effort. Each appearance at a ball involved a staggering amount of orchestration. As impressive as all that was—the transportation between balls, the pathway cleared into each party, the controlled socializing time, and then the exit path back to the motorcade—it made me wonder if it was really worth all the enormous effort and expense.

After several more brief and unremarkable appearances at additional balls, Denyse and I came to our last stop of the night: the California Ball. This was the one ball we'd been looking forward to the most. Unfortunately, at this point, all we wanted to do was shut it down for the night. My feet were killing me, but the last thing on earth I was going to do was complain to Denyse about it since she had been in heels all day.

Presidential Spirits

We each had a cup of coffee in the limo along the way and did our best to get ourselves in the mood. We were both smart enough to know we couldn't just mail this one in.

Many of our closest friends and family members were at the California Ball. When we arrived, we were ushered into a private room for ten minutes of mingling with them—which wasn't nearly enough. My brothers and sisters were all there, as well as many friends from college, high school, and even grade school, and many people I had worked with over the years. The amount of planning that went into organizing those brief few minutes blew my mind—much more organization and vetting than had gone into our wedding. For most of the guests, it was all I could do to simply make eye contact. And for that, they had flown across the country in the dead of winter and paid elevated hotel rates with three-night minimum stays. I felt an incredible sense of guilt.

But we did manage to have some fun at this ball. The dance they planned for us was "Danny Boy"—which seemed to be the song of choice at each one of the balls—followed by "Hotel California" and "California Girls," the Beach Boys tune, not the one by Katy Perry. Pretty good playlist there—right in my wheelhouse. When you dance to the first song at your wedding, you never think you're going to have to do it all over again someday—this time with much of the world watching. And much like our wedding day, I know I didn't impress anyone with my moves.

The drive back to the White House was memorable. Washington on a clear night is truly stunning. We drove past the Capitol in all its glory. And while I knew it would forever brand me as a total dork of a president with the security and transportation team, I asked nicely at first and then much more forcefully to be driven past the Jefferson Memorial, the Lincoln Memorial, the FDR Memorial, and the Washington Monument. It was all I could do to resist the compelling urge to get out and pay my respects to these legendary presidents. What I really needed most at this moment from these four iconic figures—and some of the many others who held this office—was a little bit of divine intervention and perhaps some expert advice from time to time. Now that would be something. A president can dream, right?

Chapter Twelve

January 20, 2017
The Coin and the Tradition

I think it really hit us both for the first time when the motorcade taking us home from the balls pulled onto the White House grounds and up to the entrance off the lawn at the South Portico below the Truman Balcony. It was so hard to fathom that this was now our home. This iconic venue that meant so much to the history of this country—and the world—was our house for the next four years. Unbelievable. I should have had a few more drinks.

As Denyse and I entered the South Portico, we immediately saw a now-familiar and very welcome face.

"Satch!" Denyse yelled. "You waited up for us! Did we break curfew? I swear it won't happen again."

He laughed and grinned from ear to ear. "Welcome home, Mrs. McFadden."

"It's great to be home!" she exclaimed. "You make us feel right at home."

"I hope you had a wonderful time tonight. You both deserve it."

"We did," I responded. "Very much so. But I know this is just the calm before storm. And I think that storm begins in just a few hours."

"That's what I'm here for, sir. I have a little something for you that may be of some comfort and help guide you through the next four years or more." He was holding something in a bag.

"Is it drugs or alcohol?" I asked, only half joking. "I may require a lot of alcohol during my term."

"No, sir," Satch said stoically.

"Is this what Obama was talking about this morning?" I asked. "He mentioned in the car ride over to the Capitol that you had something very meaningful to give me. Something he didn't feel comfortable just leaving in the desk for me."

Presidential Spirits

"Yes, sir, that's what this is about."

Obama became quite sincere when he told me about it. Without saying what it was, he told me it had the potential to really help me be successful. He seemed deathly serious.

"Let's go inside," Denyse said. I could tell she was merely moments away from perhaps the deepest sleep of her life, and there was no stopping that train now.

I had kind of forgotten about the Obama conversation in the midst of my nervousness over delivering my inaugural address. Now, of course, my mind was in overdrive. What could be so damn important about that little bag?

Upstairs in the presidential residence, the three of us entered the family room outside the bedroom suite.

I approached the bar. "How about a Jameson or a scotch?" I asked.

Denyse was all too happy to take that as her cue to exit. "I'll leave you two alone," she said with a smile. "I'm currently experiencing a shutdown."

"None for me, sir," said Satch. "I have a little bit of a drive ahead of me."

In that case, I passed on the nightcap as well. I couldn't have known then that my night was just starting.

It was late, so I got right to the point. "What have you got there?" I asked.

"This, sir, is something very, very special."

Satch pulled a small glass case from the bag and set it on the table before me. Now the suspense was killing me. I didn't know Satch well—certainly not well enough to have any earthly idea what this was all about. Was this something serious or just a joke—and perhaps a bad one if that?

"Go ahead and take a look at it," he suggested.

I picked up the glass case and examined it closely. Inside was a gold coin the size of a modern half dollar. The coin depicted a side profile of the head and shoulders of George Washington above the date 1792, and the words *Washington President* written in a circle along the edges. The other side showed an eagle with arrows and olive branches in its talons.

"Wow!" I couldn't take my eyes off it. "Is this one of the earliest pieces of currency in the country?"

"No, sir. It's something even more special than that. In 1792, some businessmen produced this single gold coin in the hopes of securing a contract to mint U.S. coins. In an effort to obtain approval for the contract, this exact coin was shown to President Washington. Consistent with his character, of course, he turned down the contract. He didn't want his face appearing on any coins. He felt this would be something a king would do, not a U.S. president."

"For this and many other reasons he has become my favorite president," I replied.

"There's more," Satch continued. "The gentleman told him to keep the coin, which is the only one of its kind. He did, and he proceeded to carry it around the rest of his presidency for good luck. It clearly meant a great deal to him. At the end of his second term, he made sure that it was given to John Adams, who, in turn, gave it to Thomas Jefferson, and on it went through the years, passed down from president to president. Throughout the rich and storied history of this country, this coin continued to be passed down. Through times of war, civil unrest, and peace. In times of prosperity and times of recession. It has been passed across party lines, between men who had defeated one another, between men who hated each other, and, of course, across ethnic and now racial lines."

I quickly set the coin back down on the table. *Set* might be the incorrect term. It kind of exploded out of my hands back onto the table. Satch laughed out loud.

If I had thought driving back to the White House was the moment when the full weight of the presidency hit me, I was incorrect. This moment was many times more powerful.

"It is a precious and sacred relic of our country, but it is not something to be afraid of, Mr. President. Hardly. I encourage you to keep it with you at all times. Cherish it. Rely on it for luck like Washington did, but also use it to channel the spirits of each of your predecessors. You'll need that. I suspect there truly is something supernatural about this remarkable gold George Washington coin."

I picked it back up. I'm a big believer in symbols. *Perhaps the spirit of George Washington in this White House is precisely what I need,* I thought. *If this coin can help me channel that—even if it's all in my mind—it's certainly worth a try.*

"Oh, and one more thing," Satch added, looking me straight in the eyes. "Do not under any circumstances tell anyone about this coin."

Presidential Spirits

Minutes later I collapsed on our bed and fell fast asleep—with my tuxedo still on and the Washington gold coin in my pocket—contemplating the road ahead. Maybe channeling the great Father of our Country could somehow help me navigate through political waters that appeared to be every bit as treacherous as the icy, stormy Delaware on Christmas Night 1776.

Chapter Thirteen

January 21, 2017—*1:45 a.m.*
What Is That?

A few hours later I awoke to a continuous series of faint mysterious noises. I listened as carefully as I could. At first I heard only muffled sounds, which seemed to be coming from above. I sat there stunned and a little bit spooked—shocked really. I got up and peered out the window but saw nothing. It seemed to be coming from inside the mansion. Before long, I was certain I was hearing music, voices, and laughter.

How was it possible for a party to be raging at this moment in the White House? I had heard stories of the Secret Service partying hard on the road in past administrations. They'd gotten into a heap of trouble and caused quite a stir in Columbia, as I recall. But I'm pretty sure this type of behavior in the White House would be unheard of. And there's no way on earth my sixteen-year-old son, Brett, would attempt to pull off a party like that in his first night in the White House—at least not already. I knew Brett had some game, but not *that* much. I had to investigate.

I still had the remnants of my tux on—just the pants and shirt, having long discarded the tie, cuff links, and studs. I threw on some slippers and whispered to my eighty-pound collie, Montana, to come with me. He pretended not to hear me and didn't budge. Some watch dog there, boy.

I opened the bedroom door and slowly made my way through the master suite's sitting room, which led to the Center Hall. As I proceeded, the noises got louder. I opened the door to the hall and noticed that there were no Secret Service stationed at the posts where I was led to believe they would be at night. I walked past the kids' bedrooms and past the Yellow Oval Room to the spiral staircase that led to the third floor. The noise kept getting louder and was clearly coming from above. I thought of summoning someone, but like the young protagonist in every horror movie ever filmed, I decided to go it alone. Besides, it sounded a lot more like a fun party than a mass murder.

The noises became louder and more distinct as I ascended the staircase. *Could I possibly be hearing a jazz band?* I thought. *And laughter and loud voices.* Whatever it was, it sounded like a kick.

I entered the third floor and walked toward the sound. This was a party if I'd ever heard one. What the heck was going on? I walked across to the section of the third floor that I'd been told was inaccessible—the north side that I figured housed the antiaircraft, antimissile, and other defense and security systems for the rooftop. The writing on the large door read "WHITE HOUSE STORAGE. THIS DOOR TO REMAIN LOCKED." But I knew the sound of a good party when I heard it, and there was unquestionably an impressive shindig happening on the other side of the door. As I reached for the door, an eerie feeling came over me. I wasn't about to turn back, and yet somehow, I was certain my life was about to change.

Chapter Fourteen

January 21, 2017
Something Out of Another Century

The door was very heavy—much more so than it appeared. It opened inward, and I had to push hard to get it to budge. Even then, it opened slowly. Immediately I was overcome with the smell of cigar smoke permeating the air. The distinct aroma, however, was mild compared to the incredible sight before me. I found myself inexplicably gazing inside a stunning, very well-appointed, classic period barroom. As a guy who appreciates a great pub—or at least someone who *used to*—this was a sight to behold. It struck me as something out of another century altogether—and neither of the ones I had occupied. My eyes fixated on the bar itself, which was massive. It appeared to be mahogany, or something equally elegant, and spanned a good fifty feet end to end. The grand backbar, which proudly displayed rows of all the finest spirits, extended all the way up to a lofty tin tile ceiling. Vintage rolling library ladders provided the bartenders access all the way to the top. Dimly lit gas lamps interspersed throughout the large room set the atmosphere, and the smoke billowing from the many active cigars hung in the air, obscuring the sights before me like the fog on a San Francisco summer night. Large booths with green leather banquettes and oaken tables lined two of the walls, with much larger oak tables sprinkled throughout the center of the room for bigger gatherings of men. The tavern's patrons appeared to be mostly—if not exclusively—men and there seemed to be a dress code. Some looked to be dressed in period costumes for some reason. On a small stage in the corner, a jazz singer was perched atop a barstool superbly belting out the blues backed by an ensemble band that would have been right at home on Bourbon Street. Indeed, this bar had more swagger than any I'd ever entered. And I hadn't even ordered a drink.

I wondered what the heck was going on. This was already the most unlikely and extraordinary day of my life, even before I'd happened upon

48

this spectacular find. Maybe I was dead. Or perhaps I was dreaming . . . or hallucinating. Should I summon the Secret Service? Consult a psychiatrist? Quietly return to the residence and never breathe a word about this to anyone as long as I live?

I decided to order a drink.

I meandered through the large crowded room, making my way to the bar. It was the first time in over two months that I'd been able to enter a crowd of strangers of any kind without the Secret Service tagging along. It was a little bit freeing.

There appeared to be about fifty or so men clearly delighting in the party, with several young waitresses and bartenders there to assist in that effort. The servers donned impeccable formal attire that smartly comple-mented the high-end decor. The men sported fitted, white, long-sleeved, but-ton-down shirts, black bow ties, and slim, black, flat-front trousers and shoes that appeared for all the world as if they were purchased that very day. The women wore narrow, black pencil skirts and tight, white knit shirts with deep, scoop necks. While this impressive group of ladies would have stood out in any crowd, they particularly cut quite a contrast amidst the aging male patrons.

I walked past a gentleman who was the spitting image of Ronald Reagan and sounded a lot like him too. He was deep in conversation with an old guy wearing knee breeches and white stockings. *A seemingly serious conversation with an old guy wearing knee breeches and stockings? I must be losing my mind,* I thought. *What* is *this place?* I think I saw a few others similarly dressed and a couple looked to be sporting powdered wigs, as if they'd just stepped out of the eighteenth century. This place was becoming more strange by the minute. *I need that drink right away.* Perhaps this was a cast party of some sort and some of the actors were still in costume.

Suddenly, I felt out of place for a variety of reasons, not the least of which was the fact that I was wearing a disheveled partial tuxedo and slip-pers. It appeared that many people in the room were staring at me as I approached the bar and, if I wasn't mistaken, whispering to each other about me too. But I'd become accustomed to that since my big "Jerry Maguire moment" and the whirlwind election that followed. Even so, I avoided eye contact.

I grabbed an empty barstool and sat for a second, feasting my eyes upon the majestic structure in front of me. The massive hand-carved wooden backbar seemed to illuminate every fine liquid intoxicant known to man. The wooden bar itself extended perhaps as much as a yard wide.

I glanced to my left and noticed that the gentleman sitting next to me looked remarkably like the figure on the twenty-dollar bill. I had a momentary brain lapse, straining to recall whether it was Hamilton or Jackson whose face adorned the bill. Just then, he drew the attention of the young bartender, who responded immediately.

"Another whiskey, General?"

"Yes, and bring a Madeira as well."

What the heck is a Madeira? I thought. *And this gentleman is a general?* I watched the bartender pour the tallest whiskey I had ever seen, which he quickly delivered together with what looked like a glass of wine.

Both appeared to be for the general's consumption.

"Attaboy, Old Hickory!" the gentleman to my right said to the general. "One for each hand!"

Old Hickory? I thought to myself. For a second. *Andrew Jackson?*

I looked to my right at the gentleman sitting next to me drinking water. It was George W. Bush.

Chapter Fifteen

January 21, 2017
Oh. My. God.

Oh. My. God. I buried my head in my hands and slammed my eyes shut contemplating this enormously powerful reality all around me. A feeling I can only describe as spiritual crept across my brain and left me momentarily incapable of thought. When I emerged from this state of mental paralysis, I had to come to grips with the seemingly surreal fact that not only was I the president of the United States but I somehow found myself in an old tavern in the midst of all of my predecessors, both living and dead.

I slowly turned around on my stool to face the room behind me. With my hands shaking and my pulse racing, I opened my eyes and gazed out again at the party. Directly in front of me Jimmy Carter sat deep in conversation with Harry Truman. Many of the faces were not familiar to me. I scanned the room in search of a wheelchair and quickly spotted one. Sure enough, there sat FDR, and in his left hand that distinctive long cigarette holder. The astonishing scene before me constituted what was perhaps the ultimate U.S. government and history quiz. As a closet history buff, I found it so intellectually compelling.

I located JFK, looking dapper as always in a dark suit, most likely Brooks Brothers, and narrow tie with a Heineken in one hand and what I'm sure must have been one of his favorite petit corona cigars in the other—ironic, of course, given the embargo he imposed on trade with Cuba. He stood conversing with two gentlemen—one slightly taller than him with a powdered wig, a light brown coat, a red waistcoat, and breeches. I wanted it to be Thomas Jefferson and surmised that it must have been. Thomas Jefferson and JFK. Dr. Arnold Harris, my American Presidency professor from Notre Dame, would be beside himself. I certainly was. How would one even begin to go about explaining the '60s to Thomas Jefferson? When he

51

and the other framers opted to kick the can down the road on the issue of true equality, decades like the 1860s and the 1960s became inevitable. Of course, someone would need to explain the latter half of the 1960s to JFK as well. I desperately wanted to hear their discussion.

The other much shorter, rounder gentleman with them wore a powdered wig that fell from the top of his head and the sides but exposed the bald front of his scalp. He sported a gold coat and waistcoat and gold breeches. *John Adams?* That's it! It must be. After all, he's next to Jefferson, his vice president and fierce political rival and colleague from the Washington administration. I knew that these two indispensable founders became very close in their final years before dying within hours of each other on Independence Day 1826—on our nation's 50th birthday. Perhaps he and Kennedy were conversing about the Commonwealth of Massachusetts. A couple of intellectuals, for sure, but they struck quite a contrast in appearance and style standing next to one another.

I was thoroughly enjoying every second of this remarkable scene when George W. Bush slapped me on the back and barked, "Hey Rook, Big Time here wants your drink order."

I turned back toward the bar to see the young bartender right in front of me, smiling and shaking his head, ready for instructions. He cut an impressive figure behind the bar. Standing at least six foot five with thick blond hair, he looked to be as strong as an ox. It appeared as if he could handle any trouble, but his friendly face and demeanor projected anything but intimidation.

"I really have no idea why he calls me Big Time," the bartender said cracking a smile. "But he gives everyone here a nickname. I give him great credit for getting to know the help here. Not all of these characters bother. He's one of my favorites."

"What's your real name?" I asked.

"People call me Matt . . . or Matty depending on how well they know me. But in here, out of deference to W, a lot of them call me Big Time." He laughed and shook his head. "What can I get you, Rook?"

"How about a Jameson and ginger, Matty?"

"An Irish buck! Fine choice. Coming right up."

"I've ordered it for years and never heard it called that before, but I like that name. Perfect."

"Welcome!" Matt said, extending his hand to shake. "This is the most exclusive club known to mankind—or I guess unknown would be more accurate." He laughed and darted off to make me an Irish buck.

I couldn't help but notice that Bush was looking right at me.

"First night here, Rook?"

"Yes," I responded. It was a rare moment when I was at a loss for words, but I couldn't even begin to know where to start.

"Go walk around. This is really something special—providential even—as a few of these guys would put it," Bush said as he nodded toward the patrons. "There's a ton of wisdom and experience out there. Use them. You'll need it."

"Really?" I asked. "I'd love to."

"One point of caution, though. . . . There's a lot of egos out there—massive egos. These are what you'd call alpha males," Bush added with a quick laugh. "But if you blow plenty of smoke up their arses, as they say, you'll be just fine."

With that, he gave me a fist bump and a half wink before making his way down the bar.

Matt then came back with my drink and another bartender.

"This is Jason," Matt said, putting his hand on Jason's shoulder. "But Bush and everyone else call him Haskell. Probably easier if you just call him that."

"Pleased to meet you, Haskell," I said, extending my hand out over the wide bar. "Why Haskell?"

"Not sure. No one really knows why Bush gives people the nicknames he does."

I engaged with them rather on autopilot as my mind spun out of control trying to grasp what exactly was happening to me.

"I'm so honored to meet you, sir," said Haskell. "I really respect the way you've renounced the two parties and invoked the ideals of Washington's Farewell Address."

"That's very flattering, son," I responded, a little taken aback by his bar conversation. Both these bartenders were sharp-looking kids and appeared to be just barely above college age. "How do I square away my bill?" I asked Matt innocently.

"It's all taken care of," he shot back. "Just have Congress keep raising that debt ceiling." He laughed and hustled down to the other end of the bar as I heard someone yell out, "Hey Big Time, what's a president gotta do to get a drink around here?"

Meanwhile Haskell started chatting up Old Hickory next to me. "I have so much respect for what you accomplished in the Battle of New Orleans, sir."

I had a feeling I knew why Bush referred to him as Haskell. He was a reincarnation of Eddie Haskell. George W. Bush must be a *Leave It to Beaver* fan.

I took my drink and waded into the crowd, uncharacteristically unsure of myself. The smoke was tough to handle, but was a small price to pay to attend the cocktail party of a lifetime. I saw that about a dozen or so men had gathered around a table. Quite curious, I headed over and found an opening. The scene in front of me took my breath away. I watched as General Eisenhower unfolded a map of western Europe on the table before him and proceeded to recount, step by step, the events leading up to D-Day and the options considered by the Allies, including the creation of phantom field armies and operations intended purely to divert the Axis Powers away from Normandy. And then he described in great detail how he executed the greatest military operation in history with an Allied armada of nearly 7,000 vessels and 2,500 aircraft. As dramatic as that was, the most meaningful aspect of the scene, to me, was the fact that his intended audience was not the group around the table. Instead, he spoke directly to the much taller, distinctive-looking, broad-shouldered man at his side, who was dressed in a brown wool coat that buttoned across the front with a tail extending all the way to the rear of his knees, and matching breeches. His white hair was pulled back into a pigtail, and he exuded an air of eighteenth century martial nobility. I recognized this man with the long face immediately—most any American would. George Washington.

Washington alone asked questions of Eisenhower and even interrupted at times for clarification. He appeared mesmerized. So, I'm sure, did I—as well as everyone else at the table taking this in. Eisenhower, too, appeared to relish the moment. He spoke of the human impact and the stress of the operation. It clearly took a toll on him personally. In the days and weeks leading up to the invasion, he said he'd been operating almost exclusively on coffee and cigarettes.

Presidential Spirits

Following his captivating retelling of the operation, Eisenhower looked up from the map. "This massive invasion took place on the very day my own son graduated from West Point. I knew I was sending many hundreds of boys off to give their lives or be maimed forever. But America did this not to gain anything for ourselves; not to fulfill any dreams we had for conquest. But to simply preserve freedom, and systems of self-government in the world.

"Twice in my lifetime, American boys have been called to travel to Europe to defend those values. We must find a way to work for and achieve an eternal peace in the world."

Deep in thought, Washington stood peering at Eisenhower. Something was clearly on his mind.

"Do you have another question, General Washington?" Eisenhower asked.

Washington shook his head. "General," he said, "I cannot help but stand here in awe. And to think that our men were called upon to save Britain and France of all countries—our first two adversaries. I fought them both. And in my Farewell Address, I advised on the importance of avoiding all foreign entanglements. You obviously had other ideas, but I commend you for it." Then, chuckling to himself, Washington added, "What I wouldn't give for a conversation with Lafayette about this! Whatever debt we feel we owed to him and to France is more than repaid."

Then came the most compelling moment of Eisenhower's stirring speech. He reached into his pocket and pulled out two letters—one delivered to the troops on the eve of the invasion and one held back that he intended to be distributed if the mission failed. In the latter communication—the one that was never delivered, Eisenhower accepted full responsibility for the failure of the operation. He read from that letter:

> "Our landings in the Cherbourg-Havre area have failed to gain a satisfactory foothold and I have withdrawn the troops. My decision to attack at this time and place was based upon the best information available. The troops, the air and the Navy did all that bravery and devotion to duty could do. If any blame or fault attaches to the attempt it is mine alone."

Eisenhower looked up from the letter. "A month after the invasion, I found that second letter in my coat pocket. I had forgotten about it. Thank God the boys did their job expertly and this letter was never necessary. Nothing can ever prepare a general for the soul-racking decision to send young men to their death. Thankfully with their uncommon courage and heroism, those who died did not do so in vain. We lost 400,000 men in the war."

As Eisenhower finished, he paused letting the moment linger. The group absorbed those powerful seconds in silence. I recognized General Grant, but not most of the others. I was guessing that among them were many of the other generals: the Harrisons, Franklin Pierce, Andrew Johnson, Zachary Taylor, Chester Arthur, James Garfield, Rutherford B. Hayes. I knew they were generals but had no idea what they looked like. All stood quietly in a moment of reverence.

Washington emerged, placed his hand on Eisenhower's shoulder, and broke the silence. "As I, too, had the great honor of holding an appointment in the service of our county, let me congratulate you, General Eisenhower, on these glorious events that heaven was pleased to produce in your favor and in favor of our blessed nation. You are, indeed, a true patriot and a most humble servant of the public. Your labor enables the states to continue to participate in the fruits of our revolution and enjoy the essential benefits of a civil society under a form of government so free and uncorrupted and happily guarded against the danger of oppression. I am proud to be your countryman."

Eisenhower responded, "That means everything to me coming from you, General. You have always been my hero. And I cannot help but feel compelled to mention that you, too, know a thing or two about conducting ambitious, amphibious surprise attacks at night. The Delaware in December at night had to be treacherous."

"Hear! Hear!" chimed in many of the others. Among them, I noticed Teddy Roosevelt. How could I miss TR? He was so recognizable with his rock-solid frame, thick bushy mustache, and pince-nez–style eyeglasses. He seemed enthralled by this truly remarkable firsthand account of such a monumental event in history. As I thought more about him, I remembered hearing that on D-Day, his son Teddy Roosevelt Jr. led the first wave of U.S. troops at Utah Beach. He died a month later in France at age fifty-seven. I also recalled that TR's youngest son, Quentin, died in air combat in France during World War I.

Trying for all the world not to appear like a stalker, I kept watching TR as a waitress approached. Straining my ears, I distinctly heard him order a mint julep. That threw me for a loop. I would've never guessed that was his drink. And while I would never think to order one myself, I absolutely loved that you can get a mint julep in this place. If I hadn't been so distracted by the presence of all these legendary figures around me, I would have been overwhelmed by this incredible bar!

As the group around Eisenhower's table began to disperse, I saw Ulysses S. Grant approaching Ike. "Thank you so much, General Eisenhower, for providing this account of your war exploits," he said. Then, extending his hand, he continued, "It's an honor to shake the hand of a revered military man who had a tendency to take on more casualties than I did! I only wish my own naysayers were alive to see this sweet vindication!" He smiled broadly and laughed uproariously. "Always knew I was way ahead of my time."

I made my way back to the bar. I walked right past Richard Nixon and recalled vividly watching the Watergate hearings in my youth, being cajoled into doing so by my Mom's sense of the history of the moment. Much later, of course, I saw him make somewhat of a comeback as an elder statesman in his last years.

Back at the bar, I noticed George W. hand a note written on a napkin to one of the waitresses, who then proceeded to deliver it to George Washington. My curiosity piqued.

Just then Bill Clinton, standing nearby paying close attention to all this, said aloud to no one in particular, "Look out fellas, Otter's up to something."

I leaned over at Matt and asked softly, "If you don't mind me asking, who's Otter?"

"Ha ha! That's the nickname Clinton has given George W here. No doubt you've seen *Animal House*, right?"

"Who hasn't?" I replied. "It's one of my favorite flicks. What a classic!" I thought for a few seconds then added, "Otter was the main guy, right? Tim Matheson's character?"

"Yes, yes. 'Eric Stratton, Rush Chairman, damn glad to meet you.' Watch George W operate up here. Everybody likes him—the founders, the generals, both the eighteenth and the nineteenth century guys as well as the modern guys. The Republicans, the Democrats, the Whigs—you name it. Just watch him operate. With all his nicknames and his fist bumps, he's a total Rush Chair. I'm not too sure about his presidency, but he would make the perfect frat president—which I think he probably was at Yale, but I have no idea."

I shook my head rather dumbfounded. "Awesome! I love it! You're right, he *is* the perfect Otter."

"Isn't he?"

"Wow! This place is really unbelievable." I remarked, clearly smitten by the whole experience.

I watched as Washington read the note from George W. He then gave the waitress very clear directions, and she hurried back to the bar. Washington motioned to Jefferson and Adams, and the two Founding Fathers promptly came to his side. As word seemed to spread, the music stopped and many of the early presidents began to gather around. Whatever they were up to, I had the sense that this was going to be something special.

Chapter Sixteen

January 21, 2017
Thirteen Toasts

The room seemed to instinctively come to a collective hush as Washington arose and faced the crowd. From my vantage point back at the bar, he projected an almost mystical aura in the dim light amidst the smoke that hung in the air. He commanded the attention and respect of the crowd, even the servers, before even so much as uttering a word.

"Gentlemen," he said, in a booming voice. After pausing a few seconds, he began again, "Gentlemen. Let us offer thirteen toasts—as has become our custom—one for each original state in our fine Union." The room began to buzz in approval. The entire team of waitresses and bartenders busily doled out large glasses of Madeira or buttered rum to everyone in the room. Many accepted both.

I then noticed an African American gentleman emerge from the hallway behind the far side of the bar. He took a position in the back of the room all by himself. An impressive-looking young man, he was dressed very sharply in colorful silks and knee breeches, garb that appeared to be plucked right out of the Revolutionary War period. I wondered what possible connection he had to this group. He seemed to know that something worth observing was about to transpire.

Washington continued, "Let us commence, gentlemen. Number one: to the United States of America."

The crowd echoed back, "Hear! Hear!" they cheered as they took ambitious sips from their glasses.

"Number two," Washington added, "to my dear friends Jefferson, Adams, and Madison beside me, whose labors produced the foundations of our great republic."

Adams interrupted, "Why Jefferson first, General Washington? He merely put his pen to my ideas." Everyone in the room laughed. However, I suspected that this was much more than just a joke. Adams wasn't finished, "Besides, the Constitution should be celebrated above his Declaration as our seminal document."

Well out of earshot of our toastmasters, Bill Clinton leaned over just behind the two Presidents Bush near me at the bar and uttered, "I believe Mr. Jefferson got the best of this tussle. He's up on Mount Rushmore!" They all roared with laughter, Clinton even more so than the others.

Washington, choosing to ignore the comments, simply continued, "Number three: to the memory of those heroes who have fallen for our freedom. May our country be forever grateful for her military children."

Then, looking at General Eisenhower, he raised his glass and said, "General."

Eisenhower, nodding and raising his glass, responded, "General."

Adams stepped forward. "Number four: to George Washington, the pride and ornament of his country. No other could have led both our Continental Army to victory and our newborn nation in infancy. We profoundly venerate his virtuous character."

The drinks flowed freely, as the serving staff did their best to keep the glasses filled. A waitress handed me and others around me warm mugs. I accepted it without hesitation, but she correctly surmised that I had no idea what it was.

"It's a hot ale flip," she whispered as she hustled off. It tasted like warm, bad beer with a couple shots of something serious in it.

Adams continued, "Number five: to another peaceful transition of power, which has now occurred. Another plum for the delegates to the Constitutional Convention." There were more roars of approval, but Adams wasn't finished. "Number six: to the Constitution and our laws. May Americans ever remember that law is liberty and the Constitution is the sacred palladium of political safety."

Adams was on a roll. "Number seven," he said. May the friends of America be impressed with a suitable resentment, in every instance of foreign interference with respect to its Government."

Adams, noticing James Madison waiting behind him, yielded to his diminutive colleague, who looked to be about 5'4 and couldn't have been much more than 100 pounds. "Number eight," shouted Madison—

determined not have his faint voice go unheard, "to America's singular system of checks and balances, which shall forever stand guard to control the abuses of government." Much applause followed. Madison, overcome by his colleagues' reaction, spent a moment basking in the adulation and then proudly stepped aside.

Madison's toast and that ovation for the man many consider the Father of the Constitution really got to me. This whole scene was so surreal, but to see Madison, who didn't strike me as an alpha male, step forward at this moment and offer that particular sentiment sent chills up my spine.

Washington then motioned to Ronald Reagan, who promptly stepped forward. "Number nine, sir?" Reagan asked.

"Yes," Washington said with a nod.

Reagan looked over at me. "Number nine," he said, "to our newest brother, President McFadden. In 1790, President Washington so eloquently stated that 'the destiny of self-government and the preservation of the sacred fire of liberty is finely staked on the experiment entrusted to the hands of the American people.' Now I know all my political opponents obsessed about my age, but I want to attest to this group today that I did not actually hear President Washington utter those words." The room burst into laughter. "Mr. McFadden, it is great to have another Irish American as president, although my dear friend Tip, the good Speaker, was proof enough that not every Irish American is fit for higher office." More laughter. "Young McFadden, may you preserve the fire of liberty as the others in this room have done so adeptly over the course of nearly 250 years."

The room showered the Great Communicator with applause and words of approval. He clearly owned that moniker—and the moment.

After an awkward pause, President Kennedy emerged. "I will step forward to spare you others from the unenviable task of following the Gipper. What Mr. Reagan lacks in his politics he more than makes up for in charm." JFK paused and smiled as the room laughed and then applauded. This guy was smooth as silk. And he seemed tanned, which made me wonder if he somehow still managed to get to Palm Beach in the winter.

Kennedy then proceeded in his familiar Boston accent, "Number ten: to my fellow Irish American, Daniel Patrick McFadden, perhaps the finest-named president in this room. May you have the character of General Washington, the wisdom and knowledge of Mr. Jefferson, the toughness and passion of Teddy Roosevelt, the vision of FDR, the humility, determination, and perseverance of Mr. Lincoln, and the advice, support, and encouragement of every leader in this room."

All those around me shook my hand as they drank from their glasses. Several moments passed, and then Richard Nixon stood up from the booth he had been inhabiting. In a voice so familiar to me from my youth, he said, "You all know I have been knocked down in my life. So many of us have. I fell further and faster certainly than most of you," he paused for a second then added with emphasis, "but I got up. And we all got up. For only if you have been in the deepest valley can you know how magnificent it is to be on the highest mountain." Raising his glass, he said, "Number eleven: to all who have been knocked down. May they get up, even at the risk of being knocked down again."

This seemed to strike a nerve in the room. The support and encouragement for this moment of rather remarkable vulnerability was palpable. What a powerful truth he spoke. Perhaps like most people, I tended to view the lives of presidents as largely privileged and idyllic, ignoring the struggles, the conflicts, and the utter failures. I appreciated that toast and made a vow to remember it in the lonely days that may be awaiting me.

Bill Clinton came forward from the back by the bar. Of course, he did. How could he not? "Thank you for that, Dick. As you know, I spent some time facedown on the mat as well." He smiled as he looked at Nixon. "What number are we up to now, fellas?" he asked.

A few in the group responded, "Twelve."

Clinton proceeded, "Number twelve: More than any other nation on Earth, America has constantly drawn strength and spirit from wave after wave of immigrants. In each generation, they have proved to be the most restless, the most adventurous, the most innovative, the most industrious of people. Bearing different memories, honoring different heritages, they have strengthened our economy, enriched our culture, renewed our promise of freedom and opportunity for all. May America forever be a home for all those yearning to breathe free."

Another chorus of "Hear! Hear!" followed from the group.

Applauding, Washington said, "Now we are in need of a thirteenth, gentlemen. Have we someone to provide a suitable finale?"

Teddy Roosevelt answered the call. I could sense the excitement of the room as he emerged to speak. He sported a three-piece suit with striped pants and a pocket watch chain visible in his vest. I could tell from the look on his face how much he relished this moment. "Many of you know I was once shot in the chest by a saloonkeeper before a speech." Then with great excitement, he belted out, "But it takes a lot more than that to kill a Bull Moose!" The room exploded.

Moments later Roosevelt continued, "I proceeded to give my speech that day and finished before being rushed to the hospital. With that bullet still in my chest today, I should possibly be the last person to offer a toast to a saloonkeeper and staff." He turned to face the bar and looked at the staff. "But to you fine folks, we owe a tremendous debt of gratitude. I have often said that I had more fun in the White House than any other president, and I believe I have more fun in this fine establishment too. It is such a wonderful privilege to be among these delightful employees. We are so fond of each of you. We applaud you for your labor, good humor, and patience in providing these fine spirits and fellowship. Number thirteen: to these fine Americans here at this illustrious establishment."

More applause and approval erupted from the crowd. After the speeches, some in the crowd began to exit. However, it appeared that a lingering group had no intention of stopping at thirteen. I felt I needed to call it quits. The risks for me far outweighed the rewards. None of these gentlemen had a schedule like mine tomorrow—or the weight of the free world firmly affixed to their shoulders. I looked for the servers to offer my thanks.

Many of the presidents shook my hand and greeted me as I started to break away. Harry Truman, Jimmy Carter, and Gerald Ford halted their conversation to say hello as I walked past them. Truman looked me in the eye and said, in the most earnest, heartfelt way possible, "You do what you believe deep in your heart that you need to do. Pay no attention to all the blowhards. They're not sitting in your chair."

I appreciated that so much.

Carter added, "I've read about your work with the homeless in California. I admire that a great deal."

"That means a lot coming from you, sir, in light of all you've done for so many causes in your life," I responded. What a rare and wonderful gift this evening was.

Making my way toward the door I had entered, I noticed four men emerging from a booth in the corner. I immediately recognized the first. I couldn't miss him. Who wouldn't? Abraham Lincoln. There's no mistaking him. *Holy cow! What a sight!* I had not seen him in the crowd anywhere. He must have been in that booth all night. He wore a long dark coat with a bow tie and dark vest. He was so thin that he actually appeared even taller than his six foot four inches. The mere sight of him triggered in me a rush of emotions, as it clearly would any American. I knew instantly that I would never forget this moment. I couldn't take my eyes off of him.

As Lincoln arose, I saw the others who'd been sitting with him. I only recognized one: Barack Obama. I had met President Obama four times before—once at a tech summit in Silicon Valley before I was appointed to the Senate, once on Capitol Hill when I was still a Democrat, once at Camp David several weeks ago during the transition, and yesterday morning when we rode to the inauguration together. Nonetheless, it was still such a welcome sight for me to see him here in this room with all these gentlemen.

The other two presidents with them had to be from the nineteenth century. I did not recognize either of them. I decided to go say hello. Before I could reach them, two of the waitresses caught up to me to welcome me and introduced themselves. They were young, smart, engaging, and attractive—basically perfect like everything else about this bar.

"Welcome to the Saloon, Mr. President!"

I stopped and turned around. "It is something special to be here with you," I said. "Thank you for everything tonight."

"I'm Grace, but everyone here calls me Mary Ann."

"OK. Then I guess I'll call you Mary Ann."

"President Bush nicknamed me that." She then placed her hand on the other young woman's shoulder. "And this is Tina."

"Is that your real name, Tina?" I asked.

"Yes, it is sir. Otter is way too intimidated by me to give me a nickname." They both laughed.

"He really is," said Mary Ann.

"I will definitely remember that," I replied.

"We hope to see a lot more of you around here!" Mary Ann gushed.

"Oh, I'd love to come back, believe me. I'm not exactly sure how to go about that, but I'd love to. What's it like to work here with all these alpha males?"

"Every night is an adventure," responded Tina. "In some ways, it's like an intellectual candy store. But oh my God, some of these egos are out of control. And many of them have absolutely no concept of sexual harassment. They seem to consider it sport."

"But Mr. Sheels watches out for us and tells us which ones to steer clear of," said Mary Ann.

"And that's a pretty long list," added Tina.

"Who is Mr. Sheers?" I asked.

"It's Sheels," corrected Mary Ann. "He's our boss. He's been running this place since the day it opened."

I looked around at this classic, vintage saloon. I wondered exactly how long that was.

"Haven't you met him? "asked Mary Ann.

"I don't believe I have." I answered.

"He's a remarkable guy."

"He runs a tight ship around here," added Tina. "And he takes no guff from any of these egos."

"He was here earlier, but I think he took off," said Mary Ann. "He keeps a low profile, but he's clearly in charge here. I'm not sure he likes a lot of these guys. But you should really get to know him."

"Thanks," I replied. "I'll make a point to catch up with him next time."

"Wait a second . . . ," I said. "I may have seen him. Was he standing alone in the back during the toasts.?"

"Yes, I believe so," said Mary Ann.

Just then I felt a tap on my shoulder. I turned to see none other than George Washington gazing into my eyes. "Good luck to you, McFadden," he said in a most sincere tone as he grasped my hand and gave it a firm shake. "I was a reluctant president, but a few of these folks convinced me that it was best for the country. I have a suspicion you may be too."

I was blown away and rendered effectively speechless. "Thank you, Mr. President," I said. I'm afraid that was about all I could muster up.

He smiled back. "No one called us that when we served, but I have gotten used to it here. Of course, you can call me George."

"I don't suspect I'll be doing that anytime soon, but thank you just the same, sir." I responded, borrowing a line from a new friend.

"You can call me General, then. I rather prefer that anyway."

"Thank you, General."

"Tell me, McFadden, did my gold coin survive another transition?"

"Yes!" I laughed. "There was another peaceful transition of the coin to me through a wonderful gentleman in the White House named Satch."

"Ah, yes," replied Washington. "I understand he's been handling the passage for the past forty years."

"In fact, I believe I've got it on me," I said as I pulled the coin out of my pocket to show him.

"Keep this with you at all times," Washington directed. "You never know when you may need it."

"I am honored to be the latest entrusted with its possession, General. I will try to live up to the standard it represents."

"Good luck, McFadden. Remember, we're here for you."

As Washington turned and walked away, I took a second to let what had just transpired sink in. This whole experience was exhilarating.

I looked back toward Lincoln's table, but he had disappeared. Obama was saying goodbye to the other two. The short bald one may have been John Quincy Adams. Somehow it made perfect sense to me that Obama would stay out of the way of a lot of these guys and spend a good portion of the night at a table with Abraham Lincoln and John Quincy Adams. I knew a little about the younger Adams—enough to know he was a staunch abolitionist, both as president and later as a congressman, and had represented the *Amistad* slaves in their trial and ultimately helped them gain their freedom. I loved that movie with Morgan Freeman and Anthony Hopkins. The book too.

I was dying to find out who the other gentleman was. In as subtle a way as possible, I asked Mary Ann.

"Everyone calls him General Hayes," she whispered.

Rutherford B. Hayes. I have to admit I didn't recall anything about him, but I decided that he couldn't have been all bad if he'd been seated with such distinguished company—incredibly distinguished company, I should say.

As the two waitresses scurried off, I called out, "Wait, why does George W call you Mary Ann?"

They didn't hear me.

I felt I had to leave. I thanked some of the other servers and made my way back to the side door through which I had entered. As thrilling as the night had been, it was nothing short of inspiring as well. I clearly felt the support of this group—for me and for the country. And while I wasn't exactly sure if that support could help me in any way, it made a world of difference to my mental state and to my confidence that I could, indeed, pull this off.

The last thing I heard as I approached the exit was another loud toast, this one from a voice I did not recognize.

"To our wives and sweethearts!" Then after a brief pause, "And may they never meet!"

Those who remained erupted in laughter. Even with the little I knew of the private lives of many of these characters, I'm guessing they appreciated that one as much as any they'd heard all night. I wasn't sure they'd be slowing down any time soon. I decided that I'd gotten out of there just in the nick of time. As I walked out, I noticed a large wooden sign above the door. It displayed the image of George Washington that appeared on the gold coin Satch had given me. Below that in bold letters read: "THE PRESIDENTIAL SPIRITS SALOON, SERVING PRESIDENTIAL SPIRITS SINCE 1792."

1792? Oh my God!

Chapter Seventeen

January 21, 2017
Must Have Been a Dream

With my head spinning—and not from the alcohol—I quickly descended the spiral staircase back down to the second floor and proceeded back to our bedroom suite. I looked at Denyse, who was still sound asleep in the same position as when I'd left her. If she only knew. My God, if she only knew. Montana was next to her, now in my spot. I undressed and tossed my tux pants to the corner of the room. As they hit the ground, the gold Washington coin flew out of the pocket and clanged against the wall. That wasn't exactly the level of respect Washington wanted me to afford it. Or Satch. I got up, put it back in its case, and left it on the nightstand. Then I poured myself into bed. That day—clearly the longest, craziest day of my life—left me with far too much to process, and I didn't even know where to start. I fell asleep in seconds.

***

The next thing I knew I was waking up at first light.

I quickly showered and dressed. My older son Brett was up—no sign of Jack yet— and one of the White House chefs was hard at work in the residence kitchen impressing him with a made-to-order breakfast.

"How'd you sleep, buddy?" I asked.

"Great, Dad. This is a pretty cool place."

"Did you hear anything last night? Music or talking?"

"No . . . but I fell asleep with my iPad on. Why do you ask?"

"No reason."

Denyse came out wearing a robe and followed by Montana, who bounced around the room and jumped all over the chef.

"I am so sorry. I'm Denyse. I sincerely hope you're a dog person."

"I know who you are, ma'am. I'm Sandy. And oh yes, I love dogs. But I haven't been able to get another one since my Chloe died. Someday, maybe. Me and this one will get along just fine, though. I've been enjoying some time with your son this morning. I adore your children. I think they enjoyed dinner last night."

"How'd you sleep, babe?" I asked Denyse.

"Perfectly. Nothing like twelve hours in heels and a couple glasses of wine to knock me out."

"You hear any noises or any activity?"

"Nope...slept like a rock, so I'm not sure I would've heard anything if I'd tried. Why do you ask? Did you asleep alright?"

"Maybe not the best. And I think I had a doozy of a dream. Perhaps someone slipped something into my champagne at one of the balls last night."

I hardly ate a thing at breakfast. I was still in a daze from that surreal saloon—whatever it was. Moreover, I wanted to be in the office early on day one to make a statement to the staff about the urgency of our mission and establish an ambitious work ethic. But beyond all that, I found myself incredibly fired up to get started, especially after the experience at the bar. I would think every president starts out this way before becoming hopelessly bitter and cynical. Before proceeding downstairs, however, I had to investigate the third floor. I knew full well I wasn't going to find any of the answers I was looking for, but I had to try.

At every turn, I encountered the security staff that had been conspicuously absent the night before, which only added to the intrigue. I struggled to come to grips with it all as I walked up the spiral staircase. What an incredibly powerful experience that had been. But how could it possibly have been real? I opened the door at the top of the staircase and proceeded toward the "inaccessible" wing. I tried the door and found it locked, just as the sign told me it was. I heard no music, smelled no smoke, and saw no hint of old presidents, living or dead. *Of course not*, I thought. *Even so, I had to check.* All my life I've been keenly aware that I'm a little nuts. Those closest to me know it, too, but I've done my best to shield the crazy from everyone else as much as humanly possible. I promised myself then and there that, no matter how desperately I wanted to, I would not tell anyone what I'd experienced up there on the third floor last night. And under no circumstances would I tell the vice president or any Cabinet members—they might go all Twenty-fifth Amendment on me!

I thought it best to just forget the whole episode, even as vivid, memorable, and meaningful to me as it was. Better to have the public convinced of my sanity, regardless of the truth.

I headed back downstairs. When I got to the Oval Office, I found Satch there waiting for me.

"Good morning, Mr. President. Great to see you bright and early," he greeted. "Let me know if the staff and I can do anything more to get you settled in here. That's what we're here for. How was your first night in the White House?"

"Memorable," I responded. "Unbelievably memorable."

"Did the ghosts of this old place get the better of you?"

I did a double take. *The ghosts?* "You don't know the half of it," I replied. I was pretty sure he was merely joking. But *I* wasn't. "Let me ask you something, Satch," I said, gazing up at the paintings of Lincoln and Washington. "What's the history of that third floor up there? What do you know about it?"

He smiled back at me. "Well, like everything else in this old haunted house, and, indeed, in this whole town, there is a rather *colorful* history." His smile grew as he spoke.

"Tell me more," I implored. "History always fascinates me."

"Well, for starters, Zachary Taylor housed his slaves up there—the ones he brought with him from Kentucky. That was back when you needed a ladder from the residence to access the third floor. It was more like an attic. Woodrow Wilson kept rooms up there for the young men who were courting his daughters. Can you believe that? And FDR's dear friend and longtime secretary, Missy LeHand, who is rumored to have been a whole lot more than just a secretary, if you know what I mean, lived up there as well."

"I don't imagine we're going to have any arrangements like that during my administration."

"That's good to know," Satch laughed. "Many of your predecessors lived rather interesting lives."

"And I'm sure as hell not going to put up any of Kelly's suitors in a fancy bedroom one floor above her! In fact, I was kind of hoping to use the

Secret Service to make sure she doesn't do *any* dating." My daughter, Kelly, was a freshman at Santa Clara University. I was half kidding about the Secret Service. Maybe.

"Let me show you how we've got your study set up. Most presidents these days work mostly out of that. The Oval Office is used more for meetings, signings, formalities, and photo ops."

We walked next door to check out the study, where my longtime assistant, Cathy, was already organizing the desk, bookshelves, and credenzas. She'd been with me for twelve years and had made the big move with me from the Bay Area. It was the first time I'd seen her since election night.

She greeted me as "Mr. President," which I rejected immediately. "Cathy, please." It seemed silly for her of all people to call me that.

We talked about how her husband and kids were adjusting. She assured me they would all be fine. I felt guilty about being responsible for plucking her kids out of beautiful Almaden Valley in San Jose and taking them away from all their friends. Then I got to the item front and center on my mind.

"I need you to do a favor for me," I said to her in a voice that probably sounded more serious and desperate that I intended, but I couldn't help it. "I need you to find an expert on presidential history for me. Doris Kearns Goodwin or someone like her who really knows their stuff and is willing to engage with me about it from time to time."

"Sure. Of course. I would think anyone you ask would be flattered and certainly willing to do so. How should I characterize your expectations for them? Is this for purposes of speeches or general background or something more specific?"

"Just tell them that I have suddenly become keenly interested in the lives and legacies of all of my predecessors. I'd love to have someone capable of briefing me on any part of their lives at a moment's notice."

"Sure. By phone?"

"I'd love a few hours in person at first, followed perhaps by phone, text, or e-mail communications after that." I was glad she wasn't overly curious about why I was asking.

"How soon?"

"As soon as you can pull it off."

"Shall I summon Air Force One, then?"

I could see she had no intention of altering her sense of humor just

71

because we were now occupying the most venerable office in the history of our republic.

"Better yet, why don't you contact Dr. Arnold Harris, my old professor from Notre Dame. He's an expert on presidential history—my favorite college professor. I'd love to reconnect with him."

***

That night following the late-edition of *SportsCenter*, after everyone had else had fallen asleep, I decided to venture upstairs again, just to see if that phenomenon—or whatever it was—would possibly replicate itself. This time, the Secret Service agents were at their posts as I walked toward the staircase leading to the third floor. I heard no music or voices walking up the stairs. The floor was deserted. In light of my conversation with Satch, this floor now brought to mind Zachary Taylor's slaves, Woodrow Wilson's daughters' suitors, and FDR's special friend. But no sign of them or any of the other "ghosts" I had come to see.

Very reluctantly, I concluded that I wouldn't be frequenting that mystical saloon again. *Must've have been a dream. I figured as much. How could it not have been?*

Chapter Eightteen

January 2, 2017
Charlie Company

Still haunted by that supernatural saloon, I felt the need to seek out Satch again. For some strange reason, I suspected he might be more knowledgeable about this than he was letting on. He seemed to know where all the bodies were buried around this place.

I ventured down to the basement of the White House, which necessitated an escort from the Secret Service. I wanted to try to catch Satch in his office. We turned quite a few heads on the way as we passed the flower shop, the carpentry quarters, and the other offices in the bowels of this old mansion. We stopped in front of a nondescript, lonely looking office tucked away all by itself. Its only window appeared on the door looking out at the hallway.

A light was on inside the office. I looked in and could tell in an instant who it belonged to. Photos and memorabilia adorned the walls and revealed a life well lived. A rather lonely but charming work sanctuary.

Just then I heard a familiar voice call out, "Mr. President." I turned to see Satch approaching. When my Secret Service escorts saw him, their faces lit up, and they gave him the most effusive bro hugs I'd ever witnessed. I was a bit taken aback, only because I had permitted myself to become quite proud of the relationships I had already forged with the many Secret Service agents, convincing myself I was truly a man of the people. Well, let me say this, they never embraced me with anywhere near this level of enthusiasm. It was a very humbling sight.

Satch finally got around to me. "You checking up on me, Mr. President?"

"Just paying you a visit, Satch. I needed to check out your digs."

"Come on in, sir," he said enthusiastically. I followed him inside.

I was mesmerized by all the photos on the walls. One appeared to be a youthful version of him on the mound in mid-windup; it was obviously posed. Beside it hung a photo of what looked to be Satchel Page and another I recognized of Dizzy Dean.

"Now, there's a couple of pitchers there!" I exclaimed.

"A couple characters too," replied Satch. "I don't think either of them lacked for confidence."

"'It ain't bragging if you can back it up.' Isn't that what Dizzy used to say?" I asked.

"Ol' Diz was Muhammad Ali well before Cassius Clay was."

I scanned the walls some more and spotted a Sam Cooke record cover for his anthem, "A Change Is Gonna Come." Of course—a classic. Next to that hung a photo of a young Satch alongside a lady dressed to kill in a classic convertible. "Ooh la la!" I called out. "Wow! Get a load of you!"

Satch smiled. "Senior Prom, 1964. That's my Uncle Raymond's '63 Corvette Stingray. I loved that car, and I loved that lady, of course. Always will. Made her Mrs. Satch."

"Beautiful bride. And a sweet ride," I said, trying not to let on that I wasn't the least bit interested in cars and really had no idea what a Corvette Stingray was. "Your uncle had it going on. And obviously, so did you."

"Yes, indeed. Hell of a jazz trumpeter. Very successful. He even played a bit with Count Basie. I idolized him. And that, my friend, is my dream car."

"Do they still make 'em?" I asked, even though I was quite sure that was a stupid question.

"Yes, they do, but not like the '63."

"And how about Uncle Raymond?" I asked. "Is he still with us?"

"No. He left us in the late '60s. Died way too young, God rest his soul. And I've got no idea what happened to that car. I believe my cousins may have sold it following his death to settle a few debts. But my Dina and I went to that prom in style, baby!"

"I'll say. So classy!"

"In my next lifetime, I'll have one of those all my own in my garage," Satch said with a bit of sparkle in his eyes. "And I'll coach baseball too. Just let me have the pitchers, and we'll do just fine."

"Now that's an idyllic life."

"And my Dina, of course. Wouldn't want any of the other stuff if I didn't have her too. Married her during the Summer of Love. Best decision I ever made."

"You're a lucky man."

"Yes, indeed. The only love of my life."

I noticed an eight-by-ten-inch photo of a woman on his desk in what appeared to be nurse's uniform and hat. "Dina as well, I assume?"

His face burst into a big smile. "Yep . . . her senior photo from nursing school."

"They are certainly among the most selfless, caring, consequential people in the whole world," I said. "I have no doubt the Lord has reserved a special place in heaven for nurses."

"And that's precisely where she is, sir. We lost her to ALS in 2010."

My heart sank. I should have surmised that earlier. How could I have missed that? I looked and saw that he clearly had a wedding ring on his ring finger, but still I felt terrible. "I am so, so sorry, Satch. I had no idea."

I saw a brief moment of profound sadness engulf his face, but he quickly broke free of it and perked up again. I felt terrible that I'd led him to that dark place.

Scanning the room some more, I couldn't help but notice a print of a painting of George Washington. I thought that rather unusual amidst all the other personal memorabilia, but what was even more surprising was the setting. Washington was seated at a table with Martha and being attended to by a well-dressed, handsome, young black server. From all I knew of Satch, this print—which was clearly, in part, depicting slavery—was certainly a strange choice. And oddly enough, the slave in the painting kind of resembled Mr. Sheels, whom I had briefly seen in the Saloon the night before, although I hadn't yet met him.

When Satch saw me gazing at the print, he immediately directed my attention elsewhere. "These are my boys, here." He pointed to an old grainy photo rather hidden on the back wall of his office amidst a sea of other photos. It showed about a dozen young soldiers in uniform posing in front of a tent. I walked over to get a closer look. I easily recognized Satch—one of three African Americans in the photo. The whole group of them looked so young. Most were smiling, which took me a bit by surprise.

"Vietnam?" I asked.

No response from Satch. He just sat there letting me absorb the photo, which quite obviously meant a great deal to him in spite of its inconspicuous location on a busy wall amongst many other photos. In the top right against the light blue sky, someone had written: "Marines First Bat. 5th Reg. Charlie Company."

"Marines," I said. "Impressive. But even only knowing you for a day, I can't say I'm surprised." The more I learned about this gentleman, the more I admired him.

"We lost several of those guys," Satch said, his voice cracking a bit with emotion. "Lost my best friend TJ—the one with his arm draped around me."

I examined the photo to take a closer look at the tan, muscular, young man alongside Satch. TJ was clearly mugging for the camera. The smiles of this group belied the tragic and heartbreaking nature of the predicament that they found themselves in. Hard to imagine, but the human spirit obviously finds a way. It made me feel so fortunate to have been born into a generation that largely escaped all that. For so many generations of Americans, that was just a rite of passage.

"Good-looking kid," I said.

"He was something else. Life-of-the-party personality. Kept us all laughing. He was fearless too. Many of us in this photo owe him our lives—including me. And he was no kid—had a wife and a young child back home. His wife, Christy, made me the godfather of their toddler. When we got back to the States, she got all of us together for a memorial service for TJ followed by a baptism. I gave a eulogy in the morning and read a christening prayer that afternoon."

He paused in an obvious effort to fight off tears. "I would do anything for Christy and that family. Anything—as he would have done for mine. Somehow, someday, in some way, I'll pay him back."

This little jaunt of mine to Satch's work quarters had been so telling. As depressing as so much of this clearly was, at the same time his compelling personal story inspired me.

"Such a shame," I said, not quite sure what else to say. "Heartbreaking. I'm so very sorry about all that." Then I added what I had become accustomed to saying to every serviceman or woman I encountered, "Thank you so very much for your service."

"I appreciate that, sir," he replied. "It's all a bad dream, and I'm not entirely sure why. What had it all been for? What could it possibly all mean?

Maybe Tennyson got it right - ours is not to reason why.

"I can't imagine what it must've been like to be Lyndon Johnson presiding over that war?" I asked rhetorically.

"To put it mildly, I'm not his biggest fan," Satch said candidly. "Lost so many good buddies over there. Hard to imagine having a war like that as a legacy. Inconceivable, really. You gentlemen are in a mighty messy business."

"Don't I know it!"

Searching for a segue to something positive and life-affirming, I saw a photo of a young family on the desk next to the photo of Dina. "Who have we got here?" I asked.

"That's my boy, TJ, his wife, Rene, and their kids, Hank and Dina. These kids are my pride and joy. When Dina passed Mr. Biden told me you gotta have something to do, someone to love, and something to hope for. These are my someones to love," he said with a mighty proud smile.

"From what I gather, there is no shortage of people who love *you*, Satch."

"I've been very blessed, sir."

"You are the type of person people are naturally attracted to," I added. "It comes as no surprise to me at all that Vice President Biden befriended you."

"He was very gracious with his time for me."

"Who's this?" I asked, pointing to a small painting of a dog.

"That's my yellow Lab, Jackie. Lost her years ago."

"No!" I yelled. I started to walk toward the door. "OK, that's it. I'm gonna leave now . . . and shut my mouth forever."

Laughing out loud, Satch replied, "It's no problem, sir."

"Have you gotten another?"

"Can't do it. She can never be replaced."

Seeking to end on a positive note, I pointed back to the photo of his son's family. "That's quite a pair of grandkids you've got there, Satch."

"Don't I know it, Mr. President," he said, beaming.

As I exited Satch's office, I realized I hadn't even broached the subject I had come down to explore: the Saloon. But what an enlightening few minutes I'd had with him. I wanted to explore it all so much further. I'm guessing Biden reached out because he himself had been through a good bit of personal tragedy of his own. I wanted to learn more about Dina. It sounds like she was special. I also wanted to hear more about Satch's time in Vietnam. I felt sad that he'd lost his best friend, his wife, and a favorite dog. I needed to let Denyse know all of that. She'd go to work on it right away. She's good at that.

More than anything, this remarkable soul gave me hope. What a genuinely admirable character he was. I considered myself profoundly fortunate to have him one floor away as I embarked upon the challenging road ahead.

Chapter Nineteen

January 29, 2017—2:05 p.m.
The Court Pick

Cathy came in to my private office in the study off the Oval Office unannounced. She caught me spying the news at the top of the hour on the bank of televisions in front of me.

"You asked me to make sure you were ready for your three o'clock on the court pick, so I'm gently nagging you."

"I am not ready, of course," I replied. "Nowhere near it. I wanted to get through those stacks last night, but never got to it. Please, please, *please* build time into my schedule every day so I can fully prepare for all these meetings. If I come unprepared, it makes me look like an idiot—or even more like an idiot."

"I do build in time as you well know, but you fill it. However, if you'd rather blame me go right ahead." Then she looked at me with a face of exaggerated insincerity. "I am so sorry, Mr. President. I take full responsibility. I promise it will never happen again."

I did not laugh. "I'll just get their initial thoughts and read this stuff tonight," I replied.

"And I started to reach out to Doris Kearns Goodwin as you requested but I may just need a few more specifics on precisely what you'll be asking of her. I'm no expert, but don't you think it's a little early for her to do her assessment of the McFadden presidency?"

"Ha ha, very funny!" I shot back sarcastically. "Tell her I just want to get a greater sense of the history of some of my predecessors in this crazy job. And there is some urgency. But as I mentioned last week, try my college professor first. He has all the background in presidential history I need."

My attorney general was nowhere near confirmation, but I wanted to move on the Supreme Court vacancy right away. I had the acting Attorney

General, Sally Yates, the Solicitor General Brad Wright, and the Deputy Attorney General Mark Lennon coming in to meet with me, my Chief of Staff Terri Drake, Senior Policy Adviser Karen Nevarez, and our Chief Congressional Liaison Christina Murphy.

Terri Drake stuck her head in my office a few minutes before three just as Cathy left. "You tell me how you'd like this to go, sir. Do you have a leader in the clubhouse?"

"No, not really. My interest is just that I want a damn good judge. I'm not looking for a stealth candidate like Souter whose record is shielded or a bit of a mystery. I want someone who has taken on the tough issues in a thoughtful, fair-minded way and hasn't been shy about it, but who isn't a zealot."

"Are there positions or stances on issues you are seeking here, sir? I honestly don't know how you sit on the right to privacy or if you're looking for a strict constructionist. You yourself are a bit of a mystery, I would say," She laughed as she said it.

"I'm afraid it's that mystery—that unknown, blank slate of a record—that got me elected. Had I taken enough stances on issues, I probably would've been unelectable." It may have sounded like I was kidding, but I really wasn't.

"Well, I'd caution you against selecting someone with too much of an extensive record. Confirmation will be hell."

Together we walked next door into the Oval Office.

Cathy walked the others in right at three, and we sat on the couches in front of the fireplace. I had already decided that I preferred the seat on the couch facing the glass door between the Oval Office and Cathy's space so I could see if anyone was milling about out there.

I kicked off the meeting with a mini-rant, which I guess had become my new brand. "With this pick I want it all—a brilliant legal mind with impeccable credentials, who brings a reputation for openness, collegiality, modesty, and even-handedness. Beyond all that, with this pick I'm seeking to challenge the notion that Supreme Court picks must necessarily fall into one of two camps - the Scalia camp or the Brennan camp. That may be an incredibly naive notion to express on my part, but our system of choosing justices is simply yet another by-product of the political paralysis in this country. My challenge to you today is to find me a judge with all the requisite credentials and integrity and no discernable political bias. Maybe that's a tall order these days, but I'm convinced we can find several phenomenal folks who fit that criteria."

"Are you hoping to make a statement with a woman or a particular minority?" Karen asked. "You carried the Hispanic vote and did well with women, but Clinton did better with African Americans."

"Of course, all things being equal, the court could use more gender and ethnic diversity. But my primary goal with this pick is purely and simply a stellar judge without a perceptible political compass. With this pick, I want my statement to the nation to be that it doesn't have to be a far right judge or a far left judge every time. Maybe if I'm here long enough, I'll be able to put three moderates on the bench."

Sally handed me a stack of papers. "I've got a list of dossiers of candidates here that I think you'll like. At the top of the pile is Merrick Garland."

"Obama's pick?" I asked, a bit surprised.

"Yes," Sally replied. "Hear me out for a second. He was really a sort of compromise candidate. Obama knew he had an uphill climb in the Republican Senate, so he offered up a candidate that the conservatives would not find unacceptable. He's probably the most moderate nominee any president has submitted in quite some time. He came with high praise by both sides."

"How did he appeal to conservatives? What did they see in him?"

Sally leaned forward. "He has continually ruled against Guantanamo Bay prisoners attempting to assert their rights. He also signed on to a decision in the landmark *Citizens United* case that paved the way for super PACs."

"Really? Then why the heck did liberals like him?"

"First of all, I'm not sure they *loved* him, but he would've been better than anyone a Republican president would have offered up. They figured he'd at least maybe have a chance at confirmation. He leaned left in the employment cases, frequently voting to uphold the rights of workers suing for discrimination in the workplace. However, he really would've been an unknown on many of the social issues that tend to drive these confirmation hearings."

"I'd rather have someone with a bit of a record in that area, one who is not predictable but willing to evaluate the merits of each case on their own facts." I looked around at the others. "Let me know if you come across any-one remotely resembling what I'm getting at here."

Karen Nevarez looked at me with an expression that seemed to seek my approval to contribute to the conversation.

"What have you got, Karen?"

"I've got someone you may want to take a look at. Jonathan Harper is a Ninth Circuit judge—appointed by George W and confirmed unanimously in the Senate. I think you'll find he has some of the elements you're seeking. He has famously not toed the party line for the GOP. He's had no shortage of contentious issues come before his panels and has provided some wins for both sides."

"Can you give us some examples?"

"Yes. He upset the NRA and many on the right by upholding an Oregon statute that dramatically restricted assault weapons. In his opinion, he specif-ically stated that the Second Amendment provides no protection for what he referred to as 'weapons of war.'"

Drake laughed, "Alrighty then. If you're looking to be a four-years-and-out president, he sounds like your man!"

"Tell me more, Karen," I said, turning away from Drake.

Karen carried on, "Well, any liberal friends he made in the Oregon case he may have lost in upholding a law that outlawed partial-birth abortions. Again, he wrote the opinion—he's not a grandstander, but he certainly does-n't shy away from these political minefields."

"Did the law have an exception for the life of the mother?"

"Yes, it did. The wording of the exception was, of course, one of the critical issues in the case,"

"Please get me that case."

"I have it right here," she said as she passed me a rather thick file.

"Anything else noteworthy about the record in here?"

"Yes, there is more—quite a bit more. He also incurred the wrath of the right with an opinion he wrote upholding a campaign fund-raising restric-tion. In his opinion, he went so far as to question the proposition that money constitutes speech. His opinion is peppered with a lot of language about the evils of money in politics, corruption, etc. From the little I know about you, sir, you would love it. The Supreme Court reversed it. Scalia didn't write the opinion, but he ripped him in his concurrence."

"Oh, that would be rich," added Murph, "having him take over Scalia's seat after that. Not sure it would fly in the Senate, though."

"And there's more," Karen added. "He wrote the opinion upholding California's ban on race-based admissions."

"Did he say affirmative action is unconstitutional?" I asked.

"No," Karen responded. "That issue wasn't in front of him. He merely articulated that it's permissible under the Constitution for the voters of a state to ban race-based admissions."

"Let me take a look at this guy. I like the thought of putting someone up who hasn't shied away from the critical issues of our day but has confronted them in an even-handed way."

"I'd be careful with this one for precisely those reasons," Murph cautioned. "I can see you getting hit from both sides on him. He may be the first nominee to be excoriated by both Judicial Watch and Common Cause."

"Perhaps that's the surest sign he's our guy," I said, grabbing all the homework they had prepared for me. "Please find me a dozen more respected, even-handed, courageous judges just like him. I'd be thrilled to push through someone who's not simply there to carry the water for one of the two parties."

The meeting energized me beyond belief. *This is precisely my marching orders,* I thought to myself. I hoped I wasn't underestimating the challenges that lay ahead in getting someone like this through.

Chapter Twenty

March 10, 2017
Rush

The Rush Limbaugh Show

Rush Limbaugh: Greetings, folks. Great to have you with us. Rush Limbaugh back at it. Here we are safely ensconced in the EIB Southern Command. And it's great to have you here, as always, as we kick off another week of broadcast excellence at the Limbaugh Institute for Advanced Conservative Studies. The telephone number if you want to be on the program is 800-282-2882 and the e-mail is ElRushbo@eibnet.us.

Let me cut to chase here, folks. We've had two months of this government by moderates, and as I told you the day after McFadden was elected, it has been and will be an unmitigated disaster. I predicted this, ladies and gentlemen, and it's one of the few times I hate being right.

I fear today that our RINO friends in the Republican Party—a number that seems to be growing by the day—are on the verge of caving in and confirming Jonathan Harper, McFadden's milquetoast selection for the Supreme Court. Ladies and gentlemen, the GOP is still in control of the Senate. That used to mean something. It should *still* mean something.

Harper is being sold to us as a moderate. That's how he's being branded—by McFadden, by McCain, and by Press Secretary Jed Rose. Let me tell you about the word *moderate*. A moderate is someone who lacks convictions, passion, a core set of beliefs. The dictionary spells it out for us. To be moderate is to be average, middling, common, passable, unexceptional. Well in that sense, I agree with the president. Judge Harper is unexceptional, and we should send him back. But my fear is that our Republican leaders lack the spine and the courage to make it happen.

Justice Antonin Scalia was that truly exceptional, once-in-a-generation Supreme Court justice we conservatives wished for. I have been noted to have said many times over the years that if I had not been born with my own brain, as much as I hate that thought and I'm sure you do too, but if I had to have another man's brain, I would have liked to have had Justice Scalia's brain.

I had the great fortune of getting to know him and calling him a friend. I had one particularly enlightening conversation with him years ago, and I will never forget what he said to me.

I always had the impression that there was persuasion going on in the Supreme Court chambers. So I asked him about that internal debate they must have all the time. He looked at me in an odd way, with a sort of a mild incredulity, and said, "There's no way we are going to change their minds." And by *they*, it was clear to me he was referring to the liberal justices. He meant that we are dealing with hard-core ideologues. He told me there was simply no possibility of changing the minds of the liberals on the court. They are not going to change their minds, and it is pointless to try. They are committed ideologues. And I interpreted that as a correct and proper understanding of just who those people are. They have not arrived at where they are as a result of debate. They are committed ideologues, and that's what takes me into this whole subject of Harper.

As you know—or if you don't, you have me to explain it to you—a 4–4 divided court is not always bad. If you look at it case by case, there are many instances where it's actually OK and helpful. If the court is divided, the last lower court's ruling holds, and with many cases, that could be very helpful to us.

The real test—and what we have witnessed for the past eight years here—is whether or not the Republicans will say no. They didn't do it to Obama until McConnell shut the door on Merrick Garland, and I fear they won't do it to McFadden. This is what it will come down to: Will the Republicans stop McFadden? Will they even try to stop McFadden?

All this talk about McFadden trying to find somebody who might be a little bit more moderate and may be acceptable to the Republican Party is baloney. There is no such thing as a moderate. The impact of this change will be significant. This will impact a generation or two, maybe more. This enables McFadden to shift the balance of the court toward the left, long after he has vacated the presidency. And, as Scalia convinced me, the conservatives on the court will not be able to change the minds of the others. Justice Scalia knew well that of which he spoke.

And ladies and gentlemen, listen when I tell you this: Judge Harper is no moderate. He may be labeled a moderate, but there is no such animal. Pay close attention to the so-called conservative senators. This will be the true test of whether they, in fact, have political courage or conviction. We cannot allow this to happen. We would have been better off with Obama's choice. Think about that, ladies and gentlemen. Obama selected a better judge than McFadden has.

And listen when I tell you, all this talk about bipartisanship, from Susan Collins and from Lindsey Graham and McCain—when they talk about bipartisanship, McCain says he's showing people how to get along. Let me tell you, he's showing people how to lose. Today's GOP is filled with moderate Republicans, including the leadership—especially the leadership. The GOP has undergone a transformation in the last several years. I no longer espouse what they believe. And this bipartisan nonsense is playing right into the liberals' hands. We are caving on our principles and ceding the country to the left. Don't get me started on this. The Democratic Party is responsible for the dissolution of morality in this country. The Democrats are peddling this war on women and selling it to their voters for political gain. It's the stupidest thing I've ever heard. Liberalism has become a special kind of stupid. There's so much hypocrisy on the left—don't even get me started.

McFadden and McCain lash out at all those so called bombastic people in radio. They say the hell with them, meaning us—you and me. Let me tell you, folks, the real bombast is in elected leaders running around mocking responsible patriots like you and me.

I want to reach around and pat myself on the back. I warned you about this, folks. I warned you about these milquetoast Republicans. Those Republicans who want to forge a relationship with McFadden and plan to confirm Harper are no better than liberal Democrats.

Chapter Twenty-One

April 3, 2017—2:00 p.m.
What's a Double Filibuster?

My worst fears on my court pick seemed on the verge of coming to fruition. Murph came into my office after lunch. She had a look on her face as if she'd just seen a ghost. I knew she had spent the morning working the offices in the Hart Senate building, taking the temperature of the senators on Harper. I think I knew where this conversation was headed, but my proclivity for denial was presently at full throttle.

I put my hand up signaling to stop her in her tracks. "Don't even come in here unless you have good news. I won't accept anything but good news."

That, of course, caused her to pause. "Are you serious?" she asked sheepishly with a look of disbelief.

"I've never been more serious about anything in my entire life," I responded, although I was starting to crack a smile at the sheer absurdity of that response.

She took a half step backward and studied my face in an attempt to gauge my seriousness.

"OK. Let me have it," I said, slightly defeated. "I'm ready, although I sense it will ruin my day . . . maybe even my month."

"Well, sir, even if this thing does make it out of committee, I think we are looking at a filibuster."

"By whom? Is it my buddies on the left or my pals on the right?"

"Well, that's the part that's really tough to swallow." She paused for a second, as if to allow my blood pressure an opportunity to rise to a level befitting this bombshell she was about to lob my way. "Mr. President, it's both."

"Ha ha!" I responded, shaking my head. All I could do was laugh. "That's just priceless!"

Not realizing that she clearly should've left it at that, she added, "Has the NRA and Emily's List ever seen eye to eye on any political issue before?"

"Not since the dawn of time." I jumped up and out of my chair, as if to try in vain to extricate myself from my body and this fiasco. "Am I setting new records for political ineptitude?"

Thankfully for my sake as well as hers, she let that last question linger unanswered.

I continued, "This is really truly remarkable, groundbreaking, unprecedented stuff here, right?"

"Don't do this to yourself, sir."

"I mean, we've had really truly inept and bumbling morons occupy this office who couldn't pull off precisely this level of—"

"This can't be good for you, sir."

". . . dysfunction and failure."

"Stop, stop, stop! It's not you that's inept, it's the system! If anything, you should be proud that both these extremes are displeased with you. Wear that like a badge of honor, sir! Not only is it your brand, it's precisely what this country needs." She continued with one parting shot as she exited the office. "Really, how is it even possible that the leader of the free world can actually suffer from this degree of insecurity and low self-esteem?"

That hit home. I was half joking with my little diatribe, of course, but that meant I was half serious as well. That was a red flag. Or certainly should've been.

Chapter Twenty-Two

April 3, 2017—3:00 p.m.
Twentieth Century Night

About an hour later, feeling mentally exhausted, I headed upstairs to the residence to catch a bath or a nap or just get the heck away. I don't have a particularly high tolerance for frustration, and it shows. Often.

I found the entire second floor empty except for two secret service agents. I'm sure the boys were at baseball practice. There was no sign of Denyse.

I kicked off my shoes and collapsed on the bed. With my head still spinning and trying hard to fend off a migraine, I opened the drawer of my nightstand to grab my reading glasses. I reached down to the basket below to pick up a book or magazine. I saw one of Denyse's *Vanity Fairs*. That kind of diversion promised to do the trick. I just needed my mind to go to a different place for a few hours. As I grabbed the magazine, I spotted Washington's gold coin next to the bottom of the stack. My first thought was how unappreciative Satch must think I am for never even thanking him for that or mentioning it in any way, particularly after the solemn manner in which he gave it to me. It clearly meant a great deal to him. More importantly, I thought maybe this might be the perfect time to see if this coin did, indeed, carry with it any good fortune or magic of any kind. I needed a little divine inspiration right about now. Heck, I needed a whole monastery doing Gregorian chants for me round the clock right now.

I tossed aside the *Vanity Fair* and grabbed the coin. I examined it again and thought of Washington carrying it around for luck. I decided I really needed to do that too. I placed it in my chest pocket. Within a few short minutes, I was fast asleep.

Sometime later, I opened my eyes and felt an eerie yet somehow vaguely familiar feeling. I got up and somewhat instinctively walked out of the bedroom suite and proceeded down the Center Hall toward the spiral staircase. I saw no sign whatsoever of the agents I had seen on the floor when I came up for my nap.

My heartbeat quickened as I approached the staircase up to third floor and heard voices and laughter. Could I possibly have another go at my new favorite saloon? *No—that would be far too much to hope for,* I thought. I'd convinced myself that I'd imagined the whole episode and that I was crazy—a thought certainly not far-fetched in the least.

As I neared the top of the stairs, I distinctly heard older male voices. I allowed myself to believe. I darted down the third floor hall to the secure area. The heavy door opened slowly, and there it was again—that mystical, magical bar in all its glory. Nearly empty, it looked spectacular. This time it was well lit with overhead lights turned on in addition to the gas lamps, and no presence of thick, hanging smoke. The woodwork and fixtures—now much more visible in the light—were even more stunning. Some of the servers scurried about apparently setting up for the evening, while a few musicians tested their instruments. A jukebox played vintage Sinatra. I always loved a bar that plays Sinatra. I had only set foot in this saloon once, but it already felt like home.

At the large table in the center of the otherwise empty tavern sat quite an eclectic collection of presidents. I easily recognized each of them: FDR sat in his wheelchair at one end with Truman next to him, then Carter, Lyndon Johnson, Ford, George H. W. Bush, and Nixon. Each had an active cocktail amidst multiple empty glasses before them. There was no sign of Madeira or buttered rum with this crowd, though. That was a good thing.

These men, many of whom I remembered well from my youth and young adulthood, looked much younger to me. LBJ, Nixon, Carter, and particularly George H. W. Bush all seemed younger and more vibrant than I last recalled them to be. Then it dawned on me that they appeared to me as they looked when they were in office, not as they looked presently or at the end of life as I remembered them most vividly. Perhaps someone else would have figured that out a lot quicker. Yes, certainly they would have. I knew I had to think a whole lot more about what all this means.

To my surprise, the elder Bush shouted a greeting to me. "Hey there, Rook!" He had evidently overheard his son at the bar my first night. "Pull up a chair and listen to a little bullshit about the glory days."

"What is this?" I asked with a slight smirk. "Twentieth Century Night?" I was evidently feeling considerably more comfortable this second time around.

As I sat down next to Truman, Teddy Roosevelt walked in the front door (not the side door that I used) and headed straight for the bar. I heard Matt yell out to him, "Mint julep, Mr. President?"

"Capital idea, fine sir!" TR responded with a big smile. "Let me begin with that and see where that takes us!"

The entire group greeted me very warmly as I sat down.

"How goes the battle, Rook?" asked LBJ. Apparently this nickname was not going away anytime soon.

"Tough one today," I answered. I don't know if they realized that I'd been doing my best to earn that nickname with my rookie moves every day at the office.

"No matter how bad it might be, Rook," LBJ responded, "you can be sure you've got a team of experts assembled right here at your disposal ready to help you screw it up even worse." They all exploded with laughter. Nixon particularly seemed to enjoy that one.

FDR chimed in, "And the advice you'll get from most of these fellas after a few belts certainly beats anything you'll get from them sober!"

More laughter. I thought it fascinating to witness camaraderie amongst this group, some of whom had been fierce political rivals and bitter enemies—or certainly would have been. Perhaps I could extract a powerful lesson from that. *Figuring out how best to capture it, properly articulate it, and then use it to bring about meaningful change is the challenge.* I didn't yet have the answers, but at least I knew the questions.

FDR looked over at me. "Welcome to the Children's Hour, McFadden. You look like you could use a drink." He called over to Mary Ann behind the bar, "Nurse," he yelled, eliciting more laughter, "how 'bout a cocktail for our man McFadden here."

"Be right there, sir," she responded as she shot a look to the bartender. I couldn't see, but I imagined an eye roll accompanied it.

"Please give us the latest, McFadden," requested FDR. "We're dying to learn the source of your consternation."

"Well," I began, "let's just say the Senate hasn't exactly embraced my Supreme Court nominee. The world's greatest deliberative body seems not to be a fan . . . of him or me."

"What is the essence of their objections?" asked Nixon.

"It seems I've selected someone with too much of a track record and who is not extreme enough to earn himself a groundswell of loyal, passionate support on either the left or the right."

"I made the opposite mistake," added George H. W. Bush. "I selected someone without an extensive public record or writings on important or controversial issues."

"Who still lived with his mother," added Nixon. The table enjoyed that quip, perhaps too much for Bush's taste.

Bush continued, "My point being, in selecting Justice Souter, I had chosen someone whose record was so sparse it could not be impugned, but that fact also deprived me of the track record necessary to demonstrate that he would be a reliable conservative. And, lo and behold, the son of a bitch voted with the liberals. Your nomination may be denied, but you can select another. I, on the other hand, could not."

Mary Ann arrived at the table. If she felt bothered in any way, it didn't show. "Tell me, what can I get for you handsome, powerful leaders of the free world?"

That line clearly pleased this collection of egos. Truman responded first, "Bourbon, please."

She looked at FDR. "Would you be so kind as to make me a Bermuda rum swizzle?"

"For you, Mr. President, of course! Happy to." She was flirting now.

Mary Ann looked at LBJ. "You look to me like you've been in a tavern or two in your day."

He responded right back, "Oh, I think I've *needed* a tavern or two more than these other fellas. I'd love another scotch please."

"You got it!" She looked at me. "How 'bout you, Rook?"

"How about me!" I shot back. "I'd love an Irish buck."

"Coming up, Mr. President," she replied.

I loved this bar and absolutely everything about it. It seemed any drink known to man could be summoned up in a few short minutes.

"Anyone else?" Mary Ann asked.

"I'll have a beer if you don't mind, please," Carter requested in his slow southern drawl.

"A Billy beer?" Nixon asked, clearly amusing himself.

"We can do a Billy Beer," Mary Ann answered with a proud, beaming smile.

"I'd say you have to do that, Jimmy," directed Nixon.

"Sure!" laughed Carter. "Get me can of Billy beer—the warmest can you've got!"

"And, sweetie, please bring me a good single malt scotch," Nixon added.

"Better make it two of those," Ford chimed in.

The group collectively watched as Mary Ann hurried back to the bar. For me, this whole magical scene was just what the doctor ordered after the day I'd had.

Truman brought us back to the topic at hand. "Justice Clark was my mistake, gentlemen. It wasn't so much that he was a *bad man,* it's just that he was a dumb son of a bitch!" That broke up the table.

"I erred with Oliver Wendell Holmes," Teddy Roosevelt called out rather loudly from the bar. "Monumentally. He turned a blind eye to the corruption of business on a gigantic scale. I could carve out of a banana a judge with more backbone than that."

"Mine was Felix Frankfurter," added FDR.

Nixon took his turn. "My mistake was Harry Blackmun. He gifted us a constitutional right to abortion."

Ike spoke up next. "Gentlemen, you cannot be more disappointed than I was with my appointees Brennan and Warren, maybe the two most progressive judges in the court's history. Warren was the biggest damn fool thing I ever did."

Mary Ann appeared again with reinforcements. Without any assistance, she perfectly delivered each drink to its intended recipient, until it came to Nixon and Ford.

"Let's see," she said looking at the two of them. "Single malt scotch?" She paused for an awkward second or two as both Nixon and Ford raised their hands. A little flustered, she set the drink down between them and hustled back to the bar.

"Go ahead, Dick," conceded Ford, "I'll wait for the next one."

"No, no, no," insisted Nixon. "Let me put it this way . . . I owe you one."

"You're damn right you do!" Ford responded amidst the laughter from the table.

"Now we're even," added Nixon with a laugh as he slid the drink toward Ford.

I must admit my relief at seeing them begin to drink without offering toasts. I have to think that on Nineteenth Century Night at the Saloon I wouldn't get off so easy.

After a brief lull in the conversation, Ford broke the silence. "Let me offer McFadden a contrary view on this topic. When I nominated Justice John Paul Stevens, who served for thirty-five years, I was more interested in healing the country than appointing an extreme ideologue. That said, he had told me he was a Republican, and his writings suggested a conservative slant. I had no idea he would consistently oppose the conservatives on the court throughout his entire term. That said, I am very proud to have appointed him. He was good for the court, and good for the country. I am prepared to allow history's judgment of me to rest on that selection alone."

"Well said, Mr. President," remarked Carter. "He was a tremendous choice." Carter then looked at Ike and said, "Similarly, General Eisenhower, Chief Justice Warren and his court ushered in some long overdue progress this country sorely needed in the areas of civil rights and liberties. I give you great credit for that." Then, turning to Nixon, he continued, "And Dick, I applaud your choice of Blackmun and the new era he ushered in for women in this country."

Eisenhower responded, "Thank you, Jimmy. I have to admit, I was not thrilled with the *Brown* decision, but in time I came to realize it was indeed best for the country. I disagree with the manner in which the Warren court increased judicial and federal power, but their legacy on civil rights is admirable."

I felt compelled to speak up, "I cannot tell you how fascinated I am by this discussion, gentlemen, and I appreciate it very much. As I wrestle with this, I can take solace in knowing that I'm in good company—the best company. I firmly believe the Senate will soon torpedo my selection, so it looks like I'll be back to the drawing board. Your experience in this area is invaluable to me. Any advice?"

Truman spoke up first, "Why don't you take Franklin's lead and just appoint fifteen new justices?" That generated much laughter. This group seemed surprisingly easy to amuse. The alcohol coupled with the utter lack of any discernable stress contributed mightily to that dynamic, I'm certain.

George H. W. Bush added, "I think the lesson for you from these fellas here today is that it is next to impossible to predict how someone might rule once appointed to the court. With that in mind, doing it all over again I would focus on selecting someone of impeccable character, who has a reputation for wisdom, integrity, fairness, and collaboration with colleagues. Precisely what our founders intended. I'd focus less on trying to predict a certain judicial or political philosophy. Find a truly outstanding person."

Nixon added, "Then good luck with your base!" More laughter.

These comments from Nixon and Bush spoke volumes. One could say it is all too easy for former presidents to sit back in their rocking chair and call for their successors to rise above the politics of the day. Governing in the moment in the real world—with an intensely divided, partisan electorate and an equally divided and intensely partisan Congress, eight-hour news cycles, and instant social media outlets like Twitter and Facebook—is perhaps more difficult today than ever. Moreover, all the incentives in this job seem designed to push presidents away from any instincts they may have to act in the best interests of the country.

I looked Bush in the eye and said, "I believe I did what you suggested. I picked a respected judge who is not an ideologue. Unfortunately, he had a long track record that included many instances of addressing divisive issues. In those cases, he sometimes leaned to the left and sometimes he leaned right. That track record now seems to make him unacceptable to both sides in our current political environment."

"Stick to your guns," advised Carter. "If it means you only get one term, so be it. You'll be better able to live with yourself, and perhaps you can bring about some meaningful change."

"Sage advice, sir," added Teddy Roosevelt. "It is dreadful misfortune for a man to grow to feel that his whole livelihood and whole happiness depend on his staying in office. Such a feeling prevents him from being of real service to people while in office, and always puts him under the heaviest strain of pressure to barter his convictions for the sake of holding office."

"Thank you, gentlemen, for a very enlightening discussion," I said, standing up to make my exit. I had heard what I needed to hear and felt a new sense of inspiration about my approach and philosophy—which is precisely the philosophy that got me into this in the first place. It was abundantly clear to me that the collegiality and willingness to listen to the viewpoints of others among this group far exceeded that of any present collection of politicians in Washington. *How could I change that?*

On my way out, as I stopped at the bar to say goodbye to the staff, I encountered two presidents I was unfamiliar with. One looked at me and said, "You should consider yourself fortunate to have this opportunity. When I had a chance to appoint a justice, Congress precluded me from doing so by abolishing the seat on the court."

I shot him a look equal parts sympathy and astonishment. *Could Congress really do that? Weren't nine justices ingrained in the Constitution?* As they walked away with their drinks, I looked at Mary Ann and asked, "Who was that?"

"Andrew Johnson," she replied.

"Who was with him?"

"Buchanan."

"Got it. It's gonna take me a while to get these down."

As I made my way back to the residence, I felt much better about my plight. I had a renewed sense of commitment to my convictions. For the moment at least, the political gridlock seemed to have less of a mental hold on me. And this self-assurance I was experiencing had everything to do with my little afternoon presidential happy hour. But I was still no closer to figuring out what the heck that is.

I headed back to work, reliving my second visit to the Saloon over and over in my head and searching to make sense of it all. *Was it a dream? Why was I able to open the door sometimes but not others?* As I walked quickly down the stairs, I felt something bounce against my chest in my shirt pocket. Placing my hand inside, I pulled out the gold coin. I had fallen asleep with Washington's gold coin in my pocket. I remembered that I had it with me the first night in the saloon as well. *Of course—the Washington gold coin.*

Chapter Twenty-Three

April 5, 2017—1:45 p.m.
Professor Harris

Cathy popped into my office. "Dr. Harris is here a little early. Would you like to see him now?"

Arnold Harris, my old professor from Notre Dame, was the person most responsible for my interest in government, politics, and history. He had an enthusiasm and a passion for the subject that was infectious. Had I taken his class earlier, I may have been a political science major.

I grabbed a few of the files on my desk and some writing material and walked next door into the Oval Office. A few moments later Cathy showed Professor Harris in.

"Welcome, Professor!" I was thrilled to see him.

"Mr. President," he replied. "It's great to have a Domer in the White House—a first!"

"Unless you count Josiah Bartlet, which I certainly do!" I said with a laugh. "Thank you so much for coming."

"Oh my gosh, sir," he replied as he walked around the room admiring the portraits and the photos. "The pleasure here is all mine."

"Can you and Carol have dinner with Denyse and me tonight? My boys may join us as well. I'd love to have them meet you."

"Yes, of course. We'd love to. We are staying with you as well, you know."

"Oh, awesome! I knew we offered, but I wasn't sure that was the case."

"I believe we'll be in a bedroom on the third floor."

"Wow! Perfect," I responded, "and remarkably appropriate, too, for purposes of this meeting." I think I just threw that in for my own amusement.

"First of all, you were the best professor I had at Notre Dame. I knew little or nothing about government and political science when I arrived at the university, and I left four years later with it being one of my life's passions."

"I love hearing that. Stories like that are why I love teaching. What did you have me for?"

"U.S. History, the American Presidency, and the U.S. Constitution. I would have taken more, but I was actually a business major!"

"I remember you in class." Professor Harris said.

"I don't believe that for a second," I laughed, "but it's nice of you to say. I loved your classes! You had such tremendous enthusiasm for the topic. And you wrote great letters of recommendation for me—very genuine and heart-felt."

"I always take those seriously. It's an important part of the job, particularly at a place like Notre Dame."

"I appreciated that very much. That's the type of attitude every professor should have."

"So, Mr. President, I'm dying to know what's on your mind. What have you summoned me for? I'm happy to help you in any manner you like. What can I do for you?"

"Well, to begin with, I wanted to properly thank you for the impact you clearly had on me. And for being so much more than just a professor who imparts the subject matter. You taught with a passion and enthusiasm that inspired all those of us willing to engage.

"Secondly, I'm finding that I have a constant need to know more and more of the history of this office, and, in particular, more about its previous occupants. We have historians here employed by the White House Historical Association, but I'm not sure they are what I'm after. And I have a team of speechwriters who generally know a great deal about history, but I think I'm gonna need something more specific. And everything I know and recall about you tells me you would be up to the task."

"I would love to. I am flattered. I am happy to be of help. As you may know, I'm emeritus now, so I've got a lot more time on my hands. This would be a very meaningful use of my time. How much time are you contemplating?"

"I'm not entirely sure. But we can pay you for the effort. And please don't read too much into the questions I'm asking or judge my relative lack of knowledge about history in general or the presidents. I have a good working knowledge, but it's nothing compared to you."

"Deal. I won't judge. Besides, since I taught this to you, any issue I would take with your relative ignorance on these topics would be an indictment of me as much as it would you."

"And I recall you have an obvious Democratic-leaning bias. I remember specifically some choice words you had for Reagan one day when I spoke with you after class. You didn't exactly use that terminology when lecturing to the class."

He laughed. "I don't doubt that a bit. Sometimes I let my guard down after class in discussions with the truly exceptional students." He smiled, but I saw right through it.

As we spoke a little more, I struggled to come up with a way to broach the inquiry I would be making of him without him thinking I'd completely lost my mind and running to the Cabinet to invoke the Twenty-fifth Amendment on me. Nonetheless, I started to wade in. "Let me ask you something, Professor. This may sound like a crazy question, but do you think that, generally speaking, all the presidents in history would get along? What do you think would happen if all the presidents, living and dead, could magically convene in some form of social setting?"

"Let me think about it. That's an interesting thought." He sat and considered it for a few moments. "Well, first off, I don't have to tell you that many of them hated one another—many times for very good reasons. But the majority of them would only know a handful of the others, if that. There would be party differences, north and south divisions, slaveholders and those who despised the institution, and some who disgraced the office and others who brought it honor and distinction. I would hope there would be mutual respect for each other and the country, however, a duel could break out at any time," he said with a laugh.

I laughed, but that piqued my interest. "I know about Hamilton and Burr, of course, but were presidents involved in duels?"

"Andrew Jackson participated in many. He even killed a man in a duel well before he became president. It left him with a bullet in his chest for the rest of his life."

"How lovely," I said, shaking my head. "I would think with all the divisiveness and bitterness in Washington these days, if we still had duels, there'd be no one left in Congress," I was only half joking.

"I wouldn't make the mistake of thinking it's more divisive now than ever before."

"Are you going to tell me there was a time when it was actually worse?"

"Yes, often. Bitter politics and ugly elections are a hallmark of this country. In the 1876 election, Samuel Tilden was called a thief and a 'drunken, syphilitic swindler.' Of course, the Federalists accused Thomas Jefferson of fathering children with a slave, and in 1858, there was a brawl on the House floor during a debate over whether to permit slavery in Kansas."

"A brawl?"

"Yes."

"And, by the way, those Federalists turned out to be right about Jefferson, didn't they?"

"Yes, they did," Professor Harris affirmed. "But the world didn't know that for certain for 200 years."

I found myself as fascinated talking with him as I had been back in college. "By the way," I said, "did Teddy Roosevelt ever get shot in the chest?"

"He certainly did!" And before I could ask him about the circumstances, the professor elaborated, "It was while he was giving a speech, and remarkably enough, he completed his speech before allowing people to take him to the hospital."

With that response, I felt an onslaught of blood rush to my head. My emotions overcame me as I struggled to grasp the meaning of it all. I had never heard that story about Teddy Roosevelt before—I swear I hadn't. *If I'm dreaming or hallucinating these encounters on the third floor, how could my dreams possibly involve facts and incidents unknown to me that were actually true?*

Completely mesmerized, I had to press on. "Let me ask you this," I said, "Did Eisenhower write a letter to the troops before D-Day in which he took full responsibility for the mission in the event that it failed?"

"Yes," replied Professor Harris, "but then he forgot about it until he found it in a coat pocket sometime later. Why do you ask?"

"Oh, no reason," I fibbed nervously. My hands were shaking and my head started spinning. "How do you suppose Obama would do in a room full of all of our former presidents?" I asked.

"That's a great question." Professor Harris lauded. "As you can probably guess, many of our presidents were racists. And I'm not just referring to the pre–Civil War Southerners—even some more recent presidents. For example, Woodrow Wilson praised the KKK. And the White House tapes really exposed Nixon's racist views. He had some views on race that are really quite disturbing. By the way, you should know that he also ripped your Irish race for being nothing but mean drunks."

"That's nothing I haven't heard before—or experienced firsthand! That's really unfair, though. I know many happy Irish drunks too."

The professor laughed. "You can find a whole lot of racist views if you go looking for them in our presidents—even in some areas you might not expect it. Truman admitted to being quite prejudiced when he was young, and his letters to Bess reflect very racist views. However, later in life he developed a much more enlightened view and became the first president since Lincoln to speak of civil rights. As I'm sure you know, he banned segregation in the military."

"I'm not sure I knew that," I admitted, "although it does sound vaguely familiar."

"So to answer your question, I really don't how Obama would interact with that group. Whatever he did or said outwardly, my guess is that, on the inside, he may not have much respect for a lot of them, and for good reason."

"That makes sense," I responded. "And I'm sure their racist views aren't the only reason why some of them might not be respected."

"Oh, of course. There are character flaws aplenty! But that's all of human history—particularly the human history of leaders and people in power. It doesn't take a very deep examination to uncover corruption, misogyny, hypocrisy, self-dealing, you name it. But the beauty of it is that you'll also find tremendous achievements, inspirational leadership, phenomenal vision, political courage—often from the very same folks with prominent character flaws."

"No doubt, Professor. That's what makes the study of this so compelling, at least in my opinion." I paused for a second, enjoying the moment with this gentlemen who meant so much to me. "Tell me this . . . ," I said, "which of the presidents would you most like to have a drink with, if given the opportunity?"

"I have to say I'm intrigued by all these questions, sir," he admitted. "Let me think about that for a minute."

He looked away for a few seconds then quickly focused his attention again back at me. "Thomas Jefferson. I suspect most people might say

Lincoln or Washington or possibly FDR. But of all of them, Jefferson might be the most interesting to meet and actually talk to. Because of his role in the creation of the country, his sheer brilliance, and his mastery of so many disciplines. He was a real renaissance man, you know. And more than any of that, the complexity of the man. He outwardly deplored miscegenation, yet he fathered many children with a young slave woman his daughter's age who was the half sister of his deceased wife. How about that, for starters. He stood for restraint on federal power yet exercised it liberally as President. And the man who wrote that "all men are created equal" himself possessed slaves, and ultimately opted to punt on this powder keg of an issue— bequeathing it to future generations. For all those reasons Jefferson would be the one I would choose to have a drink with.

"Yes, of course. Hard to argue with that," I said, loving that answer. "Let me ask you this, did Adams and Jefferson have a rivalry of sorts?"

"Oh, yes . . . very much so! They were fierce political rivals and even bitter enemies at times. However, they did become good friends in their elder statesman years."

"Do you think Adams resented the attention and legacy Jefferson enjoyed regarding the Declaration of Independence?"

"Yes, his letters suggest that he did."

My mind was racing. *How could it all be a dream or hallucination if I'm learning of truths that I don't even know in my subconscious?*

Just then, Cathy walked in with Terri Drake, my chief of staff. Both were sporting looks of concern. Drake came close and whispered in my ear, "There's been considerable rioting at a Far Right rally in Raleigh, North Carolina, sir. Three students who were protesting the rally were killed when a white nationalist intentionally plowed through the crowd in his vehicle. I believe this calls for an immediate response."

I stood up. Looking at Professor Harris I extended my hand and said solemnly, "I'm sorry, but I need to go. However, I'm looking forward to our dinner this evening. Thank you so much for making the trip here."

Together, Drake and I walked down the hall of the West Wing into Jed's office. He updated us on the latest reporting on the incident.

The demonstration, which was called a "Unite the Right Rally," was intended to make a statement about preserving Confederate monuments located on the grounds of the State Capitol. Many protesters carried Nazi symbols and chanted racist slogans. The right-leaning protesters had clashed with a large group of counterprotesters.

I shook my head. "This stuff is absolutely crazy," I said. "I know Lee is an icon to many, but he led an army that battled against the United States over the right to enslave fellow human beings. It's not unreasonable to see why such a statue is objectionable. Find out all you can then draft a statement for me and run it by the senior staff. This merits immediate attention."

The staff kept me abreast of the incident throughout the day. It soon became clear that the protest had been designed to stoke racial tensions. We released a statement expressing outrage over the violence and condemning hate groups. I told the staff I wanted to personally attend a candlelight vigil being planned for Monday evening in Raleigh. I also asked them to make the offer for me to attend any formal memorial service held for the poor young students who were killed.

Later that night, I lay awake in bed clutching the Washington gold coin and listening hard for any signs of activity from the floor above. Perhaps I was feeling my oats a little bit, but I felt eager to see if I could engage some of my new drinking buddies on matters of race.

Chapter Twenty-Four

April 35, 2017—11:23 p.m.
A Little Bit of Soul

Sure enough, not long after I lay down, I heard music and voices, which brought a smile to my face. I felt as if I'd cracked the code with my gold coin and perhaps this provided the final, definitive evidence of that.

I needn't be too proud of myself, though—I mean, it didn't exactly take a genius to figure it out. I eased my way out of bed so as not to disturb Denyse and Montana—although I'm fairly convinced little or nothing can roust either of these two from a sound sleep. I eagerly jumped up and made my way to my favorite new watering hole. This time I definitely had an agenda—other than simply immersing myself in the sheer spectacle of it all. While that in and of itself would certainly serve as a compelling motivation to belly up to that bar every night, I suddenly wanted more. I had at my disposal the sum total of all firsthand knowledge of this immense challenge I had undertaken. All of these men had assembled together apparently just for me—and seemingly with little or no compunction about sharing their experiences for the good of the country and mankind. My God, I wish DC was like this. But I needed to use this powerful tool at my disposal and see if somehow I could re-create that vibe inside the Beltway.

The joint was hopping when I arrived. Full house. A jazz band belting out the blues. I could see Bill Clinton playing tenor sax alongside the Saloon's house musicians. It looked to me like he may have been cozying up to the lead singer between songs, with no objections from her. The band appeared to be sporting a few of the other presidents who took turns playing different songs. A couple of them that I didn't recognize intermittently chimed in on the violin, another at the piano, and one even appeared to be on a trombone. However, none played with quite the swagger of Clinton, who seemed to excite the band as much as he did the crowd.

I stood at my side-door entrance and took a minute to just absorb this wild spectacle in front of me. The smoke was back, which didn't thrill me, but it created a hazy, dimly lit glow that achieved a mystical quality worthy of the spirits who frequented this swanky, supernatural saloon. Everywhere I looked, I saw laughter, smiles, and people having fun. However, I saw nothing even marginally resembling an appetite for serious discussion. Following a little Miles Davis, the band stopped and Clinton took the microphone.

"Gentlemen," he said, looking over at Obama, "we have amongst our ranks some legit soul, and I may need a little help from you to coax him up here. The band's gonna do a little 'Sweet Home Chicago' and we want to have a true South Sider on vocals."

Obama immediately shook his head and repeated "No, no, no" as George W. Bush bear-hugged him from behind and aggressively pushed him forward. A few of the band members—another saxophonist and a bass player—rushed to assist. Obama laughed loudly and reluctantly gave in, realizing he had no choice. He took the microphone shaking his head but smiling ear to ear.

"There was plenty of soul up here already without me," he began, looking around at the band. From what I could see, three of the band members were African American—the saxophonist, the bassist, and the female lead vocalist. "And by that, I refer primarily to Bubba here, who, as many know, is widely considered our first African American president."

Obama's remark about Clinton got a hearty laugh. When the pianist and electric guitarist started to riff, Obama added, "My apologies to Jake and Elwood," and then belted out on cue, "Come on . . . baby don't you wanna go . . . " He nailed it, as did President Bubba on sax by his side. The waitresses all danced with George W while the bartenders delivered more drinks. Now this was a party, baby!

George W then requested Al Green's "Let's Stay Together." It didn't take much convincing for the band to start playing. George W obviously must've known of Obama's spot-on Al Green imitation. Obama burst into a big smile and obliged. He stopped after a few verses, raising his hands up, shaking his head, and remarking, "I can't sing a song like this to a room full of dudes," but the group approved wildly—even though the vast majority of them had never heard of Reverend Al.

Presidential Spirits

I couldn't help but wonder how many Silicon Valley CEOs and Hollywood producers would've jumped at the chance to raise a mint for the Democratic Party to watch this incredibly memorable moment. In fact, how telling was it that these modern-day presidents put aside their complicated on-again, off-again histories, rivalries, and campaign scars to produce a wonderful moment for this group and for each other with no political or monetary motivation. Perhaps that was the most remarkable aspect of the evening and, indeed, of this otherworldly saloon.

Franklin Pierce, clearly feeling no pain, approached George W several times over the course of the next half hour, hoping for a shot at the microphone. W finally relented when the band took a break following an impressive rendition of "Soul Man" that brought the house down. Stogie in hand, Pierce proceeded to belt out an unrecognizable, forgettable drinking song a cappella, causing no shortage of laughter amongst the crowd, as much at him as with him. Next, Nixon took a turn at the piano, playing something classical that I wouldn't even attempt to identify, while Jefferson ad-libbed impressively on the cello alongside him. That particular duo would've made for quite a photo if only I'd had a camera or cell phone. Another president I did not recognize accompanied them on the violin. Each seemed to enjoy it immensely.

Jefferson then took a turn on the violin and, after conversing with Nixon, they played a selection they said was from composer Joseph Haydn. I won't claim to have recognized the music, but they did a really impressive job of it. I loved that they discovered music they both appreciated despite being born more than a century and a half apart. By this time, I had consumed a few drinks, which admittedly makes me a little more inclined toward hyperbole, but I couldn't help but comment to a few of my predecessors nearby. "How about this unlikely twosome!" I gushed.

"Indeed," responded Buchanan. "Mr. Jefferson seems as proficient at musical instruments as he is with languages."

"How many does he speak?" I asked.

"Six," Monroe replied proudly. "Greek, Latin, French, Italian, Spanish, and English."

Moments later, John Quincy Adams leaned over to me and said, "Mr. Jefferson is indeed a scholarly gentleman, but keep in mind his fancy for telling large stories. He claims to have learned Spanish simply by reading

Don Quixote on a voyage to France with a translation book."

I laughed—more at the love-hate thing going on between Jefferson and the Adams family than the underlying comment.

Before long Clinton reappeared with his saxophone for a little "Heartbreak Hotel" with the female vocalist. Nixon stayed at the piano attempting to accompany them on the fly with only mixed success, but he certainly got a kick out of it. Jefferson decided he'd better call it quits. Perhaps he really is as smart as the history books suggest.

I decided to slip out early and head back to the residence. I passed Mary Ann on my way out. "Was Mr. Sheels here tonight?" I asked. "I still haven't met him."

"I don't think I saw him. He generally keeps a low profile—doesn't exactly love a lot of these guys."

"That's odd," I said.

"Not really," she replied. "You know about his background, right?"

"No. I don't believe I do."

"Before he started running this place, he was a slave. In fact, in the early years when he first started working here, he was still a slave. He manages the whole joint now, though."

"Wow!" I replied. That was a whole lot to contemplate.

"That's really fascinating," I added. "The Presidential Spirits Saloon is run by a former slave." I let that sink in for a minute.

"Kind of ironic, huh?" Mary Ann said.

"Or maybe not so ironic. I've really gotta meet this gentleman. I would absolutely love to get to know him."

George W saw me sneaking away toward my personal exit and came charging after me. "Hey Rook," he yelled. "Where do you think you're going?"

"I've got another big day tomorrow, so I think I'd better head out before having any more drinks."

"You don't need to drink, Rook! Do you see any drinks in my hand? I'm having more fun than anyone here, and I'm sober as a judge."

"Don't get me wrong . . . I love this place! And I promise I'll be back if you'll have me. I might even take a turn with the band . . . if I have enough liquid courage."

"You should definitely come back, McFadden. Use these guys. They are willing to help—all of them."

"I promise, I will. Thanks so much!"

Bush's face lit up. "That's my boy!" he said as he wrapped his arm around my shoulder. He had a way of making you feel like you were lifelong friends, even though you barely knew each other.

"I'll get the band ready for that," he added. "What shall I have them rehearse?"

"Oh, I'm afraid I have a very narrow range, but I could probably pull off a little 'Thunder Road' or 'Hotel California' . . . perhaps 'Margaritaville.' That is, if I've had enough 'presidential spirits,' of course. And, more importantly, if everyone else has had enough! It appears as if a couple of these boys like to drink!"

"You should see when folks like Jackson, Buchanan, Pierce, and a few of the others get rolling. It's truly a sight to behold."

"I don't doubt that for a bit."

With that, I proceeded to walk back toward my door, but not before taking one more glance again at this spectacular scene. I got such a kick out of being there and witnessing all this. *My God,* I thought, *if the country—our culturally divided and politically paralyzed country—could get even the tiniest glimpse of this scene, wouldn't that begin to make a difference?* I had to figure a way to capture this and deploy it to bring about meaningful change. Just look at how these rivals interacted, worked together, and even enjoyed each other's company when they weren't faced with an election or trying to pander to their base.

This was a productive evening for me—aside from all the fun I'd had. I hadn't learned anything from engaging them in conversation or seeking out their advice, as I had hoped. But the scene that unfolded in front of me clearly ignited something inside me. It was just a purely and uniquely American celebration. *There has to be a way to tap into that and unite the intransigent factions of this country.* While I had no idea how to bring that about, I had a new sense of commitment to that cause combined with a fresh belief that it was, indeed, achievable.

I walked away fixated on that thought and the question it begged. *There has to be a solution.* And I needed to come back and meet Mr. Sheels.

Chapter Twenty-Five

April 11, 2017
Healing Week

(AP Memphis 2017) President McFadden's "Week of Racial Healing" continued today as he visited the National Civil Rights Museum attached to the Lorraine Hotel in Memphis where Martin Luther King Jr. was killed. King was assassinated by a gunman while standing on the balcony of the hotel nearly fifty years ago. The visit is the latest in a series of hastily planned events designed by the president to focus the nation on racial healing in the wake of last week's violent protests in Raleigh concerning the presence of monuments to Confederate soldiers on the grounds of the North Carolina State Capitol. The protests also transpired against the backdrop of a series of controversial deaths nationally involving black males at the hands of law enforcement. The president's week began with a eulogy delivered at the memorial service for Caroline Wilson, one of three counterprotesters who was killed when a man who had voiced racist, pro–Nazi views plowed his vehicle into a group of counterprotesters attending a "Unite the Right" rally. At the White House on Tuesday, the president met with representatives of the Black Lives Matter movement. Wednesday he traveled to Dallas to meet with the widows of five police officers who were ambushed last year by a gunman who stated that he wanted to "kill white police officers."

***

Presidential Spirits

CNN's *Anderson Cooper 360°*

Anderson Cooper: Welcome back to our roundtable. Tonight we are examining the president's attempt to focus the nation's attention on race relations and bring about some measure of healing and national progress on issues that have plagued this country since its inception. Van, how do you think he's doing?

Van Jones: Anderson, while he may have the best intentions, I think this whole thing was very reactionary. It seems to have been slapped together at the last minute, and it really has the look and feel of something almost impulsive, as opposed to a thoughtful, well-considered, and organized national dialogue. These problems have crippled our country for centuries and certainly won't be solved in a matter of just a few days.

Cooper: Aside from the lack of planning and organization for this on the part of the White House, do you take issue with the message—with McFadden's message and the tone he's striking?

Charles Jackson: I certainly do, Anderson. This was not the week to visit the Dallas police widows. We always find excuses for cops who kill young, unarmed African American males. We bend over backward to find justification because we refuse to entertain the notion that our revered officers are anything but good men doing impossible jobs who need our support. We have a problem in this country with police brutality against young minority males. Visiting the widows furthers the narrative that nothing is more important than shielding our vaunted officers from unfair criticism. McFadden can't simultaneously fly the Black Lives Matter flag and a Blue Lives Matter flag. It doesn't work that way. He needs to grow a spine. The issue facing us is law enforcement's mistreatment of young black males all over America. Video from smart-

111

phones has enabled us to confirm what we have long suspected to be true.

Shelby Fontana: Anderson, I would add that McFadden
has been silent while many states have recently passed
laws banning race-based admissions in higher education.
And the justice department appears to be siding with an
Asian American plaintiff challenging Yale's admissions
policies as the case heads to the Supreme Court this fall. I
object to both his tone and his message, and I question
whether this particular white male is the best person to be
facilitating our national debate on race in this country at
this particular moment.

***

The Sean Hannity Show

Tucker Carlson: It's time now for Sean Hannity.

Sean Hannity: Great show tonight, Tucker. Good job, sir.

Carlson: Great to see you, Sean. No shortage of critical
topics to dive into tonight. Have at it, my friend.

Hannity: Alright. Well folks, we're gonna tackle them all,
so buckle up. We have an incredible show for you tonight.
We have a window into McFadden's true feelings on the
racial divide in this country, and you won't want to miss
this. The more we see of McFadden, the more he comes to
resemble Barack Obama. Then we'll expose the continuing hypocrisy of the liberal mainstream news media by
showing you how CNN Fake News Reporter and liberal
activist Jim Acosta has gone completely off the rails. It's
the latest example of how the partisan press has lost all
credibility. Then we'll get into the latest with the NFL and
why the owners better manage their players or risk losing
their ratings, which they may never get back.

But first, it's time for tonight's breaking news opening

monologue. Tonight we start with explosive news reported by our own Cindy Walsh involving the president's
recent powwow with the radical leadership of the extremist group Black Lives Matter. As you may have heard, our
president chose to dignify the radical extremist and racist
movement Black Lives Matter with a personal invitation
to the White House. Let's be clear about who this group is.
They are every bit as reprehensible and bigoted as the
KKK. They chant "pigs in a blanket" and "fry 'em like
bacon" at their rallies, and these same leaders who dined
with our feckless president have repeatedly refused to distance themselves from these chants and this despicable,
hateful conduct. So let's start by calling this organization
what it is, a domestic terrorist group.

Tonight, FOX News reporter Cindy Walsh reports that on
Tuesday evening, McFadden not only welcomed this ter-
ror organization into the Oval Office, he made promises to
them in private that he would never utter in public because
he would be exposed as the true Obama–Pelosi Democrat
we've come to know he is at heart. We report tonight that
President McFadden caved to their demands on virtually
every issue they raised with him, and that, among other
things, he assured them he would continue a direct,
behind-the-scenes dialogue with them, that he would
encourage the justice department to initiate federal criminal inquiries into a handful of high-profile police miscon-
duct cases, and that he would push to have Confederate
statues removed from federal property. This, ladies and
gentlemen, is outrageous. McFadden would never hold a
Klan reception in the White House, and the self-righteous,
sanctimonious media hacks would go into cardiac arrest if
he ever did.

The media's tendency to hyperventilate over all these race
issues is feeding right into the hands of this extremist
group, and, let me tell you something, it has got to stop.

Our police officers, who put themselves in the line of fire every day, are under siege, and our own president is providing aid and comfort to the enemy. I thank Cindy Walsh for this terrific reporting, which you won't hear from the fake news media.

Fine Americans like Rudy Giuliani are being attacked by the fake news media simply for uttering the words "all lives matter." The very name Black Lives Matter is racist on its face. It implies that police lives don't matter or matter less, that Hispanics lives don't matter, that white lives don't matter, that Asian lives don't matter. If you bothered watching the fake news media in the past twenty-four hours, which I do not recommend, you won't hear this there. The media in this country has zero credibility, and we have known this for over a decade. And we've been exposing the media for what they really are: fake news. They are frauds. They are partisan hacks. And frankly, they're nothing more than extensions of the Democratic Party and all things liberal. Pretty much all they do is parrot liberal talking points. They hate Conservatism. They hate anyone who dares to challenge their liberal, radical left-wing agenda. And, perhaps even worse, it seems that they have found in our president someone they can manipulate to promote their extreme agenda. I am worried tonight for our country. But rest assured, ladies and gentlemen, we will continue to hold McFadden, this Obama-wannabe, accountable and call him out every night.

Chapter Twenty-Six

April 11, 2017—1:47 p.m.
America's Original Sin

Quite ironically, I needed some healing of my own after Healing Week. I hadn't slept soundly in days. The country was awash with deep racial unrest, and all my attempts to quell it or even make a dent were falling flat.

I came up to the residence to catch a nap in the afternoon, deep in thought concerning this great national divide. I contemplated a visit to the saloon. Given America's track record on issues of race, I was fairly certain my predecessors were the last ones I should be approaching for advice in these matters. However, something inside me made me want to confront them and get some answers. And the history buff in me was fascinated to engage them. Who knows, maybe there would be some enlightenment, perhaps from an unsuspecting source. Before long I was up on the third floor, slowly pushing open that heavy door to enter the Saloon.

The Saloon was well lit and largely empty that afternoon. A jukebox provided soft background music. I loved the playlist—heavy on Nat King Cole, Tony Bennett, Dean Martin, and Ella Fitzgerald. Again, I found the oval table in the center of the room occupied by a fascinating collection of former presidents, this time spanning our entire history. I recognized Jefferson, John Adams, John Quincy Adams, Madison, Jackson, Lincoln, Truman, Kennedy, LBJ, Carter and Obama. Mary Ann seemed to be providing the proper libations to keep the conversation and opinions flowing.

Matt's face brightened as he saw me approaching the bar, "Irish buck?" he inquired.

"Let me start with a beer this afternoon. Do you have anything on tap from Gordon Biersch?" I asked.

"Absolutely," Matt shot back with a huge smile on his face. "Love their beer, and they have the all-time champion marketing campaign: 'Never trust a skinny brewer.' How about a Märzen?"

"Yes, please," I responded, "in your biggest schooner."

"Sure thing. Mary Ann will bring that over in a second."

I sat down in an empty seat with Obama to my right. A few people looked up at me and smiled to welcome me to the table, but with many private conversations going on at once, I quietly took my seat, politely choosing not to interrupt. I wanted to hear all of them.

LBJ was regaling the group with stories of his ranch and how he would indoctrinate each new group of visitors to the property. While driving them around on a tour of the estate, he would proceed down a road toward the lake. As they neared the water, he would act like the brakes on his car were failing. He would start screaming as if in full panic mode as he plunged the vehicle full of his guests at high speed into the lake. Only well after they hit the water did they realize that the car was an amphibious vehicle. Johnson roared with laughter as he described the fear in the eyes of his unsuspecting invitees.

He then turned to Kennedy and told him how hapless his brother Bobby had been handling a rifle on the ranch when Johnson took him on a deer hunt. JFK smiled and laughed, but deep inside, I'm not sure how amused he was with this anecdote.

While I had been straining to keep track of all the conversations, I had difficulty hearing what appeared to be a fairly serious discussion between Obama and Lincoln. *My God, I need to hear this!* I thought how utterly fascinated most of the world would be to listen in on the two of them. As I shifted my entire focus to that conversation, I distinctly heard Obama say, "Tell me what Frederick Douglass was like."

They had my full attention now.

"He was a remarkable gentleman and an effective advocate," Lincoln began. "I considered him to be one of the most meritorious men in America. At times he was my fiercest critic. He questioned my character and honesty, said I was timid as a sheep, and called me racist. He pressured me persistently in public without ever letting up. A passionate advocate for the cause of complete emancipation. In time we came to respect and even admire each other, I believe. He recruited scores of Negro soldiers to fight for the Union and pressed us to provide equal pay, rations, and promotions. We corresponded often. He penned frequent missives to my attention and often authored criticisms in newspapers. I initially resisted a great deal of that which he advocated, such as enlisting Negro soldiers, but ultimately relented. In time he had a profound influence on me."

"He influenced your decision to enlist black soldiers?" Obama asked.

"Yes, he certainly did."

"How difficult was that decision?"

"We were in desperate need of men. Losses and casualties were considerable. Many of the men had two-year terms of service that were expiring. They all desperately wanted to go back home. Desertion was rampant. Ultimately, this was a decision borne of necessity." Lincoln paused in thought, and then continued, "My vice president, Mr. Hamlin, argued with great zeal for enlistment of Negro soldiers. His son, who was an officer in the Union Army, came to the executive mansion with a delegation of officers to volunteer to work with Negro troops. And some of our generals had already started using them."

Lincoln saw that I was listening closely now to the conversation. Then, looking back at Obama, he continued. "You are kind to ascribe to me all the most noble motives, as many of our colleagues in this establishment often do. My charge was to provide the generals sufficient men, weapons, and supplies to carry out this victory. That provided the primary impetus for my decision."

A few others at the table were now obviously attempting to hear Lincoln's words. I looked around and saw that other presidents were arriving and filling in around us.

Lincoln carried on. "Later, when Mr. Douglass learned that we were contemplating a plan to end the war that included a tenet espousing perpetuation of slavery, he angrily objected. He was correct, of course. Had I done so, I would have certainly been damned for all eternity. Nearly 200,000 Negro warriors had bravely fought to preserve the Union, and I could not— I would not—return them to slavery. The politics of the moment had forced my staff to consider that proposition. However, in the end, the world shall know that I will keep my faith to friends and enemies, come what will."

By this time, the whole table was listening, and presidents who had been at other tables pulled up chairs nearby. Lincoln saw that the room was transfixed on his every word. "Mary and I invited Douglass to tea at the summer cottage, and I enjoyed spending time with him very much. He was unwavering in his belief in the equality of all races, including Indian tribes, and of women. He was an esteemed writer and orator with an uncommon appreciation of music.

"As I mentioned moments ago, the gentlemen in this room are always quite effusive in their praise referencing my character and morals. However, Douglass and some of the leaders in the Negro community were initially unwilling to support my bid for the Republican nomination in my campaign for reelection. They viewed me as fickle and blamed me for stalling on emancipation, on enlisting Negro soldiers, on pushing for equivalent pay, and for my unwillingness to advocate for full voting rights."

"We all wrestle with the interplay between what is right and political expediency, sir," Clinton declared boldly as he glanced around the room. "None of the tremendous admiration for you held by those in this room, and, indeed, by virtually every citizen of this country, is misplaced. The fact that the politics of the day may have slowed your ability to achieve your moral objectives does not diminish the fact that you eventually prevailed. Viewed against the backdrop of the place and time in which you served, your achievements were monumental."

"Hear! Hear!" echoed several in the group raising their glasses.

Clinton continued, "Whether it's slavery, treatment of Native Americans, civil rights, women's rights, gay marriage, you name it, change comes gradually, and it can be challenging to get out in front of it. I found myself in similar terrain and was slower than I should have been on gay rights and gay marriage."

"Wait, we're letting homosexuals marry each other?" Nixon asked incredulously. An audible gasp could be heard in the room.

Given my present predicament, I desperately wanted to keep the focus of this little happy hour on race issues. "If you don't mind, let's address the gay marriage issue later," I pleaded. "I'd like to discuss that, too, but right now, I need to get some advice on what to do about the racial divide in our country. It's been nearly 250 years, and we still can't sufficiently come to grips with this as a nation."

"It has been correctly termed 'America's original sin,'" added Clinton. "One in which I would venture to say each of us here has been compelled to address in some form or fashion."

"I agree, Mr. Clinton," stated John Quincy Adams, becoming quite animated. "Slavery is the great and foul stain upon our North American Union."

My heart was racing. I couldn't believe I was a witness to this scene. Competing thoughts wrestled back and forth within my head. I wanted to speak up with some fairly pointed questions, but I didn't want to derail this conversation from its natural course. I wanted to see how much ownership of this problem some of these gentlemen would cop to. I had no idea which of these two powerful impulses within me would win out.

With great emphasis and no shortage of passion, Adams continued, "The inconsistency of the institution of slavery with the principles of the Declaration of Independence is glaring. But slavery was seen by the delegates to the Constitutional Congress and lamented. No insincerity or hypocrisy can fairly be laid to their charge. Never from their lips was heard one syllable of attempt to justify the institution of slavery. They universally considered it as a reproach fastened upon them by the unnatural stepmother country and they saw that before the principles of the Declaration of Independence, slavery, in common with every other mode of oppression, was destined sooner or later to be banished from the earth."

James Madison sat up, looked at John Quincy Adams, and then added, "Let's consider the origin of our slave population. That evil commenced when we were in our Colonial state. Our Colonial legislature attempted to prohibit the import of more slaves into the Colony. These were rejected by the Crown. Mr. Jefferson's original text of the Declaration of Independence set forth an indictment of the merchant slave trade placing blame squarely at the feet of the 'Christian King of Great Britain.' The provision was removed at the insistence of Georgia and South Carolina."

The elder Adams spoke up, "An imperfect compromise was forged between northern and southern states, without which we would have had no Union, no independence from England, and no freedom. However, for this we paid a great price, for we left unsettled within our borders an evil of colossal magnitude to be rectified only at great hardship by our children and their children."

Lincoln came to the founders' defense. "All honor to Jefferson," he said as he looked directly at Jefferson, who had been quiet throughout this discussion. "To the man who, in the concrete pressure of the struggle for national independence by a single people, had the coolness, forecast, and capacity to introduce into a merely revolutionary document, an abstract truth, and to embalm it there that today and in all coming days it shall be a rebuke and a stumbling block to the very harbingers of reappearing tyranny and oppression. Within his eloquent prose—including that all men are created equal - lay the principles upon which to defeat this scourge on our Union's soul."

Many in the room welcomed Lincoln's remarks. Some in the group shouted, "Hear! Hear!" while raising their glasses.

Jimmy Carter rose to challenge them. He looked very different to me than the Carter I had come to know in photos over the past couple of decades when he'd be visiting Haiti or working with Habitat for Humanity. This Jimmy Carter was much younger-looking, his skin free of wrinkles and streaks of gray in his hair rather than the white hair I was now used to seeing.

"Gentlemen," Carter said, "even if we grant that it may have been best for purposes of establishing an independent Union to defer on the issue of slavery to future generations—which I'm not entirely certain I'm willing to do—that can't possibly absolve us from all our overt discriminatory actions that followed: allowing slavery to expand to the west, withholding voting rights, permitting segregation and Jim Crow laws, not to mention all the personal hypocrisy in so many of our personal lives on matters of race." That set the room abuzz.

Obama decided to enter the fray. "Mr. Adams, you mentioned that the Founders' decision not to resolve these issues inflicted great hardship upon their children and grandchildren, who themselves had to rectify it. That, I would suggest, pales in comparison to the hardship inflicted on the children and grandchildren of those who were slaves at the time."

The silence was deafening, even though the saloon was now packed with presidents.

Obama continued, "Many of our vaunted Founding Fathers—as well as other leaders who followed—clearly recognized how truly heinous and deplorable slavery was, yet many still held hundreds of slaves for themselves, and flogged them, sold them, separated them from their families, and hunted them down as fugitives when they dared to flee to freedom. And in some cases, fathered children with them and condemned those children as well into a life of slavery—their very own children, mind you. They railed against the spread of the slave trade yet advocated for the spread of slavery to the new territories under the false premise that this would bring about the end of slavery under some misguided notion of diffusion."

Andrew Jackson grew defiant. "These gentlemen did not possess tools enough to rid us of this scourge delivered to us by the Crown. Theirs was neither the time nor the place to eradicate slavery. They brought us independence. Purge one evil at a time. To do otherwise would have destroyed the economy of the South and crippled our ability to prevail against the Redcoats."

The faces and expressions in the room were now quite unlike anything I had seen before in this enchanted saloon. They silently screamed both obstinance and denial.

Jimmy Carter reentered the discussion. "Some principles and some fundamental truths, President Jackson, are worth risking the political and economic consequences. Simply parroting the will of a misguided populace is hardly leadership. Anyone can do that. Are there not more noble objectives than merely sustaining your power? There's a reason we created this as a republic, isn't there? I know it wasn't by accident."

Jackson snapped back immediately, "Perhaps, Mr. Carter, that type of thinking helps explain why you may have been removed from office after only four years, just as Mr. Adams was. I am pleased that our nation had political visionaries like Messrs. Jefferson and Madison mapping our nation's future rather than shortsighted zealots like yourself."

Our frat president Otter attempted to restore some order. "Gentlemen," he called out, raising his hands up palms out as if to restrain the gathering force of the confrontational energy permeating the room. But for me, watching these two sons of the South square off over this issue was absolutely captivating.

"I agree with President Jackson," another president stated emphatically. I looked over to see who was standing by Jackson in this moment. It was the other Andrew—Johnson. He continued, "I strongly opposed black suffrage. Allowing the Negro to vote would have substantially diluted the white vote, particularly in the South, with devastating impact."

Someone cried out, "Mary Ann and Tina, we're gonna need a whole lot more liquor here." The crowd took a collective breath.

As the servers reappeared and people talked amongst themselves, Grant leaned over to me, pointed at Johnson and whispered, "Have you met that gentleman?"

"Gentleman is not really the word I would use to describe him," I responded. "What an idiot. Yes, we met briefly."

Grant shook his head in disgust. "Doesn't belong in this room, if you ask me. I succeeded him, you know. I refused to ride in the carriage with him to the inauguration. He was an easy act to follow. Should've been impeached—and damn near was—missed by only one vote. Pay no heed to him."

After more drinks had been distributed, James Monroe emerged from the back of the crowd that had gathered around the two center tables. "Emancipation at any point would surely have led to civil war," he said, "as it eventually did. We did work hard to bring about change. Emancipation in my time also would have resulted in bedlam, insurrection, lawlessness, and violence. Presidents Jackson, Madison, and I all worked with the American Colonization Society to repatriate freed slaves back to Africa. We worked hard forging solutions to this vexing circumstance that befell us."

Jimmy Carter spoke up. "With all due respect, sir, your solution to rid us of blacks by transplanting them to Africa was as misguided as the one President Jackson deployed to rid us of the Cherokee." Then, looking directly at Jackson, he added, "History doesn't refer to that migration as the 'Trail of Tears' due to the great joy it brought to the Cherokee Nation."

Lyndon Johnson looked over at the Virginians—Jefferson, Madison, and Monroe—who were now all seated next to one another, and calmly chimed in with his distinctive Texas drawl, "You fellas undeniably created a bold, audacious vision for this nation at great risk to your own safety and that of your families." He glanced over at the two Adamses as well before returning his gaze to the Virginian presidents. "And Mr. Jefferson expressed these ideals in the most magnificent and poetic prose imaginable. However, it is undeniable that collectively you boys had a blind spot, and you knew it. Your slave labor made you each personally quite wealthy and in some cases, shall we say, satisfied other desires as well," he added with a sly laugh. "Some of your colleagues at the time even lamented that slavery would forever shape your legacy and that of the country. And that it has."

Thomas Jefferson, whose voice and words I most wanted to hear, particularly now after really being called out by both Obama and LBJ, spoke softly with a surprisingly high-pitched voice, but the room palpably hung on his every word. "Gentlemen," he said, "slavery is a moral and political depravity. I reflected at the time that God is just and that his justice would not sleep forever. I struggled with this in my time. We all did. We knew of this great evil and ultimately chose not to use our power to defeat it.

"And yes," he added, somewhat sheepishly, "I will not deny to this group the reporting about me that appeared in the *Richmond Recorder* and all the Federalist journals."

Wow! I thought. *What an absolutely stunning admission we've just witnessed.* It may have been the least well-kept secret in the history of the nation, but nonetheless, that was an absolutely monumental confession played out before our very eyes, even as vague and cryptic as it was. It was clear to all what he was admitting to.

John Adams, of all people, was the first to come to his defense, although in a rather backhanded way. "At the time, my friend Mr. Jefferson, I posit that there was not a planter in all of Virginia who could not reckon among his slaves a number of his children."

"Gentlemen, gentlemen, gentlemen," cautioned Nixon. "Before we go too much further down this treacherous path, perhaps a lesson in moral relativism is in order here. I think we should eschew the tendency by liberals to judge our leaders in the past by present-day standards and mores. There are no universal, objective, moral truths. Instead, moral propositions are rooted in the particular social, cultural, and historical circumstances that exist at the time."

"Spare me the platitudes, Mr. Nixon," Clinton spat back. "Let me ask you this, what amount of moral relativism justified your position that abortion is murder except when one parent is black and the other is white, in which case you claimed it was not only permissible but necessary? Tell me, was that something that you think would hold up to the light in any era? That's a delicious dichotomy there, boy. I don't care what century you are in, Mr. President, that dog won't hunt."

Tina had been serving drinks, and I noticed that she had been lingering long over the tables and taking it all in. "Hey boys, can I chime in here? Given the utter lack of estrogen in this room, would you care for a woman's view?"

The room fell silent. Many faces appeared startled, but more than a few smiled approvingly, although I'm quite certain at this moment she didn't much care whether anyone approved.

"Someday, one of our fine sisters will walk through that door over there," she pointed back at the door I used, "and that will be a glorious day for this nation you all built and really for the world as well. But until then, I'll give you a point of view that's sorely lacking at this nightly dude party of yours."

I was loving this. More smiles greeted her now among my more contemporary colleagues, but I also noticed no shortage of incredulity in the expressions of many of the others.

"In short, there's a word for sex with one's own slave. It's called rape. You can pretend that you are their soul mate or that they adore you and look up to you and are just dying to be with someone as rich and powerful and, by the way, as old as you. But there's no consent there. How could there possibly be? Someone you own, who has to obey you lest they be disciplined, who can't leave your property or else they'll be hunted down and whipped into submission, cannot possibly consent. And you do need consent, guys."

She wasn't finished, "And by the way, if you guys are gonna cover abortion, I want to come back for that discussion too."

With that she marched away with a smile on her face that cut quite a dramatic contrast to the looks of horror on the faces of the other staff and many of the presidents in the room.

"That woman needs to be fired, pronto!" James Polk uttered emphatically.

"Fire her for what . . ." Kennedy retorted, "expressing her opinion? How truly *un*-American that would be."

"She's a barmaid in a saloon for God's sake," chirped Cleveland.

"As the only one among us born in a tavern," replied Van Buren, "I take exception to that."

How fascinating to see where the lines were being drawn here and on what basis. And now I knew why I'd seen Van Buren tending bar with Matty on occasion.

"I can speak with her," John Adams volunteered. Then, breaking into a smile, he added, "I have some experience with a strong personality of her gender."

"As do I, of course," Clinton quipped with a grin.

"Someone needs to talk to our man Sheels about her," barked one president. I wasn't sure which one.

"Well, I for one welcome her thoughts," continued Adams. "My dear Abigail always implored upon me to 'remember the ladies.' I quite think we didn't heed her directives. We should be wise to allow Tina time to speak her mind with us."

President Reagan, whom I had observed angling for precisely the right moment to join in, finally spoke up. "Nancy was not only my best friend but my closest adviser. Without her at my side, I never would have been included amongst the likes of you gentlemen in this august fraternity." After a moment of thought, he continued, "I should add that Maggie Thatcher was certainly the one on the world stage whose voice and friendship I trusted the most. And I had the great privilege of being the first of us to appoint an outstanding female jurist to our Supreme Court—Sandra Day O'Connor. So I too welcome Tina's thoughts."

JFK, sporting a bit of a smile, added, "I love you boys dearly, but I can't be the first among us to think that we need a lot more of the fairer sex in this room. I trust none of you will blame me for preferring the company of Miss Tina and the other young ladies to the likes of Mr. Taft, Mr. Arthur, and Mr. Cleveland." That drew plenty of laughter. Perhaps a bit too much from Clinton, who I suspect harbored a bit of a "man crush" on Kennedy.

I thought it quite amusing that it took a discussion on sexism of all things to knock us off the topic of racism. I felt I'd gotten what I came here looking for. I can't say I received any enlightenment apropos to my predicament, but, alas, I had set my expectations remarkably low, and in that sense, those expectations were not disappointed. Still, it was incredibly compelling to see all that play out. Professor Harris would have been captivated—although he would've also been chomping at the bit to join the fray. But any American who has ever struggled to come to grips with that great founding hypocrisy of our nation would've loved to witness the scene that had just played out before my eyes. How could a nation created by embracing the very highest ethical ideals and most lofty notions of freedom choose to ignore the most contemptable treatment of other human beings known to mankind? It was so fascinating to hear the justification directly from those involved.

Chapter Twenty-Seven

April 11, 2017—4:08 p.m.

We Can Make You Better

I jumped up and headed for the bar. I happily high-fived Tina as I passed her. I was pleased to detect not the slightest trace of regret in her eyes. Good for her.

That spirited discussion and Tina's participation had combined to create quite a stir amongst the bartenders and waitstaff. Matt couldn't hold back. "Holy Cow!" he called out to me. "What's going on out there? I haven't seen anything like that here before. And, oh my God, is Tina riled up! I really thought your addition to this group was going to bring them all together, not tear them apart."

"Oh, so you're pinning this all on me?" I protested.

"I'm just sayin' . . . never saw this sort of thing at all before you came around."

"Where'd Otter go?" I asked. George W had made a beeline for the bar after Tina had said her piece, but I hadn't seen him since.

"He's back in Mr. Sheels's office," Matt said, pointing to a side room back behind the bar. "Go ahead and join them."

Why not? I thought to myself. I was dying to meet this guy Mr. Sheels.

As I approached the office, I could see George W sitting inside talking to a young, sharp-looking, African American gentlemen seated behind a desk. Bush motioned for me to come in as I got closer.

"Hey, Rook . . . have you met Sheels?"

"I don't believe I've had the pleasure," I responded, reaching out my hand as I entered the room.

"Great to meet you, Mr. President," Mr. Sheels said as he stood and extended his hand.

Bush turned to me. "So, Rook, I was just explaining to Sheels here that

126

Presidential Spirits

Tina spoke up a bit out there and challenged a few of the gentlemen, so he might be hearing about it from some of our esteemed colleagues. Of course, her views on women are going to challenge a few of these guys. Heck, June Cleaver's views on women would push some of these old timers' buttons. But we need a few more like her around here! I told him not to worry about any of them—I've got Big Daddy under my thumb, so to speak. And between the two of us, we're all good."

"Who's Big Daddy?" I asked. "Your Dad?"

"No, no, no," he shot back, almost angrily. "Man, you really are a rookie. Haven't you been paying attention? Big Daddy—the Father of our Country . . . GW . . . the Big Cheese . . . *that* Big Daddy."

"My bad. I need a program to keep up with you and all the nicknames."

"No problem, gentlemen," replied Sheels. He seemed annoyed at Bush's irreverence. "We value Tina and hold her dear. I appreciate the alert, Mr. President. I'll mention to her that her job is safe, although knowing her, I'm certain she's not at all worried." He laughed.

"Thank you, sir. You're a good man, Sheels," declared Bush, as he turned to head back to the bar.

I decided to seize my moment with Mr. Sheels, "Did you hear any of that out there this past hour?"

"No, sir," Sheels responded. "I keep my head down and run this establishment the best I know how. I tend to allow them their space and keep some distance. I respect a lot of those guys, but I don't care much for some of them. But that's alright. Things do seem to be getting better here with each new addition. Got a whole lot better after they got to know Obama. And we hear great things about you, sir."

I glanced up at the wall behind him, which displayed a reproduction of the Declaration of Independence. Next to that hung what appeared to be three pages of framed rough handwriting. I walked closer to get a better look at it. "What is that?" I asked.

"That, sir, was given to me by Mr. Lincoln. Take a closer look."

I leaned in to read it closely. It only took the first few words to recognize it. "Wow!" I said. "How cool! The Gettysburg Address. Is that a reproduction of Lincoln's personal notes?"

"No," he responded. "It's the original."

"What?" I exclaimed with disbelief.

"Lincoln wrote out five originals to give to people close to him, but no one ever located the folded version he pulled from his pocket on the battlefield the day he delivered it. That's it right there."

"Oh my God!" This whole place and experience was the coolest, most unbelievable, mesmerizing, supernatural experience I could've ever in a million years conjured up. I had a thousand questions, each of which I was strangely fearful of asking.

Sheels interrupted my thoughts. "Sounds like you boys got into it a little bit out there today."

"That's putting it mildly," I quipped.

"Is that what you were looking for?"

"Not really . . . although I'm not entirely sure I know precisely what I *was* looking for. Certainly not that, though. I get that in DC every day—or any other town in America these days."

"What did you learn from it? Did you get better? Use this place to better yourself. You can make us better, and we can make you better. That's what we are here for."

OK, there's another one, I thought to myself. I knew I had to thoroughly dissect that statement at some point, but unfortunately my brain was not quick enough to do it on the fly. *That's what we are here for? What the heck is this place? How did it get here? And what exactly am I supposed to do with it?*

"What did I learn today?" I asked myself out loud in response to his question. "I guess I learned again what I already knew—how terribly hard this all is. Even the seemingly easy stuff—the obvious, principled stuff—can be wrought with complications and unworkable politics."

"You were expecting something easier?" he inquired with a knowing smile.

"Yes, to some degree. We grow up with these lofty notions of democracy, and people paint for us an absolutely idyllic view of our country and its potential. I admit that I'm a dreamer and an optimist, but all my dreams and optimism have just been flattened by an oncoming political train."

"Do not lose hope, sir, or that optimism of yours. You let them win when you do that. So take what you can from this place. Soak it all in. Have a mint julep with Teddy Roosevelt, smoke a Cuban cigar with JFK, listen to the founders talk about the American Revolution. Be a little kid in a candy store here. But realize that for all the exalted and mythological status these larger-than-life personalities enjoy up on the pedestals we've placed them on in this country, your own views and instincts are just as enlightened and will be your very best guide. Be true to yourself, Mr. President."

Wow! I was not expecting that from him. I'm not sure what I was expecting, but definitely not that.

"Thank you. I will do that." I said.

At that moment Tina appeared in the doorway. "Come in, Tina," he said. Then, looking at me, he added, "Let me spend a few minutes alone with Tina, if you don't mind."

"Of course," I replied as I stood up to leave. "Right now, I need to get back out there anyway and find a way to lighten the mood and get them all together again. Any ideas?"

"You'll think of something, I'm sure. I don't know you well, but I have faith in you."

I liked Sheels.

Chapter Twenty-Eight

April 11, 2017—4:52 p.m.
America's Pastime

I left Sheels's office and returned to the bar. I desperately needed to summon up a little levity for the group following that heated conversation. I noticed Mary Ann, Haskell, and Matt at the bar, so I figured that was a good place to start.

Haskell called out, "What'll it be, Mr. President? Something to remind you of home? A California cabernet? A Sierra Nevada? A mai tai or margarita?"

"How do you make your margaritas?" I responded.

"I make them precisely the way you want them, sir."

Haskell is definitely someone who aims to please, I thought. Perhaps a bit too much. "Do you use real lime juice?"

"Squeezed fresh each day, just for you, sir."

"Do you use sugar?" I asked.

"Do you like sugar?"

"I can't stand sugary margaritas."

"No, sir. Agave nectar only. I would never dream of putting sugar in a margarita, sir. Couldn't agree with you more about that. By the way, I love what your administration is doing to fight obesity, Mr. President."

"Yes," I said with a laugh, "if I could only get the country to use more agave and less sugar . . . therein lies the answer."

Mary Ann, looking quite bored with this banter, left us to make her rounds.

"What kind of tequila, sir? We've got anything known to man."

"How about some Rey Sol Extra Añejo?" I asked, testing his claim.

"Coming right up, sir!" he shot right back without missing a beat.

"No, no, no," I responded, "I was just testing you. That is so impressive that you have it, but I'm not looking for anything that pricey. Just some 1800 would be fine. I'm not sipping it straight."

"We've got that too. Coming right up, Mr. President."

I needed some light conversation. "Are you guys baseball fans?" I asked.

"Absolutely!" Matty replied.

Haskell couldn't help himself, "I'll bet you were quite a ballplayer in your day, Mr. President."

"Nothing special, really. Got cut from my college team,"

"There must've been some mighty impressive talent on that team. I can only imagine there was, sir, if they cut *you*."

I couldn't help but laugh out loud in response to all this. It was as funny as it was personally sad. "I'm not sure about that," I said. "But I love it like nothing else."

Haskell slid the finished product over to me. "Try this on for size, sir," he said, obviously quite proud of his creation.

"Perfection," I responded after taking a sip. "Very nicely done. You've done this before, I gather? And I like all the pulp in there."

"I figured you would, sir."

OK, at first this Haskell character annoyed me a bit, but I was now starting to really enjoy him. "You'll go far in life, kid," I told him. "I'm as convinced of that as much as I know anything in this world."

"Thank you, Mr. President. That means a lot coming from you, sir."

I glanced out at the tables and noticed that the presidents were still gathered around as they had been during our earlier lively discussion.

"Speaking of baseball, would you like to watch a game, Mr. President?" Matt asked.

"Sure, why not?" I responded, looking around for a television. "You got a TV in here?"

"Have I got a TV?" he answered, before repeating again, even louder, "Have I got a TV? Hey Haskell, the leader of the free world wants to know if we've got a TV!"

"Funny you should ask, Mr. President," Haskell replied, as he reached down to press a button underneath the bar. Pretty soon, a massive television slowly started to emerge in front of the backbar at the far end of the bar. It gradually slid toward us, coming to rest directly in front of us. I'm not good at estimating, but it was easily a good eight feet by six feet. Nifty little thing to have at your disposal.

"What game would you like to watch?" Haskell asked.

"Wow!" I replied, taking several steps back to take it all in. "You know I'm a Dodgers guy, but it's not about me. What game do you think these guys would like? Yankees? Red Sox. I'm not sure what's even on right now?"

"How about the Dodgers and the Yankees, sir?" Haskell asked, fiddling with a rather sophisticated-looking remote as he looked back at the screen.

"Oh, they wouldn't be playing each other tonight," I responded, thinking these guys must not really be that into baseball. "It's a little early for the World Series."

"I'm talking about the World Series," Haskell replied.

The next thing I knew, the screen showed Reggie Jackson at the plate facing Bob Welch with the Dodger Stadium crowd on its feet in the background—a game I instantly recognized as being from the 1978 World Series. I also recalled that this particular at bat, this game, and this World Series didn't end so well for me as a Dodger fan.

"First of all, that's really cool what you did there. But that's not a Dodgers–Yankees series I want to relive," I protested.

He fiddled with the remote. "Is this more to your liking?" he asked.

The next thing I knew, we were watching a banged-up Kirk Gibson come off the bench and limp his way into the batter's box trailing by one with two outs in the bottom of the ninth of Game One of the '88 Series. The A's had Dennis Eckersley, their ace reliever on the mound looking for the save. After working the count to full, taking a few pathetic cuts in the process, Gibson practically just threw his bat out over the plate and connected with a backdoor slider that disappeared into Dodger Stadium's right field pavilion for a walk-off homer. We watched Gibson pumping his fist repeatedly after rounding first base. NBC's Vin Scully let the moment speak for itself before adding, "In a year that has been so improbable, the impossible has happened."

"Greatest home run in baseball history," I said confidently.

"No way," came a voice from behind me. It was George H. W. Bush. "How about Bobby Thompson's shot heard 'round the world. Or Ruth's called shot against the Cubs at Wrigley Field in the '32 Series?"

Presidential Spirits

Another very familiar voice behind me spoke up. "Bill Mazeroski's home run to beat the Yankees in the tenth inning of Game 7 of the 1960 series was the greatest home run in baseball history."

I turned back to see the speaker—Richard Nixon—amidst of sea of presidents who had filled in behind us, all lured by the spectacle of this crystal clear, high-definition television and the magical baseball moment it displayed.

Haskell was only getting started. Soon we were watching Carlton Fisk approaching the plate at Fenway Park to lead off the twelfth inning of Game Six of the '75 World Series.

"I recognize that ballpark," uttered Kennedy with a smile that evidenced a good bit of pride.

Ronald Reagan joined in. "What you are about to witness, gentlemen, is the climatic ending to what clearly is the greatest single game in baseball history— the Cincinnati Reds against the Boston Red Sox, 1975."

General Grant commented, "I welcomed a professional baseball club called the Cincinnati Red Stockings to the White House."

"They're one and the same," Nixon pointed out. "The Cincinnati Reds franchise started as the Cincinnati Red Stockings,"

The bar went silent as Haskell turned up the volume to hear Dick Stockton's call.

Kennedy leaned over at the two Adamses, "We Massachusetts boys are rooting for the fella with the bat in his arms, gentlemen. I can explain later."

Carlton Fisk swung at the second pitch and lifted it down the line in left. Stockton's call was simple. "There it goes . . . a long drive. If it stays fair . . . home run!"

The bar erupted in applause, as if we were watching it live. Matty and Haskell were beside themselves with glee over this new amusement they had stumbled upon and this captive audience.

We remained transfixed as the slow-motion replay showed Fisk emerge from the batter's box, watching the ball along with everyone else in the park, jumping up and down as he danced toward first base while frantically trying to will it to stay fair with his arms.

"And Carlton Fisk had a lot of little boy in him right there, Joe," Stockton exclaimed, talking to color commentator Joe Garagiola.

Kennedy looked at Otter and said, "Please tell me my boys from Boston

133

finished the job in Game Seven."

"I wish I could say they did, Mr. President," Bush responded.

"But clearly the Sox have won one since, have they not?"

"Yes, of course," Obama added, smiling ear to ear. "The Sox won it all in 2005."

"Very funny," responded Bush Sr. "He's referring to the Red Sox, not your White Sox, as you well know."

Addressing Kennedy, Bush Sr. finished his thought. "The Red Sox, you'll be thrilled to know, did finally break their curse, and since then have won two more."

"Marvelous!" Kennedy proclaimed, flashing a very satisfied smile.

Haskell then took control again and gleefully hopscotched around through baseball history. We watched those epic home runs by both Bobby Thompson and Bill Mazeroski. We tuned in to the final out of Don Larsen's perfect game in the 1956 World Series, seeing the iconic image of Yogi Berra leaping into the pitcher's arms after the final out. Next, Haskell showed us Jackie Robinson stealing home in the '55 Series by successfully sliding underneath Yogi's tag. Many in the group argued that the ump had gotten that call wrong. I am pretty sure that's the first time anyone on earth has ever seen this replay in high definition, full color, super-slow-motion, and I can tell you in my unbiased opinion that the ump got it right.

We showed no sign of stopping. Half the room relished viewing these epic moments in baseball history, while the other half marveled over the technology of the television itself. We then traveled through this magical television to Wrigley Field for the 1932 World Series to watch Babe Ruth's supposed "called shot." It wasn't lost on me that the scene we were watching took place seven years before the first televised baseball game. We all saw Ruth clearly pointing at something, but it could've simply been back at the pitcher, as they seemed to have had words during that at bat. Inconclusive.

George H. W. Bush asked Haskell to pause the TV for a second so he could address the group. "I met the Babe in 1948 when he donated a copy of his memoir to the Yale Library. He presented it to me, as captain of the Yale baseball team, before one of our games. He was dying of cancer at the time and looked terribly gaunt—a shell of his former self. However, he still had a twinkle in his eye as he said to me, 'You know, when you write a book like this about your life, you can't exactly put everything in it.' We both laughed."

JFK looked at the group and remarked, "I suppose a few of the boys here would say the same." The whole room got quite a kick out of that.

As Haskell fiddled a bit more with the remote control, Ronald Reagan turned to the group and said, "I called that World Series game between the Cubs and the Yankees when Ruth hit that home run. I was doing radio re-creations for WHO in Des Moines. I was no Vin Scully, but then again, I wasn't even at the ballpark and had to rely on my imagination."

"I threw out the first pitch at that game," said FDR. "It was a great win for New York. And yes, the Bambino definitely called his shot!"

Nixon stood up and looked at the group. "I love baseball. It helped me get through the darkest moments of my life after resigning the presidency. The Angels even invited me into the locker room when they won the division. I had beer and champagne dumped on my head!"

To that Warren G. Harding gave a boisterous laugh and said, "In my day, I have to say, I had many a drink dumped on my head—but always by women rather than ballplayers!" That drew laughter and applause.

Nixon continued, "If I had to do it all again, I may well have been a sportswriter."

Ike, standing next to Nixon, put his hand on his shoulder and looked at the group. "Dick knows how much I love baseball. Not making the baseball team at West Point may have been the biggest disappointment of my life."

"Sounds familiar to me," Herbert Hoover began. "I played baseball very briefly for Stanford my freshman year. After a couple of games at shortstop, they made me the manager!" That drew some hearty laughter. "We lost thirty to nothing to the San Francisco Pacifics—the local pro club. I had a few errors that day, as I recall."

"They call that having a cup of coffee with the club," added George W.

"While my wife was a much bigger baseball fan than me," Hoover continued, "I know well the profound impact this great game has had on our country. I would even venture to say that, next to religion, baseball has had a greater impact on American life than any other institution.

"On further reflection, as much as I love baseball, I must conclude it did not love me," Hoover added with a smile. "Babe Ruth endorsed my opponent, Al Smith!" More laughter.

FDR raised his hand. "As many of you know, when our nation was drawn into the Second World War, I wrote to Commissioner Landis and expressed my personal opinion that our country needed baseball at that time more than ever as a respite from the stress and unpleasantness of the great conflict. While Judge Landis and I did not often see eye to eye, we agreed that this great game should continue, and that it did." Many in the room clapped in approval.

"Thank you for mentioning that, President Roosevelt," said George W. "Following 9/11, when our freedom and our very way of life came under attack on our soil at the hands of a group of cowardly terrorists, I needed to attend the World Series and throw out the first pitch as a symbol to all and a powerful statement that our cherished way of life lived on, undeterred." The presidents all applauded loudly.

"Jeter's last words to me before I went out there were "Just don't bounce it in front of the plate," he added, laughing. "How about that for pressure? But I walked right out there, bypassed the little temporary rubber they had set up in front of the mound and threw a perfect strike from the actual mound! What a moment!" More applause.

He continued, "I also had the great privilege of co-owning the Texas Rangers, which, the way I love baseball, was a dream come true."

"Is that a semi-pro team?" asked FDR, a statement which drew howls from Nixon, Clinton, and Obama.

"No, sir," replied the younger Bush. "That's a major league ball club."

Teddy Roosevelt arose and walked over in front of the massive television screen. "I know all you fellas revere your "grand ol' game." He paused for effect. Then, raising his voice sharply, he added "But I rather think its soft!"

Amid some laughter, he continued with no shortage of passion. "Pansies. All of them! I've never seen such a mollycoddle sport in all my life! Not a man's game like boxing or football. Some of these teams are named for colored stockings for God's sake."

George W. Bush yelled over to the bar, "Haskell, show us some of the more vicious sides of the game. Can you pull up Pete Rose and Ray Fosse on that fancy TV of yours?"

"Happy to do so, sir," replied Haskell, clearly thrilled with this challenge.

We all watched as Pete Rose rounded third and came charging home with the score tied in the bottom of the twelfth inning of the 1970 All-Star Game. Catcher Ray Fosse set up in the baseline well in front of the plate. Rose lowered his shoulder and barreled into Fosse, knocking both the ball and the glove out of Fosse's hand and separating the catcher's shoulder.

Teddy Roosevelt, obviously pleased, declared, "Now you have my full attention, gentlemen."

Haskell gleefully showed the room a few more of baseball's more violent moments, including the Dodgers–Giants brawl at Candlestick Park when Giants pitcher Juan Marichal hit Dodger catcher Johnny Roseboro over the head with a bat, and Kansas City Royals' slugger George Brett exploding out of the dugout at Yankee Stadium and being restrained from attacking a home plate umpire who had just nullified his home run off Goose Gossage for having pine tar that extended too far up his bat.

"I like that Brett fella!" TR shouted approvingly while pointing at the screen. "Would've been a welcome addition to our boys charging up San Juan Hill."

"And ours at Pointe du Hoc," added Ike.

"We had quite a few just like him," TR continued. "Oh, but we had a bully fight that day."

Obama looked at Haskell and said, "Perhaps tomorrow night we introduce President Roosevelt to the WWE!"

Clinton, laughing hard, responded, "I imagine many of our colleagues from the nineteenth century would pick up the rules of baseball long before they would ever understand the concept of the WWE!"

Jimmy Carter then addressed Haskell, adopting a more respectful and professional tone than the others. "Perhaps you could show us some of the iconic moments in which baseball became woven into our national fabric."

Haskell smiled but with a nervous, pensive look, lacking the confidence he'd displayed when summoning up the violent moments.

"I'll help you, kid," George W said, hopping easily over the wide bar as if he was mounting a horse on his Crawford, Texas ranch. He took the remote, and suddenly, we were transported to Yankee Stadium on July 4, 1939, with Lou Gehrig approaching a microphone set up on the infield, wiping away tears. The video appeared in spectacular color and showed Gehrig's entire speech, not just the most famous quotes.

George W set the scene. "For those of you unfamiliar with this story, this is Lou Gehrig, one of baseball's greats. A fellow Ivy Leaguer by the way—like all of us—are there any in here not from an Ivy?" he laughed and looked around, stopping when he came to me. "Oh right, McFadden's not an Ivy Leaguer." Then he added amid much laughter, "Although you Domers all seem to think Notre Dame is an Ivy League school!"

Becoming much more serious, he finished the setup. "Anyway, this poor ballplayer, who'd been nicknamed 'the Iron Horse' as a testament to his exceptional strength and durability, was stricken with ALS at the height of his career. This is his farewell speech to the game and the fans. He died a short time later."

Bush let the video roll and we heard Gehrig begin to address the capacity crowd:

> "Fans, for the past two weeks you have been reading about the bad break I got. Yet today I consider myself the luckiest man on the face of this earth.

Gehrig concluded his powerful, heartfelt, speech in barely a minute but it will live on for an eternity. We then saw Babe Ruth walk over and give him an enormous bear hug. I noticed many in the room tear up. It was refreshing to see. If that doesn't do it for you, nothing will.

George W then transported us all to Dodger Stadium on a sunny afternoon in 1976. Vin Scully's familiar voice provided the call as two fans ran onto the field, spread an American flag on the ground, and attempted to light it on fire. Suddenly, Cubs outfielder Rick Monday sprinted onto the scene, swooped up the flag, and darted away before the protesters could ignite Old Glory.

Ronald Reagan punctuated the video, "Sometimes actions speak louder than words."

"There's an awful lot of stars on that flag," remarked one of the presidents that I did not recognize. "My goodness, how many states have we got now?" It may have been Tyler…or Arthur.

Bill Clinton approached George W and whispered something out of earshot of the crowd. The younger Bush nodded his head approvingly and fiddled with the remote for a few seconds.

"A little context is again in order," spoke President Clinton. "In 1947, Jackie Robinson changed the face of baseball—and, in doing so, the face of

America—by becoming the first African American to play major league baseball. Prior to that, as many of you know, African American players could only participate in the Negro Leagues. Jackie received countless death threats and incurred racial slurs, but he persevered amidst it all."

"What are we looking at here, Otter? Is this Jackie's first game?" asked Clinton.

"No, not that, Bubba, but another priceless moment. This one's from the first time the Dodgers played the Reds at Crosley Field in Cincinnati that year."

We could hear quite a ruckus from the crowd as the Dodgers took the field in the first inning. Bush continued, "The racial epithets directed not only at Jackie but also at the guys playing with Jackie triggered this iconic act of love."

As the crowd chatter increased, Dodger shortstop Pee Wee Reese walked over to Robinson, stood next to him, looked up to the crowd, and put his hand on Jackie's shoulder."

"How did the fella make out?" asked Woodrow Wilson, one whom I knew had not been, shall we say, the most sensitive about issues of race.

"Oh, Jackie did alright for himself," added Obama. "I would say this little experiment was a success."

"You think?" asked Clinton, with a wide grin.

Obama looked at Wilson. "Jackie became an MVP, a perennial all-star, and landed in the Hall of Fame."

We continued on like this for another hour and a half. We watched clips of several presidents throwing out the first pitch, including Truman throwing with both his right hand and his left, and Obama placing a White Sox hat on to throw out the first pitch at a Nationals game. He airmailed it way over the catcher's head.

We watched Ronald Reagan take the mound in a scene from the movie *The Winning Team,* which costarred Doris Day. Many of the guys unloaded on Reagan for that performance, as well they should have.

Next, we saw a clip of Herbert Hoover tossing out the first pitch at the 1931 World Series. The game took place during Prohibition and we could clearly hear the crowd chanting, "We want beer!"

"Now that's a cause I can embrace," shouted Grover Cleveland, raising his beer before setting it back down next to multiple empty mugs.

Obama, still sitting next to Lincoln, turned to him and said, "You would have been good at basketball, Mr. President."

"Basketball?" Lincoln replied. "I don't believe I'm familiar with that. You'll have to tell me about that game sometime."

Obama looked over at George W. "I would love to see what kind of reaction we'd get from some of the good ol' boys in here if your boy Haskell teed up some modern-day NBA highlights!"

Bush laughed out loud. "Let's not push our luck. We may have actually generated a little progress here tonight."

"Make sure I'm here for that one," Clinton requested. "I want to be seated right next to Andrew Johnson."

That was my cue to leave. I figured there was no stopping this night, and I needed to get back and face my real-world problems. These guys didn't have that weighing on their minds anymore. I was overcome, however, by the camaraderie amongst this group. What a tremendous bonding moment this evening had proven to be after all, and it was all made possible by that most–American of games. I couldn't help but believe that if fierce rivals and enemies could see past that and become what I considered to be respected friends and colleagues then certainly the country could do so. How could I package the goodwill, mutual respect, and genuine concern for the country clearly on display in this room and deploy it for the benefit of the nation? I remained utterly unsure as to how to go about it, but even so, I was all the more certain that it could, indeed, be done.

I approached the bartenders, who had Jefferson and Washington behind the bar with them, clearly mesmerized by the technology of the television.

"Another absolutely classic evening, gents," I exclaimed. "Priceless stuff!"

"Oh, you don't know the half of it," Haskell replied with a huge smile. "Every night in this joint is one for the ages!" He paused for a moment before continuing, "Your idea to shift the focus to baseball was brilliant, sir—very unifying. Great message and lesson for us all. It's so helpful to stop every now and then and realize there's more that unites us than divides us."

I accepted the compliment, knowing full well that if I thought about it long enough, I'd realize it was much more his idea than mine. I decided then that Haskell would make a perfect chief of staff someday.

"Let me ask you this," I said, alternately looking at both Haskell and Matt. "What if instead of baseball, I had asked you guys at the beginning of the night if you were football fans?"

Haskell's face lit up. "Come back tomorrow night, sir."

I fist-bumped many of the presidents on my way out. I'm sure we have Otter to thank for that or possibly Obama. The thought that I'd ever one day be fist-bumping Chester Arthur is a bit too much for me to comprehend right now.

I glanced back on my way out the door and saw that the boys were all still gathered around the enormous television screen. They were dumb-founded watching mascots made to look like four of our iconic presidents race each other during the middle of the fourth inning at National's Park. It was clearly one of baseball's wackiest traditions. As much as I wanted to see someone try to explain to these gentlemen why some of them had been cho-sen to be depicted with massive foam caricature heads and participate in a foot race around a baseball field every night, I decided it was best to depart. Besides, I didn't want to be there when Teddy Roosevelt realized that his mascot was the most hapless racing president of them all.

I heard them all cheering as I walked away. I smiled and shook my head. I still wasn't convinced that I hadn't completely lost my mind. The only thing crazier than me thinking that I was in a room full of all the former pres-idents was me believing that they were watching themselves being parodied with giant foam heads at a ball game and cheering loudly for each other. This was something I decided I could never tell anyone—not even my psychia-trist—the one I now realized I desperately needed to start seeing! However, whatever it was, it was clearly working for me. And that kind of made it irrelevant what it was and whether it meant I was crazy. At least that's what I was telling myself that night.

I took one look back inside as I shut the door. I spotted Sheels lingering inconspicuously in the back, taking it all in with a big smile on his face. We made eye contact, and he flashed me a thumbs-up sign.

Chapter Twenty-Nine

April 12, 2017
Christopher Sheels

Cathy buzzed me on the intercom she and I shared. I picked up. "I have him on line two for you, Mr. President," she said.

I clicked on line two. "Professor Harris," I said with enthusiasm, greeting my favorite prof. "How are you, sir?"

"I'm doing just fine. Following the news closely and thinking a great deal about you."

"I appreciate that, sir. Unfortunately, I'm getting hit pretty hard right now by both sides. There seems to be a whole lot of that lately."

"You wanted to be president, sir," he reminded me.

"Did I?" I couldn't really remember at this point. I kind of thought that maybe I didn't. I just kind of woke up one day and here I was, completely surrounded by a couple dozen Secret Service agents 24/7, who, despite their weaponry, couldn't seem to shield me from the daily barrage of artillery fire that I'd been taking from the press and from an ever-expanding army of anonymous social media accounts.

"Either way, I've got a few questions for you today, Professor," I said. "They may seem rather random to you, but they are fairly important to me."

"No problem, Mr. President. Fire away! I'm happy to be of service. It is truly the honor of a lifetime."

"I appreciate that so much. Thank you. . . . So, what do we know about Thomas Jefferson and the slave woman who he seems to be linked to? Was there anything to that?"

"Her name was Sally Hemings, and history's judgment on that has changed just in the last few decades. Sally was the daughter, believe it or not, of a slave woman and Jefferson's father-in-law—so she was technically Jefferson's wife's half sister."

"Whoa! . . . The plot thickens."

"Yes, indeed . . . although this really transpired after Jefferson's wife, Martha, passed away. When Jefferson received an appointment as Minister to France, his daughter and Sally later joined him. According to Sally's son, that was where a relationship ensued. By the way, Sally was only sixteen years old at the time, and in France, she was considered a free woman.

"The story received widespread circulation in the newspapers at the time, and many reports called him out for it. However, no one had any real proof, and who's to say the accounts weren't politically motivated? Years later, one of Sally's children gave an interview in which he said his mother claimed that Thomas Jefferson had fathered all seven of her children. By the way, she named one of those children Thomas and another James Madison Hemings. However, it is fair to say that the issue was an open question until recently, when DNA analysis on Sally's heirs matched DNA evidence from the Jefferson family. While it's still possible that other Jefferson males fathered those kids, I suspect history's presumption about it has shifted and that he is now generally considered to be the father of at least some of Sally's children."

"Is there any evidence that he ever admitted it?"

"It does not appear that he ever admitted it during his lifetime. And we have extensive records of letters he both sent and received, as well as daily journals he kept. He left no evidence of it and certainly no admission. If he ever did admit it, that has since been lost to history."

"Do you think he would admit it if he were here right now?"

"I'm not sure what you mean by that. I don't quite know how to answer that. As I said, he did not admit it as far as we can tell."

I decided to push my luck and press a little further on this. "I guess I mean that if he had been confronted about it by his peers, would he have admitted it?"

"Well, I think the record shows he was confronted by the press, and, in fact, he didn't admit to it. I'm not sure how else to respond."

I chose to move along. "Were Lincoln and Douglass close? And do you think Douglass pushed Lincoln toward allowing black soldiers in the Union Army and toward total emancipation for the slaves?"

"Well, they were fierce political rivals, of course, and their debates became legendary. Are you asking if his opposition pushed Lincoln?"

"No, actually, I was referring to Frederick Douglass, the former slave, not Stephen Douglas."

"Oh yes. Frederick Douglass was very politically active for the abolitionist cause, and he pressured Lincoln often, both privately and publicly. Although I do believe they achieved a level of respect for one another."

I thought quietly for a few moments.

"You're quite interested in slavery today, sir," Professor Harris declared.

"Yes, I would say so. I should probably learn a little more about the lives of slaves. If there are any books you could suggest for me, I'd love to read up a bit on it. I need to know more."

"There are fascinating stories you can read about, sir. In addition to Frederick Douglass and Sally Hemings, there's Dred Scott . . . and William Carney—who won a Medal of Honor fighting for the Union in the Civil War. And then there's Margaret Garner, who slit the throat of her two-year-old child rather than allow her to be returned to slavery, and Oney Judge, one of Washington's slaves who served George and Martha during his presidency. She famously escaped to New Hampshire and, for the remainder of her life, managed avoid their extensive efforts to capture her."

"I've never heard that story. Did Washington have any other notable slaves?"

"Not many as famous as her, but a few. Harry Washington was one who escaped and then fought for the British Army. There's William Lee, who served right alongside Washington throughout the long Revolutionary War. And then there's Christopher Sheels, who served—"

"Wait, who? What was the name you just said?"

"Christopher Sheels."

"*Sheels?*" I responded.

"Yes, Christopher Sheels."

Oh my God! I couldn't believe what I was hearing. My head was spinning as it labored to figure out what this all meant.

"What do you know about him?"

"Well, not a lot. As a young man, he served as a waiter and bartender for Washington at Mount Vernon. Washington liked him very much, and took him to Philadelphia to serve as a valet while he was president. History books note that when Washington was on his deathbed, Christopher Sheels was right there by his side."

After a few moments of awkward silence, he asked, "Why the astonishment, sir?"

"Oh, nothing in particular," I fibbed, knowing a full explanation was out of the question. "How would I learn more about some of these folks?"

"I'll work on it for you, Mr. President. I'd be happy to do so. But if you don't mind me asking, what's your angle on this? If I know what you're after, I can more clearly focus my search on what matters to you most."

"Sure. Just get me the most you can find on Christopher Sheels. . . . And let me ask you this . . . ," I said, "is it possible that Christopher Sheels appeared in a painting with Washington?"

"I'll check on that for you as well. I know there are a least a few paintings of Washington with his slaves."

"Thank you, Professor. I can't tell you how enlightening this has been for me. Really, I can't." I laughed to myself.

"I'm so delighted to hear that, Mr. President."

That exchange had just completely blown my mind. This had to be the same Sheels. He'd been a bartender at Mount Vernon for God's sake. And, oh my God, Professor Harris was the perfect one-stop American History source for me. He seemed to know everything!

"One more thing, Professor."

"Sure."

"And this might sound random, but did Teddy Roosevelt hate baseball with a passion?"

"I haven't the foggiest idea, sir. Why do you ask?"

I didn't really know how to respond. There was another brief but awkward silence.

"You know I enjoy speaking with you, Mr. President," Professor Harris said, "but what's really behind all these questions, if you don't mind me asking? It seems like a whole lot more than merely random curiosity."

"Oh," I responded, unsure of where I was going with my reply but confident that if I just started talking, I'd end up in a good place. "I've had the opportunity to participate in some rather remarkable discussions about political and historical events, and often I don't feel as well versed on some of the particular topics we're discussing as some of the others in the room."

"Terrific! You know I love that, and I can only imagine how useful that must be for all that you have to tackle in this job. I'm pleased I'm not your only conduit to history."

"Oh, I've got quite a conduit, that's for sure!" I said with a laugh. Then I added, under my breath, "I'd say it's the mother of all conduits."

"What did you say, sir?"

"Oh, nothing. Just thinking out loud again."

Chapter Thirty

April 13, 2017—1:14 p.m.
Evelyn Lincoln

"A couple things, sir," Cathy said, greeting me as I returned from lunch in the residence. "First, Professor Harris called. And second, Murph is back from the Hill and needs to see you on the budget negotiations."

"Professor Harris called? Please get him on the phone right away."

"But Murph is—"

"Please see if you can get him. I just need a couple of minutes, then I'll be out there."

"Are you sure?"

"Yes. I'll be quick."

Moments later, the professor was on the phone. "Professor!" I said eagerly.

"Why don't we just make this a daily occurrence."

"I would love to."

"My former students and colleagues don't believe me when I tell them we speak regularly. I hope you are OK with me mentioning that."

"Sure, as long as you don't tell them what we talk about. They'd think I'm crazy."

"You mean like I do?" Professor Harris said with a hearty laugh.

"Ha ha! You've probably known that since I was in your classes."

"I have some follow-up information for you," he said.

"Wow! That was quick!" I was thrilled. "What did you find out?"

"So, Christopher Sheels was technically a dower slave of Martha Washington," the professor began.

"What does that mean?" I asked.

"It meant that he became Washington's by reason of his marriage to Martha through her deceased husband, but upon her death, he would be returned to her deceased husband's heirs. But Christopher Sheels worked directly for Washington as a waiter and bartender at Mount Vernon and then as a valet and body servant for him in Philadelphia during the presidency."

"What else do we know about Sheels?"

"His mother, a slave named Alyce, was a seamstress for Martha Washington. Washington must have thought highly of him to make him a waiter, bartender, and body servant. Only trusted and respected slaves worked inside the mansion."

"Did you find out if he appeared with Washington in any paintings?"

"While they can't be certain, historians believe he is depicted in some paintings by Edward Savage, a prominent portrait painter from Massachusetts."

"Is one of those a painting of Washington and Martha dining and being served by a slave?"

"Yes, as a matter of fact."

"I thought that looked just like him," I mumbled.

"Excuse me, sir?"

"I mean, I've seen that painting, and the slave seems to fit his description. Do we know what happened to him later in life?"

"There appears to be no record of him later in life—which is odd, since we do know what happened to so many of the other Mount Vernon slaves. For him, that information appears to have been lost to history, unfortunately . . . like he dropped out of sight."

"That's fascinating. Thank you so much, Professor."

"Why this fascination with Christopher Sheels, if you don't mind me asking?"

At that moment, with what can only be described as impeccable timing, Cathy popped her head in. "Murph and her group are ready and waiting for you out there, sir."

"Sorry, Professor, but I've gotta go. Thank you so much!" I hung up a little abruptly, and then turned my attention to Cathy. "Did Murph look happy?" I asked.

"Oh, that's impossible for me to tell," Cathy replied. "She's a tough one to read."

"You must have sensed something, though? Anything? I'm dying here."

"No. She had a fairly blank face and a benign mood. But if you were the standard, I'd say she was positively rapturous." She smiled, apparently quite proud of that comment.

"Would it kill you to be just a tad more respectful toward the leader of the free world? Do you suppose Evelyn Lincoln made cracks like that to JFK?"

"Are we comparing ourself to JFK, now?" Cathy smirked.

"You would be wise to channel a little more of your inner Evelyn Lincoln, my dear. She worshipped her boss. She had photos of JFK hanging on the wall behind her desk, for God's sake—and that's while she worked in the White House right outside his office."

"Well perhaps if I worked for him I would too." Clearly she wasn't backing down.

"He certainly has a style and a charm about him," I replied. "I mean *had*, of course. At least from what I've read and seen on TV."

"They're waiting for you, Danny," Cathy reminded.

"I'm on my way. . . . But remind me to get you some photos of me to hang in your office. Perhaps one of me delivering my inaugural address, one of me relaxing on the dock at Lake Almanor, one of me pitching to the boys—"

She turned around quickly and walked away with impressive pace.

I raised my voice to have the last word, "My next assistant is going to be unbelievably respectful."

She was well out of earshot.

Moments later, I entered the Oval Office and looked right at Murph. Much to my dismay, she avoided eye contact. To me that spoke volumes.

I took what had become my usual seat, opposite the glass door to Cathy's entrance. We were joined by Chief of Staff Terri Drake and Senior Policy Adviser Karen Nevarez, as well as Budget Director Ben Morales.

"Let me have it, Murph," I said.

"I think we have our work cut out for us with this, Mr. President. I'm fairly certain the leadership on both sides have really effectively cut us out and are negotiating this thing on their own. Our proposals are not even really on the table. Your notion of a 'grand bargain' to permanently fix the budget for the next few generations doesn't even seem to be on their radar. You may not want to watch any cable news today—you're getting destroyed by both sides."

As if that wasn't enough to lay on me, she continued. "Worse yet, I think they are down a path for a short-term solution, and it will be really hard to dial it back."

"Is there any good news?" I asked. "Are they at least united in their vitriol against me? Have we managed to unite Congress and the country after all?" I was only partially kidding.

"No," she responded humorlessly. "We're getting hit from both sides for reasons that are diametrically opposed to one another. They are no closer to a deal than they were when we engaged them about this two months ago."

For the past two months, Republicans and Democrats had been negotiating on a deal to avoid the latest fiscal cliff—a combination of raising the debt ceiling coupled with what we hoped would be a budget deal that would amount to more than just another temporary fix. We proposed a lasting framework that would eventually bring us to a balanced budget and begin to chip away at our national debt. Our proposed grand bargain would address big picture structural issues that had inflated the national debt to unsustainable levels. As a centrist, I felt I was uniquely positioned to propose real cuts to both entitlement spending and the defense budget. We coupled all that with a plan to dramatically scale back the massive federal workforce. We felt that these cuts, while painful to be sure, were essential to the long-term fiscal health and sustainability of the nation. I believed our proposals were as reasonable as they were necessary. We advocated for a means test for social security—so the benefits would target those who needed them most. To cut the massive defense budget, we sought significant reductions to worldwide troop levels and challenged the notion of being perennially ready to engage in two major wars simultaneously. The deadline to avoid a government shutdown was the following day.

I looked at the frustrated faces around the room. "Is there any silver lining at all?" I asked.

"Well, if it makes it any easier for you," Murph replied, "I'd say there might be."

"Well what is it?" I demanded. "I need to know."

"I'd say that they definitely seem to hate each other as much as they hate you."

Karen and Ben couldn't contain the laughter they were trying in vain to hold back. However, at that moment I was simply unable to grasp the humor.

Presidential Spirits

"OK," I said slowly without changing my defeated expression. "I don't believe that helps me in any way whatsoever, but thanks for trying."

Chapter Thirty-One

April 13, 2017—9:46 p.m.
A Genetic Cocktail

CBS Evening News

Scott Pelley: Good evening, ladies and gentlemen. Our top story tonight comes from Capitol Hill. With no time to spare, Congress has finally come together to pass a bill on the budget. That's the good news. The bad news is that the bill they passed simply extends a government shutdown—the date upon which the government will run out of authorized funding pursuant to the most recent continuing resolution—by two weeks, and only marginally raises the debt ceiling.

These continuing resolutions have become the norm in Washington, with this being the seventh such resolution since the end of the last fiscal year. Lawmakers took to the senate floor to engage in the time-honored ritual of assigning blame to the other party. While senators took turns berating their colleagues, President McFadden's grand bargain solution was roundly derided by both sides, with some legislators knocking him for what one senator termed "an utter lack of effective leadership."

President McFadden has not yet signed this short-term bill. He has until midnight to do so to avoid a government shutdown. He has stated emphatically that he is not willing to sign any more temporary fixes. However, sources inside the White House indicate tonight that they believe, from a political standpoint, he has no choice but to approve the measure again.

***

I entered the Saloon and instantly felt better. This supernatural establishment was beginning to become incredibly familiar to me. And what an escape it was—almost addicting.

Matt yelled out at me as I approached, "What's shaking, President McFadden?"

"Vetoed my first bill tonight, Matty. In fact, I vetoed the hell out of it!" I burst into laughter and Matt did too.

"I am purposefully plunging us directly into a government shutdown. I think that calls for a drink."

"That's what I want to hear, President Mac."

Mary Ann approached and gave me a hug. She's always so positive, generously flashing that infectious smile. I exhaled hard. Haskell walked down from the other end of the bar. "Great to see you tonight, Mr. President. It's always a special night when you're here."

"What's happening in here tonight?" I asked.

"Quite a bit," responded Mary Ann. Pointing to the stage, she said, "Kennedy is speaking over there about his handling of the Cuban Missile Crisis. I've heard it a few times, but it's still pretty interesting. You know—with the world being on the brink of annihilation and all—that never gets old."

Then she pointed to the opposite corner of the tavern. "Over there, you've got your usual suspects playing cards. And there's a bit of a challenge in the bar tonight between Washington's own whiskey distilled at Mount Vernon and Andrew Jackson's from the Hermitage."

Haskell looked at me and said, "Many of your colleagues tonight are siding with Big Daddy—the Father of Our Country—for obvious political reasons. But knowing your integrity, sir, you'll make a purely principled decision uninfluenced by politics."

All I could do was shake my head and laugh in response to that. I loved this bar. No wonder I was becoming addicted. *What the hell is this place, anyway?*

"Pick your poison, President Mac, Virginia or Tennessee?" Matt asked.

"Let me start with the Hermitage."

"Thank you," cried Mary Ann, clearly relieved by my choice. "I'm kind of afraid what might happen if Jackson loses this one."

"I'm with you there," I responded. "We wouldn't want this charming saloon to see its first duel."

"Too late for that, sir!" Mary Ann shot back.

My jaw dropped, "No way! There's actually been a duel in here?"

"You don't see Millard Fillmore around here do you?" she answered.

"Oh my God!" I blurted out, completely and utterly astonished.

Mary Ann shrieked. "I'm just kidding, sir!" She laughed uncontrollably, seeming very impressed with herself, and for good reason—she had me hook, line, and sinker.

"How can you be the president and be so gullible?" she said, still laughing.

"You have to realize, of course, that for me to actually believe I'm mingling with every person who ever served as president of the United States, living or dead, then I must be fairly easy to deceive."

Tina walked up to us with yet another beautiful, young server accompanying her. "We have someone we'd like to introduce you to," she said.

"I'm Danny McFadden," I said, extending my hand out to her.

"I know who you are, Mr. President. It's great to have you with us here. Call me Ginger. That's not my real name, of course, but Otter gave me the nickname, and now that's all anyone here calls me."

She looked a little bit like a young Ann Margaret in *Bye Bye Birdie*, which, if you've ever seen the movie, is not a bad look. It made sense to me—giving a redhead the nickname Ginger, although it certainly wasn't the most clever or original moniker I'd ever heard.

I glanced over at Mary Ann and then it hit me. "Alright," I said, connecting the dots. "Bush named you two Ginger and Mary Ann. Now I get it. Do you ladies even know that reference?"

"We've seen some reruns," Mary Ann quickly responded.

"I'll call you whatever you prefer if you think those nicknames are in any way demeaning," I offered. Having witnessed a lot of harassment in the workplace in the past twenty years, I knew enough to tread lightly.

"I'm fine with it," Ginger said. "Everybody loves Otter. He makes this place fun."

"Yeah, the nicknames aren't the demeaning part of working here," Tina added.

"Alright," I said. "Let's talk about that. I want to help."

"I'll fill you in another time," replied Tina. "But I appreciate your concern."

"Yes. Please do. I'm happy to help. I've done my share of addressing such issues in my career."

I made some more small talk with Matt while the ladies made their rounds. A few minutes later, Ginger returned and handed him a drink ticket. She looked stressed . . . and annoyed.

I read Matt's lips as he whispered to her, "You doing OK, sweetheart?"

"No, as a matter of fact!" she barked back. She knew the rest of us could hear, but apparently didn't care. "A few of the grandpas in this old folks home are in desperate need of a good neutering."

"What can I do about it?" Matt asked. "I can talk to Otter or Big Daddy about it . . . or Sheels. If it's really bad, I'll bypass them all and go straight to Tina."

I stepped in and looked at Ginger. "I'm happy to go see if I can talk some sense into these folks," I suggested.

"No, no. I can handle it. Please don't," Ginger begged.

Even so, I grabbed my all-too-tall glass of Tennessee whiskey and walked in the direction of where I felt the likeliest culprits were gathered. I took a seat at a table in the center of the bar just as Kennedy's talk at the far corner ended. Most of that crowd came and joined us at tables nearby.

Within moments, Mary Ann, Tina, and Ginger arrived with drinks. Most everyone was having whiskey tonight. Some had obviously already had their share, as I suspected from Ginger's conversation with Matty.

As the ladies returned to the bar, the conversations at our three middle tables turned to them. I strained my ears attempting to follow all of the colorful discourse, which came fast and furious. The alpha males could not help themselves.

"You see the way she was looking at me, fellas?"

"I have to admit the thought of separating one of these beauties from the herd has crossed my mind."

"The redhead has that 'come hither' look."

Jimmy Carter spoke up, "Gentlemen, these ladies are young enough to be our granddaughters! Let's show them some respect."

"And that coming from the man who famously 'lusted in his heart,'" cried a voice I couldn't identify.

They quieted down as the ladies came back again with drinks.

I watched Ginger closely; she was as sweet and flirtatious as can be. As she came near me, I motioned for her to come close. "I thought these guys made you sick to your stomach," I whispered.

"Oh, they do, sir," she whispered back, momentarily losing her evidently manufactured smile. "But remember, it;' a tip-based industry."

Mary Ann also thrilled these gentlemen with her infinitely sweet, genuine disposition and alluring smile.

After LBJ thanked Mary Ann for the drink, he added, "What nationality are you, sweetheart?"

"I'm a little bit of everything, Mr. President. My dad's family came from Mexico. My grandma on my mom's side is Filipino, and my grandpa was African American. How's that for a genetic cocktail?"

"Let me tell you, honey . . . ," Harding said in response to overhearing all this, "it works."

"That's one cocktail I'd sure like to taste," uttered LBJ. Then, raising his voice for all to hear, he added, "What time do you get off tonight, sweetie?"

Mary Ann laughed and smiled all the more. "I'm sure you can do much, much better than me, Mr. President." She turned quickly and hurried back toward the bar.

"Well played by the young lady," remarked Kennedy, seemingly amused at the rebuke of his vice president.

Harding added, "Tough luck with her, but it appears the redhead is game, Lyndon."

George W. Bush chimed in, "Hate to disappoint you boys, but I'm afraid she's taken. I do believe she is making time, so to speak, with Big Time."

"That doesn't scare me," added Harding. "He's merely a barkeep."

"Really?" Obama asked, incredulously. "Are you kidding me right now? I understand we all have high opinions of ourselves, and in some cases, for good reasons. But, Christ, have you seen that guy? Dude looks like he works out five hours a day, seven days a week. You know I love you, Mr. President, but I'm just keeping it real here."

Another voice added, "And perhaps there's another reason they call him

Big Time."

Much to everyone's delight, Tina had overheard the last part of this tawdry conversation. She had approached the table from behind Harding's back, out of view of him and a few of the others, where she stood quietly taking it all in.

All eyes now diverted to Tina in great anticipation. Our feminist heroine did not disappoint. "Gentlemen," she called out, commanding everyone's attention. "I don't even know where to begin." Looking directly at Harding, she said, "Some of you think that because you were president, these smart, sweet, beautiful young waitresses will easily succumb to your eminently awkward advances. Let me tell you something—it's a new era. It may have taken almost 250 years, but women are a tad more empowered these days. The good ol' days in which presidents, CEOs, Hollywood moguls, and other powerful men could use their positions of power to prey on young women, then deny it, cover it up, and attempt to ruin anyone who deigns to expose it, are coming to an end.

"You folks may have gotten a pass while in office but, in case you didn't notice, it's now game on for historians. I would advise against reading some of the latest biographies being penned about you."

Tina let her remarks sink in for a few moments before going back for more. "Secondly, how deliciously delusional it is for some of you to think you'd even have a chance with someone like her. Yes, you're presidents, but look around you . . ." Tina paused and peered around the room. Then with increased passion and volume, she continued to let 'em have it. "You're in a room full of presidents! You guys are a dime a dozen in here. And just because a cute woman smiles at you when she takes your drink order doesn't mean she wants to be your date for the evening or your soul mate."

Her comments divided the room three ways. As she walked away, many of us started applauding. Some were outraged. But a decent number of the men were really just amused to see a few colleagues get dressed down by a strong woman, whether or not they appreciated the broader significance of the moment.

One of the guys called out to Harding but clearly intending for the whole room to hear him, "Hey Warren, I want to be here the night you try to get somewhere with Tina. Sheels could sell tickets to that event."

That comment broke up the room. Clinton in particular seemed to enjoy it.

I looked at George W. Bush, and while pointing at the speaker, I silently mouthed, "Who is that?"

He read my lips and mouthed back, "Garfield."

I gave him a thumbs-up. He smiled, pointed back at me, and half-winked. *There's a guy who knows his role in the room and relishes it.*

I found the whole scene so captivating. I really didn't want to leave. And what a kick it was to see a young woman call out a few of these guys. I regretted not speaking up in her defense—not that she was even remotely in need of an assist from me. I tried to convince myself that I would've spoken up if she hadn't returned to the bar immediately following her smackdown.

As much as I didn't want to, I needed to get back to reality. I hadn't had a chance to discuss my latest political predicament tonight, but for some reason, this place was remarkably therapeutic for me. As I walked away, I heard someone yell, "Hey President Mac."

I turned to see Tina approaching. "Thanks for the support," she said.

"Are you being sarcastic?" I asked, as feelings of guilt raged inside me.

"No, I mean it. Your words to Ginger were appreciated, and I saw you clapping after my little rant there. So I just wanted to say thanks."

"Well, thank you for that, but in both cases, it was really nothing."

I wasn't being modest—it really was nothing. Perhaps women are so used to never having men jump in to show support when issues such as these emerge that they see any sign of support—no matter how small—as a big deal. I needed to file that realization away for more analysis later.

"I love what you said tonight, Tina," I said. "I want to hire you."

"That's music to my ears. That really sums up what this is about—trying to get powerful men to trade their primal instincts to want to sleep with us for a desire to hire us, work with us—or for us—and respect us as peers."

"I do see that happening in this next generation. The younger folks really get it," I said.

"No, I mean now, sir," she scolded with a suddenly somewhat annoyed tone. "We're not waiting around for another generation."

"Of course. You are absolutely correct," I responded, terribly disappointed in myself. "Of course," I repeated. I felt as if I'd just flunked a test—one I should've been well prepared for.

"Yes, I am," she declared.

I think I needed to just shut up. *Stop talking now.*

When she started to walk away, I stopped her. "What are you doing in this bar, Tina? And in this job?" I asked. "What are all you bright, competent, engaging kids doing in this place anyway?"

"Are you kidding me?" she asked. "I get to interact with all these sexy old men on a nightly basis."

I looked at her with a rather blank stare.

"That's a joke, Mr. President," she said. Again I felt stupid. This sharp young woman clearly intimidated the hell out of me. "But seriously," she continued. "I have a profound influence in this role. I can shape opinions."

"Sure," I granted her. "I can see that, and you do it quite adeptly. But what good does it really do at this point to shape Harding's view of women? He's been out of office for nearly a century."

"His is not the opinion I am aiming to influence," she countered. She paused to let that sink in, fixing her gaze right into my eyes.

OK, now I was freaked out again. That small but powerful exchange blew my mind. *Was this whole saloon designed just for me?*

Perhaps because she saw me awash in emotions and no shortage of anxiety, she moved on. "There are other reasons to stay here, too, of course. I've got a good bit of vanity in me, as you know, and staying here means I'll never age, never get wrinkles, never hit menopause. And I have the nightly pleasure of rejecting the advances of all these guys—not just Harding, but Garfield, Clinton, LBJ, JFK. . . . Although I have to admit that one night I may just have to give in with him," she said, half joking. Or at least I think she was.

She then added, "And under no circumstances can I leave until I see a see a sister walk through that door of yours over there, so I may be here a while."

I laughed, but then I immediately realized it wasn't really funny, nor was it intended to be.

"This group desperately needs a woman's voice," she continued, "and that's not to say all women's voices are homogeneous. But for God's sake, how about just one after 250 years?"

"Well, we got closer than ever this year, but I'm afraid I didn't help that particular cause. I may have been the spoiler in that."

"Well, if you prevented Hillary, you also prevented Trump. You spared the country and the world from seeing what that unmitigated disaster would have been."

"I'm not sure about the disaster part, but I do feel he would've just played to his base. As she would have as well. And that's kind of the point of my whole political existence—we've gotta have presidents like Washington who try to unite the whole country and not just seek to rack up wins for one particular side.

"You're a really sharp person, Tina," I continued. "If you don't mind, answer me this: What the heck *is* this place?"

"What do you mean? This country? This bar?"

"This bar. What the heck is it?"

Just then FDR yelled out, "Nurse, we need another round over here."

"Hold that thought," Tina said with a smile as she darted off to attend to my predecessors, leaving me no closer to an answer. *What the heck is this place anyway?* I was so unbelievably intrigued.

Chapter Twenty-Two

April 15, 2017
Shutdown

There is a unique problem inherent in being a president who is neither a Democrat nor a Republican. When the shit starts hitting the fan, as it inevitably does—and as it was at this particular point in my presidency—rather than align with your party in publicly placing blame squarely on the other, you are seemingly on an island unto yourself, taking incoming fire from all sides.

"You've gotta publicly defend yourself, sir," Jed beseeched me. It was only day one of the government shutdown, but it seemed like it had already been going on several months. I had Jed, Murph, and Terri Drake in my private office desperately seeking a path to anything that could resemble victory.

Jed was adamant. "You're getting destroyed by all in the ideological press, sir. Cable news is having a field day. You've got FOX and MSNBC looking practically indistinguishable. I know you don't like to publicly attack others, but you can't just sit back and let this happen."

"You know I despise the Washington blame game, Jed," I responded emphatically. "There are few labels I detest more intensely than 'whiner'."

"No one will ever confuse you with a whiner, sir. But they won't be confusing you with anybody at all if you're out of office. I'm trying to help you here. As your press secretary, it would be malpractice for me not to strongly urge you to go on the attack. You've got the higher moral ground. That's your identity. That's your brand." He let that sink in for a few seconds before picking back up. "Here's a page of talking points for you. We've got our allies out there pushing back with these points, but they're a dwindling group these days."

"I've got a long list of calls for us to make to Capitol Hill this evening,

Mr. President," added Murph. "Can you give me a couple of hours?"

"You got it. Cathy cleared my schedule."

Jed stood up. "I've gotta go," he said. "The White House press corps awaits. The crazy thing is that the mainstream press seems to agree with us on the need for a long-term fix. But this has really become such a feeding frenzy for the two extremes. And unfortunately, that's where all the passion is."

"When is the briefing?" I asked.

"As soon as I walk in. Thinking of joining?" Jed looked pleasantly surprised.

"I may just do that. Any advice?"

"Be brief and stick to the big picture. They'll hammer you with the short-term fallout and immediate consequences—of which there are many. Your play here is for history and the long-term . . . you know, the pesky little matter of the national debt that for decades neither party has seemed to care about."

Jed got to the door and turned back to us. "Wish me luck," he said. Then, cracking a big smile, he added, "Feel free to come bail me out anytime you like, Mr. President."

I entered the briefing room amidst a frenzy of reporters raising their hands and shouting questions at poor Jed. It was such a quintessential American scene. So central to what makes this country great. So why did I despise it so much?

Jed shot me a look of relief as a smile came across his face. "Ladies and gentlemen," he began, "looks like the boss will be taking it from here. Please be gentle with him." Jed had an enviable way of not letting this stuff really get under his skin. Unfortunately for me, it wasn't contagious.

I took the podium as a sea of reporters shouted questions at me. They settled down as soon as I started to speak. "Let me begin by saying just a few words. I was elected with a nonpartisan wave of support that stood as an unequivocal rejection of the polarized, destructive party politics our country has devolved into. I come without party allegiance, but rather, with the country's best interests as my driving force. There is nothing about this seventh consecutive continuing resolution that addresses the long-term, systemic budget and finance challenges that confront our nation. Had I signed this deal, I would've merely been enabling that dysfunction. Failure to address these matters, particularly our expanding debt, will dramatically impact our financial sustainability, our place on the world stage, our prosperity, our military readiness, and our ability to preserve the American dream for future generations. I did not veto this bill in a vacuum. I warned Congress well in advance of signing the latest continuing resolution that we would no longer accept short-term fixes. No one else in our system of government has the power to force Congress to confront this . . . or the responsibility to do so. Without me taking these actions, in the present political context members of Congress have no incentive to attempt the type of long-term grand bargain we need to bring this country forward. To the contrary, they see even attempting such bold action to be fraught with political peril."

I paused and looked around the room. When my eyes landed on Jed, he flashed me a thumbs-up and a big smile. I continued, "I know that was long-winded, but that's the most concise expression of why we are where we're at and why I now adopt this position. I had intended to take questions, but there is nothing I care to add to that. I know there are severe short-term consequences for many as a result of this shutdown. For that, I am sincerely sorry. We have done our best to mitigate against the worst of that. However, failure to take a stand on this would amount to political malpractice on my part."

I looked over again at Jed, whose look of relief had suddenly shifted to sheer panic as he realized he wasn't quite off the hook. "With that, ladies and gentlemen, I will hand the podium back over to Jed, who would be happy to entertain all questions you might have."

I stepped away from the podium, leaving a sea of shouting reporters. As Jed approached, he paused for a second to whisper in my ear, "You son of a bitch."

I couldn't decide whether it spoke well of me that a staffer felt comfortable hitting me with that or it was an absolute indictment of my leadership skills. Regardless, I left the room and couldn't help but laugh out loud. Why not? It sure beat crying, which I could have been doing just as easily.

Chapter Twenty-Three

April 22, 2017
Largely Irrevelant

NEW YORK TIMES

MCFADDEN RELEGATED TO SIDELINES AS CONGRESS SEEKS BUDGET FIX

by Alan Rappeport

April 22, 2017—In a remarkable rebuke to President McFadden, both houses of Congress voted today to override the president's veto of the latest continuing resolution on the federal budget. This override effectively ends the government shutdown, funding the government for an additional two weeks and providing lawmakers additional time to reach a more permanent budget agreement.

Leaders in the House and Senate also announced they have made some progress toward a long-term deal. It appears that the Democrats are willing to support some form of additional across-the-board tax relief measure in exchange for Republican concessions on Democratic spending measures. It is telling that the White House apparently has not been involved in those longer-term discussions. The president's agenda for aggressive budget reductions and his staunch opposition to both the new Republican tax cuts and the Democratic spending measures seem to be largely irrelevant to these negotiations.

Chapter Twenty-Four

May 2, 2017
The One Who Added the Pitcher's Mound

My Oval Office meeting with King Abdullah II of Jordan went very well. I never tire of meeting world leaders on behalf of the United States. What a profound privilege. We covered Syria at length—the latest concerning its civil war, Russia's continuing influence, and the de-escalation zone on the southern Syrian border with Jordan and Israel. The meeting was largely for the photo op, since the substantive content of our get-together had been brokered well in advance. We spent an hour and a half in the Oval Office, the last fifteen minutes in front of the reporters and cameras. We then broke to prepare for a joint press conference in the East Room, where each of us was planning to give a statement before answering a few questions.

As the crowd was being ushered out of the Oval Office, I glanced outside the windows to see my son Jack and two other kids pitching to my son Brett out on the lawn with Satch behind the mound coaching them. It warmed my heart to see such a beautiful sight. Installing that mound was clearly the best improvement I'd made to the White House. I figured if Nixon could add a bowling alley of all things, no one would complain if we added a pitcher's mound and a home plate. What's more American than that, for God's sake. *When all is said and done, if nothing else, perhaps that mound will be my lasting legacy. People will say, "Let's see, McFadden . . . wasn't he the one who added the pitcher's mound?"* I decided that wouldn't be all bad—except that inevitably half the country would say we built the mound too high and the other half would say it wasn't high enough.

Jed Rose and a few of his White House Communications staffers who had been supervising the brief media moment in the Oval Office appeared. Chief of Staff Terri Drake, Secretary of State Cynthia Miller, and National Security Adviser Jim Garza followed closely behind. They all looked like they meant business. Even so, they were no match for the allure of the "boys of summer" out back. I couldn't help myself—I tore off my coat, loosened my tie, and hightailed it outside. All involuntarily—just following a primal instinct. I could see the look of utter exasperation on Jed's face as he very quickly assessed the scene in front of him. It didn't make matters any better when I called back to him, "Don't let them start the presser without me." His jaw dropped what seemed like half a foot. If I had thought it through thoroughly, which I purposely refused to do, I may have felt some guilt about it. But even then I certainly would have concluded that, of all the guilty pleasures pursued by inhabitants of this office at the expense of the job over the years, this had to be among the most harmless.

Jack was pitching from the stretch with Satch perched just behind the mound calling balls and strikes. I yelled out to the boys, "Pay attention to what that old guy says! He may seem ancient to you guys, but he was a baller in his time!" The boys watched as several Secret Service agents scrambled to take their places around us.

Satch called back as I got closer, "We've got some real talent here, Mr. President."

Seeing me approaching, Jack sprinted over to weathered baseball bag nearby and pulled out my old Wilson A2000 infielder's glove that I'd had since high school. If there's anything I own that means more to me, I certainly can't think of it at the moment.

"This is my grandson, Hank," Satch said, as another teenager settled in on the mound, taking over for Jack.

"Great baseball name," I replied, "although more of a slugger's name than a pitcher's."

"Oh, he can hit, sir. You better believe he can hit!"

"Love it!" I said turning to Hank. "Don't let them force you into specializing. Pitchers get a raw deal when it comes to getting at bats. Break the mold."

Satch then pointed to the other kid. "And that's Dom. He's family too."

I waved to Dom, a small but solid blond-haired kid about the same age as Hank. He was standing next to Brett near the plate. I wondered how exactly he was connected.

"I got a new pitch, Dad," Jack said, flashing a confident grin.

"Courtesy of Coach Satch?" I asked. "Tell me about it."

"It's a splitter, but he throws it very differently from how you taught me."

"Word of advice, dude, on matters of pitching, always defer to a guy nicknamed Satch," I conceded willingly. "And on a whole lot of other matters, too, I might add."

"Your boy's getting some pretty good lateral movement on that pitch," Satch declared proudly, "which is gonna prevent guys from barreling up. It rides in on the lefties and floats away from the righties."

"Let me know what we owe you," I said looking at Satch. "In Silicon Valley, parents of youth pitchers pay a king's ransom for private coaching like this."

"Well, maybe that'll be where I end up then. I'm always searching for my next chapter."

"There's worse places to be than the Bay Area."

"No way I could afford it."

"As long as you teach kids that pitch, you'll be able to afford it."

"Here . . . ," Satch motioned to me, "stand next to me and watch this movement."

Rather effortlessly, Hank threw what appeared to be a fastball to Brett. As the ball approached the plate, it exploded right to left and dropped a few inches in the process.

"Unhittable, son!" pronounced Satch. "Absolutely unhittable. That's just not fair."

"Nothing quite like having someone who believes in you, Hank," I said. "Good for you. You are lucky to have a stud like that as a grandad."

"Feel like tossin' a few, Dad?" Brett asked, reading my mind.

"I don't have the shoes for it," I responded. "But what the heck. Why not?"

Then looking over at Jack, I said, "Here buddy, warm me up a bit."

A few moments later, I was trying out out all the old pitches from the rubber. I saw Cathy approaching from the corner of my eye. I ignored her, although with her I knew I did so at my own risk. I respect her too much to mess with her, so after a few more tosses, I decided to meet her halfway.

"Look, Boss," she began. She almost never called me "boss," so I knew she meant business. "I've got your entire staff screaming at me to do something. As if I actually have some influence over you." She spoke calmly and softly, but her words suggested an urgency. "I could go on and on about how pretty soon you'll be keeping the king of Jordan and the whole White House press corps waiting, but I'll spare you those details . . . just tell me what you want me to say to them."

"I'm coming, Cathy," I whispered to her. "I'm sorry. I don't expect anyone to understand," I paused, my cadence coming to a crawl, "but this is awesome." I looked right into her eyes and said as earnestly as I've ever expressed any truth since I first learned to speak. "These last fifteen minutes have been among the most special and therapeutic moments of my life. I needed this after dealing with all the dysfunction of this town. I'll be in there in a minute."

"I can tell, Danny. You look happy for a change. I do understand. Take your time. You forget I'm a baseball fan too. And I share your pain more than you know."

"Yes, it's baseball as a complete escape, but it's also the unmistakable bonding baseball brings about. I'm in the moment with my boys, and that is so special to me. And in a very spiritual sense, I'm somehow also in the presence of my dad and my brothers and all my very best friends that I played this game with through the years. I love how much it matters to me and to these kids and to my entire family. So few things in life can match that. Love you, Cath."

"You stay out here as long as you need to, sir. Seriously now, world affairs can never measure up to a McFadden family baseball moment." She smiled as she said this. I could tell she was mocking me—as she is all too prone to do—but at the same time, I knew she completely understood. She turned around and walked back alone to face the wrath of my staff. I do love her. And God I love baseball.

Chapter Twenty-Five

May 3, 2017
Dom

We tried to have a family breakfast on Wednesday mornings every week whenever I was in town. I really looked forward to those, and so did Denyse. I'm not sure the kids did, though, since it meant an earlier wake-up call. Wednesday breakfasts were especially good. Sandy did it right and spoiled the heck out of all of us, knowing exactly what we all like.

The boys rolled out of bed last, as usual. Sandy, Denyse, Montana, and I had all been gathered around the table for quite some time before they finally emerged.

"How's your country, Dad?" Brett asked with a smile, as he always did.

"It's just as much yours as it is mine, dude. And *divided* is probably the most apt description for it, but I'm trying to change that."

I kind of hated talking shop with the kids. I needed my parenting time with them to be an escape from the job—if you could call this a job. I'm sure there's a much more appropriate word for it.

"How did baseball go yesterday?" I asked.

"Awesome!" Jack shot back.

"What do you think of Hank and Dom?"

"They're a couple of ballers, Dad," responded Brett. "Mad respect."

"Can you guys hang with them?"

"We did on the baseball diamond and in the weight room afterward, but they schooled us in *Fortnite*. Dom was a beast."

"What the heck is *Fortnite*? I'm almost afraid to ask."

"Dad, where've you been?" Jack said, displaying an annoyed look I was all too familiar with.

"I'm not saying you're out of touch," Denyse added, grinning broadly, "but even *I* know what *Fortnite* is, Daddy." She was evidently quite proud of herself.

"Let me guess," I said. "I'm gonna say it's not something involving exercise or even athleticism . . . or anything educational or character building."

"Why do you always do that, Dad?" protested Jack. "You know it's none of those things, and you're just trying to make us feel bad."

"Now that's unfair. I'm just trying to parent the best way I know how and steer you down the right path in life. Is that so wrong—to be a dad who loves you and wants the very best for you?

"Look at our family motto," I continued, pointing to an old wooden sign hanging in the kitchen that I'd had custom-made years ago. "It says 'The McFaddens—that clean, healthy family that loves each other, reads a lot, and prays.' I have a hunch that *Fort Right* doesn't exactly fit within one of those core family virtues."

"It's *Fortnite*," Jack barked back at me.

"OK, but you're not denying my underlying assertion. And by the way, I'm proud that I don't know what *Fortnite* is. It sounds like I don't want to know."

"Mom, please tell him to stop," said Jack, but it could just as easily have been Brett.

"Tell me about Dom," I asked, satisfied that I had guilted them enough about playing video games. I wasn't trying to prohibit them from playing them altogether, I just didn't want video games to make them less physically active or less inclined to pick up a book. A dad can dream, right?

"Dom is a great kid. I feel really sorry for him, though," Jack answered.

"Why is that?" I asked.

"His dad just died."

"What? Really? How do you know that?" Now I was really curious.

"He told us."

I looked at Denyse, and she shook her head suggesting she was just as surprised as me. "I don't even know who Dom is," she said.

"Does he go to school with Hank?" I asked.

"No," Jack responded. "He lives in Virginia. And I don't think he has a mom, either. He's staying with Satch for a while."

"Is he really a family member? Satch kind of introduced him that way."

"I don't think so," said Brett. "Hank didn't seem to know him that well.

We liked him a lot, though."

"How can you not like a guy who's so dominant at *Fort Right*?" I said, now intentionally mispronouncing the name. "Gotta admire that, right? Nothing but respect for that."

As usual, I had taken it one step too far . . . or maybe two or three. But I did need to know the rest of the Dom story. Everything about Satch intrigued me.

Chapter Thirty-Six

May 4, 2017
God I Love this Bar

I knew I needed another night in the Saloon. I wasn't just despondent about my utter inability to bring about any of the change the country so desperately needed, I was beginning to worry that this political divide would never be overcome. And it was all going down on my watch.

The mystical aura of the place instantly upgraded my mood, as did the now-familiar sight and smell. Even the cigar smoke was strangely soothing. And the reception I got. The bar staff always welcomed me like an old friend that they hadn't seen in years. Being a parent of kids just a half a dozen years younger than some of them, I wasn't exactly accustomed to such a reception from that generation. I'm certain they treated all the presidents that way, but that did not diminish its effect upon me.

It looked like a full house. I went straight for the bar, where JFK was sitting on a barstool chatting with George W and Mary Ann as Haskell took drink orders behind the bar. I could hear Haskell talking to Kennedy as I approached.

"Sir, please tell me about saving all those lives when *PT 109* went down off the Solomon Islands."

"Now Mary Ann here doesn't want to hear about a little thing like that," JFK responded coyly.

I looked at George W, who was laughing hysterically and shaking his head.

"That Haskell is a beaut," I commented.

"Oh, you don't know the half of it," George W replied, setting down his water. "Watch this." He walked over to the nearest table of presidents and whispered something in their ears.

Within moments, three presidents I didn't really recognize got up and approached the bar near us. All three motioned as if they wanted drinks. Haskell jumped into action.

"Drinking tonight, General?" he asked the first one.

"Yes! With Mrs. Hayes not around, I believe I'll have one of your best beers."

"Coming right up!" Haskell responded. "By the way, I was so moved by your account of the conversation you had with the Confederate soldier during the Battle of South Mountain while you both lay next to each other severely wounded."

"I am impressed with your knowledge of that incident, young Haskell," President Hayes said. I'm certain these guys thought his name really was Haskell.

That's an American story for the ages, Mr. President."

"I rather agree with you there," responded Hayes.

Then, addressing the next president in line, Haskell inquired, "Your usual, President Fillmore?"

"Yes, please."

Haskell poured a tall glass of water as he said, "What remarkable vision you had, sir, in opening up trade with Japan for the first time ever."

"It has worked out quite well, hasn't it?" They both smiled broadly.

Looking at the third president, Haskell did not disappoint. "General, would you care for a whiskey?"

"You read my mind, young man."

"How inspiring that you became a war hero and a president with no formal education, sir." Haskell offered.

"Ah, but I achieved that station precisely *because* I had no formal education, not in spite of it."

"Well said, sir," Haskell replied.

Surveying the scene in front of us, George W leaned over and whispered to me proudly, "Never gets old."

We looked at Big Time, who was standing behind the bar and laughing so hard he was almost crying.

"Who was that last one?" I asked.

"Zachary Taylor," George W replied. "And Haskell can go pretty deep. Watch him. He never gives the same compliment twice."

"How is that even possible?" I asked.

"We'd like to challenge him some night and have William Henry Harrison come up and order from the bar a dozen times and see how he does with that."

"Why Harrison?" I asked.

"You realize he was only president for 32 days, don't you?" George W retorted, laughing out loud. "My money's on Haskell, though. He's the best. There's no one even remotely like him. Best hire Sheels ever made. Born to work in a joint like this. All these men need their egos stroked on a regular basis.

"Sometimes when I'm really depressed, I just come in here, sit down, and order a drink from him. And I don't even drink!" George W continued. "Picks me right back up. And I swear he knows my presidency better than I do—or at least the good parts."

George W suddenly jumped to attention. "Here comes Big Daddy himself."

George Washington approached the bar with Madison and Monroe in tow.

Washington was tall and impressive in appearance. His voice and manner of speaking, however, were not what I would've expected. Even so, he clearly commanded the respect of everyone in the room.

Washington looked right at me and said, "Good evening, McFadden." A rush of adrenaline came over me. I froze as I have done once or twice in the presence of a true idol, torn between letting them be or telling them how much they mean to me. In this case, I chose the latter.

"You have inspired me so much, sir. Your Farewell Address still rings as true today as it did when you delivered it," I felt I was blathering.

"I'm flattered. However, I must correct you. I did not deliver that address. I wrote it as a letter saying goodbye to the American people and left the written text with a newspaper to publish. Actually, Mr. Madison here helped me write the first version, which I intended to give when my first term ended. However, as I saw factions emerging that could divide the country, I agreed to stay on for a second term."

"Well, I think it's fair to say we have some fairly established 'factions' dividing the country right now. We would be wise to heed the advice given in your address."

"Persevere, young man. I was not immune to great criticism in my time.

I placed my countrymen first in order. Bow not to those factions. Rely upon the goodness of the cause and the aid of the supreme being. Have courage, my friend."

The three Virginians then turned their attention to Matty, who stood waiting to take their orders.

Out of earshot of them, the younger Bush leaned over at me and with a big smile said, "He took the words right out of my mouth."

Washington's few, soft-spoken words to me in that brief moment clearly amounted to the most powerful and inspirational pep talk of my life. No one could possibly surpass that particular source for providing me a moral compass and help summon the courage to stick to my convictions. Powerful stuff. *My God, I love this bar!*

Chapter Thirty-Seven

July 2, 2017
Déjà Vu All Over Again

Yogi Berra might say it was déjà vu all over again. With the latest continuing resolution on the budget about to expire, the country, once again, faced an impending government shutdown with seemingly no hope for a permanent agreement of any kind—let alone one that started to reestablish the type of fiscal responsibility the nation so desperately needed. In addition to assembling Murph, Terri Drake, and the budget team as I had previously, I had also invited a handful of congress members who shared both our disdain for these ill-advised short fixes and our bold vision for a grand bargain. We met in the Roosevelt Room of the White House to assess the state of things in the face of yet another fast-approaching deadline.

Representative Anne Romano, a Republican from Ohio, who may have worked harder than anyone over the course of the past two weeks to forge some sort of productive long-term fix, spoke for the group: "This time, I actually believe they'll pass a long-term resolution, thanks to your prodding and shaming campaign. That's the good news. The bad news is that rather than reaching an agreement in which both sides have sacrificed something, they seem to be gravitating toward just giving in to each other and blowing up this deficit even further."

"Unfortunately, I have to agree," Murph added. "Despite my most sincere and impassioned pleas, I'm afraid what we're about to see is increased spending on all sorts of entitlement measures and pet projects for the Dems and serious tax cuts, increases in defense spending, and border control enhancements for the GOP."

"Lovely," I replied dejectedly. "We are, indeed, irrelevant here as the *Post* has been suggesting. Did anyone convey to them that they'll face another veto?"

"I'm not sure they fear that anymore, Mr. President," Romano replied.

An hour later, after the congressional delegation had left, the rest of us remained to assess the situation.

"I think you've gotta veto this, Mr. President," warned Ben Morales, my budget director. "This is your wheelhouse. Their budget amounts to government malpractice. Stand up against it. This is an easy one."

I laughed and shook my head. "That's easy for you to say. My numbers seem to be plummeting by the minute."

"Are the numbers why you're doing this?" Drake asked. She continued before I could reply. "Since when are those even relevant? Is my faith in you as the antidote to the dysfunctional Washington political dynamic misplaced? Don't fail me now, sir."

"You're right, Drake. Of course, you're right," I said, looking over at her. "This may be one of those hills worth dying on."

Chapter Thirty-Eight

July 9, 2017
Canterbury Tales

Congress overrode my veto again. They had their long-term budget agreement, but it was certain to exacerbate the national debt. I knew I needed another night in the Saloon.

I was painfully aware that I was beginning to use my new favorite watering hole as a bit of a crutch, or perhaps *escape* was a better word for it. Either way, the joint was jumpin' as I walked in. A lively New Orleans jazz band energetically provided the mood. I took one look around, exhaled, and suddenly the weight of the world within me levitated and began to float away. *I love this place!*

Tonight, the Saloon had the look and feel of my first night here. Tons of activity. Oozing energy, and it looked like the full waitstaff was working. I liked those kids a lot.

At the large table in the center of the room, Thomas Jefferson seemed to be holding court in front of a dozen or more presidents captivated with rapt attention. I wondered about the topic of the night. With him, the possibilities were endless.

I also noticed two tables of presidents playing poker. Included among them were some of the "heavyweights"—Washington, Lincoln, Grant, Teddy Roosevelt, and Harding at one table, FDR, Truman, Eisenhower, Nixon, and Obama at the other. How thrilling to see that mix of ideologies all coexisting happily over a game of cards. I again thought to myself: *There's a message in here somewhere for me to decipher, and it will solve the nation's political tribalism. I just have to figure out how to unlock it.*

I looked around for Sheels. I really needed to get to know him. Perhaps he held the key to understanding what this place was all about. If he didn't, then maybe he knew who did. Not locating him within the bar, I started to make my way back toward his office.

Presidential Spirits

Tina, Ginger, and Matty saw me coming. "President McFadden," Matt called out as I walked by. "Great to see you, sir."

"We need to see you more often! Where have you been?" exclaimed Mary Ann. The staff made me feel like Norm entering Cheers every time I walked into this place.

"Oh, I've had a few things on my plate," I responded. I didn't really feel like getting into all the details of my budget nightmare.

"Is Sheels in?" I asked.

"Yes," responded Matt. "He's in his office. Can we bring you something?"

"No, not tonight, guys. Brutal day at the office."

"All the more reason why you need a cocktail," said Ginger. "I've been waiting for an opportunity to serve you."

"That's awfully nice of you, Ginger," I said, realizing a little more how appropriate that nickname was. "I will definitely take a rain check."

"Great seeing you guys," I said, walking back toward Sheels's office.

I found Sheels there with John Quincy Adams, who was just leaving. Adams looked at me and said, "He's all yours, McFadden."

Turning back to Sheels, he said, "Please inform me when you'd like to study it in more detail, and we shall speak again."

"Yes. I will do so," Sheels replied.

That brief exchange got my curiosity raging. I'd already found myself needing to know absolutely everything about Sheels, but now I had to find out what this was all about too.

"Welcome," Sheels greeted as he stood up and motioned for me to take a seat.

Dressed in his usual garb of colorful silks, he was an impressive-looking gentleman. He looked to be in great shape, appeared to be no older than his mid-thirties and had a very confident presence about him. He took a large book off his desk and placed it in one the few vacant spaces on a massive bookshelf behind him that took up the entire wall and must have contained 500 titles.

"What are you reading?" I asked.

He smiled. "*The Canterbury Tales.*"

"Chaucer? Wow . . . I'm shocked!"

"You were expecting something different?"

"I'm not sure what I was expecting. I really don't know you very well. But no, not *The Canterbury Tales*—that's quite a book there. Such an ambitious work. I love the whole concept of that story. And I love how Chaucer places himself in the story, even using his own name."

"I found that to be a little arrogant, if you ask me," Sheels responded. "But that's the quality I most deplore in people. At times, he seems to confuse his own life with that of his character—particularly toward the end."

"You think? I didn't really get that at all. I guess he could've disguised the name a little bit to—"

"Yes, I think it's quite arrogant."

"Why read Chaucer then?"

"President Adams. He took it upon himself long ago to educate me. He taught me to read when I was just a slave waiter in this bar. Do you see all these books behind me?" He turned toward the massive bookshelf. "He selected most of these for me, and we've read many of them together—and scores of others as well."

"Wow!" I exclaimed. "That is truly extraordinary." I scanned the vast array of books behind him. "Looks like you're quite a bibliophile."

"I am now," he said with a smile. "No one bothered with my education until President Adams came into my life. I owe him a great debt of gratitude."

"You speak quite well for someone with no formal education."

"I've spent years and years with him. Decades really. I'd call that quite formal."

"Was he ever a professor?"

"Yes, actually. He and his father both taught at Harvard."

"I've heard of it," I said with a smile. I'm not sure why I was attempting to get him to laugh. He struck me as a fairly serious guy, particularly it seemed, when it came to this particular topic.

"Many others here have sought to help with my education and brought me books—his father, Lincoln, Taft, Wilson, Kennedy, and Obama, to name a few. But John Quincy Adams has devoted the most time and attention to me. I have spent years with him working on my reading, writing, and speaking."

"How is your Middle English?" I asked, cracking a smile.

"It's adequate, as is my French. I'm studying Mandarin too and attempting Swahili. I sometimes speak French with Jefferson and Mandarin with Hoover."

"Herbert Hoover speaks Mandarin?" I asked, quite shocked.

"He spent a few years working in China as a mining engineer."

"Who on earth within this saloon can possibly speak Swahili to you?"

"None of the presidents, but Mary Ann is learning it with me. It'll take us both some time, but here we've got nothing but time." He smiled. I was relieved to see that smile.

"Speaking of that, I understand you've been in this establishment since it opened."

"I have indeed."

I paused to contemplate the enormity of that for a second.

"Why you?"

"I was Washington's valet while he was president. He trusted me. He was hard on everyone—his employees and his slaves—but I worked hard for him. He appreciated that. I met his standards. He liked me."

"Had you worked for him at Mount Vernon?"

"I was born at Mount Vernon. My ma was one of Mrs. Washington's spinners. She had no education of any kind, but she was the smartest person at Mount Vernon."

"I have so many questions. Did you know your father?"

"He was a wagon driver at Mount Vernon. He was a poor, white man and was never a father to me, at least not in the sense you would think of a father. Not even close. He left Mount Vernon when I was young. I began doing labor for General Washington before I was ten. I worked hard and was eventually allowed to work inside the mansion as a waiter and as Washington's body servant."

"How were you and your mom treated by the Washingtons?"

"We were treated like slaves, of course, but working inside the mansion was much better than working outside, and working at Mount Vernon was better than working at many other Virginia plantations. But we were slaves, not humans. We received no schooling or religious or moral training, and we weren't taught how to swim like the white children, so many slaves drowned. Having the general's trust and respect meant my ma and I knew them better, so they were often kind to us, and we were fed better than the others. But we knew if we escaped, we'd be captured, forcibly returned, and beaten. And we always lived with the fear that, at any moment, we could be sold and separated from our families."

I was so moved by this. How could you not be.

"General Washington liked me so much that he brought me to Philadelphia when the capital moved there from New York during his presidency. I served as his valet. His important guests liked me—people like Franklin, Jefferson, Madison, and the Marquis de Lafayette. Because Pennsylvania was a free state, there was a large free black community in Philadelphia. There was a Pennsylvania law that any black man living there continuously for six months became free. For that reason, every six months we were returned to Mount Vernon and then brought back a few weeks later.

"When Washington first opened this Saloon, he told me I was the one he wanted serving the presidents. I have worked here since that opening night. I started as a slave waiter and bartender."

"Are you here now of your own free will? Could you leave if you wanted to?"

"Yes, I am free now and have been since the Compensated Emancipation Act freed all slaves in the District of Columbia in 1862. Lincoln, the two Adams, and a few of the others convinced Washington to give me my freedom following that."

"But you're still here."

"Yes, I'm still here."

"Why are you still here?"

"I'm here now of my own free will and that makes all the difference. I am respected now and entrusted with running this bar. They knew they needed to do that to keep me here. I love the staff I have assembled and what we do here. However, most importantly, while I don't care for many of these gentlemen, my presence here in this tribute to America is a constant reminder to them of the unspeakable sins of America's past. As much as they crow about all they've done in the name of freedom and liberty, I stand as an unavoidable reality check—an inconvenient truth, to borrow a phrase from one of our recent vice presidents. For that reason, it's very important that I stay. You speak often about causes. That is my cause."

Wow. I was incredibly moved by this gentleman. The more he spoke, the more confused I became about Washington, my hero.

"It must have been quite a day when Barack Obama walked through that door," I said.

"Yes, sir, it certainly was! However, I'll wait until there is true equality between all the races in this country before I walk out that door for good. That will be the finest day."

"Do you suppose that will ever happen? I asked. Is it even possible?"

"So long as men have to keep asking that question, the answer is most assuredly no."

Chapter Thirty-Nine

Nine Months Later—April 20, 2018
Barbara Bush

NEWS

(AP Houston) History will be made tomorrow as six living presidents gather together for the funeral of former First Lady Barbara Bush. It will mark only the second time in history that six living presidents have assembled together. Jimmy Carter, George H. W. Bush, Bill Clinton, George W. Bush, Barack Obama, and Danny McFadden will all attend the funeral for the beloved Mrs. Bush. Following the funeral, they will spend time together and pose for group photos with their wives.

***

They all looked so old—each and every one of them. Jimmy Carter, now in his nineties, looked so much older than the gentleman I had come to know in the Saloon—although I have to say this older Jimmy Carter looked and acted much younger than I would expect of a ninety-year-old. The first President Bush looked much, much older too. He was confined to a wheelchair and was so much more frail than the vibrant person I had become acquainted with. Clinton seemed much older too. Obama looked just a little bit older, and good old Otter still seemed to be in pretty good shape. I guessed that he must have been riding his bike quite a bit at his ranch. I made a mental note to find out exactly what he did to keep in shape. I know he gave up drinking, but I'm not sure I'm quite ready for that degree of sacrifice. However, seeing them all like this confirmed what I had already concluded—somehow in my favorite saloon, all my new drinking buddies appear not to age after their presidencies. I'm sure that's meaningful in some manner but that reason at the moment escaped me.

Presidential Spirits

I didn't want to miss this funeral. Barbara Bush was such an iconic figure—a first lady and a mother of a president—and that family may not be finished. Unpretentious in spite of her vast wealth, she always enjoyed such great approval from the American public. The decision to attend the funeral came very easily for Denyse and me.

I have to say, though, this well-hyped moment of the gathering of six presidents and the requisite photo op was not nearly as special to me—or as special as the media was making it out to be—considering that I had many nights under my belt where I'd congregated with forty-four other U.S. presidents. Six was nothing. A half a dozen presidents together was nothing more than a very slow and boring night at the Saloon.

In advance of the photo gathering Obama did not hesitate to come over to greet Denyse and me, since I knew him the best of any of the presidents in this group—in the real world, that is. In the Saloon, I had come to know George W the best, but I had never actually met him in real life.

"Thank you so much for being here," George W said. "It really means the world to my family."

It should not have been surprising to me, but this George W's interactions with me were decidedly less familiar. His tone and demeanor were much more formal than they were in the Saloon. The twinkle in his eye and the "Rush Chair" persona were nowhere to be found. Of course, the occasion certainly did not warrant them. But, as crazy as it sounds, part of me was clearly hoping that somehow I'd get a knowing look or glance from him.

Obama seemed the most interested in how I was doing. "You stick to your guns there. I respect the way you've stood up to so much of the partisanship. You are a breath of fresh air."

"Thank you so much, Mr. President. That means a great deal coming from you. However, I'm not certain the country quite agrees with you."

"The country does, my friend, even if the parties do not."

I had to seize this rare opportunity. "Let me ask you something," I said. "Did you ever wish you could interact with all those who sat in that chair before you when you were agonizing over the various decisions?"

"There's no question," he responded. "I spent many a late night upstairs in the White House trying to channel the ghosts of Lincoln and the others."

Alright, I thought. *That was a pretty telling comment.*

"Ever have any success?" I asked, wondering if it was even remotely possible that we were talking about the same thing.

"I may have convinced myself that I did," he answered.

Is that an admission, I wondered. What a response. *Is he trying to tell me something here without actually telling me? How would he realistically answer that any other way?* But I didn't think I could ask a more direct question about it, fearing he'd have me committed.

"How's my boy Satch?" he asked, bringing a halt to my runaway thoughts.

"I love that guy!" I raved. "He's a gem."

"He runs a remarkable organization," said Obama.

"Yes, he does," I replied.

"There are certainly some truly unbelievable aspects of that White House, that's for sure."

OK, was that a thinly veiled reference to the Saloon? I wanted desperately for him to be referring to that. Perhaps he's telling me without telling me, so to speak.

Then. looking right at him, I added, "The White House seems kind of haunted at times, doesn't it?" It was as much a question as it was a statement. I fixated on his face, trying to gauge his reaction.

"Yes, it does. A lot of history walking around in that old mansion." His statement was nondescript, and he was looking away from me when he said it, but then he glanced quickly at me as if seeking to gauge *my* reaction. Or was that only in my head?

I don't know if this exchange got me any closer to what I was searching for, but it did, at least, keep the notion alive.

Later, while speaking with Bill Clinton, I decided to be a little more blunt about it. "When you were president, did you ever wish you could just ask some of your predecessors what they were thinking? You know, get their advice and suggestions on the issues of the day?"

Clinton looked over at me and paused for a second before responding. "I did feel I knew precisely what the ones I respected would do in certain situations."

Alright, I thought. *That's as good as an admission, Now we're getting somewhere.* "How did you know that?" I asked, hoping I was onto something.

"Why do you ask?" he said with an sly smile. Just then, the photographers called us for the photo op. "Let's talk about this later," he said, as we were ushered away for the group picture. My moment was lost.

I later had the opportunity to spend a few moments with the first President Bush. He was amazingly gracious given the occasion, but I could tell there was a profound sadness about him. During our several minutes together, I told him I'd heard a secondhand account of him meeting Babe Ruth and asked him if it was true. He confirmed every aspect of the story he'd told in the Saloon. I knew I'd never heard that story anywhere else before. The Saloon simply couldn't be explained away as a very vivid dream.

It was hard seeing the elder President Bush in that condition, struggling both physically and mentally. It made me ponder questions far more consequential than just the Saloon I was so obsessed with.

However, I desperately needed to know for certain if these gentlemen had experienced the Saloon when they were president, and if they could shed some light on what it all means. I just wished I wasn't so afraid to ask.

Chapter Forty

May 2, 2018
Once a Marine, Always a Marine

My meeting in the Oval Office with the Joint Chiefs of staff was running late, and I knew my staff and a team of congressmen were waiting for me in the Roosevelt Room. I didn't want to keep them waiting too long because we really needed them on a variety of issues, and, frankly, I needed all the friends in Congress—and in life, for that matter—I could get.

I had heard each of these impressive, smartly dressed gentlemen give their assessments on the state of the world with particular attention to North Korea, Syria, and Ukraine. I sat there rather in awe of this scene. It seemed surreal, like an out-of-body experience. Here I was a political neophyte, and very fortunate right place, right time Silicon Valley guy who now held the key to America's nuclear launch codes.

I was closing my folio and putting away my pen—in a not-so-subtle signal that I needed to move on—when Paul Selva, air force general and vice chairman of the Joint Chiefs of Staff, interrupted. "Sir, may I give you some advice?"

"Absolutely," I responded.

"Please stop calling it '*the* Ukraine.' It's a common misconception—an honest mistake. Many Americans, including some in Congress, say it that way, but it's a surefire way to upset Ukrainian Americans, who consider that a throwback to their days as part of the Soviet Union when the country was referred to as the Ukrainian Soviet Socialist Republic."

"Thank you very much. That's exactly the kind of stuff I need to hear, so don't be sheepish about it. I'm going to make myself look uninformed enough on my own, so anytime you can save me from doing so is greatly appreciated. I won't make that mistake again."

We all rose and shook hands to conclude the meeting. Just then, Joseph Dunford, the chairman and general of the marine corps, glanced out the window. "Is that Satch?" he asked.

I looked out the window and, sure enough, there was Satch with Hank and my boys playing ball on the lawn again. It looked like Dom was with them as well. "Yes," I responded. "He's quite a pitching coach—quite a guy too."

"You don't have to convince me of that," General Dunford replied. "How well do you know him?"

"I'm getting to know him well. Love him. He's a remarkable gentleman. Why do you ask?"

"Do you know about his war record?" the general asked.

"I know that he served in Vietnam."

"Yes, I'd say he served alright. Medal of Honor recipient!"

"What?" I'm sure my jaw dropped six inches.

General Dunford's facial expression turned deadly serious. "You haven't heard the story of that day, sir?"

"No," I responded. "Unbelievable. He hasn't said a word about it. I can't say I'm completely surprised, though. He is so modest and unassuming. But I need to hear it. Please tell me."

"Do you have a minute, sir?"

"For this, I've got nothing but time."

I sat down, prompting the Joint Chiefs to return to their seats as well.

"Satch is actually something of a legend in the Corps," General Dunford began, speaking quite noticeably with enormous pride. I could see he relished the opportunity to recount the story. "In the spring of '67 his Fifth Marine Regiment carried out a search-and-destroy mission in the Que Son Valley. The object was to use Satch's Charlie Company as bait to engage the North Vietnamese and draw them out, at which time other units would hit the enemy with a devastating air and artillery assault. Needless to say, an extremely dangerous mission.

"Following a bloody initial encounter with the North Vietnamese which killed the platoon leader, Satch's platoon retreated to a defensive position. Satch took charge. He called in tactical air strikes with a squawk box and threw smoke to direct their fire. Over the objections of his men, he repeatedly ventured back out into no-man's-land, crawling through devastating machine-gun and small arms fire to drag wounded marines to safety. At one point, his rifle was blown to pieces right out of his hands. When helicopters showed up, he ran alongside them on the battlefield picking up more wound-ed, twice disposing of North Vietnamese soldiers charging the chopper in hand to hand combat. He took a bullet through his left shoulder puncturing his lung and incurred extensive shrapnel wounds to his legs and face from grenades. In spite of these injuries, he insisted on being the last to board the medevac. When he finally came aboard, he collapsed. His platoon feared for his life."

"My God," I responded, with a tear forming in my eye. "He is the most gentle, humble, and personable soul imaginable. I cannot believe that's the same gentleman out there now teaching my kid how to throw a splitter."

"It is hard to adequately convey how much respect I have for him," General Dunford declared, equally overcome with emotion. "He is a marine's marine, sir."

"Unbelievable. I'll never quite understand how someone learns to com-partmentalize such an intensely savage and inhuman chapter of their lives."

"Not all marines do, unfortunately. I think Satch struggled at first—both physically and mentally. They thought he might not survive initially, so they awarded him the Distinguished Service Cross, which can be processed much more quickly. It was only years later that his fellow marines organized an effort to lobby Congress to award him the Medal of Honor. That was a no-brainer. Gerald Ford, who presented the medal to Satch, was so taken by him that he personally offered him a position on the White House grounds staff. He moved up from there fairly quickly."

"It's so great to have an ex-marine as White House chief usher," I said.

"You mean a marine as chief usher," Dunford corrected. "There's no such thing as an ex-marine, Mr. President. Once a marine, always a marine."

"Of course, General. My apologies. *Semper fi.*" I felt I needed to work the motto into the conversation so he'd think I had at least the tiniest bit of street cred. I'm not sure I pulled it off, though.

I shook hands with the generals and then hustled off to the Roosevelt Room. But I just couldn't get my mind off Satch. *What a truly phenomenal person.* Made me proud to be an American. I only wished all that heroism could've been employed for a more noble cause—or at least a more winnable and justifiable war. I think America did wrong by Satch and his generation, but that doesn't for one second diminish what he did for his fel-low marines and for his country. I'm lucky to know him—and not just

Presidential Spirits

because he can teach my boys how to toss a nasty splitter.

Chapter Forty-One

May 3, 2018
Two Strikes Against Him

Cathy buzzed me on the intercom. "Satch is here for you, sir,"

"Sweet!" I responded. "Send him in, please."

Moments later, Satch came lumbering into my private office wearing a big welcoming smile. *God, I wish I had his approach to life.*

This time, I paid more attention to the scars on his face than I ever had previously. And I had even more admiration for him than I did before.

"How are you, sir? he asked politely.

"I'm hanging in there. Thanks for coming over so quickly. Have a seat."

"Anything for you, sir," he took his seat and pulled his chair a little closer to my desk.

"First of all, thanks so much for working with Brett and Jack. They love it, but I'm afraid every coach they'll have from this point forward will be woefully inadequate by comparison."

"You are far too kind, sir. You've got a couple of high character boys there."

"It's a work in progress, but I'll accept that. Thank you."

"And Kelly introduced me to her boyfriend last night."

"What???" I sat up and leaned forward. "Michael? You met him? Oh my God! She seems to be hiding him from me—purposefully, I might add." I shook my head. "So tell me . . . what's he like? Is he even remotely worthy of her?" I said that with a smile, but only to make it appear to him like I might be kidding.

"Well, yes. I liked the young man very much, sir," Satch confided. "They asked me if I thought you would like him. I wasn't quite sure how to respond, though. You see, he's not a sports fan—not in the least . . . not even close . . . not even a little bit. Knowing what I know about you and your boys, I wanted to tell him that he already has two strikes against him, but I didn't think he'd know what that meant."

I know he said that intending to make me laugh, but, at this particular moment, I couldn't bring myself to do so.

"Let me ask you this," I said, hoping to change the subject. "Who is Dom? The boys tell me he may have lost his father recently."

"I'm afraid so, sir. So tragic. Respiratory depression caused by opioid overdose. Heartbreaking."

"Oh my God! I am so sorry to hear that. Does he have a mother?"

"No sir. She's been out of the picture since he was a toddler. She struggled with narcotics. Abandoned the family. I believe she may be in jail. In any event, she's not a viable caregiver."

"I recall that you mentioned he was family. Is he part of your family?"

"He is now, Mr. President. He's the grandson of a dear friend of mine who died alongside me in Vietnam. I was his daddy's godfather."

"What was his grandfather's name?"

"TJ Manzanetti. A real legend in the Corps."

"I think you've told me about him. TJ was your best buddy, right? The one you named your son after?"

"Yes, sir."

"Who's caring for Dom now?"

"You're looking at him...for the moment, at least. Talk about a work in progress. His grandmother Christy is planning to take him, but her grief over her son's death is fairly debilitating at the moment. I owe her husband my life, so I'm proud to step in and help for the time being—honored really. It feels right to me to be doing this." He paused a moment before adding, "Besides, I'm rather lonely in that big old house of mine ever since I lost Dina."

A look of sadness momentarily engulfed his face, but then he quite consciously snapped himself out of it. "I've learned to live with that, even though I must say happiness has been hard to come by since then. But I am figuring it out."

"Happiness can be quite elusive," I said. "You appear to be navigating that quite admirably."

"When I lost Dina, I told myself I would mourn like hell for three months then find my new mission—a new purpose. I threw myself into my work and this place. Like my guy Andy says in *The Shawshank Redemption*, you either get busy living or get busy dying. Right now it's this job and these people that keep me going. But I am still very aware that I need to find my next chapter—my last chapter. It's time. I don't want someone to run me out of here when I'm in a wheelchair. Better to leave too early than too late."

"You've got a job as long as I'm here."

"Well I appreciate that, Mr. President. I may just stay as long as you're here. But as much as I'd like to, I know I can't do this forever. I do need to figure out that next chapter. It will be the last one, but I'm determined to make it the best one."

"I love your determination about that. It's inspiring. And I have no doubt you'll find that next chapter."

"And you, sir? You've got all the money in the world. They made you president without you ever even seeking it. You've got an awesome family. If you are finding happiness elusive, you need to reset those expectations."

"I'm smart enough to know all that, Satch. But for some reason, that doesn't seem to help me. Right now, I am absolutely being driven by unrealistic expectations. The country is a divided, dysfunctional mess. And I'm on the clock, as Roger Goodell would say. What am I gonna do about it? I can't be happy unless I find a way to lead us out of this cultural and political civil war."

It felt good venting openly to someone who wasn't beholden to any party, ideology, or gerrymandered constituency.

"But you're trying . . . you're giving it your all. Others are so jaded from years of bathing in this cesspool that they don't even *see* the problem. Worse yet, some can see it but are too busy profiting from it to do anything but oppose solutions. Take a step back, sir. Take twenty steps back if you need to, but. don't allow this job to suck the life, joy, and happiness out of you. Think of your grandmother and what she would've thought knowing that a mere two generations after she arrived in this country, her grandson became president."

"I know," I responded with frustration surely written all over my face. "I understand that in an intellectual and logical way, but it doesn't seem to help. And just look at this—I asked you to meet with me so I could see if there are things in your life I can help you with, but then somehow, the conversation gets turned around to my own struggles, which—as you so aptly pointed out—are nothing compared to what virtually every other human who ever walked this earth has faced."

Satch looked over at me with a wise, knowing smile. "I'm no Wall Street guy, but I think happiness is a lot like the stock market. We focus altogether too much on the day to day and even the year to year—you know, the fleeting, temporary swings—and in doing so, we miss the long-term trends. If the market drops 800 points in an afternoon, you've got people looking to jump off a bridge. Doesn't seem to matter that their stock may have risen ten times that in the last ten years, all they focus on is their grief over this incremental loss. Conversely, those whose stock rises 800 points in an afternoon may be over the moon, even if they've gradually lost their life savings during the previous ten years."

"I've never thought of it quite that way, but there's a lot of truth to what you're saying. That's very helpful. However, I am also painfully aware of the passage from Luke, which states that much is expected from those to whom much is given. I have been granted a treasure trove of privileges, luck, and circumstances and am one of but a tiny handful of people who possess both the desire and the potential to help solve these problems for our country. That very real weight of the world on my shoulders makes it a little challenging to take those twenty steps back you've suggested, but nonetheless, I must do so every day . . . for my own sanity."

"But enough about me," I added after a brief pause, "For God's sake, how can I help you and Dom and Christy?"

"I'll let you know, sir. And I appreciate the offer, but you've got bigger issues in front of you to deal with."

Satch rose to leave. He seemed uncomfortable every time I tried to steer the conversation toward him, but I genuinely wanted to help. It spoke so well of his character, but it was beginning to annoy me a little bit. Even so, he did seem to operate for me as part psychologist and part happiness coach—two things I was desperately in need of at the moment.

Chapter Forty-Two

July 10, 2018
Bohemian Grove

The presidential limo, which is affectionately referred to as "The Beast," sped up the 280 north of San Jose surrounded by an impressive armada of identical decoy "Beasts," SUVs, and police vehicles. This remarkable vehicle had eight-inch-thick armored doors, armored floors in case of grenades exploding beneath the car, and foam that sealed the gas tank in case of puncture. I was told it got four miles per gallon at most. It also came with a fridge that they kept stocked with plenty of replacement O positive blood for me – if that should ever happen to come in handy. I was really hoping it wouldn't.

I had spent a significant portion of my life in traffic on this very road in Silicon Valley, so I had a special appreciation for this particular escort. We were heading to Atherton for a breakfast fundraiser—this one sprinkled with an extraordinary collection of Silicon Valley illuminati, former 49ers greats from the glory days, and other local business titans. Denyse had managed to get a short list of some of our best friends from the Bay Area an invite, which, amazingly enough, annoyed our political people well beyond what should be considered reasonable. But we were in town, and there really wasn't a better method of connecting with them given all the security concerns.

I don't hate fundraising like a lot of folks do. I love interacting with people—particularly at events like these at the unbelievable home we were headed to. I feed off of interacting with people, and I get energized by a crowd—a supportive crowd, I should say. This was going to be one of those. What I don't like is the expectations that come with the lion's share of the big gifts our fundraisers were seeking. I don't like that it now costs a half a billion dollars to run for president and takes two years of one's time—both to canvass the country for the votes and also, more importantly, to generate the money to fund the operation and crush your opponent with negative ads. The American way. However, I'm sure that's the last thing my new friends at the Saloon intended when they set this system up.

At the fundraiser, I enjoyed seeing my old friends Ronnie Lott and Brandi Chastain, whom I had gotten to know through my involvement with their REACH youth scholarship program in San Jose. I felt a bit sheepish about involving them, and all their pals in the area for that matter, because I didn't know if their politics lined up with the cause I happened to be championing. In most cases, I suspect their appearance here was out of friendship. I spent a few minutes with a collection of old colleagues from Google and a few other tech giants, as well as some former staff members from my days as a senator. But other than giving my speech, most of my time was spent one-on-one at a table on the balcony with a succession of titans who paid handsomely for their five minutes.

Before we knew it, Denyse and I were back in The Beast heading north to a lunch fundraiser in Marin County, where our time was even more choreographed. The home and grounds were breathtaking, of course, and Denyse and I spent the entire time talking with, smiling at, and glad-handing the 200-plus guests. Ninety minutes later, we were back in The Beast. Upon entering the limo we exhaled, as much mentally as physically.

"How'd that go?" I asked.

"I met a couple whose daughter lives on Kelly's floor at Santa Clara," Denyse replied. "I'm sure I spent a great deal more time with them than your team wanted, but I just loved hearing them talk about meeting Kelly and how impressed they were with her. They say she's handling all of this so well."

"I'm guessing they don't mind having two Secret Service agents living on their daughter's floor, either. Probably keeps some of the shenanigans in check."

"I would hope so," Denyse agreed. "And they love Michael too."

"Great! Love hearing that! Makes my day. The whole world will know him before I do. All I know is what I read online in *People* magazine. I have to say I'm not thrilled with their little game of hide-and-seek with me."

"Honey, they're college kids," Denyse assured. "From what you've told me about your college years, you weren't exactly winning awards for rational behavior and maturity."

"If I gave the kids a pass for repeating every bad behavior I ever engaged in, I'd be a worse parent than I was a youth."

Our next stop was the Bohemian Grove, an ultra-exclusive, somewhat secret, century-and-a-half-old elite private men's club which congregates for three weeks every summer in a gorgeous setting along the Russian River an hour north of San Francisco. I was to be the featured speaker at the lakeside afternoon chat. We had a couple hours to get there and the police escort to overwhelm any traffic obstacle.

Denyse and I both spotted an In-N-Out Burger as we approached Highway 1. "Did you get a chance to eat anything back there?" she asked. I knew full well what she was suggesting.

"Nope. Haven't eaten a thing since last night. I'm absolutely famished!"

Like a couple of synchronized swimmers, our heads turned in perfect unison as we looked back at the In-N-Out we were speeding by. I quickly pulled out my cell phone to check the time then made a snap decision that we could pull this off. *I wish I could be as certain of all my decisions.* I picked up the limo phone to connect with the transportation captain for the trip. "Eric," I said, "we've got a bit of an emergency here."

"What's the problem, Mr. President?"

"It's the First Lady. She's demanding In-N-Out!"

At that moment, Denyse screamed at me and punched me in the shoulder—with much more power than I ever thought possible. Her new White House personal trainer must be making a difference.

"It's fairly serious, Eric. She said take me to In-N-Out or lose me forever,"

Denyse grabbed the phone out of my hand and said with a laugh, "Don't listen to him, Eric."

"We'll see what we can do, ma'am. We are specially trained for precisely these types of emergencies."

"Eric, please tell me you know that this was all his idea."

"Your secret is safe with me, ma'am."

Denyse hung up the phone. Forcefully. "Why are they all so loyal to you?"

She calmed down as the great funeral procession of a motorcade made a right, followed by another right and traveled down a residential street before making a third right, and then a left to return to the In-N-Out Burger.

Presidential Spirits

It was quite a scene.

Eric buzzed us again. "I doubt you need a menu, right?"

"Uh . . . no . . . we won't be needing a menu. Can we go through the drive-thru?"

"You know better than that, sir."

"How about just this one time?" I pleaded.

"I don't report to you, sir, and I could lose my job."

"If he fires, you I'll fire him and hire you in his place."

"Don't push him, Danny," Denyse scolded me as she slapped me on my newly sore shoulder.

"He knows I'm just kidding."

"First of all, you're not 'just kidding,' and anyone who knows you knows that. And anyone who doesn't know you had better assume that you're not kidding lest they risk losing their job."

"OK, we know exactly what we want. I'll take a double-double and a chocolate shake. Denyse will have a cheeseburger, animal style, and a Diet Coke."

"Anything else, folks?"

"I'll take a large black coffee too," I said. "I need to wake up."

"We'll get on this right away, sir."

"Let me ask you this, Eric. How can we try to keep this on the down-low? I don't want these Bay Area folks to know I'm such a carnivore."

"I don't think I can help you there,"

"And we can't really say it was grass-fed, I suppose. In-N-Out should use grass-fed beef, at least in the Bay Area."

"I can't help you there, either, sir."

Within minutes we had our first In-N-Out burgers since we'd left California.

"What are you going to say to the Bohemian Grove folks?" Denyse asked, plowing through her animal style burger.

"It's all about our great political divide."

"Right up your alley. Prepared remarks?"

"No, I'll be speaking from the heart. I could give that speech in my sleep."

"So could I!"

"Which reminds me," I said. "I've been meaning to tell you about these

199

very vivid dreams—"

Denyse interrupted, "I assume it's a very liberal crowd."

"Actually, this club is really conservative," I said. "It's kind of been a Republican bastion for the longest time. Nixon, Kissinger, George Schultz, Colin Powell, Karl Rove, you name it, they were all members. There are some liberal members, too, like Chris Matthews. And Ken Burns spends time there as well. But for the most part, it's very wealthy conservatives plotting their political takeover of the world."

"How will you be received?" Denyse asked, a bit concerned.

"With skepticism, I'm sure. There's a lot of great people there, but I'm afraid they're more concerned with winning their political battles than attempting in any way to unite us."

"All the more reason for them to hear the Danny McFadden dissertation."

"Well, they're gonna get it today!" I exclaimed. "And I may give them a bit of an earful about opening up their ranks to women as well. It's gotta happen. When I was invited there as a guest years ago, I couldn't help but think what a shame it was that women weren't allowed."

"I'm fairly certain the joke is on those guys, though," she said with a smile. "I'm sure they have no idea what the women in their lives are really up to during the three weeks they're away at the Grove."

I laughed out loud at that. "Perhaps that explains why it has flourished for 150 years."

After devouring our lunches, I nervously began wading into a subject I was not altogether comfortable talking about. "So, I've been having some really crazy dreams lately. At least, I think they're dreams—very vivid, incredibly lifelike dreams."

"First of all, before you go any further, am I in these dreams?"

"Uh . . . no, not really," I hesitated. "It's really more of a—"

"Is there another woman in these sick dreams of yours?"

"Of course not! I would never in a million years . . . ," then pausing for effect, "tell you about those dreams. I may not be the smartest guy around, but I'm smarter than that." I laughed again. I'm not sure she did.

Just then, my cell phone buzzed. It was Terri Drake. She didn't bother saying hello.

"Justice Kennedy is stepping down from the court," she said with an urgency in her voice.

"Oh my God," I replied. "Of course, only the most centrist judge would resign with me as president." I thought for a second then asked, "Tell me about the politics of replacing him."

"I just got off the phone with Murph about just that. With Scalia's seat still unfilled, the conservatives are now down on the court 4–3. I suspect you'll find them more willing to back off their filibuster now and ease a bit on their litmus test."

"We'll still need Democrats to get to sixty votes."

"Well, that's what we need to talk to you about. Republican senate leaders are hoping to meet with you to discuss the nuclear option."

"Eliminating the filibuster?"

"Just for Supreme Court appointments, not for everything," Drake clarified. "That would enable you to get an appointment passed with a mere majority. The Democrats as you know already eliminated the filibuster for other federal judgeships."

"That's against everything I stand for, Drake! The filibuster forces a spirit of bipartisanship. Without it, I'm afraid as a nation we would just tack far to the left with one administration and then reverse course and tack far to the right with the next, all the while losing ground as a nation to the other economic superpowers due to that dysfunction."

"Before long you may not have a Supreme Court, sir."

"I'd rather have no Supreme Court than have the Senate go the route of ridding itself of this essential procedural check!"

"I understand your point, sir, and it is admirable. But I'm just warning you—in the strongest of terms—that if you want to continue to be president and if you want to continue having a functioning government, then you must have a functioning Supreme Court."

"Our partisan divide has ruined the reputation of the Supreme Court! How many 5–4 decisions on fundamental, critical issues can we continue to accept?" While I wasn't screaming my voice was certainly gaining volume. "Thoughtful, principled, nonideological Supreme Court justices are extinct thanks to our partisan tribalism. The branch that was supposed to be most immune to partisanship is now swimming in it. This is a hill I'm prepared to die on."

"I'm gonna start calling you Kitty, sir, because you'll certainly need nine lives or more to survive all these deaths on all these political hills."

A few moments after we hung up my phone rang again.

"Who's that?" Denyse asked, before I answered.

"McCain."

McCain and I had developed a mutual respect, but he did not have an active role in the administration. He had settled into a position of a trusted adviser and even, at times, a mentor. However, as much as he did famously cross the aisle at key moments, he was still a conservative Republican, and ideologically much more conservative than me. Even so, he and I were unquestionably aligned when it came to wanting the very best for the country, and he made it clear that was his driving force—more than any desire to kowtow to the party leaders.

Additionally, he had been diagnosed with a brain tumor, and had pulled back from his already limited role since then, spending most of his time in Arizona. I was more than happy to encourage him to be with his family at his ranch in Sedona. There was never a thought of him stepping down. I loved all that he he stood for—it fit in nicely with my message, which had been heavily influenced by him in the first place.

I addressed him as I always did when I answered, "Senator." I couldn't get used to calling him anything else.

"Mr. President."

"It's so great to hear from you. How are you doing?"

"I'm fighting every day, sir."

"I knew you would be. I expected nothing less. So am I. However, I sincerely hope that you're having more success in your battle than I am in mine."

"You are having success," he replied. "You still have decent approval numbers, Mr. President, even if you can't seem to get Congress to budge on anything. When your approval plummets to a level below paid staff and blood relatives, then you'll know you're in trouble." He laughed. "I know," he added. "I've been there." It was great to know his famous sense of humor was alive and well.

"Denyse and I are in Northern California heading to the Russian River for a talk I'm giving at the Bohemian Grove—addressing a number of your kind."

"You'll certainly find a fair share of conservative true believers there, sir."

"Oh, I'm loaded for bear!" And I'm ready to get on my high horse about tribalism and the future of our country, and I may even take on their exclusion of women from the Grove."

"I would advise against that, Mr. President," he responded, laughing. "I sincerely hope you are kidding."

"I'll get a sense of the crowd and see how I feel first, but I'm somewhat compelled to push the issue."

"I want to chime in on an issue that may be presenting itself," McCain said, changing the subject. "I fully expect the Republicans in the Senate to seek a deal with you on a justice now that both Scalia and Kennedy's seats are empty. I believe you'll see an offer to compromise on a moderately right-of-center conservative coupled with their plan to eliminate the filibuster to get him through."

"Yes, sir," I replied. "I believe that's the direction they're moving in."

"I'd like to offer my opinion on that, if I may," McCain suggested.

"I'd love to hear it,"

"I firmly believe it will be a dark day in the history of the U.S. Senate when the filibuster is abandoned. The Republicans opposed Harry Reid when he and the Democrats pulled that stunt to appoint judges to the appeals court in 2013. This is not the time to throw away more than 150 years of senate history."

"I appreciate that very much, Senator. Again, that's what I love most about you—your willingness to break with your own party when you believe it is warranted."

"I've made a lot of errors, Mr. President," he responded, "but I've served my country first. Hopefully honorably."

"I wish there were a whole lot more in Washington like you, sir. And I wish you had joined the ranks of our presidents. You would have done quite well in that exclusive club."

"I appreciate that," McCain said. "I will be in Washington next week, Mr. President."

"Super! I'll alert Cathy to get you on my schedule."

"Don't bother. I've connected with her myself. That's quite an assistant you've got there."

"Ha! I guess that's one way of putting it," I laughed. "You are correct, of course, but she seems to have missed the class on being incredibly defer-ential to your boss."

"She is whenever it matters, as you well know. And you wouldn't want it any other way."

"I look forward to seeing you next week, Senator. We are praying for you every day. Plan on staying in the White House with us. Please give my best to Cindy."

"How's he doing?" Denyse asked as I hung up the phone.

"I'm not sure. It's tough to tell with him. He seemed upbeat . . . said he's coming to Washington next week."

"You need to do something for him, Danny."

"I do. I know I do."

We both paused in thought.

"My heart breaks for him—and for the country. This guy is clearly one of the most admirable public servants in our history. His record as a senator in my view even eclipsed his heroism in Vietnam. I owe it to him to come up with the consummate expression of appreciation on behalf of the coun-try."

"I have faith in you, Danny."

"Good . . . at least somebody does."

Chapter Forty-Three

July 22 2018
The Ghosts of Andrew Jackson

We took the McCains to 1789 Restaurant, an upscale spot in Georgetown. I stayed up late listening to McCain regale me with stories culled from every segment of his remarkable American life. It was such a special night, the memory of which I knew immediately I'd always cherish.

Before climbing into bed moments after bidding him good night outside the Lincoln bedroom, I grabbed my Washington coin. Sure enough, within a few brief minutes I heard activity emanating from the floor above. The timing could not have been more perfect. I had to give this a shot.

I jumped up and threw on some slacks and a shirt. I decided it would be too awkward for me to rap on McCain's door at this hour. In what amounts to a gutless display coupled with somewhat of an abuse of power, I asked the night steward to summon the vice president for me from the Lincoln bedroom. I could see a decided look of distress on the steward's face at this order, to say the least, but he nonetheless carried it out, and a few minutes later a disheveled McCain reappeared. I could still hear the sounds from above. I had the coin in my left hand.

"What the fuck do you want now, McFadden?" he asked with a smile.

"Humor me," I said. "Just follow me." We walked toward the spiral staircase.

"Do you hear anything?" I asked.

"No, sir. But I've always assumed this place is haunted. Are the ghosts of Andrew Jackson and his drunken cronies raising hell here at night?"

"Well, Senator, it's funny you should say that."

As we walked up the spiral staircase, the noise went silent. When we walked across to my entrance there wasn't a sound to be heard. I tried to open the door, but it wouldn't budge. No party, no presidents, no saloon. I was crushed, but not altogether surprised. Terribly disappointed, though. It would have been an incredible experience for him—one he deserved so much more than I did. And oh my God, would he have delighted in it!

I must have been pushing my luck trying to bring a visitor into the Saloon. Apparently, this magical saloon door opens only for presidents. What a bummer.

Chapter Forty-Four

July 23, 2018—1:13 p.m.
The Canine Paradox

I returned to the residence after a long day and was promptly greeted by Montana, who seemed about as agitated as a chill, fluffy collie can get. Something was clearly up. He darted over by the staircase to the third floor and began pacing back and forth, eyes fixed upstairs. As I approached him, I heard familiar noises from above. For some time now, I'd been carrying my Washington coin with me at all times as instructed. Not because it was lucky—my God not that. Quite frankly, I was having no luck at all. However, I wanted to be ready whenever my favorite watering hole got rolling. With the coin in hand, I proceeded up the staircase with Montana leading the way. He had never acted like this before, which made me really curious about what was going on.

Montana beat me to the top of the stairs and then made a beeline to the Saloon entrance. While he pawed aggressively at the door, I pushed it open and then couldn't believe my eyes. The Saloon looked like a giant indoor dog park. Montana darted away from me immediately like a bat out of hell and disappeared into a sea of dogs that had overrun the entire bar. The presidents and saloon staff were scattered amongst them, clearly enjoying every part of it and egging them on. The dogs had the run of the place, and they clearly knew it.

My first reaction—and, honestly, my only possible natural reaction—was to laugh. The scene in front of me was absolutely hysterical. There was no order of any kind to the dogs' stream of consciousness as they scampered about. This was a room full of joy and happiness if ever there was one, for both the dogs and the presidents. There looked to be way more dogs in the room than humans. I saw many of the presidents calling dogs by name. Suddenly it hit me. Could these be the presidents' own dogs? *Oh my God.*

President Ford approached me. "You ever see anything like this before?" he asked.

"I love it! I always knew there was a dog heaven! I've been telling my kids that for years."

"I love your dog," Ford said. "She's a collie, right?"

"Yes." People always seem to think collies are shes. I guess because of Lassie.

"We have many of those in here. I love Dash, Benjamin Harrison's collie. Coolidge and Hoover have collies too. So does LBJ."

"Any of these yours?" I asked.

"Yes," replied Ford. "I have two goldens: Liberty and her puppy, Misty. Misty was actually born in the White House. And by the way, every president in here has a dog. How remarkable is that? Every single president has had a dog in the White House. Some of these presidents are scoundrels, of course," he said with a smile. "Many of them actually. But I like to think that says something good about them all. We definitely do have more in common with one another than we have differences."

We sat and took it all in for a few minutes. "What's your collie's name?" Ford asked.

"Montana."

"Named for the state?"

"No, the quarterback."

"Ah . . . I was afraid of that. You're a Notre Dame guy, right? You *do* know I'm a Michigan man, right?"

"Yes, I do. An all-American lineman, correct?"

"That's ancient history."

"I love ancient history, sir. And I love the Michigan–Notre Dame rivalry. Nothing signals the arrival of fall better than those two teams hooking up in early September."

Just then we were joined by Matty, wearing a sizeable smile. "So glad you could make it here tonight, Mr. President. There's nothing quite like Dog Day. Are you acquainted with any of these characters?"

"Yes, but not their dogs," I responded with a smile.

"That's President there," Matt said, pointing to an enormous Great Dane. "He's Franklin Roosevelt's. Teddy owns a bunch of these dogs. His bull terrier, Pete, tore the pants right off the French ambassador in the White House one day. People swore he was trained to keep the reporters away."

Presidential Spirits

Then Matt pointed over at a crowd of presidents gathered around LBJ. "Check this out," he said. "I know exactly what he's going to do next."

LBJ reached down and picked up a beagle by its ears. Reactions ran the gambit from laughter to outrage and everything in between.

"It's good for him!" LBJ yelled to the disbelievers, not convincing anyone.

Matty added, "His two beagles are named Him and Her."

"Clever names, but that strikes me as animal cruelty there," I responded. "There must be a million stories about all these dogs out there."

"You know it," Matty replied before pointing to a giant Newfoundland. "There's Veto, Garfield's dog."

"What a classic name for a president's dog," I laughed.

"Yes. . . . You think he was trying to send a message?"

Matty then pointed across the room. "Two of those many black-and-tan coonhounds of Washington's are named Drunkard and Tipsy—aptly named, I would say, for an establishment such as this. Harding would take his dog, Laddie Boy, on the golf course with him, and the dog would retrieve his errant drives and return them to his fairway. Not sure how he managed to teach him that."

"I could use a few of those dogs," I sighed.

"I could go on and on about all these dogs."

"Is Nixon's dog Checkers here?" I asked. "The one who was the subject of his big speech?"

"No, she isn't. Although she's certainly one of the most famous dogs owned by a president, but Checkers was never in the White House. She died before Nixon became president. You see that impressive looking Irish setter over there?" Matty asked as he pointed over near the bar. "That's King, the dog the Nixons had in the White House."

Truman approached us and looked at Matty. "You giving McFadden here the lowdown on all these hounds?"

"Yes, I am, Mr. President."

"There's a lesson in this for you, McFadden," Truman added with a smile. "If you want a friend in Washington, get a dog."

"I am painfully aware of that, sir. My big tan-and-white collie is out there mixing it up. Some nights the sight of him is just what I need at the end of a long day. Most nights, actually. And this saloon, of course."

I heard a voice from behind us. "Good for you, McFadden." I turned to see it was Calvin Coolidge. "Any man who does not like dogs and does not want them about does not deserve to be in the White House."

"I'm with you on that, Mr. President."

I spent the next hour just taking it all in. I tossed a tennis ball just to watch a whole pack of them stampede across the room. It was kind of unfair, though—the retrievers seemed to have such an advantage. Some slid out of control on the hardwood when they'd try to stop quickly or turn on a dime. More than anything, I was struck by the sheer joy of it all. More joy than I had seen in the Saloon before—or for that matter, anywhere else in the last few years. Dogs sure seem to have this whole happiness thing figured out.

I saw Obama seated at a table with Lincoln and John Quincy Adams, and took the opportunity to go say hello. Obama saw me approaching, stood up, and gave me a bro hug. There were only a couple of us in the room who he could even try to pull that off with. "Have you got a pup out there, Mr. President?" he asked. The thought of Obama, or any of these guys, calling me that still floored me.

"Oh yeah. That big fluffy collie out there. Our second dog. When the first one passed the kids wouldn't let us go without another."

"Ha, ha. I know that well. I was feeling my oats a bit on election night. Got caught up in the moment in my acceptance speech and promised Malia and Sasha in front of all the world that we'd get a dog. I was venturing out of my comfort zone but I never regret it."

"That was a great move," I responded. "My kids identified so much more with you and your family when you got Bo."

"Yes. There's a lot to be said for that.

Mary Ann was clearly as big a hit with these dogs as she was with the presidents. I found her sitting on the ground midway between the stage and the bar in what appeared to be the most heavily trafficked dog route, and they all stopped to express their affection for her as they came by. None of that surprised me. Ginger remained secluded behind the bar. That didn't really surprise me, either.

"Who's the biggest dog lover among the presidents?" I asked Mary Ann.

"Oh, that's easy. Washington," she answered without hesitation. "About a dozen of these babies are his. You should see how he is around Tipsy. She's running around here somewhere. She's his pride and joy." She scanned the room but couldn't locate Tipsy in the sea of dogs.

"You can tell an awful lot about a person by how they treat their dogs," Mary Ann continued. "And the guys say he once called for a cease-fire in the middle of a battle to return a British general's dog to him. I've loved him ever since I heard that."

"I'm not sure I really believe that," I replied. "I think I'm gonna have to check with my professor on that one."

"Teddy is big dog person too," she said, ignoring my skepticism. As a handful of dogs competed for her affection, she looked as joyful as her companions.

"Do you know many of these dogs?" I asked.

"Yes, I do," she responded. "I love Dog Day."

"Who is that massive dog with Buchanan over there?"

"Ha! That's Lara. She's his Newfoundland. She's enormous, but she's such a sweetheart."

"That is awesome!"

"And that's Clinton's chocolate Lab Buddy with them."

"I remember Buddy. I'm just shocked that Montana was able to get in here. I've tried to get people up here before to no avail."

"Dogs are special," she added. "They've got all the best qualities of people—loyalty, trust, friendliness, bravery, happiness, love—without any of our fatal flaws. How much better would the world be if dogs were running the show? I mean, think about it. No egos or narcissism, no hidden agendas—they're completely transparent."

Tina, who was standing nearby, then added, "No dishonesty. No ultra-complicated personas. No intensely debilitating insecurities. And they're motivated by factors beyond just sex, wealth, and power."

"Hold on there," I said, whirling around quickly to look back at Tina. "I was right there with Mary Ann for her part. Sounds like you've had some issues with a few humans. And by humans, of course, I mean men."

"Ha! No . . . mostly just the men in here. And yes, I've have issues with more than a few of them."

We both looked back upon this priceless scene of dogs and presidents.

I thought to myself how fascinating this place was and yet, so mysterious. I was still figuring it all out. I said to Tina, "It is interesting that dogs can be in here, but as far as I can tell, the only people permitted to set foot in this tavern are presidents. Are all these pooches the same dogs these men had while serving as president?"

"Yes. From what I gather, these are the dogs they had in the White House. And, in Washington's case, while he lived in Philadelphia and New York as president."

"So, does that mean when it's all over for me as president that not only will I still be in this bar every night from here to eternity, but Montana may be here with me on occasion as well?"

"Yes, sir!" Tina affirmed.

"I like the thought of that. That's the best news I've heard in a long time."

"Maybe not for all eternity,"

"You don't think so?"

"I would think for the duration of our country or perhaps this form of government."

"That might not be very long, I'm afraid."

Tina laughed, but I wasn't trying to be funny.

"Dog lovers have such a roller-coaster of a life," I said. "The very best thing about dogs—how much we grow to love them—instantly becomes the very worst thing when they're gone all too soon."

"Yes," responded Mary Ann, suddenly looking very sad. "That is the canine paradox. I hate the canine paradox."

Tina then added, "I've never missed an ex-boyfriend nearly as much as I've missed my dogs."

"OK, Tina," I said. "Your gonna need some therapy for that man issue you're harboring."

"No, sir. I am right at home with my rather enlightened outlook on your gender. A therapist will only try to teach me that I should love men more than I do dogs. Why on earth would I possibly pay for that?"

"OK. I'll stop encouraging you," I said. Then after pausing for a few seconds, I added, "I'm thrilled Montana will be with me in the Saloon for the duration after my term."

"Yes! And what a sensational addition!" Mary Ann gushed with great enthusiasm. Then she added in much more courtly fashion, "You are too, sir, of course."

I brushed over that unintended slight. "So if I get another dog, that dog would be with us in the Saloon as well?"

"Absolutely!" said Tina.

"Oh, please get a bunch of them!" Mary Ann implored.

"Alrighty then! That'll be a tall order with Denyse. She loves Montana, but I'm fairly certain one is her firm limit. I'll have to get Kelly, Jack, and Brett on it."

Feeling the need to get back, I ventured out into the mosh pit of dogs to retrieve Montana. I immediately realized this was going to be a lot more difficult than I'd imagined. I swear Montana saw me coming but acted as if he didn't see me. He ran to the other side of the room, seemingly encouraged by his buddies. Even man's best friends were plotting against me in organized factions.

Sensing my frustration, Matt appeared with a couple handfuls of pretzels. "Like most of the men in this room, I've learned these dogs can be bought," he said with a laugh as he handed me the pretzels.

I waved one in front of Montana, stuffed the rest in my pockets, and hastily proceeded across the bar toward my exit. Unfortunately, so did half the dogs in the room. I must have appeared every bit like the Pied Piper as I hustled toward the door followed closely by this enthusiastic pack of canines.

But my challenges were just beginning. As I slowly pulled the heavy door open, four or five noses immediately filled the crack. I quickly pushed the door closed. This was going to take some thought.

I walked about twenty feet away from the door and emptied my pockets of all the pretzels onto the floor. I then immediately grabbed Montana by the collar, and made a mad dash toward the exit. The dogs pounced on the pretzels like kids at birthday party on a newly smashed piñata. Pushing Montana through the doorway first, I turned and looked back at the scrum. Just before the door shut completely, I spotted something shiny amidst all the dogs and pretzel crumbs—my Washington coin.

I instinctively flung the door back open and sprinted over to grab this precious artifact. Pushing my way through the horde of dogs, I saw it again. But before I could get my hands on it, Rollo—Teddy Roosevelt's huge St. Bernard—knocked me flat on my behind. I quickly seized the coin, sprung to my feet, and dashed back to the door, which had sat there wide open in my absence. With dogs everywhere, I somehow managed to get the door closed without crushing any paws.

I looked around but saw no sign of Montana. He had either escaped somewhere on the third floor out of my sight, returned to the dog party, or quickly bolted down the staircase. I tried to get back into the Saloon to look for him, but the door would no longer open. That's what I was afraid of. I never knew when the door would open and when it wouldn't. I guess I hadn't completely cracked that code quite yet. I quickly descended the staircase to the second floor. A security guard posted there smiled and greeted me.

"Did you see a dog run by?"

"Yes, sir," he answered. I breathed a huge sigh of relief.

Then he added, "They went that way."

I stopped in my tracks. *They?*

Chapter Forty-Five

July 23, 2018—3:25 p.m.
Who Let the Dogs Out?

Suddenly all I could think about was how I would possibly explain this and what kind of havoc it would cause. And, interestingly enough, for a guy who holds himself out as Mr. Transparency, the epitome of integrity, the last thing on earth I knew I needed to do at this moment was tell the truth. It only took a few panicked seconds of thought for that to become abundantly clear to me. This must be how Nixon felt in the White House after the Watergate break-in or Bill Clinton following the emergence of the blue dress as they scrambled to avoid the truth at all costs. I suddenly felt a rather disturbing kinship with each of them.

I looked back at the security guard. "How many did you see?"

"Three, I believe. Montana and his two friends. How many should there have been?"

"Yes, three," I replied, trying to sound nonchalant. I could practically feel my nose growing as I said it.

At that moment, two more dogs came barreling down the staircase and scampered past us in search of the others. I could hear Denyse in the residence screaming at the boys. "Where did you boys get this pack of dogs?"

I heard Brett yell back, "Mom, I swear we had nothing to do with it!"

That only prompted her to elevate her decibel level. "You guys are gonna have to do better than that! Where did they come from? You take them back to wherever you found them right now!"

Then I heard Jack ask innocently, "Oh, please can we keep 'em, Mom?" Bless his heart.

"Shut up, Jack!" replied Brett. "Let's just get these guys out of here."

"Where are we going to take them?"

"I don't know. But we'll figure something out."

I heard them marching toward the entrance to the presidential residence, frantically herding these very excited canines.

They saw me when they got to the stairwell. "Dad, what's going on?" Brett said with no shortage of panic in his voice. "Mom's really pissed."

"And we didn't even do anything!" added Jack.

I was still utterly without a plan to explain this, let alone address it. "First take them outside," I said, completely winging it. "Run the hell out of them. Then one of you go find Satch and tell him I asked you to have him find a way to care for these guys for the time being."

"What if he asks where they came from?" asked Brett.

"Just tell him you think they ran down from the third floor. And tell him I seemed really nervous about it."

If I wasn't so panicked about my predicament, I would've thought it was hilarious watching my boys running through the White House chasing after five dogs. I could only imagine what sort of pandemonium was about to be unleashed on the White House staff and security. And I was kind of worried about what would happen to the dogs. My God, what if I couldn't get them back to the Saloon? That would definitely spell the end of my bromance with all my new drinking buddies.

I considered just walking down to the Oval Office and pulling the "I'm-busy-being-the-leader-of-the-free-world" card, but I knew I'd have to face this sooner or later.

I was still out of eyesight of Denyse, but I heard her talking to Sandy. "Is my husband around here somewhere, Sandy? I thought I heard the boys talking to him."

"I'm not sure, Mrs. McFadden," Sandy responded. "I can go check for you."

The security guard looked right at me. We could both hear this conversation, and he could sense my uneasiness. He smiled at me. For a moment I considered coming clean with Denyse, but I chickened out. Instead, I texted her: *"C u in about an hour. Dealing w/ a bit of an emergency."* Then I high-tailed it in the direction of the Oval Office.

She texted right back: *"Do you know anything about these dogs?"*

I knew I couldn't even answer that. I needed to decide what to say. *She already knows I'm a little crazy, She knows that better than anybody, but I'm sure she doesn't think I'm so batshit crazy that I think I can talk to dead pres-*

idents. I'd think she was completely nuts if she told me she was regularly sip-ping chardonnay with Dolley Madison, Jackie Kennedy, and Mamie Eisenhower.

I thought about it for few minutes then for some reason I decided to text her back: *"I'll talk to you about that when I get back."*

As I walked toward the Oval Office, I saw a few of the dogs running outside in the Rose Garden. There appeared to be a team of security person-nel chasing them. I guess at least I now knew I really wasn't just imagining or hallucinating the Saloon. These dogs were very real. I texted Satch but got no response.

Moments later, as I sat on the couch in my private office, a security staffer buzzed in on the intercom. Cathy was away from her desk. "Mr. President," he said, "the First Lady is here to see you."

"God dammit!" I muttered to myself in utter exasperation.

"Does that mean you don't want to see her, sir?" the staffer responded, making a completely reasonable assumption based upon my response.

"No, no, no," I shot back. "I'm happy to. I was angry at something else—not the fact that she's here. Please show her in. I'll meet her in the Oval Office. And I love her very much."

I don't know how convinced he was of that.

I waited a minute or two but then realized I could no longer put it off. *I guess I just have to tell her the truth.* I got up and walked slowly into the Oval Office.

Denyse was already seated on the couch, wearing on her face the most discernible "what the fuck" expression I had ever seen. As I approached the couches, I noticed Jack outside in the Rose Garden with a pair of dogs. I went over and let them in. The dogs burst through the crack in the door as soon as I started to open it and bolted over to Denyse, leaping up onto the couches and nuzzling next to her.

"Oh my God, Dad!" Jack said, breathless with excitement. "You should see these two run. They caught three squirrels in five minutes."

"Holy cow!" I responded,

"Can we keep 'em?" Jack blurted out.

"No. I'm so sorry. We need to get them back to their owners. They're not ours,"

"What kind of dogs do you think they are?"

"I'm guessing some sort of hound or retriever,"

Jack looked up at the painting hanging on the wall that showed Washington seated on his horse while on a hunt with two sprinting dogs following closely behind. "Hey, these guys look just like those two in that painting!"

I turned to look at the painting. "No, I don't think so," I responded.

"Dad, they look *exactly* like those two!"

"I think those are a completely different breed."

"No, Danny. Look at that," Denyse added. "I agree with Jack. These two dogs really do look just like the two in the painting. Same size, same faces, same coloring."

"Dad, maybe they're descendants of Washington's dogs! How cool would that be?"

"I guess that could be possible," I said.

"So, Danny, please tell us where these animals came from," Denyse demanded.

"Well," I answered with great uneasiness, "it's kind of a long and complicated story."

"I've got nothing but time, dear," she replied with more than a hint of attitude. "Start talking."

"I'm kind of taking care of them for their owners for the time being."

"*Really?*" she responded incredulously. "In the White House? Someone asked the president of the United States to dog-sit? I think you're gonna have to do better than that, Danny."

"I can't really say."

"So what, you mean to tell me these are some kind of CIA dogs or something? Yeah, that makes a lot of sense. That clears it all up." Sarcasm was dripping from her words.

At that moment we saw Brett and Satch appear through the window at the door facing the Rose Garden. I was all too happy to jump up and go let them in. Behind them, a team of security officials had corralled the rest of the dogs, including Montana. I called to Montana, and he came running.

"Thanks for all your help, folks," I yelled out to the security staff. "Give us just a couple of minutes here and I'll be back out."

Montana darted inside as I let Brett and Satch in.

"Hello, Mrs. McFadden," said Satch. He looked back and forth at the two of us, seemingly attempting to size up the situation. "It's been quite a day around here," he said, perhaps just to gauge the reaction.

Neither Denyse nor I bit on that comment. All the while, I was reading him, trying to ascertain whether he recognized these dogs, which would tell me everything I needed to know about his knowledge of the Saloon.

"If you'd like, sir, I can take care of these guys. The staff would be happy to care for them until we find their owners."

"Where did they come from, Satch?" asked Denyse.

"There was an event with a bunch of dogs on the property here, and I'll bet there was some confusion and these guys were left behind. I think I can help get them back to their owners. Would you like me to do that, sir?"

"Yes, please," I responded.

He whistled and clapped his hands. "Hey Tipsy, Drunkard, come here." They hopped off the couch and came running.

Satch knew their names, I thought. *Amazing.* I knew enough to know that was a huge piece of the puzzle, but wasn't sure exactly how it fit, and I didn't have time to dwell on it at the moment. I knew Denyse would soon be cross-examining me, so I needed plausible answers as soon as possible that didn't make her want to have me committed.

As Satch reached for the door to let them out, he paused. "Uh . . . Mr. President."

I turned to look at him.

"I believe this one here is pregnant," he said with a look of astonishment.

Holy cow! I thought to myself. *Could this get any more complicated?*

He took the dogs outside.

"Hey boys . . . ," Denyse began, "would you please take Montana upstairs so Dad and I can talk for a few minutes?"

"Sure, Mom," Brett said.

As Montana and the boys made their way to the door, I hastily ran through a number of options in my head. I had some quick decisions to make...

Chapter Forty-Six

July 23, 2018—4:12 p.m.
When All Else Fails, Tell the Truth

I really didn't blame Denyse one bit for demanding to know what was up. I was just finding myself right smack in one of those crazy situations I always seemed to get myself into—through absolutely no fault of my own.

Denyse wasted no time. As soon as the door shut behind the boys, she looked at me and began her interrogation. "Alright . . . you want to tell me what's going on here? I've never seen you act quite *this* strangely."

I spent several moments in deep thought before saying anything. Unfortunately, that pause only made it worse. She saw the deathly serious look on my face and I could see her mentally jumping to conclusions. Even so, I struggled to decide how to begin.

"Are you having an affair?" she blurted out.

"What? . . . No! Absolutely not. . . . How could you even—"

"Do you want a divorce?" Her mind was racing out of control now, not that I blame her.

"Wait . . . what? How did we go from having a handful of strange dogs in the house to me having an affair?"

"All I know is that I've known you for twenty-five years, and I've never seen you act anywhere near this peculiar around me."

I still, inexplicably and perhaps tragically, struggled for words.

"And it really seems to me like Satch was trying to cover for you just now. You two seemed to be giving me different stories—always a red flag, just so you know."

"First of all, Satch would never cover for me if I *was* having an affair— which I'm not!—he'd definitely take your side, as would everyone else we know. Let's take a walk. I promise I'll explain all this."

That bought me some time. We walked outside past the South Lawn toward the tennis courts. I felt myself breaking a sweat, as much from this crazy predicament I'm sure as from the late afternoon heat and humidity. I knew my only option at this point was the to tell the truth. *There is nothing to be ashamed of, right? But that doesn't mean she still won't think I've gone completely bananas.*

We sat down on a bench in the Children's Garden. A group of Secret Service agents scrambled to take their places amidst the trees nearby. I barely noticed them anymore.

"I'm going to tell you the truth here."

"Would you like a medal for that or something?"

"No—I just mean what I'm about to say might make you think I'm crazy or hallucinating or something, or it might make you think less of me."

Her expression and her attitude softened. "Nothing you can say will make me think less of you, Danny." She put her hand on my shoulder. "I don't know what the hell is going on, but I'm still your biggest fan. I was just really put off by you not being straight with me about whatever you're about to tell me. And, by the way, it better be worth it."

"Oh, believe me, it is."

I pulled out the Washington coin and held it up so she could see it. "Do you remember what this is?" I figured that was about as good a place as any to start.

"Yes," she said. "That's the special coin you told me Satch gave you to bring you luck. How's that working out for you?" The question reeked of both attitude and sarcasm.

"Well, yes, it's not exactly lucky in the sense of bringing me good luck. But I don't think that's its purpose."

"Oh, this coin has a *purpose*? What a remarkable thing. That's quite a coin."

I couldn't blame her for being annoyed, but I realized that the longer I took with this explanation, the more sarcasm she would throw at me.

"No, listen to me. This is terribly hard for me to say out loud to anybody, but especially you." I took a deep breath and exhaled. "Denyse, something supernatural is happening to me, and it's been going on since I became president . . . since I was given this coin."

I had her attention.

"I haven't been able to tell you or anybody—not even those I think might know about it." After one more brief pause, I finally took the plunge.

"This coin has permitted me to access a room on the third floor of the White House where I am able to interact with all of the former presidents—even the dead ones. At first I thought it was a series of dreams or hallucinations, but now I know it's much more than that."

"What do you mean you interact with former presidents?" She started to look a bit worried.

I took another deep breath. "If I have this coin with me and hear noises coming from the third floor, when I go up there, instead of entering what we know to be the restricted access portion of the third floor, I enter a sort of supernatural saloon. Every former president is in there. It is the most amazing, mysterious, and, yes, the craziest thing ever. But it is also the most compelling, life-affirming, and inspirational thing I've ever witnessed."

"What do you mean when you say you interact with them?" Denyse repeated, speaking more slowly this time.

"I speak to them, I drink with them, I joke with them, but I also learn from them. And I had no idea how much respect I had for this country until I spent some time up there."

"You're telling me you speak to Abraham Lincoln . . . and Franklin Roosevelt?"

"Yes! And George Washington and Thomas Jefferson and Teddy Roosevelt. John Kennedy. Ronald Reagan. I talk to them all!" I exclaimed, relieved to finally tell someone. "And you know what the best part of it is? They are so much less partisan than the clowns I deal with here every day. And they want me to be successful—and this country to be successful! After some of the days I've had in that West Wing, I desperately need that experience on the third floor. It centers me. Reminds me why I'm here. Inspires me. And it leaves me more determined than ever to find a way to move us beyond this debilitating partisan divide."

I studied her face to try to gauge how this was playing with her. "Oookaaay," She said. An awkward silence followed for a few seconds that seemed to me like minutes. Suddenly her face brightened up. "So what's the scary part? That sounds pretty darn cool to me."

"You don't think I'm absolutely frickin' nuts?"

"Danny, I've known you were different since the day I met you. You're a dreamer, and that poor brain of yours doesn't seem to be able to turn off or relax for even a moment, so I'm sure this is just a mechanism it has created to allow you to cope with the enormous pressure you're feeling. And if it's helping you get through it—and it sounds like it is—then baby, I'm all for it."

"First of all, thank you for not thinking I'm crazy."

"I didn't exactly say that, but—"

"This is really not just in my head. It's very real!"

"I'm certain you think that, and I'm OK with that."

"No, no, no! You don't understand! I know this is real. I've learned things about these presidents in the Saloon—little-known facts or stories that that turn out to be true. Things I've never heard or read about. Like that Teddy Roosevelt walked Eleanor down the aisle on her wedding day or that John Quincy Adams swam naked every morning in the Potomac or that Monroe crossed the Delaware with Washington and was injured in the ensuing battle. I learned all those things from talking to these guys in the Saloon and only later found out it's all true."

"The human brain is an incredible thing, Danny. I'll bet you knew all those things at one point in your life and stored them away in your subconscious, and now they're coming out. You know, they say we really only use 40 percent of our brains—"

"OK. Alright. I get it. When this all began I thought the very same thing. However, something happened today that let me know *unequivocally* that this is real—not just some figment of my imagination."

"And what was that, dear?" she asked, playing along but still looking rather skeptical.

"You know those two dogs you saw today that caught three squirrels and looked a lot like the dogs in the painting of Washington on a hunt?"

"Yes. How do they fit into all of this?"

"Those two *really are* Washington's dogs!"

"Huh?"

"All of these strange dogs running around here today are from the Saloon. It's a long story, kind of, but I brought Montana into the Saloon this afternoon, and all the presidents had their dogs in there with them. As we left to come back, I accidentally let some of them out the door and into the White House."

A fresh look of shock came over Denyse's face.

Speaking very slowly, she said, "So you mean to tell me," she paused, "that all those dogs," another brief pause, "came from that Saloon you're talking about?"

It was as if she was talking to a small child. I guess I didn't blame her. That's precisely why I had tried so hard not to tell anyone—even Satch, even the former presidents at Barbara Bush's funeral, who certainly must've known.

"Can you show this Saloon to me?" she asked.

"I'm afraid not. I could try of course, and I'm willing to do so. We can go right now. But I tried to get McCain up there, and it didn't work. It only seems to work when I'm alone with the coin in my hand and I hear the noises. I think all three of those things have to be working together."

"But you got Montana in?"

"Yes, yes, I did. Look, I don't make the rules on this. I'm merely telling you what I've come to learn about this by trial and error and by talking to the staff."

"*Your staff* knows about this?"

"No, no . . . not *my* staff. The staff who work at the bar."

"There's staff in the bar?"

"Yes, bartenders and waitresses."

"There are waitresses?"

I could see where this might be going. "Yes, there are. They're probably half my age—at least in appearance. I guess no one ever really ages in the Saloon. And they have their hands full with that crowd of alpha males."

"Are the waitresses attractive?"

Why did I know she was going to ask that? I thought hard about my answer before responding. "I've never really noticed." That was a bit of a white lie. Or perhaps maybe not white at all. "But I love *you*, babe, not some imaginary waitresses."

"Or not so imaginary, as we seem to be finding out."

Now that attractive waitresses were part of the deal, the Saloon was suddenly very real in her mind.

"By the way, I think you would love the bartenders if that makes any difference. I wish I could introduce you to all of them."

"So what are we going to do now with these dogs? Are you supposed to return them to your 'saloon'?"

"I tried, but the door wouldn't open. It doesn't always open for me. I think I need to keep trying. I'm not worried . . . at least not yet. Meanwhile, I'm not sure what to tell any of the White House staff about who they are or where they came from. Satch will handle it for the time being."

"Great. I'll let you take care of that."

"By the way, I haven't told you perhaps the craziest part of all,"

"That can't possibly be true, but go ahead and tell me anyway."

I took yet another deep breath. "One of Washington's former slaves runs the Saloon."

"What?"

Chapter Forty-Seven

July 24, 2018
Germantown and General Howe's Dog

Cathy got Professor Harris on the line for me as soon as I got my morning coffee. "Professor Harris," I said. "Thanks for taking my call."

"Mr. President, great to hear from you! What can I do for you?"

"Professor, today I want to ask you about presidential dogs."

"Ha ha! Great subject."

"What do you know about them?"

"I know a little bit. I know that each president had at least one while living in the White House, which in and of itself is rather remarkable," the professor began. "Of course, there have been some very memorable presidential dogs. And very memorable stories. George and Barbara Bush's springer spaniel, Millie, published her own memoirs, which appeared on the bestseller list and sold more copies than Bush's own memoirs did. Once in a campaign speech, Bush famously said of Clinton and Gore that Millie 'knew more about foreign affairs than these two bozos.'"

"Ha! That's hysterical!" I replied. "Anytime you can work *bozo* into a campaign speech I've gotta think that's political gold."

"Harding, who knew well America's love of dogs, also used that to his political advantage by placing a picture of his dog Laddie Boy on a campaign poster. He also commissioned an official portrait of the dog."

"What do you know about Washington's dogs?"

"He had many. Washington loved dogs. He hunted with them. Lafayette gave him some large French staghounds that Washington bred with his black-and-tan coonhounds."

"Do you know anything about Washington and a dog at the battle of Germantown?"

"Oh, yes, yes. There's a very famous account of British General Howe's dog straying across enemy lines. Washington took the dog into his own tent and fed, brushed, and cared for it. When they determined that it was, in fact, Howe's dog, a temporary cease-fire was called so the dog could be returned to General Howe."

"That is quite a story. I've gotta think that makes Washington a kind of patron saint of dog lovers. It's certainly an example of how certain innate human qualities such as the love of a dog can transcend even war. That's really incredible."

"Isn't it?"

"Reminds me a little of the stories you told in class about cease-fires and caroling between troops of both sides on Christmas during World War I," I said.

"Yes—the Christmas Truce on the Western Front. It's fair to say, however, that while General Washington may have felt a dog was worthy of a cease-fire, he certainly did not believe that Christmas warranted one. His much-celebrated crossing of the Delaware and defeat of the Hessians at Trenton took place on Christmas night. If anything, he took advantage of the holiday, and the drinking that took place by the Hessians on Christmas clearly helped his cause."

"Fascinating. For Washington, the love of a dog transcends war but Christmas does not."

"Yes, I think that's fair to say," the professor replied. "Let me ask you this: what prompts these questions about dogs and the presidents?"

"Let's just say it's been a topic of conversation quite frequently lately."

"There is some literature out there on this topic, Mr. President. I can come up with a list and pass it along, if you like. You might find it interesting to see what kind of dogs each of the presidents had."

"Oh, no thank you, Professor. I appreciate that, but I have a pretty good source of information on that at my disposal here."

Chapter Forty-Eight

July 25, 2018
I'm Suddenly in the Mood for a Colonoscopy

The next day I was in my private office when Cathy buzzed me. "Mr. President."

"Yes."

"Are you alone?"

"Yes, and I've rarely felt more alone in all my life," I responded, laughing.

"Well maybe this will be welcome news, sir. Satch would love to stop in for a few minutes. I told him there's a small chance you may have some time this morning, but I hedged to give you an out in case you'd rather not."

"I appreciate that very much. What would I do without you?"

"Oh, you and I both know this place would be a total shitshow without me," Cathy howled, quite impressed with herself.

"Who says it's not a total shitshow now?" I retorted.

She laughed. "What should I tell him, sir?"

"Of course I'll see him. I'll meet him in the Oval Office."

Moments later, Satch entered the Oval Office and brightened my day as he always does.

"I'm so sorry to spring those dogs on you," I said.

"I love dogs. The staff loves them too. We're happy to handle them for you for as long as you wish."

"The staff is taking care of them?" I asked, feeling sheepish about this.

"Yes, all except the pregnant one."

"Tipsy?"

"Is that what you call her?" he asked.

"*You* called her that when she first stormed through here," I reminded him.

"I'm not sure what you're talking about," Satch countered.

"You know where these dogs came from, right?"

"I don't concern myself with that. I'm just happy to care for them as long as you'd like us to, Mr. President."

"You're caring for the pregnant one yourself?"

"Yes. I have her at home with me now and I bring her here every day. She's in good hands."

"Who should I contact when the right time arises for me to return them?"

"The residence manager on-duty at the time can help with that, sir."

"Alright. I need to get them back as soon as I can. That's good to know. Thanks."

"I heard you spent some time with the vice president recently," Satch asked. "How is he?"

"Well, he's certainly seen better days, but knowing his story, I'm sure he's seen many worse ones as well."

"Everyone is asking about him."

"Let me ask you something. I need to do something special for him— something deeply meaningful. Do you have any suggestions?"

"Let me think about that one. How long will they be here?"

"About a week. Not sure what I could do for him that would be worthy of him. You know what?" I said. "He deserved to be president, even if just for a night."

"I agree, sir."

I thought for a few moments. "Perhaps I could formally resign in January during my last week in office. However, I'm afraid he may not make it that long." I paused again before continuing, "I just wish there was a way of just making him president for a night without me formally resigning."

"Well, you know, there is a way you could do that now if you really want to," Satch said. I immediately perked up.

"What are you getting at?" I had no idea where he was going with this.

"I'm talking about the Twenty-fifth Amendment, sir, which states that he becomes president temporarily if you're incapacitated in some way, like while you are in surgery or something. It's been done. George Bush transferred power to Dick Cheney while he was undergoing a colonoscopy. In fact, he did that twice."

229

"Oh my God," I responded. "I shudder to think of Cheney as our president."

"Reagan did it for a surgery too."

I sat up straight. "Huh . . . the Twenty-fifth Amendment. I thought that's just when the Cabinet gangs up on me because they think I'm crazy,"

"It's for more than that, sir. You can temporarily transfer power and get it back."

"Hmm . . . the Twenty-fifth Amendment. Wow! That might be the answer! That just might work," A smile quickly spread across my face.

"Of course it would work," Satch replied. "Like I said, it's been done at least three times before that I know of."

"No . . . I was thinking of something else. But yes, you're right. It would certainly work."

This was worth a try. When I returned to my private office after speaking with Satch, I buzzed Cathy. "Cathy, please summon Dr. Connor. I'm suddenly in the mood for a colonoscopy."

"That's an overshare if I've ever heard one," she replied, appropriately so. "I'll contact him right away."

I had a scheme in mind to give McCain the gift of a lifetime. If he could incur merciless beatings in the Hanoi Hilton, the very least I could do on behalf of a grateful nation is take one for the team. So to speak.

Chapter Forty-Nine

July 26, 2018
God, I Hope This Works

The following day, I met Drake, Cathy, and McCain in the Oval Office to execute the formal documents necessary to temporarily transfer power under the Twenty-fifth Amendment.

"How was your night, sir?" McCain asked.

"It was fine," I responded.

"Any trouble with the solution?" he said with a smirk.

"What do *you* think?" I looked at him, and he laughed. "That stuff is absolutely brutal,"

"I've done it many times, and I'll say this: the Vietnamese should have tried that stuff on us over there. They may have gotten a lot more out of our guys!"

Cathy placed my daily briefing folio on my desk. "We've cleared your schedule for the day, sir. Dr. Connor and his staff are available in the medical unit of the Old Executive Office Building whenever you're ready."

"Is anybody ever really ready for that?"

We proceeded with a formal, videotaped signing ceremony, choreographed by White House Counsel Brian Benedict. While not exactly top secret, they nonetheless wanted to keep it under wraps and simply inform the world after the fact when power had been successfully transferred back. The whole thing took less than a minute. How is it that the leader of the free world can effectively transfer all the powers of his or her office so much more quickly, easily, and painlessly than a doctor can examine someone's colon?

"Do you have some time for me, Senator?" I asked McCain.

"Anything for you, my friend, but kindly address me as Mr. President from now on," he replied.

I laughed. I certainly should have seen that coming. "Seriously,

231

though," I said, "if you could give me a couple of hours right now—"

"Uh . . . I refuse to hold your hand through this procedure, if that's what you're getting at," McCain interrupted, laughing out loud again at his own humor. "My loyalty to you is unquestioned, but that's a personal and professional line I will not cross."

Cathy was on to me. She had some fairly sharp instincts, particularly when it came to me. She walked over and leaned in close to me. "Would you care to bring me in on this, or are you going to keep me in the dark on this one like you usually attempt to do?" She at least knew enough to whisper that.

I chose to ignore her. Her stare grew more aggressive.

"It's classified. I wish I could tell you." She wasn't buying it, but it didn't matter.

Looking at McCain, I said, "Can you meet me in the residence in twenty minutes?"

"Certainly. I'll see you then."

I motioned to Cathy, and she followed me into my private office. "Can you go talk to Dr. Connor for me? I'm sorry to keep them waiting, but I've got something I need to take care of first. I'll get down there as soon as I can. Please apologize for me."

"Sure," Cathy said.

"Tell him I'll explain in person when I see him."

Minutes later, I met McCain outside the presidential residence, and we walked up to the third floor together.

"We trying this again?" he asked.

"Bear with me on this," I said.

The door would not budge. Perhaps this thing opens to the Saloon only for a president attempting to enter alone, I thought. I had one last plan to unveil.

"Do me a favor," I said, pulling the Washington gold coin from my pocket. "I'm gonna go undergo this procedure, but I want you to do something for me."

He looked at me with an even more puzzled expression on his face than before. However, it was becoming obvious that he found the whole thing quite amusing. He took the coin and examined it closely.

"I'll explain everything about this coin later, but whatever you do, don't lose it." Then walking toward the couch, I said, "Come here, please. Sit here for a while. When you hear noises coming from that room over there, try the door again. Make sure you are by yourself as you attempt to enter. And promise me that you won't ever tell anyone anything about what you see in there."

"I'm beginning to think you are as crazy as all your critics on both the right and the left have been saying you are," he laughed, but I could tell he was intrigued. "You realize, of course, armed with this story I could make this temporary Twenty-fifth Amendment promotion of mine much more permanent."

"That might just be the best thing that ever happened to me," I replied, only half joking. "Be careful what you wish for."

"What on earth am I going to encounter behind that door?"

"Well, I'm not sure how earthly it is, but trust me, if I can pull this off for you, it will be the treat of a lifetime."

"I place my blind faith in you, my friend. I'll do what you say. I have almost no expectations about this, and that might be an overstatement. But I will do this out of loyalty to you, coupled with the fact that I now have literally nothing to lose."

I left him on the couch, studying the coin, and started back downstairs to the residence. I paused for a moment at the top of the stairs and thought of his spirit in the face of his obviously fatal disease. I knew I would not be of the same mind-set if stricken with a similar ailment. I had considerable work ahead of me to get my mental house in order, but that was not my most pressing issue at the moment. *God I hope this works!*

Chapter Fifty

July 26, 2018
The Vice President Is Missing

I spent a groggy afternoon following the procedure meandering in and out of sleep watching the Dodgers and the Cubs from Wrigley Field. At about five o'clock, I wandered up to the third floor to check in on my little scheme. Glancing at the couch, I saw only McCain's wallet, keys and cell phone. He must have achieved success. *Wow!* I was elated. *God I hope I was right.* Stumbling upon this Saloon was absolutely the most incredible thing I had ever come across in my life and to be able to share it with John McCain meant the world to me. Who else on earth could possibly be more deserving?

I returned to the residence, figuring I'd check on him again in about an hour. A little while later, there was a rap at the door. "Mr. President," a security staffer called through the door, "I've been asked to tell you that Terri Drake is hoping to have you return to the Oval Office with the vice president to execute the transfer of power back to you."

"OK," I responded. "Give me a few minutes, and I'll be right there."

"And Mr. President," he said, "one more thing. Is the vice president with you?"

"Is the vice president with me?" I replied. "Is that what you asked? Uh . . . no . . . he's not. We're very good friends, of course, but he's not in the bedroom with me."

I laughed to myself, but then I started to really worry as I foresaw perhaps some more deception ahead, and I didn't really need any more of that at this time, by the way.

I got dressed to returh to the Oval Office. On my way I stopped up one more time by third floor. McCain's things were still there. I had dropped him off eight hours earlier. I hustled down to the Oval Office and found Drake and Cathy with Secretary of State Cynthia Miller.

Presidential Spirits

Drake greeted me, "Great to see you, sir. Hope you're feeling better. We'd love to arrange the transfer of power back to you, but no one seems to know where the vice president is, including his wife, Cindy. I know that sounds really crazy, and perhaps even a little unprecedented, but this has been a rather unprecedented day around here. Remarkable even by our standards."

"I'm sure he's just fine wherever he is," I responded. "He's the ultimate survivor and has gotten himself out of some of life's biggest pickles."

Drake came close to me and spoke softly so only I could hear, "Having him disappear while you were under kind of defeated the purpose of transferring power in the first place."

She had a point, of course, but I had an entirely different purpose in mind. I guess I didn't realize he'd be up there so long. "This one's on me, Drake," I said. "Don't blame him for this. I can't explain it to you right now."

"Well, regardless of that, we want to complete this transfer of power back to you before the close of business today. Since he's not here to sign it, the secretary of state will sign instead."

"Is that valid?" I asked.

"We checked with Brian's office, and they stated clearly that having the secretary of state sign right now is more than sufficient," replied Drake. "The salient element, according to Brian, is that you sign and deliver the document to the House and Senate. We'll get the vice president to sign another one when we locate him.

"Answer me this," Drake continued. "Should we initiate a full search? There's no video of him leaving the property.

"Let's hold off on that for now," I suggested. "I hate to be cryptic about it, but trust me on this—at least for now."

***

Later I had dinner with the family in the residence, then Denyse and I watched several recorded episodes of *Modern Family* with the boys. I was killing time and trying to focus on other things, but all the while, I was becoming rather obsessed with McCain and his whereabouts.

We all headed to bed by ten thirty. By then, McCain had been gone about twelve hours. The longest I'd ever spent up there was perhaps three or four hours at most. My thoughts of worry were beginning to be overcome by a bit of jealousy. I certainly wasn't about to go to bed without seeing how this played out. Armed with one of my favorite books—John Avlon's *Washington's Farewell Address*, I camped out on the couch in front of the Lincoln bedroom. Before long, I fell asleep.

At 3:45 a.m. I awoke to the sight of a rosy-cheeked John McCain standing in front of me with a smile as wide as the Potomac. His clothes barely clung to his body evidencing an epic and memorable night. His grin quickly morphed into a look of profound earnestness. "Thank you," he said. Then again, a moment later, "Thank you."

He did not appear drunk, but seemed exceedingly happy. *Mission accomplished,* I thought. The sight of him like this warmed my heart. It was the kind of feeling that can only be derived from giving to others. The look on his face was my reward, and I loved it.

"Thank you," he repeated one more time. "You have provided me with such a singular experience—the gift of a lifetime. I don't know how to even begin to thank you or where to start in describing just quite how it impacts me at this particular stage of my life." He collapsed into the couch next to me.

"I don't know where to begin my questioning," I said. "I'm not sure we're even supposed to talk about it."

"They didn't want me to leave!" he said jubilantly.

"What?"

"They literally begged me to stay."

"Who did?"

"Teddy," he said with a big smile. "He's everything I ever thought he would be and more! "And Grant . . . Over a few bottles of whiskey, he regaled us with stories of the Civil War—Vicksburg, capturing Fort Henry, the Overland Campaign. We could have gone all night!"

"You did!" I exclaimed. "Are you even supposed to drink with your treatments?"

"I did tonight!" he laughed uproariously. "But I'm pretty sure Tina and Ginger figured it out and watered down my drinks considerably. They didn't want me to leave, either!"

"Wait," I said. "Are you sure? They have never once suggested that I stay longer."

"Sheels instructed the bartenders to keep the place open."

"Holy cow!" I said, my emotions vacillating between jealousy, disbelief, and a tinge of anger.

"Tina wanted me to go home with her."

"What??" I blurted out, much louder than I cared to.

"I'm kidding, sir!" McCain said, exploding with laughter. "They love you, and they all made a point of saying that."

"Thanks for adding that, even if it's not true." That made me feel a little better, but somehow I was quite bothered by all this. I know that didn't speak well of me.

"Lovely ladies," McCain continued. "And that Haskell is something else."

"Sounds like you really got around up there."

"I made the most of a once-in-a-lifetime opportunity."

"Do you have the coin?"

"What coin?" he asked.

"The Washington gold coin," I said, a bit exasperated.

"I may have misplaced it," he added. "I'll see if I can come up with it in the next few weeks."

I knew he was kidding. "By the way, you need to stop in the Oval Office and sign the transfer back."

"I don't know . . . I'm gonna be quite busy tomorrow. Cindy has a whole day planned for us around town."

I was ignoring him at this point.

He pulled out the gold coin and admired it for a second. "So this thing has been passed down from each president?"

"Pretty inspiring, huh?"

"Magical. Destiny. I'm afraid I wasn't worthy of that fine saloon. But I am forever in your debt, Danny." He placed the coin in my hand and slapped me on the shoulder.

I pointed to the likeness of Washington on the coin, "So did you meet him?"

"I did indeed, sir! I got completely tongue-tied, I'm afraid. I've never experienced anything like that before. But what a truly magnificent figure! There was no mistaking him in that room. He wondered who the heck I was. I'm not sure I impressed him."

"John, if he'd had the opportunity to become acquainted with your legacy, both in war and in politics," I responded, "I'm certain the admiration would be mutual."

"You are too kind."

We said good night outside the Lincoln bedroom. As I started to walk away, he called out to me, "Oh . . . one more thing, Mr. President."

"What's that?" I said, turning back around.

"He wants his dogs back."

Chapter Fifty-One

August 1, 2018—8:45 p.m.
Please Don't Answer It

After a good bit of begging, our Secret Service captain permitted Denyse and me to have a brief after-dinner drink on our private terrace at the posh Shangri-La Hotel in Paris. Less than a mile from the Eiffel Tower, the view was something right out of a movie. The sun was setting to our right, and the Eiffel Tower looked magnificent in the twilight directly in front of us. Although this was mostly a business trip, this brief little romantic interlude was precisely what the doctor ordered—particularly after that unpleasantness and confusion with the dogs.

This was our first opportunity to be alone on this whirlwind trip, and we could not have asked for a better setting. This trip to Paris was a first for both of us, and so far, we loved everything about it. President Macron and his wife, Brigitte, had rolled out the red carpet. We'd had a private tour of the Louvre and a State Dinner at the Palace of Versailles. Tomorrow we were traveling to Normandy before heading off to Ireland.

"Can we just stay right here for two weeks?" Denyse asked. "Right here on this terrace. This alone is worth all the headaches, right?"

"Perhaps if I have a few more glasses of wine I will think so."

"I love this French wine. Please have some more."

"I hate to rain on your parade," I said, "but I'm fairly certain the travel staff brought these bottles of wine on the trip for us from Washington. But they are from France originally."

"So this wine has been around the world and back just for us. This has to be my all-time favorite bottle of wine."

"How much of that have you had?"

"Can I help it if I'm a little carried away in the moment? Exhale, Danny. Enjoy the moment. You've got it pretty good, you know."

"I'm sorry. Yes, I know . . . we are incredibly blessed. It's just hard to

239

see that sometimes. But it's never more clear than right now in this setting."

My phone started buzzing.

"They need to let us have a minute to ourselves here," Denyse complained. "Please don't answer it."

I reluctantly let it sit on the table unanswered. It continued to buzz.

Denyse's frustration grew. "I'm gonna throw that thing into the Rhine."

"The Seine."

"I'll throw it there too."

My personal phone buzzed too. I looked down and saw it was a text from Kelly. *"Dad, promise me you'll do something about this. Enough is enough."*

Something was obviously going on. As I started to click on the *New York Times* app, my official phone rang again. I saw it was Jed. "What's up, Jed?"

"I'm sorry to bother you, sir. I have Terri Drake with us on the line as well."

"What's going on?" I asked.

"Another high school shooting. This may be the worst yet. Dozens are feared dead."

"Where was it?"

"Mayton, Florida."

"Did they apprehend the shooter?"

"Two shooters. Both were killed by SWAT officers but not before killing dozens of their classmates. There could be as many as fifty dead."

"Oh my God. When was it?"

"Just a few hours ago. We have a prepared statement ready for release and a tweet from you as well.

"I wish I had known earlier. Drake, please arrange for me to speak with the school's principal, the mayor, and the governor. And Drake, let's come home right now."

"Of course, Mr. President," Drake responded. "Just to be clear, though, the Irish have been planning your elaborate 'homecoming' this weekend for months. We were supposed to keep it a surprise, but I think they've got Bono and Van Morrison lined up to play for you and President Higgins."

"I'm not sure about the optics of attending an elaborate party in Ireland when funerals are being planned in Florida," added Jed.

"Forget the optics," I responded. "The country is gonna require some real leadership in the way of healing for that region first before coming together on some real solutions to this national affliction. I need to come home right away."

Chapter Fifty-Two

August 6, 2018
Facta, Non Verba

Five days later, I stood with Denyse and four Secret Service officers in the sacristy at Father Damien Catholic Church in Mayton, Florida, attending the funeral for Megan Grimes, an English teacher and the girls' soccer coach at Damian High. She'd been shot twelve times when she charged the shooters as they entered her classroom where she had holed up with over sixty students who sought refuge in her room. She managed to wrestle with one before being taken down by the other in a hail of bullets. The momentary disturbance enabled all but six of the students in the classroom to escape.

We had learned a great deal more since the first news of the shooting. Forty-seven people died—mostly students attending summer school and athletes participating in summer workouts. Another twenty-three suffered injuries. The two shooters were rising seniors at the school—longtime friends who had never really fit in with the crowd. They had experienced a fair amount of bullying and had fantasized about exacting some sort of revenge—they even left a bit of a social media trail. They had also developed a sick fascination with the Columbine shooters. One of the shooters was eighteen, which in Florida was old enough to legally purchase the two AR-15 rifles used in the attack.

An older priest entered the sacristy accompanied by a much younger man wearing a black suit and a what looked to be a Labrador retriever tie.

"Mr. President," the priest said extending his hand, "God bless you for coming. I'm Monsignor Connolly." He had an Irish brogue, as dozens of priests I've known through the years have had. If it weren't for the circumstances of this particular occasion, I'm certain he would have had a twinkle in his eye as well. "Let me introduce you to Beth's husband, Bruce Grimes."

My heart stopped for a second. I was overcome with a sadness that slowly evolved into anger. I was momentarily at a loss for words. My natural abilities were much more suited to making good times better than to making trying times easier.

"I am so sorry for your loss," I said, shaking his hand and looking into his eyes. "I love your tie," I added. "I should have figured that Beth was a dog person."

Just then a young woman, who was obviously with them, entered the sacristy with a baby and a toddler. Bruce introduced them. "This is Beth's sister Colleen, my son, David, and my daughter, Liz."

Gazing upon those shattered lives, a healthy tear welled up quickly in my eye. Bruce and Colleen seemed pleased to meet me, which was unimaginable to me. In that moment, I could not detect grief, but I'm certain they had been bathing in it over the course of the last five days, with no relief in sight.

I managed to muster up some words. "I admire your sister as much as I've ever admired a human being," I said to Colleen.

She smiled but said nothing.

"Can I ask a favor, Mr. President," Bruce asked.

"Anything," I responded.

"Can you say a few words today?"

My trip here, though hastily organized over the past thirty-six hours, had been nonetheless highly choreographed. The White House media people and my political people were in agreement that I would attend and offer support but not speak. This had been thought out and debated amongst the staff and firmly decided. Besides, no one had asked me to speak.

Before I could respond, he added, "It would mean a great deal to us."

From the look on their faces I could tell how much this meant to them. At that moment, I would've done anything they asked. How could I conceivably say no?

"Of course," I said. "When would you like me to speak?"

"We'll call you up after the eulogies."

I consider myself an adequate public speaker, but only when I have time to fully prepare. I'm not nearly as good when speaking off the cuff with no opportunity to craft a coherent message. Like now, for example. For the first time in my life, I was happy that Catholic masses last so long.

The musical folks entered the sacristy and diverted the attention of

Monsignor Connolly and the family. We had a few minutes before being seated, so I texted Jed: *"Please prepare a few talking points or thoughts for me to give at Beth Grimes' funeral right now."*

Moments later he responded: *"We'd rather not have you speak, sir. I would avoid it."*

"Dude, send me some talking points ASAP!!!" I'm not sure he sensed my impatience with him, but I hoped I was conveying it.

As Beth's husband left out the side door to accompany the casket and start the ceremony, he turned to look at me and said, "Can we please do something about this, so she doesn't die in vain?" He walked away before I could respond.

They seated us in the front row, which, although I understood, I felt entirely unworthy of. Behind me sat folks who were forever bonded with this amazing, courageous, young woman, some of whom perhaps had her to thank for their survival. I caught a glimpse of a bank of cameras at the back of the church. I had no doubt my remarks would be broadcast live. While I rarely had nerves when speaking publicly, I knew this could be an exception.

It was a terribly, terribly sad occasion. I felt profound grief for this remarkable young woman, for her family, for this community, and for this country. How could meaningful solutions to this ever-increasing problem be so elusive?

Monsignor Connolly absolutely crushed it. His positive, hopeful, faith-affirming remarks at the outset of the ceremony and the homily struck precisely the right tone. This was indeed a celebration of Beth's life.

My phone vibrated, and I saw a text from Jed: *"If you must speak, your best play here is to focus on her courage, her selflessness. A hero and role model—even before her actions last week. A revered schoolteacher and coach. Molded young lives. Rave about the community coming together at this time of grief. Our better angels. Light springing from the darkness. The very best of the human condition responding to the very worst. I caution you to steer clear of any politics at this moment."*

While that provided a few points to think about, it was hardly what I was hoping for. As nonchalantly as a sitting president could possibly do from the front row, I googled the Latin translation for "actions, not words," which escaped my memory at the moment. I wondered how Lincoln, Kennedy, Reagan, and all the other illustrious orators of our history handled such situations without Google.

As is his custom when asked, after communion Monsignor Connolly sang an incredible rendition of "Danny Boy." Beth's maiden name was Finigan, and he said this was a lullaby in her house growing up. I don't imagine any person watching this scene, whether in this church or around the world, could do so without sobbing. But it was therapeutic. I cried for this family, and I cried for this country.

Monsignor Connolly's rendition of "Danny Boy" set a tone for the eulogies to follow. Last season's women's soccer MVP, who was just starting her freshman season at the University of Texas, had come home for the service and gave the first of many heartfelt eulogies. A parade of current and former students and team members followed, some of whom had been in the classroom during the shooting and owed their lives to this remarkable woman.

"She completed us."

"The greatest person I have ever known."

"My twin brother and I are alive today because of her selflessness."

"I can only repay her by living a life dedicated to others as she did."

Some directed their remarks directly to Bruce, David, and Liz. "We promise to be there for you whenever you need us for the rest of your lives. Even that cannot begin to repay Beth for her actions."

Then it took a turn—a bit of an angry turn. One said, "How long will we let people purchase weapons such as these?" The packed crowd at the church applauded long and hard.

The next student was more bold. He left the podium, walked over to the other side of the altar in front of where I was sitting, and, with no need for a microphone, said emphatically, "President McFadden, we are glad that you are here. We really are. However, with all due respect, we need your support in Washington. You and our other leaders are failing us. If this doesn't inspire you to act, please don't bother showing up at the funeral services for next month's high school massacre or the one the month after that."

Finally, Beth's father took the podium. He started by stating that it was the greatest privilege of his life to be her father. Then, as impossible as it must have been for him, he proceeded to tell his favorite stories of Beth's childhood. Teaching her to read, amazingly, at age four. Trick-or-treating alongside her when she was dressed as Cinderella at age six. Walking with her hand in hand to go sign up for her first soccer league at age eight—a short walk that changed both their lives. Somehow he managed to list all these moments and more without losing it. The same could not be said of the congregation.

He smiled when he recounted hosting her pre- and post-senior prom parties, which she attended with Bruce, whom he described as "her first and last boyfriend." He got big laughs when, after pausing a few seconds, he added, "There were many more in between, of course."

He finished by looking directly at me and stating forcefully, "Please let her heroic actions and her tragic death give rise to real solutions." That garnered tremendous applause.

It was my turn next. *How can I possibly follow that?*

My short walk to the podium from the front row seemed to take forever. I was still quite uncertain of the direction I would take, but the framework for this short speech would be supplied not by my communications team, my political people, or a teleprompter. For this, I would rely solely on the course provided by my heart.

I looked at the family. "Bruce, David, Liz, Colleen, Mr. Finigan, and all the rest of the Grimes and Finigan clans, I am truly honored to have an opportunity to speak for this remarkable, inspirational woman. I think it is particularly appropriate that we are in a parish named for Father Damien, who himself sacrificed his life coming to the assistance of the lepers in need.

"One of the most powerful of all Latin phrases is *facta, non verba*—three little words but when put together pack a mighty punch. Deeds, not words. Let us be known by our actions, not our words. That phrase will forever define our Beth. Beth was an exceptional American hero whose truly exemplary actions in the face of that all-too-American problem will forever distinguish her. She decided in a split second that the lives of her students were well worth the price of her own life.

"While grief and, yes, anger, are prominent in our minds today—and those aren't going away soon—please allow your hearts to summon some of life's other prominent emotions. You'll find those to be more powerful and lasting. Allow yourselves also to be glad that you had the opportunity to know her, to be happy your friendship brought her joy, to be proud of her remarkable courage and selflessness, to be grateful that you could share her life with her, and to be inspired by the manner in which she lived her life. Focusing on these things helps us to overcome the other emotions that can tend to dominate at a time like this."

I looked out at the congregation. I was at a bit of a crossroads. I could sum up right now. I saw the bank of cameras at the back of the church and in the choir loft, each with its little red light illuminated. I made a split-second decision to follow my heart's urgings. Not anything near the courage Beth displayed, but for me, it was something. Looking straight at Mr. Finigan in front of me, I continued. "It is the worst possible indictment of our political system that we cannot do even the simplest things to move the dial on this issue. This week, in the wake of this tragedy, we've heard many a commentator and legislator suggest that this is the price of our freedom. Nonsense! Let me tell you something," I paused for effect, "the price of freedom was paid in the carnage of young American lives in places like the beaches of Normandy, the Forest of Argonne, and the island of Iwo Jima, not in the young American lives lost in Rooms 214, 216, and 218 of the STEM wing of Father Damien High School!"

The crowd began to applaud, and I saw activity among the reporters in the back of the church.

"Let me tell you something more, Mr. Finigan, your beloved Beth did not die in vain. No, sir. She lives on in all the lives she touched in her lifetime and on that fateful day—all those she saved—and all those worldwide that she inspired. And, mark my words . . . out of her actions—her facta— will spring the national political will to finally tackle this terrible American affliction. And it's not just automatic weapons that are to blame, it's our culture of violence and bullying and school safety and proper parenting and mental health and following up on signals and tips. But yes, it is also access to guns, particularly automatic weapons. Especially that.

"If Beth Grimes can risk her life confronting this incredibly disturbing American problem, certainly myself and a majority of legislators in Washington can risk their seats."

At this point, most people in the church were on their feet. Again, I could have stopped. This was another clear stopping point. But that's the problem when Jed is a thousand miles away, and I'm taking orders only from my heart. So I carried on, "I have spent the duration of this Mass in awe of this remarkable and heroic young woman. If she had been one of our marines at Pointe du Hoc or the Tet Offensive, she would clearly warrant a Medal of Honor. I have decided in the last several minutes to create a national Medal of Honor to acknowledge those who join in her fight to defeat this pandemic of senseless violence, with Beth as its first recipient."

Then I looked directly at her coffin. "Beth, may your split-second decision to sacrifice your life, which clearly saved dozens of others, serve as the inspiration to drive the national resolve to fashion a comprehensive approach to rid our country of this epidemic of violence, and thereby save a multitude of others in your name."

I stepped down, hugged the family members, and felt completely at peace with my not-so-brief remarks. I had an idea of what would be coming at me now as a result of this, but it's fair to say I didn't know the half of it. At that moment, I didn't much care about all that. I sat back down in my seat in the front pew and started to cry. *Sobbing* may be a more apt term for it.

Chapter Fifty-Three

August 6, 2018
The Wild Wild West

I hadn't even settled into my seat for the return trip on Air Force One before the outrage from the gun lobby commenced. It came fast and furious, and it was all too predictable. I was "politicizing these deaths," "trampling on the Constitution," "demonstrating my true leftist ideology," "exposing my hidden agenda to take everyone's guns away from them," "purposefully ignoring the true causes of this problem." I saw that Jed had called. Five times. I asked the travel secretary to get him on the line.

Picking up the phone, I said, "How'd I do, Jed?" I braced for a bit of a scolding, But I had long ago made it crystal clear to him that he was to say, "It wasn't so bad," even when it clearly was.

"You spoke well, Boss," he conceded. I braced for the inevitable qualifiers. "I'm not sure you helped yourself with your new congressional friends we've been courting in the swing districts. I think you've teed up a fierce political battle."

"That shouldn't be what this is about. People on both sides will seek to make this a binary choice, but it's not. Please fashion a strategy for me to make that clear. We're not choosing between taking everyone's guns or arming every citizen with an AR-15. There exists a multitude of reasonable alternatives."

"I suggest we do that soon, sir. We'll map out a strategy for you. Enjoy the flight."

We got back to Washington late, but if ever I needed a night in the Saloon, this was it.

***

I entered the Saloon and, amidst a familiar cloud of smoke, saw a gathering of presidents congregated around the table in the middle of the room. Bypassing the bar, which I'm fairly certain was a first for me, I went directly to join them.

It was an outstanding collection of my predecessors. All the Founding Father presidents were there: Washington, Adams, Jefferson, Madison, and Monroe. With them sat Lincoln, Garfield, McKinley, and Kennedy—each of those guys knew a little bit about gun violence. Many of the recent presidents were there as well: Ford, Reagan, Clinton, both Bushes, and Obama. And the two Roosevelts. I couldn't have ordered up a more appropriate cast for this discussion. Funny how that seems to work in this place.

Washington welcomed me. "Come join us, McFadden."

"I'd love to, General," I responded.

"The younger President Bush asked us all to convene for you," he said.

That Otter is amazing, "I appreciate that very much, gentlemen." I answered.

"Tell us the latest," Washington asked.

"I'm not sure quite how to explain it to you gentlemen." I began. Then I looked over at Clinton, the Bushes, and Obama. "Those gentlemen know what I'm about to say. I'm not sure any of the others would understand."

Mary Ann, Tina, and Matty appeared—I think as much to hear the discussion as to get anyone's drink orders. I loved them for that. I turned to the three of them and said, "No drinks for me tonight, but please join us for this discussion. I need advice and opinions from a diverse array of viewpoints, and look around me, this is a fairly homogeneous group."

I passed up the opportunity to attempt to explain the concept of diversity to the early presidents, opting instead to dive right into the subject at hand: gun violence. "Over the course of the past couple of decades, and perhaps much longer, America has become a place where gun violence is rampant. Homicides related to guns are commonplace in our inner cities. Approximately 40,000 Americans die each year from gun-related injuries. Additionally, and perhaps most troubling, in the past three decades, we have had more than ninety mass shootings—where a shooter kills four or more victims.

"We now seem to have grown numb to stories of school shootings— where a disgruntled or disturbed current or former student at a school opens fire upon the students in an effort to kill as many as he can. Young males are almost always the perpetrators. Often the weapon of choice is an automatic weapon—one that can fire continuously as long as the trigger is held down.

Presidential Spirits

"America has always had a definite gun culture, and it shows. We have by the far the greatest percentage of gun ownership in both aggregate ownership and guns per person—more than any other country.

"I cannot think of a debate more intense in America today than the arguments pertaining to what to do about gun violence. At the extremes, there are people on the far left who want to do away with guns altogether, and on the far right there are many who want no restrictions of any kind on gun possession, including automatic weapons, viewing it as a sacrosanct right rooted in the Second Amendment.

"I just attended the saddest memorial service I could ever imagine for a young schoolteacher. She was savagely gunned down in her classroom by two of her own students who used automatic weapons to kill forty-seven of their classmates and teachers."

That drew an audible gasp in the room. I could see I had the presidents' complete attention. Mary Ann began to cry.

"One of the shooters was eighteen years old, so he was able to legally purchase the weapons in the State of Florida a week before the massacre. They used semi-automatic AR-15 rifles, which, depending on the magazines used, can shoot between thirty and a hundred rounds without reloading.

"I have to do something about this. I need a multipronged approach that addresses law enforcement, mental health, the violence in our culture, and parenting, but must, in my opinion, also include the availability of these guns."

"My worst day as president," added Barack Obama, "was hearing that twenty first graders had been shot in the most brutal way, in their school where they should have been safe. Every time I think of those kids it gets me mad. And by the way, it happens on the streets of Chicago every day." After a brief pause, Obama continued, "I thought the Sandy Hook school shooting would be a catalyst for some action by Congress. I didn't expect that you'd see some huge movement on gun safety legislation, but I thought, well they're gonna have to make some effort. And the fact that it didn't even get the kind of hearing and votes that you would have expected, that it didn't generate a debate, that you actually had no bipartisan legislation sponsored . . ." He stopped, shook his head, and looked down. "So disheartening. America is the one advanced nation on earth in which we do not have sufficient common sense gun safety laws."

251

"My position on the right to bear arms is well known," Ronald Reagan said. "But my own experience with gun violence influenced my view. I was lucky. The bullet that hit me bounced off a rib and lodged in my lung, an inch from my heart. Twice they could not find my pulse. But the bullet's missing my heart, the skill of the doctors and nurses at George Washington University Hospital and the steadfast support of my wife, Nancy, saved my life.

"Jim Brady, my press secretary, who was standing next to me, wasn't so lucky. A bullet entered the left side of his forehead, near his eye, and passed through the left side of his brain before it exited. I am a staunch defender of the Second Amendment, and I am a member of the NRA. But I supported the 'Brady bill'—a gun control measure named for Jim adding background checks and a waiting period, and I supported the assault weapons ban as well."

"As you know, we got the assault weapons bill passed," said Bill Clinton, "but it came at a tremendous political cost. We whipped the bill ourselves, in the White House, because the Democratic leadership was too skittish on it. It passed by one vote in the House. But it cost Speaker Foley his job. And it cost Jack Brooks, who had been in the House for forty-two years, his job. We lost fifty-three seats in the midterms. All for a ban that expired in ten years. And it did expire. Our president and our Congress shamefully let it expire."

Clinton paused for dramatic effect, then continued. "But it is a fight worth having. No president should have to go to Columbine or to Springfield, Oregon, or to Jonesboro, Arkansas, or to any of the other places I have been, to comfort these devastated communities. It's tough enough to comfort the families of our servicemen and women who die in the line of duty," he said. "Children have no duties except to their studies and their families. Our duty is to protect their lives and give them futures."

"I am the president you are referring to, Bill," stated George W. Bush. "I did think we ought to extend the assault weapons ban but was told of the fact that the bill was never going to move because Republicans and Democrats were against it. Both parties in Congress opposed it. It wouldn't pass."

"With all due respect, you could have fought for it, really championed it," responded Clinton.

George W continued, "The best way to protect our citizens from guns is to prosecute those who commit crimes with guns and keep guns out of the hands of those who shouldn't have them. As much focus as assault weapons tend to get, mass shootings and deaths from assault weapons are just a tiny fraction of overall gun deaths."

I had to respond. "I hear that argument made all the time—that an assault weapons ban won't solve the overall gun problem in America, so there's no use bothering with it. I know it won't solve the overall problem, but why is that the standard? I'll tell you what it will do—it will make a difference in these school shootings and these mass murders. What if there was a wild animal or infectious disease that wiped out a dozen or more schoolchildren in their classrooms in front of their teachers and classmates once every two or three months. The deaths would still be dwarfed by the number of deaths from cancer and other diseases in the country, but you can be sure Congress would nonetheless scramble to take some action to directly address that specific part of the problem."

I looked at the early presidents seated around the table. "I'd love to get your thoughts on the Second Amendment generally and this particular problem we are facing, including the notion, firmly held by so many today, that the Second Amendment protects a person's right to own an assault weapon—a weapon that can shoot dozens of bullets a minute—over a state's right to regulate them for the safety of its citizens."

James Madison was the first to speak. "The great mass of respectable people who opposed our Constitution before these amendments disliked it because it did not contain effectual provision against encroachments on particular rights, and those safeguards which they had been long accustomed to have interposed between them and the magistrate who exercised the sovereign power. One such right being the right of the people to keep and bear arms.

"I have said many times," Madison continued, "we were not afraid of putting guns in the hands of our people. In our view a well-regulated militia was the best security of a free country. Those best acquainted with the successful resistance of this country against the British know well the advantage of being armed. It is an advantage the Americans possessed over the people of almost every other nation."

"I agree," added Thomas Jefferson. "What country can preserve its liberties if their rulers are not warned from time to time that their people preserve the spirit of resistance. Let them take arms. The tree of liberty must be refreshed from time to time with the blood of patriots and tyrants. I hold that a little rebellion now and then is a good thing, and as necessary in the political world as storms in the physical."

"Perhaps," I responded, "that after nearly 250 years of peaceful transitions of power, with the notable exception of the Civil War, the notion of a militia or rebellion threat to preserve liberty as the primary justification for the right to bear arms has gradually given way to one of self-defense and defense of property, in addition to the hunting aspect. However, all too often these days, these incredibly powerful killing machines are being used not in self-defense or for hunting but to slaughter other lawful, innocent citizens."

"Let me add the views I expressed at the time of the drafting of the Bill of Rights," said John Adams looking over at Madison. "I recall that our purpose with the Second Amendment was to place arms in the hands of citizens to be used in private self-defense or by partial orders of towns, counties, or districts of a state. To suppose arms in the hands of citizens may be used at individual discretion is to demolish every constitution and lay the laws prostrate, so that liberty can be enjoyed by no man; it is a dissolution of government."

"Gentlemen," said Jefferson, scanning the room, "let us not forbid the carrying of guns. Such laws disarm only those who are neither inclined nor determined to commit crimes. They make things worse for the assaulted and better for the assailants; they serve rather to encourage than to prevent homicides, for an unarmed man may be attacked with greater confidence than an armed man."

"I agree with you, President Jefferson," added Reagan. "I firmly believe in the right of every man or woman to own a gun. But I don't believe McFadden is suggesting that we forbid the ownership of guns entirely. I think he is specifically referring to these automatic weapons. I believe that a machine gun or an AK-47 or any other gun designed to kill dozens of people quickly is not a sporting weapon or a gun needed for the defense of the home."

"Mr. Reagan, I have the utmost respect for you, sir," said George W. Bush, "but how can we outlaw automatic weapons when so many are already on the streets—perhaps more than two million by some estimates.

We can't put the genie back in the bottle."

Again, as much as I was there to get a sense of the room on these issues—particularly from the founders—I felt compelled to respond. "In so many of these cases, the shooter merely walks into a shop and purchases the weapon," I said. "Like they did last week. You can't tell me that in every such case, these assailants—many of whom are teenagers and loners or outcasts—would have the wherewithal to acquire such weapons through black market channels. If we can prevent even one mass shooting, or lessen the impact, would that not be worth it?"

Washington had been listening carefully to the discussion and taking it all in. "Tell me again what constitutes a mass shooting?" he asked.

"A gun crime that results in the death of four or more people. There have been at least ninety such incidents in America since the mid-1980s. In the deadliest case, a gunman opened fire with automatic weapons at a concert in Las Vegas, killing fifty-eight people and injuring nearly 500. In a gay nightclub in Orlando, a shooter recently killed forty-nine people and injured another fifty-three."

"What kind of nightclub?" asked Washington.

"A gay nightclub. I need to cover that with you folks too, but I'll save that for another time."

"Make sure I'm here for that, Mr. President," Tina shouted from the back. I wasn't aware she was still lingering. No one appeared to be drinking throughout this discussion.

"The list goes on," I continued. "The school shootings include thirty-two killed at Virginia Tech, twenty-six at Sandy Hook Elementary in Connecticut, which Obama mentioned, and now forty-seven as I mentioned at a high school in Mayton, Florida."

"There is no end in sight to this list," added Obama. "With these guns McFadden refers to, a shooter can get off a hundred rounds in under two minutes. I don't believe this type of firepower was contemplated when you gentlemen crafted the Second Amendment."

"This is a human problem, not a gun problem," said Bush Sr. "I do not oppose gun control because I am insensitive to the kind of brutality that hospital staffs see every day. I do so because I believe gun control does not work. The actual solution lies far beyond the power of lawmakers in the vast territory of the human mind. There it is either adopted in moments of anger or thrust aside in the impulse to kill."

"I agree that it cannot be solved entirely by lawmakers," I responded. "There is a powerful culture that needs to change, and mental health care issues to address, as well as bullying and education, and a real need for leadership nationally. And I agree that we can't and shouldn't seek to prohibit all guns. But I'm with your friend Mr. Reagan, sir, on seeking to restrict these automatic weapons. To me and to a lot of people, that's a no-brainer."

I paused and looked around. "Who in this room stands opposed to an assault weapons ban? I seek no ban on pistols or rifles or shotguns. This is not a slippery slope toward eliminating all guns."

"Go for it, McFadden! Godspeed," said Clinton. "But realize you are taking on a powerful lobby, and the political consequences will be real."

"Get it done this first term, and then go back to Silicon Valley and enjoy your life," added Obama. "Michelle and I will come visit."

"I would have done so if I felt it would pass," said the younger Bush.

"Your proposal seems to be an eminently reasonable and necessary restriction on this important right," stated Adams. "This does not infringe on the right we established in crafting the Second Amendment."

"I admire your courage, McFadden," said Kennedy. "I trust the word of my colleagues here that it may ruin you politically. However, sometimes history produces the vindication of one's reputation and principles after such a stand. But only sometimes."

"Allow me to confer with my fellow Virginians," said Jefferson, who then huddled with Madison, Monroe, and Washington.

Moments later, Monroe spoke, "I have properly considered your position. However, if landowners possess lesser weapons, I should think they have lesser proclivity to defend themselves from invaders and lesser propensity to stand up to tyranny."

"President Monroe," I said, "these days I think the weapons of choice in standing up to tyranny are the Internet and social media, and those won't be used to slaughter any schoolchildren. But my credentials to speak are nothing compared to yours, sir. You and your colleagues created a country from scratch that has stood the test of time for 250 years."

"Ah, but you are the president, sir," replied Monroe.

The Virginians whispered amongst themselves again. The discussion came to a halt with all eyes on the four of them. After about a minute,

Washington turned back toward the rest of the room. "I stand with McFadden," he said.

The other Virginians did not appear so convinced. However, Washington's vote of confidence was all I needed. I knew enough to know that a lawyer shuts up and immediately exits the courtroom when a judge rules in his or her favor. I stood up to walk away, but that's when I heard LBJ's Texas drawl.

"Not good enough, McFadden," he admonished from the back. I hadn't even seen him come in. "I'm from Texas where we love our guns. But if we are to keep guns out of the hands of the criminal, out of the hands of the insane, and out of the hands of the irresponsible, then we must have licensing as well. If the criminal with a gun is to be tracked down quickly, then we must have registration in this country. The voices that blocked those safeguards when I was president were not the voices of an aroused nation. They were the voices of a powerful lobby, a gun lobby that prevailed. We must seek national gun licensing now."

"Whatever that lobby was in 1968," I responded, "in the past fifty years it has grown to become the most passionate, effective political organization of our time. Its members not only contribute but organize and vote to oppose any restriction, and its leadership strikes fear in the hearts of legislators. They have moved the dial on this issue so significantly that gun registry is not even remotely politically feasible, basic data collection on guns is nearly impossible, and politicians get run out of office for even deigning to oppose military weapons in the hands of civilians. The public is with us on an assault weapons ban, even if Congress isn't. That's where I can find the middle ground. And that fight alone will be costly enough."

As I walked away, I saw Matty and Tina waiting for me near my exit. "Well played, sir," said Matty with a fist bump. "You can do worse than having Big Daddy state publicly that he stands with you. He doesn't exactly dole that out every day."

"That may have been the greatest moment of my life right there," I replied.

"I don't know," remarked Tina, casting a wet blanket my way. "I just think we're all selling out on this. The kids that die every day on the streets of Chicago and Baltimore and every other major city in this country are not being killed by assault weapons. If you had any fight in you at all, you'd organize a party and a national movement to stand up to the NRA."

"Love you, Tina," I said with a wide smile as I closed the door behind me. She had a point, of course. She always does. I wasn't sure if I loved that about her or hated her for it. I think both.

Chapter Fifty-Four

August 11, 2018
Run It by Lincoln and Washington

Ten days following the school shooting at Father Damien High, I stepped to the podium at the front of the House Chamber. Rather than travel to one of the dozens of schools that had been turned into crime scenes by these various school shooters over the years, I wanted to come directly to Congress to make this heartfelt appeal on their own turf. Congressmen and women had been privately voicing support for our gun initiatives, but public endorsements were scarce.

I knew it would take every ounce of charisma and inspiration I could muster, and even then, my efforts might prove futile. But I just couldn't live with myself if I didn't lay it all on the line for this. I owed it to the country, to myself, and, perhaps most of all, to Beth Grimes.

Transcript of President McFadden's speech to the House of Representatives, August 11, 2018

Mr. Speaker, I come here today to challenge the House leadership to pass a very simple, very reasonable, very responsible, comprehensive assault weapons ban. It does not establish a national gun registry, take guns away from anyone, or impact standard handguns, rifles, or shotguns. It does prohibit the manufacture and sale of automatic and semiautomatic weapons, as well as high-capacity magazines. While this won't prevent all assault weapon crimes, our hope is that it will prevent or reduce the severity of some of them. We can no longer live with these terrible tragedies and justify them as merely the price of freedom.

The founders' experiences with the tyranny of the British Monarchy led them to construct a government whereby gun ownership, largely related to militias, was paramount. It's fair to say the impetus for this was to establish an additional check on the government. In fact, it seems that some of them even contemplated the idea that a revolution or uprising every generation or so was healthy. Today, the notion that a heavily armed citizenry can viably act as a safeguard against tyranny is outdated. We now are routinely forced to suffer the consequences inherent in making these killing machines available for general purchase. Every two or three months, another community is torn upside down by someone who has lost all hope and seeks to lash out at society in the most outrageous manner possible. Our freedom to own firearms, which is rooted in our Bill of Rights, is now in conflict with our duty to safeguard our children in our public schools. As with our other important constitutional rights, this right is subject to reasonable restrictions.

These measures I am proposing will not lead to a slippery slope whereby we will soon seek to eliminate all guns. Such an action would, indeed, be unconstitutional and would require no less than a constitutional amendment—a very high hurdle to clear. It is undeniable that the establishment of a right to bear arms gave rise to a national culture of gun ownership for hunting, self-defense, and personal safety that cannot and should not be tampered with. And the Supreme Court in the Heller decision really for the first time clarifies that this right to bear arms does exist unrelated to service in any militia. It is not, however, an absolute right that cannot be restricted when pitted against other legitimate and critical rights and goals like the overall safety and well-being of the population and our duty to protect children in public schools.

Poll after poll reveals that the citizens of this country overwhelmingly favor these measures. More importantly, common sense suggests that they could, indeed, have an impact—not necessarily in solving all of the nation's issues related to gun violence, but in lessening the impact of many of these mass shootings.

Put simply, this body has been too afraid of the NRA to act. I came here today to say that we can and should be better than that. Try to recall what exactly it was that prompted you to run for Congress in the first place. I'm certain it wasn't so you could sell your soul to the highest bidder in order to hold onto your seat. I'm not naive to the consequences of taking on the NRA. Yes, on this issue, it may exact serious political damage. But was your desire to represent this country ever solely about you? If you're a Republican, go back and read the words of your patron saint—the great Ronald Reagan. He supported all the measures contained in these proposals, and he was an NRA member and ardent defender of the Second Amendment. If you're worried about the backlash from the Far Right, cloak yourself in the words of the Gipper, and see if they still oppose you.

If you intend to oppose these measures or prevent them from debate on the floor, I have a favor to ask. I encourage all of you to go home at the break and check in with the local grade school and high school in your home-town. Then ask yourself if you are able to sit in that first grade classroom—with children the same age as those who were savagely slaughtered in Sandy Hook with their teacher shielding their bodies—and explain to them how any eighteen-year-old should be permitted to walk into any gun shop and obtain an assault weapon.

Please join me, the vast majority of your fellow citizens, the American Medical Association, the International Association of Police Chiefs, and the American Federation of Teachers, in finally taking some action as a first step to combatting this deplorable and uniquely American predicament.

***

Murph and I had blocked out the rest of the day to make phone calls to lobby Congress to get something meaningful started in the legislative process. The national outcry following the shooting had been furious, but the national conversation was starting to wane. I had hoped my impassioned plea on the House floor would be the impetus to kick-start a call to action.

Our first three calls met fierce resistance, which really got my Irish up. With two years in office under my belt, I found that my tolerance for frustration was now virtually nonexistent.

Murph flipped to the next page of phone numbers. "Don't lose hope," she implored me. "I started with some of the more challenging ones. Let's get a few wins under our belt then return to that first page."

"A few wins? At this point, I'd settle for anything that wasn't an embarrassing blowout."

Cathy connected us with Congressman Metcalf, a Democrat from Ohio. He occupied a swing district that had seen two mass shootings in the past two years, both involving AR-15s. If we had any chance at all of generating a groundswell of support for this effort, the line of congresspeople behind us would certainly have to begin with people like him. Unfortunately, his first words were not encouraging.

"I know why you're calling."

"Of course you do," I replied. "And you know as well as I do that this stuff has gone on long enough. It's time we do something about it."

"Before you get too far here, let me cut to the chase. I can't be with you on this. I can't touch it."

"How can you possibly say that?" I was incredulous. "Your district is the poster child for this bill. We all know this is a no-brainer."

"But it won't make a dent in the gun problem. Assault weapons account for less than 3 percent of gun-related murders. Handguns are the culprit, and you're not seeking to ban them."

"No one is saying this will solve the entire gun problem. But is that 3 percent too little to care about? If it prevents or lessens just one of these mass shootings that ruin lives and destroy communities, isn't that alone worth it? I'm sorry, Congressman, but to say you oppose it just because it doesn't solve *all* gun-related issues is just a cop-out."

"I've got a brutal election ahead of me, and, the truth is, if I push this with you, I'll lose votes—it's as simple as that. On the other hand, if I pass on this, in all likelihood it'll never come up for a vote anyway, and I'll be no worse off than I am now."

"*Really*?! Is that what all this is about? Is your endgame and ultimate goal just to preserve your seat? Is that why you ran for office place?"

"Oh that's mighty easy for you to say. You managed to waltz into that job without ever taking any positions. You just wait until you try to get reelected. I'll call you back then, and we'll look through all the issues and see if every stance you've taken is principled and unrelated to your own political survival."

"I'm not naive to political realities. I'm just saying if you can't stand up and be a part of the solution on an issue that has impacted your own district as much or more than any other in the country, then what's the point of being a politician anyway? I'm sorry. I thought you were better than that. You had a real chance to lead on an issue that's starting to define this nation."

"You're sure talking a good game here. But mark my words, your high and mighty rhetoric will crumble as soon as your own consultants try to chart your path to reelection. I don't envy them, by the way. Good luck with that."

"If you think I'm here to sell out my principles, you obviously aren't paying attention. I seem to be setting new records for presidential struggles, and it's not because I'm compromising on what I believe is best for the country. I'll look forward to your call during my reelection campaign. Have a good day, Congressman."

Murph looked a bit alarmed. "Alright, let's break for a while. Perhaps a year or more." She smiled and said, "We may be in a bit more trouble here than I imagined."

"If Metcalf is a hard sell," I said, "this is gonna be a chore."

"I'm afraid you'll expend too much political capital on this, and at the end of the day, it will go down in flames. The NRA has made it clear to all Republicans that they'll fund their primary opponents if any of them sign on to this."

"We knew that going in," I reminded Murph.

"But if we can't even get someone like Metcalf on board—"

"Then what's the good of having political capital at all if you can't spend it on something like this!"

"Well sure . . . you can spend it all and die on this hill. That's certainly an option. Or you can save it and live to fight another day for another valuable cause near and dear to your heart."

"I'm starting to wonder what's the point of fighting another day within this broken system. Rather than pick a fight and fail on issue after issue, we've gotta think bigger. We've got to bring about a fundamental change in the system itself. At this point, I really have nothing left to lose, right?"

"That sounds terrific in principle," Murph agreed. "But what does it really mean? What can you possibly do to transform the system or bring about that kind of change?"

I stood up, turned, and stared out the window. "There's gotta be people smarter than me and more savvy at this that can answer that for me."

Murph had no answers. She looked up at the portraits of Washington and Lincoln on the wall. "If only you could run this by those gentlemen."

"Yes," I said, brightening up a bit. "If only there were a way to do that. Great suggestion, Murph."

Chapter Fifty-Five

August 11, 2018
Peaceful Warrior

I entered my favorite saloon and couldn't believe my eyes. The tables that usually filled the middle of the room had all given way to exercise mats, and more than two dozen of my predecessors were struggling mightily to keep up with Mary Ann, Ginger, and Haskell, out in front attempting to lead the group in a yoga session. As far as yoga goes, it was not the most ambitious program, but many of these gentlemen were clearly out of their element.

I took a seat next to Sheels, who was at a table with Clinton, FDR, Obama, and Truman, watching this fiasco and laughing hysterically.

"Get a load of Taft over there in the corner," said Clinton. We watched Taft struggling mightily to maintain his balance. The table erupted in laughter.

"What the hell is going on?" I asked.

"For months, they've all been promising the ladies they would do this with them. The truth is, I think most of these guys just wanted a chance to check out the waitresses in their yoga outfits."

Every thirty seconds or so, Ginger called out another yoga pose. "Happy baby....Butterfly....Cow face....Half lord of the fishes."

I looked over and saw several of the men sitting up motionless on their mats simply ogling Mary Ann and Ginger before them. Creepy. Or perhaps a few were gazing at Haskell. Some of them seemed to be holding their own—Otter appeared to be in really good shape. Teddy Roosevelt was giving it a valiant effort. It looked like he thought it was a competition – one that he was winning. JFK struggled to keep up amidst some back pain.

Most of the older guys were in their street clothes and hadn't even removed their hard shoes. Lincoln was certainly not the most limber of these gentlemen, but God love him for trying. Grant had a tumbler of whiskey on the mat right next to him and a stogie in his mouth. I don't know much about yoga, but I've gotta think that's a novel approach to the discipline. Not sure you see that every day. *Classic! Only in the Saloon.*

I turned to Obama and said, "You seem to be in pretty good shape. Why aren't you out there?"

"Oh, I'm way smarter than that," he answered, breaking into a big smile. "I tend to stay in my lane . . . That's clearly well outside my lane."

"I think it's safe to say it's a good bit outside those fellas' lanes as well," added Clinton.

Moments later the yoga session ended and we were joined by half a dozen or so of the participants. For reasons that escaped me, they all seemed rather proud of themselves. Kennedy, sporting a Harvard sweatshirt, called out to me as they approached.

"How is our resident Fighting Irishman? You couldn't stoop to a bit of exercise with the boys out there tonight?"

I laughed. "Is that what you call that display we've been watching?"

Kennedy, Carter, Reagan, Grant, Eisenhower, and Lincoln settled in around us.

"I have always maintained that *Fighting Irish* is a demeaning and derogatory term," said Carter, "and that Notre Dame of all places should go the way of the Stanford Indians and the St. John's Redmen and move forward."

"Well, gentlemen," added Obama, "we happen to have the Gipper right here. We should get his thoughts on it."

"You know," responded Reagan, "that may be the role for which I am best remembered. That or *Bedtime for Bonzo*." That drew a hearty laugh from all, but none as hard as Reagan himself. "I was the Errol Flynn of B movies, you know." Reagan, noticing the blank looks on the faces of Grant and Lincoln, added, "McFadden here is a graduate of Notre Dame, and their sports teams are known as the Fighting Irish."

Carter shook his head. "Again, I've always felt that mascot reinforced an offensive stereotype about drunken, brawling Irishmen."

"As I understand it," replied Kennedy, "and correct me if I'm wrong, McFadden, the nickname derives from the Irish Brigade, a group of Irish immigrants from New York, who fought for the North in the Civil War. There's nothing offensive in that."

"Those fellows served the Union with great distinction," added Lincoln.

"That group was a force to be reckoned with," said Grant emphatically. "And they were a hard-drinking lot to boot. Their chaplain, Father Corby, was a Notre Dame alumnus who later became president of the university."

"I love that story!" I exclaimed. "I'm ashamed to say I didn't know it, but that's a perfect explanation for the nickname. I have no idea if that's why we are called that, but it makes perfect sense. There's a statue of Father Corby at Notre Dame, as well as a hall named after him there. Not to mention a great bar as well now that I think about it. Another world-class saloon."

"A statue depicting him blessing the troops before combat stands on the battlefield at Gettysburg as well," said Ike. "Mamie and I had a home near the battlefield."

"How about that?" I said. "The things you learn in this place."

"That's what we're here for, McFadden," added Kennedy.

I was there on this night for a specific reason, and it wasn't to learn about the Fighting Irish or watch Cleveland and Taft attempt a downward-facing dog pose. It might not have been the smoothest transition, but I needed to get to my objective for the evening. So I scooted my chair back from the table and scanned the entire group that surrounded our table. "I need your help, gentlemen."

"We are at your service, McFadden," replied FDR.

"I've got to figure a way to fix the enormous partisan divide in this country. The two main parties have each become more extreme as independents abandon them. They've gerrymandered the districts to ensure they'll continue to thrive, and partisan media outlets help fuel the divide and profit handsomely from it. On top of all that, special interests use their money to absolutely own half of Congress. Rather than simply try to do my best within the system, I'd love to devote my energy and attention to trying to bring about an entirely new political dynamic within the country—one that is not nearly so self-destructive."

I looked at them to see if what I was saying resonated at all. I continued, "I guess I was hoping you gentlemen might devote some time to helping me kick-start a process to bring about an entirely new political dynamic that builds up the country rather than dividing it. Without some sort of massive, monumental jolt to the system, I fear we may be the greatest threat to ourselves going forward."

FDR turned to Obama and Clinton. "Are you gentlemen familiar with this political dynamic he speaks of?"

"All too familiar, sir," responded Obama.

"I'm game, McFadden," FDR volunteered. "This group of political minds can devote some time and attention to this vexing predicament of yours—and of ours. I should think we'd be pleased to do so."

"Where on earth will we ever find the time?" Clinton quipped, trying to hold back a smile. He gestured toward a few of the presidents still attempting yoga, struggling to maintain a "peaceful warrior" pose. "Don't you think we're entirely too busy as it is?"

They all laughed. Laughter was always so easy to come by in this tavern. This entire scene in front of me was absolutely hilarious. But what I was requesting here was something much more elusive than humor. And it was something deadly serious.

Obama looked at me and gently nodded his head. "We hear you. I think we can put our heads together on this and give you the collective wisdom of this room. It may take a us a while, perhaps a good while, but as President Roosevelt suggested, we would be happy to do it. And besides, it would be good for us."

"Well, let me tell you, it would be great for me, and, I suspect, great for this country as well." I scanned the entire table. "And that would mean the world to me, gentlemen."

"We'll commence work on this right away," said Franklin Roosevelt. "Have patience, my boy, but if there's an answer to be produced in this room, we shall uncover it."

I wanted to hug every one of them, but I settled for fist bumps—awkward fist bumps, but I'll take it.

I never thought I'd experience something as incredible as drinking with every former leader in the history of this great country, but I suddenly had a feeling I was about to embark on something that would eclipse even that.

Chapter Fifty-Six

August 15, 2018
America's Role on the World Stage

We all enjoyed the flight back from Brussels. Too keyed up to sleep, I left Denyse in our suite at the front of the plane and walked back to the Senior Staff Room where Jed was briefing the six folks who'd made the trip on all the favorable media coverage we were getting back home. The staff was sprawled out all over this surprisingly spacious conference room. This style of travel never gets old.

We needed the positive coverage desperately. It was a godsend. To be honest, I found it therapeutic to get away from the Beltway for a few days. Besides, I felt a tremendous sense of accomplishment in the spirit of collaboration we were met with and the work we'd accomplished. One of the first things we had done as an administration was appoint a task force to determine the full extent of Russia's attempt to interfere with the 2016 election. After just a few months, we appealed to the NATO alliance to tackle this jointly because evidence came to light that the Russians had significantly tampered with elections not only in the United States but in more than a dozen European countries. The task force became international. With this two-day summit, we successfully began expanding NATO's core mission to prioritize cybersecurity, specifically interference with elections and attacks on the digital infrastructure of other countries. An international team led by a collection of Silicon Valley security experts presented to the NATO partners. They outlined a comprehensive approach to identifying and countering threats as well as obtaining buy-ins from the world's premier tech and media companies to ferret out election hacking, false and misleading social media campaigns, bot farms, and other common means the Russians and others employed to sow division and impact the electorate.

It was all smiles as I entered the Senior Staff Room.

Jed greeted me first. "It's all positive back home. Great job. Rave reviews from both the liberal and conservative media."

"Maybe we should have just stayed over there," I responded.

"That's the lesson here, Boss," said Drake. "Murph says Congress is lining up behind you on this like nothing you've ever embraced."

***

I entered the Saloon that night amidst no shortage of activity. A crooner was slaying it with a playlist from the Big Band Era. Very Sinatra-like. Nothing wrong with that. I sauntered up to the bar. Before I could get Ginger's attention, Thomas Jefferson approached me.

"Please sir," he said in a very serious and formal manner, "tell me the very latest in communications, travel, and technology."

"Holy cow!" I exclaimed, taken aback. "Where do I even begin?"

As I thought for a second, Ginger jumped in. "What can I get you, Mr. President?"

"Any chance you guys have a Sierra Nevada?"

"Don't insult me like that! Of course we do," she said, hustling over to the impressive bank of taps.

"How much do you know?" I asked Jefferson. "Where did you leave off?"

"President Obama kept me up-to-date throughout his term, but I know of nothing since then."

"Wow, this is all very fascinating to me," I said. "Do you know what a drone is?" I asked.

"Yes," he answered. "Obama gave us a splendid talk about them a few years ago."

"Well," I said, "some companies are investing heavily in them as a means of delivering goods directly to homes or businesses. Additionally, I have seen many articles lately speculating that drones will solve our traffic issues and that people will eventually travel primarily by drone. Do you know about traffic?"

"Yes, I do," he said with a laugh. "We had some traffic in Williamsburg and Richmond."

"With all due respect, sir, I think you have no idea—"

"President Nixon gave a talk about what he called the energy crisis and the long lines to purchase gasoline and the traffic that ensued."

Presidential Spirits

"OK . . . so with drones in three-dimensional space, there would be infinitely more potential routes to take to and from work."

At that moment I noticed Ginger and Matty way down at the other end of the bar set my beer on a drone, which then elevated directly up in midair before taking a flight around the entire main room of the Saloon before landing perfectly on the bar directly in front of me. All that was mind-blowing for me to see. I can't imagine what was going through the mind of a guy who hailed from the eighteenth century. Within moments, everyone in the bar had congregated around us.

The questions came fast and furious. I saw Matty and Ginger out of the corner of my eye dying laughing.

"This, my friends, is called a drone," I said, knowing full well my expertise in this particular field was not going to run much deeper than that.

I struggled to find my next words with no idea where I was going to start or finish. I'm quite certain I had a pained look on my face.

To my great embarrassment and also my great delight, Thomas Jefferson stepped in to save the day. "This is an unmanned, aerial vehicle that is controlled remotely through the use of onboard sensors and radio wave technology on the electromagnetic spectrum. Four rotors installed on the drone consist of spinning blades and provide propulsion. The rotors push down on the air, which, in turn, propels the rotor upward into the air and back and forth. Through these rotors it can hover, climb, or descend."

"You took the words right out of my mouth, Mr. J," I said with a big smile. Otter had convinced Madison and Monroe to call him that, and, for some reason, in this moment I felt I could do so as well. "I see you *have* kept abreast of the latest technology."

"Indeed," responded Jefferson. "Nature intended me for the tranquil pursuits of science by rendering them my supreme delight."

At that I just smiled and shook my head. I got such a kick out of talking with these guys. Especially him.

Matt maneuvered the drone out over the main floor of the Saloon, where it followed Mary Ann, hovering right over her head as she made her rounds. She laughed out loud when she realized they were messing with her, then she hilariously managed to ignore this obnoxious thing suspended in midair just a few feet above her, remarkably maintaining her cheery disposition while continuing to take drink orders. I thought to myself that neither Tina nor Ginger would have been nearly as forgiving. Matt clearly chooses his foils wisely.

The presidents all followed the drone, leaving me alone again with Jefferson.

"Please, McFadden, I'd care to know much more," he asked me. "Tell me the latest in medicine. Are we closer to a cure for cancer? What new fossils have been discovered recently? Have we learned more about the origin of man?"

I needed to extricate myself from this conversation in the most inconspicuous way possible. These questions were not exactly in my wheelhouse. "Can we discuss this later?" I asked. "I'm hoping to organize a bit of a group discussion tonight."

"Yes, of course, Mr. President," he responded. "But let us reconvene on these matters soon. I shall be eager to hear."

Needless to say, I did not share in his eagerness for that conversation. Of course, I could tell him about the very latest *Jurassic Park* movie, but somehow I didn't think that would exactly suffice. Historians may have gotten his relationship with Sally Hemings wrong for 200 years, but they certainly nailed his intellectual curiosity. I did enjoy getting to know him, though. He reminded me a lot of my dad. The intellectual curiosity part, not the Sally part. At least not as far as I know.

I then found Washington and asked if he could arrange to have the group assembled to talk a bit about foreign policy. It was a discussion we had been intending to have for months. Within minutes, Washington was on it.

"Gentlemen," shouted Washington, commanding the attention of the room. "As you know, President McFadden has been requesting that we assemble to discuss foreign affairs. I ask you kindly to please gather for this important discussion."

The music stopped, and slowly all the presidents gathered, finding seats near the large mahogany table in the center of this impressive Saloon, where Washington and I and many of the others were already seated. Many paused at the bar to grab one or more drinks on their way. Minutes later, Washington looked over at me, nodded, and said, "You may proceed, McFadden."

"Thank you, General, and thanks to all of you. I just returned from a NATO summit. I know many of you attended such summits through the years. Currently, we are tackling the issue of cybersecurity, election meddling, and attempts to sow discord in other countries through social media campaigns. Russia is the main culprit. Our intelligence officials have concluded that the Russians waged a comprehensive cyber warfare campaign to interfere with the 2016 presidential election and create chaos and division throughout our country."

"Hardly the first time a foreign nation has sought to interfere with our elections," responded Nixon.

"It happened in my first election," added Adams. He then looked at Washington and Jefferson.

"I view that tale to be greatly exaggerated," responded Jefferson.

"On the contrary, the French openly favored my friend, Mr. Jefferson," replied Adams. "The French Minister to the United States, Pierre Auguste Adet, publicly disparaged the Federalists and authored notes for publication in our newspapers. In addition, France terminated relations with the United States and implied that failure to elect Jefferson might result in a state of war. Fortunately, this only served to embolden my support."

"I warned the nation in my Farewell Address of the dangers of foreign entanglements," said Washington. "My comments were in part motivated by France's attempts to intervene in that election."

"Might I remind my fellow presidents," added Jefferson, "that without the valiant assistance of the French—and their money—we would still be a part of the British Empire."

"In all matters of foreign affairs," responded Washington, "I advised that it is unwise to implicate ourselves in the ordinary vicissitudes of Europe's politics or the ordinary combinations and collisions of her friendships or enmities. Our detached and distant situation invited and enabled us to pursue a different course. A firm policy of neutrality is preferable."

"Whether or not the French get a pass in the election of 1796 for their vital role in support of our Revolution," said Reagan, "I hardly think the same should apply to the Russians in 2016."

"It is only as a result of your efforts, President Reagan," I said, "that the country is now merely Russia and not the Soviet Union."

"Thank you very much," replied Reagan, "but rather than me, it was our collective strength: our military, our system of government, our people, our allies. Peace through strength. The Soviet Union ran against the tide of history by denying human freedom and human dignity to its citizens."

"We are familiar with the notion of peace through strength," replied Adams. "Strengthening our military and creating a permanent army and navy in my time helped us avoid a war that would have ruined us."

"I concur," added Teddy Roosevelt. "As many of you know, my foreign policy approach was to 'speak softly and carry a big stick,' with an emphasis on the big stick.'"

"When did you ever, even one day in your life, speak softly?" FDR asked incredulously, eliciting laughter from all. That only encouraged Franklin to dig even deeper. "Eleanor remains convinced that you believed yourself to be the bride when you escorted her down the aisle at our wedding." More laughter.

"Believe me, Franklin," Teddy continued, "I did my damnedest on that short walk to persuade her to turn around and flee while she still could. I'm certain that with another ten feet of aisle, I would have had her convinced. Had you selected a large church for the wedding, you'd certainly be single still today!"

The room was clearly very entertained by the banter between these distant cousins.

"I'm proud that she kept her own name," Teddy added. "Ahead of her time, that girl. Our Miss Tina here would be quite proud of her too."

Tina, Ginger, and Haskell had just appeared with multiple bottles of Silver Oak cabernet. "Oh, we love Eleanor, gentlemen," said Tina, thrilled at the shout-out and what she clearly considered an invitation to join the conversation. "Some might argue she should be the first woman added to this old men's club. I'll have to bring that up with Mr. Sheels."

Reagan, now standing next to the servers, addressed the crowd. "To Mr. Jefferson and all you other lovers of French wines, your true education as a wine connoisseur begins today. This is some of California's finest. You would love the Napa Valley. As McFadden has been challenging us all to abandon our prejudices and shed our personal biases, I implore you to do the same as you indulge in this rare treat from what is truly God's country."

After a few sips, Jefferson responded. "Thank you very much, President Reagan. Certainly an adequate selection. Very adequate, in fact. An ideal food wine. Perhaps an early drinking vintage." Even someone like myself who happily knows very little about wine and abhors wine snobs could see that Jefferson was clearly slighting California wine.

Presidential Spirits

Seeing this, Ginger looked at Haskell and said, "Go tell Big Time I think we're gonna need a lot more wine tonight. All top shelf. The very best of both France and California. I think I know what's about to happen here. It's game on."

As amused as I was by all of this, I knew where it was going and I needed to bring it back to what I wanted to hear. I had been dying to engage them all on their view of America's role on the world stage since that first night hearing Ike detailing the D-Day invasion to the generals. "Gentlemen," I said in a booming voice, "please indulge me a bit more regarding American foreign policy. I'm afraid we didn't even scratch the surface."

The room settled down and their body language suggested that they, indeed, were willing to reengage on it. "OK, so where were we?" I asked.

Truman spoke up. "Add my name to the peace through strength crowd," he said. "The strength displayed by our military, including the use of the atomic bomb, brought about peace. The atom bomb was no great decision. There were more people killed by firebombs in Tokyo than dropping of the atomic bombs accounted for. It was merely another weapon in the arsenal of righteousness. The dropping of the bombs stopped the war, saving millions of lives. The fighting in the Pacific was brutal and costly. The planned invasion of Japan, Operation Downfall, would have been barbarous with unprecedented casualties on both sides. I think its usage not only brought about an immediate end to the war but has to this day acted as a deterrent to help preserve peace in the world."

The room was awkwardly silent, and I felt the need to facilitate a bit.

"We had certainly moved away from Washington's neutrality proclamation and isolationism by then," I said.

"You think?" Clinton deadpanned.

Jefferson, turning his attention from wine to foreign relations, stated, "In my time, we sought to establish an empire for liberty as she has never surveyed since the creation; to rival and surpass the British Empire. We endeavored to achieve that by means of our example to others, through our expansion westward and to the north, and in our foreign intervention. I am persuaded no constitution was ever before so well calculated as ours for extensive empire and self-government, and to make barbarism disappear from the earth."

"I find your notion of an empire for liberty so appealing, Mr. Jefferson,"

275

added John Kennedy, "reminiscent of John Winthrop, who from the tiny ship *Arbella* traveling to the New World in 1630, told his shipmates there shall be a city on a hill with the eyes of all people upon it. America can and should serve as a beacon of light for other nations. For what Pericles said to the Athenians has long been true of our great American experiment: 'We do not imitate—for we are a model to others.'"

"So well stated, President Kennedy," said Ronald Reagan. "I invoked that same Winthrop image of a city on a hill often—a shining city whose powerful lights guide freedom-loving people everywhere. The lady in the harbor faces outward toward the rest of the world. That is no accident."

"Mr. Jefferson," Kennedy continued, "I believe you and your colleagues did, in fact, create that empire for liberty you dreamed of."

"You have that right, Jack," said Reagan. "Some these days would use the term *American exceptionalism* as an expression of something dangerous or arrogant. But ever since this grand American miracle commenced, no nation has liberated more people, provided more hope, elevated living standards higher, or stood as a greater force for good in the world than America. I would not shy away from that term but embrace it."

"May I contribute something, President Reagan?" asked James Monroe.

"By all means, sir. Please do," Reagan replied.

Monroe stood up to address the crowd. He stood perhaps a bit over six feet tall, a sharp-looking gentleman with broad shoulders and a distinctive, angular sort of face. He also had a personal charm and way about him that endeared him to others, certainly to me.

Monroe paused momentarily before speaking. He had the full attention of the room. "Mr. Adams and I—the younger Mr. Adams, John Quincy Adams, my secretary of state—adopted a more aggressive posture in relations with foreign nations, particularly in the Americas. We sought to make the New World safe for liberty and our republican system of government. I declared that the American continents, by the free and independent condition which they had assumed and maintained, were no longer to be considered as subjects for future colonization by any European powers. Henceforth, any act to establish new colonies in our hemisphere would be considered as the manifestation of an unfriendly disposition toward the United States. We also publicly supported and formally recognized the independent republics in South America who were seeking liberty."

Presidential Spirits

"I had something to contribute to that effort, President Monroe," Andrew Jackson said, quite proudly.

"Indeed you did, General Jackson," Monroe concurred, "prompting Spain to finally agree to give up Florida."

"Skillful diplomacy evidently runs in the Adams family," Lincoln added. "I commissioned the services of yet another member of the illustrious Adams clan, Charles Francis Adams, to help ensure that Britain would not officially recognize the Confederacy or intervene on its behalf. That foreign alliance proved critical."

Teddy Roosevelt then stood and addressed the group in a loud voice. "As we all know, we tussled mightily with Spain in my time as vice president. Our victory in that war added immensely to our sphere of influence. When I took over as president, America had become an unquestioned international power. Inherent in that profile was a responsibility to act accordingly. We needed to move beyond the isolationist policies of the previous century. As the Monroe Doctrine prohibited European nations from interfering in Latin America, we resolved to preserve the peace by exercising international police power in Latin America as well, including intervention by force if necessary."

Roosevelt clearly commanded the room as well as any of these men. One of the great pleasures this Saloon afforded me was the ability to see this passionate, bundle of rock-solid energy speak. I got such a kick out of him.

He continued, "Our new elevated role on the world stage led to me to negotiate an end to the war between Russia and Japan."

"For which you rightfully won a Nobel Peace Prize," added Barack Obama.

"Yes, sir!" responded Roosevelt. "In that time we also added the Panama Canal. I took the isthmus, started the canal, and then left Congress not to debate the canal but to debate me. All these actions solidified the United States even more as a world power. This young giant of a nation now stood on this continent clasping the crest of an ocean in either hand. Our country, glorious in youth and strength, looked upon the future with the eager eyes of a strong man about to run a race."

I looked around, wondering if everyone else was as inspired as I was. A quick glance across the room confirmed that they were. *My Gosh,* I thought, *I wish every American could experience what I was seeing.* I just love the image TR painted of America as a vibrant young man before a race.

I jumped in, proudly wearing my facilitator hat. "That strong young man soon found himself smack in the middle of a couple of very challenging races."

"Quite obviously, gentlemen, one such challenge occurred during my presidency," recalled Woodrow Wilson. "We were called upon to send our boys overseas to make the world safe for democracy. We entered the war with Germany with no selfish ends to serve. We desired no conquest, no dominion. We sought no indemnities for ourselves, no material compensation for the sacrifices we freely made. Those Americans gave the greatest of all gifts, the gift of life and the gift of spirit, for the cause of humanity and mankind."

"Elsewhere," Wilson continued, "we intervened frequently in the affairs of Latin America. I was determined to teach South American republics to elect good men."

"And how did that work out for you?" Kennedy asked with a bit of a knowing smile.

"Next question," answered Wilson, prompting laughter throughout the room. "I also spent six months in Europe negotiating the war peace and pushing for the formation of the League of Nations. Ironically that time away hampered my efforts to ensure its passage at home by two-thirds of the Senate in the proper form, and the United States did not join."

"Woodrow," said Franklin Roosevelt, speaking from his wheelchair, "I gave hundreds of speeches advocating for the League of Nations. But my support was less about the high ideals of the concept than the practical realities of failure to join. The world that confronted both you and I certainly was a dangerous one. In my administration, we employed a Good Neighbor Policy to bring about friendly relations with Latin America. In my early years as president, America still had a strong isolationist sentiment from the bitter taste of the Great War.

"That of course dramatically changed with Pearl Harbor. I firmly believe, as I stated while I was president, that I presided over a generation that indeed had a rendezvous with destiny." Then with great emphasis, he added loudly, "Those boys of ours did nothing less than save the world!"

"Hear! Hear!" Cheers erupted and applause spread throughout the room, which FDR allowed to grow. He looked very different than the images

I'd seen in history books. He appeared to be a much larger man, and his blue eyes had been obviously been well hidden by those black and white photos.

FDR continued to address the room, "As the war in Europe drew to a close, and I met with Churchill and Stalin to negotiate the postwar world peace, it became clear that political conditions thousands of miles away could no longer be avoided by this great nation. The world was becoming smaller—smaller every year. The United States exerted tremendous influence in the cause of peace throughout the world. We formed the United Nations, which would require strong leadership by the United States if it was to prevent another war, as the League of Nations had failed to do."

FDR then looked over at Washington. "With all deference to President Washington's missive to avoid foreign entanglements," he said, "in this version of the world order, we now believe the United States must continue to exert its influence, but only if we are willing to share in the responsibility for keeping the peace. It will be our own tragic loss, I think, if we were to shirk that responsibility." More applause followed.

"Indeed, it is a different world, gentlemen," conceded Washington.

"That influence must be exerted as much at the diplomatic table as in the stockpiles of weapons," cautioned Eisenhower. "For going forward, the United States and, indeed, the world must learn how to compose differences not with arms, but with intellect and decent purpose." The great significance of the unlikely source of this particular message was not lost on any of us.

Ike continued, "In the councils of government, we must guard against the acquisition of unwarranted influence, whether sought or unsought, by the military industrial complex. The potential for the disastrous rise of misplaced power exists, and will persist, and can be exacerbated by stoking the worst fears of the people. We must never let the weight of this combination endanger our liberties or democratic processes."

That seemed to get a rise out of Richard Nixon, who then said, "I believe my 1960 opponent stoked some of those worst fears in playing the missile gap card over and over. As we all know, there was no missile gap. And it cost me the presidency."

All eyes looked to Kennedy to see how he would respond.

Jimmy Carter jumped in. "Are you sure you want to be the one, Dick, to be calling out election dirty tricks?"

"Gentlemen," cautioned Washington, "civility please."

279

Truman got us back on track. "Ike," he said, "I believe that NATO is a terrific example of the U.S. exerting its considerable influence at the diplomatic table with intellect and decent purpose. During my presidency, we constructed NATO along with eleven of our staunchest allies to establish freedom from aggression and from the use of force in the North Atlantic community, but we were also striving to promote and preserve peace throughout the world."

"Our alliance with our NATO partners," Obama proudly added, "has been a cornerstone of U.S. foreign policy now for nearly seventy years now, in good times and in bad and through presidents of both parties. Standing together, shoulder to shoulder, we rebuilt Europe from the ruins of war, prevailed in a long Cold War, welcomed new European democracies into our ranks, and brought peace to the Balkans."

Then, looking at Truman, Obama added, "Well done, Mr. President."

"My favorite moment in this esteemed drinking establishment," pronounced Kennedy, "was learning from the elder Mr. Bush the news of the fall of the Berlin Wall followed by the reunification of Germany, the tumbling of the Soviet Union, and the establishment of democracies in Eastern Europe. When I traveled to West Berlin in 1963 to give a speech in front of nearly a half a million Berliners, those wishes were merely all-too-distant dreams. I made it clear on that afternoon to Khrushchev and all the world that the people of Berlin would not face this communist threat alone."

The room vigorously applauded Kennedy's words, He continued, "In my time as president, General Washington, we became embroiled in a foreign entanglement of the highest magnitude. For thirteen days in October of 1962, the world stood on the brink of nuclear peril. At that moment, sir, it was clear that America stood unequivocally on the side of liberty, for which we would indeed pay any price."

"In that moment, President Kennedy," added Obama with a good bit of passion in his voice, "the world inched closer to the brink of nuclear disaster than it ever had before. Many hawks were advising you to take aggressive military action. Your steady hand in guiding this ship of state toward a peaceful resolution will long be remembered in the annals of human history."

Obama's statement hung in the air. What a moment. I think people were reluctant to follow that. I was enjoying this discussion immensely. I looked up at the bar and saw that all the servers and bartenders were spellbound—which is telling since they serve these folks every day and can't really be starstruck. I'm guessing by their reaction that these types of discussions were rare.

As I glanced around the rest of the room, I noticed something else very telling: Sheels had come out of his office and was very nonchalantly sitting in a booth away from us all, partially hidden, but well within earshot. Of course, he was. What a scene this was, indeed.

LBJ broke the silence, "I feel compelled to say my piece here before y'all," he said. "I reckon now is as good a time as any. I regret that mistakes made with our involvement in Vietnam completely overshadow the success of our Great Society. To begin with, Jack should have had more than 18,000 military advisors over there in the early 1960s. And then I made the situation worse by waiting eighteen months before putting our troops in. By then, the war was almost lost. Another mistake was not instituting media censorship—not to cover up mistakes, but to prevent the other side from knowing what we were going to do next. My God, you can't fight a war by watching it every night on television."

That, of course, provoked a response from John Kennedy. "In the final analysis, Lyndon, it should have been their war. The people of Vietnam. They are the ones who should have had to win it or lose it. We could help them; we could give them equipment; we could send our men out there as advisors, but in the end, they were the ones who would have to win it—the people of Vietnam themselves—against the Communists."

"The Vietnam War's most damaging impact," explained Nixon, "was upon the psychology of the United States as a truly formidable world power. It left the United States so crippled psychologically that it was unable to defend its interests in the developing world—the battleground in the ongoing East-West conflict. It tarnished our ideals, weakened our spirit, crippled our will, and turned us into a giant and diplomatic dwarf in a world in which the steadfast exercise of American power was needed more than ever before. It enabled the Soviets to go on the offensive—adding Angola, Ethiopia, Mozambique, South Yemen, Nicaragua, Grenada, and Afghanistan to their empire."

A long silence fell upon the room following Nixon's words, but the facial expressions communicated loud and clear the lingering emotions and psychological scars of that war. Nixon had crystalized the impact internationally, while glossing over the colossal domestic impact of all the young lives lost, not to mention the other social costs—mental health, civil unrest, and distrust in government.

Sensing the mood of the room, Nixon jumped back in. "Gentlemen," he said, "things improved from that low point. Our trip to China in 1972 changed the world. I believed that a balance of power in the world was the best way to ensure lasting international peace. We chose to put aside China's communist ideology, which had kept our nations apart, and focus instead on our common interests. Neither of these two great nations wanted to dominate the world. We could both develop in our own ways on our own roads. I believe that type of balance of power is best. We must remember that the only time in the history of the world that we have had any extended periods of peace is when there has been a balance of power. It is when one nation becomes infinitely more powerful in relation to its potential competitor that the danger of war arises. Our opening to China reshaped the geopolitical map—adding a third pillar to the world order—altered the balance of the Cold War, and paved the way for China's new engagement with the world."

"Similarly, Dick," Reagan added, "through four summits or meetings and dozens of letters between Gorbachev and I, we were able to develop a relationship and a trust that allowed him the space to enact the reforms that ultimately led to the breakup of the Soviet Union. People may focus on our rhetoric, our military buildup, and the economic sanctions, but the relationship developed between the leaders should not be missed in that equation."

"This has been fascinating, gentlemen," I said, preferring to cut it off then rather than continue on through Iraq I and II, Afghanistan, al-Qaeda, and ISIS, each of which I am all too familiar with. "This has been far and away the single most impressive American foreign policy lecture I could ever asked for. I have a thousand follow-up questions, but I don't want to keep you here all night, and that's quite enough shop talk for you gentlemen for one evening. This has been unbelievably enlightening. I love the powerful images you've conjured up—Jefferson's empire of liberty, Teddy Roosevelt's young man, glorious in youth and strength, about to enter a race, and Reagan and Kennedy's retelling of John Winthrop's vision of a shining city on a hill. I'm afraid that powerful young man is no longer so young, and that great shining city has lost some of its luster. But this exercise tonight has unquestionably inspired me—my God, how can one not be inspired by all this rich history? I want to reestablish that American exceptionalism which seems to have developed a negative connotation. Like many of you, I believe America's best days lie ahead of us, but not without a considerable amount of vision, commitment, effort, and diplomacy. Thank you for this valuable discussion.

"I hope to reassemble you all as soon as you are ready to help me address the present state of political dysfunction in the country. But after tonight, I cannot help but think that my faith in this group is not misplaced."

"We have commenced a process," said Washington, "to pursue a productive solution for you and for our beloved county. We shall apprise you of our resolution in due time."

"I can't thank you all enough," I said, standing and addressing the whole crowd. "Take your time. There is nothing more important than getting this right."

I started to leave but turned back. "However, before I head back to the residence, can we get an update from Ginger on who is winning the present war between Napa Valley and France?"

Chapter Fifty-Seven

August 17, 2018
Promise Me This

My heart was as heavy as the Beast itself as we pulled up in front of the Up the Creek Bistro Wine Bar a little after noon. This place seemed just about as far away from the Beltway as one could possibly get. Sitting all by itself along the side of a desolate two-lane desert road, at first glance this unassuming old rustic eatery hardly seemed a place befitting one of the most celebrated senators in our country's history. The motorcade and police escort that delivered us to this spot seemed a bit of overkill. So did the Secret Service agents positioned both inside and out. Not a whole lot of civilization around us. There couldn't have been more than a half dozen cars parked in the dirt lot out front.

A gentleman came out to greet me with a broad smile as I approached the front door. "Pleased to have you here, Mr. President. Welcome to Cornville!"

"It's so great to be here! Is this restaurant yours?"

"Yes, I'm Mario—one of the owners."

"It is a real pleasure meeting you, Mario. My buddy raves about this place you have here."

"That's great to hear. People don't make a fuss about him here. I think he likes that. We just enjoy having him around—and all those who come to visit him. We've had a number of senators and a few generals, but no presidents…until now."

Mario led me inside. I instantly loved the place. Had the feel of a very nice desert cabin. Chestnut-brown-stained wood columns framed huge windows that extended from floor to ceiling, nicely displaying the views of Oak Creek and the Verde Valley. Cornville, Arizona. This was navy brat John McCain's adopted hometown.

Mario led me to a corner table where the vice president sat alone reading Ron Chernow's biography of Ulysses S. Grant.

"I see you're reading up on your new drinking buddy."

McCain looked up and instantly set the book down, discarded his glasses, and struggled a bit to stand and give me a hug. "Have you read this yet?" he asked.

"I wish I had the time."

"You really should. Of course, why bother reading about the guy when you can just venture upstairs and have a whiskey with him."

I sat down across from him and could see a discernible difference in his health and appearance from the last time I saw him just a few weeks before in Washington. I knew ahead of time that this would very likely be goodbye, but seeing him this way was even more heartbreaking than I had imagined.

"I love your little corner of the world, here, Senator."

"Cindy and I have grown quite fond of it."

"Is there anything I can do for you, Senator?"

"You have done quite enough. That party in the Saloon you got me invited to had to be the most glorious experience of my life. I don't know how you manage to ever leave that place. I'd be tempted to spend every night up there!" He looked at me and shook his head. "Hard to believe you'd fly all this way to see me when you could just walk upstairs and be with them."

"That's a great point. And the waitresses up there are a kick too."

"I was talking about the waitresses."

I loved his sense of humor as much as I loved everything else about him. It helped me at this moment especially. How telling that he was coming to my aid at a time like this. His expression grew more serious. "Actually, I do have one request of you."

"Anything. Just name it."

"Really? Anything?"

"Of course."

"Hold that thought. I'll let you know what it is before we're done here today."

Another gentleman approached the table. "Jim, come on over," McCain said as he motioned to him. "Meet the leader of the free world."

I stood up to shake his hand.

"Jim O'Meally," he said. "Such a pleasure to have you here. I'm the piano man, a co-owner of this place, and the main entertainment."

"He plays a mean piano, McFadden."

McCain and I spent the next glorious hour talking nonstop, covering the most eclectic collection of topics imaginable—from Napoleon to Buddhism to the Arizona Diamondbacks to the mating habits of the California condor. All the while, McCain was barking out a list of equally random song requests to his buddy Jim on the piano, who was all too willing to oblige. McCain provided vocals on "Some Enchanted Evening," and I joined him for "Danny Boy." Needless to say, we didn't impress anybody. Neither one of us had a drop of alcohol, but any observer would've sworn we were half drunk.

For some reason, I just couldn't ask him about dying. I didn't have the heart—for him or for me. I think that's another one of those flaws of mine. Perhaps one of the bigger ones. But we were clearly having so much fun. For some inexplicable reason, McCain kept trying to get Jim to play something by ABBA, which Jim persistently refused, but each time he did so, McCain roared with laughter. I had no idea what was behind that, but it was still hilarious to me.

Eventually the discussion turned to more serious, pressing issues, but we blew right past the part about dying.

"Who are you thinking of replacing me with—as if anyone could ever really replace the likes of me?"

"No one could, of course. Ever. That goes without saying."

"Thank you for those words. However, I'm convinced both you and Cindy will have replacements all moved in before my first memorial service has begun."

I laughed. I think that was the appropriate response. It was awkward for me. I made it that way, not him.

"That will be a challenge, to be sure," I replied. "I would need a moderate, or at the very least, someone with a rep for crossing the aisle. And I don't think one would give up a seat to serve a president without a party. I would likely approach someone like Leon Panetta. What do you think of that?"

"A fine choice."

"He actually helped lead me to you in the first place."

"Great man. He certainly fits your 'country first' mantra. Worked well for presidents of both parties. Respected by all. Perhaps he would even warrant you undergoing another colonoscopy."

I laughed. "No way, baby. That is a rare form of human sacrifice I endured only for you, my friend."

"What advice do you have for me?" I asked.

"In life or in politics?"

"Life first."

"With all due respect, my friend, you need no advice from me in that department. I see your devotion to your wife and kids. You are a great husband and father. And a great friend. You are also the most genuine person I know—which serves as a fault in politics but speaks so well of you in life. And that matters more. Same goes for your honesty. That doesn't help you in this business, either. You are clearly motivated to bring about a better life for others. No sir, you need no advice from me on life.

"Politics will present a much greater challenge for you. To this point you haven't compromised on your core values. Maintaining that standard will get increasingly difficult in the months ahead, I'm afraid to say. Your campaign for reelection will be brutal. God I wish I could be here for it. You know how I love a good fight for a righteous cause. And I love the political ground you have staked out."

I did not respond, opting just to sit back and take it all in.

He continued, his passion increasing with every sentence. "We've got to fix this, Danny. *You* have to fix it. In the history of this country, we've always had a leader rise to the occasion in those moments of greatest peril. We've always managed to have someone emerge to demonstrate powerful leadership in such moments. It just so happens that the threat at this moment comes from within. And it's just as dangerous as any we have encountered before. It may not completely destroy America, but it will undoubtedly diminish it. It already has. Whether it's our national debt, our lack of coherent immigration policies, the simmering racism and bigotry that persists, or any other critical issue of national importance, our deep national division and political dysfunction renders us incapable of governing effectively. And, worst of all, it will forever erode our ability to stand on the world stage unabashedly as the chief advocate for liberty and all the freedoms we hold dear."

I wished somehow I was recording this. I knew that no matter how effectively I tried to recount this moment later, I would not be able to do it justice. This alone could inspire the country to get behind my crusade.

He wasn't finished. "You can be that person. Fate has put you here. No one else is better situated to pull this off. There is a nastiness in the country that wasn't here a decade or more ago, and it's only getting worse. It has to be fixed!

"You asked what you can do for me, Danny. This is the answer to what you can do for me. And not just me. Do it for your country . . . for your family . . . for the world."

He paused and looked directly into my eyes. "Promise me you'll heal this country."

"When I asked what I can do for you," I responded, "all I really meant was can I get you a martini or something."

He laughed long and hard. It was great to see him laugh.

"Of course I will—that's my answer. But you know, I'm not one to make promises I'm not certain I can keep. That's that genuineness about me you were just commending."

"That's not good enough," he said with a look of intensity that contrasted sharply with the mood he had worn since I walked in the door. "Promise me you will."

"Yes. I am trying."

"Promise me you'll not only try, but you'll succeed."

I knew I was not getting out of Cornville without a solemn promise. "I can do that," I said. "I will do that."

"Great. That's all I need. Just that." He laughed out loud again. It was a beautiful sight. He looked out the window at the scenery. "You like to talk about hills worth dying on. This is the mother of all those hills.

"Do not betray your values in the process. The pressure to do so will be intense—insurmountable at times—particularly without a party or an established base. But best to channel Polonius, 'To thine own self be true.' In watching you, however, something tells me you are quite familiar with that quote."

"OK. You got me. I'm up for the task. But I have no illusions about how achievable it is. The thought of pulling it off without your steady advice, support, and inspiration seems impossible. Without you, there is no one in DC I can turn to with the knowledge, experience, and political acumen to shepherd me through this and have my back."

"That, my friend, is where you are sorely mistaken."

"OK, smart guy. Name one person who fits that profile that I can trust, is accessible, and has the desire to help me see this through at any cost."

"I can do you better than that. I can name forty-four of them."

Chapter Fifty-Eight

August 25, 2018
Crying Hard for the Country

I took my seat at the head of the long table extending across the Roosevelt Room, right beneath a large painting of Teddy Roosevelt leading the Rough Riders from atop a rearing horse during the Spanish–American War. I knew I would need him at my back during this meeting, but even then, the two of us might still be outmatched.

I had guilted several members of the House and Senate Republican leadership to come over to explain in person where they had landed on our proposal for a broad federal ban on assault weapons, bump stocks and high capacity magazines. It had been three weeks since the horrific shooting in Mayton, Florida, and the story was fading from the news. I was deathly afraid that once more, despite the national outrage, no action would be taken.

Reading their faces gave me no encouragement. "Thank you for coming, gentlemen. I appreciate it very much."

All eyes turned to Senate Majority Leader Mitch McConnell.

"We are pleased to be invited to discuss this in person, Mr. President. But I don't want to waste your time. I'm not going to bring this up for debate unless we have sixty committed votes in favor of it."

"Well hold on a second, Senator," I replied. "I just got off the phone with your Republican colleague Senator Cornyn who said he felt there'd be 70 votes in favor of it. But when did the Senate decide there can't be debate on a bill until you have a filibuster-proof majority? If that's the case, what possible purpose can debate even serve? Surely you don't need to discussion for bills where passage is a fait accompli."

"I disagree with that assessment, sir. Senator Cornyn must have been talking about the House bill that addresses background checks and mental health. I'm certain that's what he was referencing."

"But you won't bring that up, either."

"Well, that one doesn't have a majority of Republican senators in favor of it."

"Wait, so even though it has seventy U.S. senators who favor it, you'll prevent even a discussion of it unless your party independently has a majority? Let me ask you this, Senator, why did you run for office in the first place? To serve your party or to serve your country?"

I wasn't screaming, but I'm certain my voice could be heard halfway down the hallway.

"With all due respect, Mr. President, I find that to be about as naive a statement as I've heard in all my years in politics. I know you haven't been in politics very long, but—"

"Before you finish with that outlandish thought, Senator, I would suggest my lack of political experience only enhances my credentials to address this political bullshit. You've been at this game far too long if you are trying to sacrifice the will of the American people on the altar of your almighty party."

I scanned the room. "Are all of you on board with his approach?"

"Mr. President," said Senator John Thune of South Dakota, "we voted a very similar bill down before Mayton. I don't know why we need to have another vote unless something has changed."

"Something *HAS* changed!" I shouted back. "That's exactly my point! In Mayton, Florida, there are forty-seven coffins filled with teenagers whose lives were cut short by these weapons. To say nothing of all the lives they touched that have also been ruined in the wake of this tragedy! More families and communities torn apart! That's what has changed!"

"I understand your passion and your outrage," said Senator Marco Rubio. "My heart aches for my fellow Florida residents whose lives have been altered by this. If I believed that this bill would prevent these types of incidents, I'd be the first one to sign on. I do not believe it will make a difference."

"Help me understand that," I said. "Why don't you think it would matter? I'm not saying it would prevent all mass shootings. Maybe not even a majority of them. But what if it prevented a dozen? Or even just one? Or what if, as a result of this bill, someone only managed to kill eight kids in a school with a handgun, rather than thirty with an assault weapon? Would that not be worth it?"

Senator Rubio refused to give an inch. "There are millions of these AR-15s already on the streets. People will get their hands on them or other weapons just as effective as these."

"People can get their hands on surface-to-air missiles, too, if they try hard enough. Should we sell those at Walmart now too? After all, missiles don't bring down commercial jetliners, people do, isn't that right?"

"Let's focus on the thing we have broad agreement for," Rubio responded. "Background checks, mental health, enforcing the existing laws we already have on the books. A middle ground. Isn't that what you stand for? The middle?"

"I am with the vast majority on this—the ones who want to ban these things. Just because the majority of elected officials from your party don't support it doesn't mean the majority of Americans don't."

"This bill will not be effective at addressing the gun violence issue in America," Representative Mitch Rudnik of Nevada argued. "Gun deaths from assault weapons make up only a tiny fraction of all gun deaths. Less than 500 a year out of as many as 40,000. We should be looking at black-on-black crime. Look at what's happening on the streets of Chicago every day. This bill will do nothing to address that. Everyone is so fixated on assault weapons, but to me, that's just grandstanding for the cameras. We need to be looking at the poverty levels, the breakdown of African American families, and mental health."

"That is such horseshit! Just because we can't solve the entire gun problem with this bill then that means we disregard it? The question shouldn't be does it solve all gun deaths. The pertinent question is: Does it solve any? If it prevents even one mass shooting, is that alone not worth it?"

I took a second to calm down, but I wasn't finished yet. "I'm sorry, but since when are hundreds of deaths annually something not worth addressing in and of themselves, particularly when children and young adults are the most likely victims. Meanwhile, if an E. coli outbreak in lettuce sickens even a small handful of people, we'll immediately recall all similar lettuce nationwide and move heaven and earth to get it all off the shelves. By contrast, if one politician deigns to even mention a legislative fix following one of these ungodly incidents, they are eviscerated for politicizing the tragedy."

"For me, what this all boils down to is a fundamental right guaranteed by the founders in the Second Amendment," said Rudnik.

"That's revisionist history," I responded. "The Second Amendment dealt with state militias. You know who created an *individual* right to bear arms?" I paused for a moment for effect. "Scalia did," answering my own question, "in the Heller case."

"The founders were solidly in favor of a right to bear arms," countered Rudnik. "Ronald Reagan would be rolling over in his grave right now if he could hear you."

"All that is utter bullshit!" I yelled. I was losing my temper, but I intentionally allowed myself to do so. "These are all NRA talking points that they've forced down your throats along with the endless piles of cash they've thrown at you to do their bidding! Reagan, the Lord and Savior of your party, opposed assault weapons. Look it up!"

"With all due respect, Mr. President," responded Rudnik, "you have your history wrong."

"And I take exception to your insinuation regarding campaign contributions," added Rubio. "I have had this position since I entered public life. People and organizations support me because they believe in the positions I advocate. I don't advocate those positions because they support me."

"How could anyone ever possibly tell the difference, Senator?" I replied, my passion at full throttle again. "You are losing your teenagers to this—in your own state, for God's sake. If you had any integrity about you, you'd refuse all NRA money to avoid even the *appearance* of being bought and paid for."

Rudnik stood up. "I'm going to leave now. We came here today as a courtesy to calmly explain our principled, nuanced position on these complicated issues, only to be lectured by you, scolded and yelled at. All of this from the self-proclaimed king of civility, respect, and consensus. But I'm not surprised that all those lofty notions of yours get abandoned behind closed doors when the cameras are off."

"That makes two of us at this table who are hopelessly disappointed, Senator. I will always have a decidedly uncivil reaction whenever I see the debilitating effects of lobbyists taking over this country. I don't apologize for my reaction to that affront."

Just then I saw Cathy enter the room. She had a look of seriousness in her eyes that I had never seen before. And she didn't seem worried that she was interrupting a critical meeting. I knew something really important must be afoot. I motioned for her to come to me. "Pardon me for a second," I said to the group.

She came close to my side, leaned in, and whispered in my ear. "I am so, so sorry to have to tell you this." She paused. I turned to where I could see her face and saw that she was crying. When she tried to speak, her voice cracked. She couldn't get the words out. I braced myself for the worst. She gathered herself and then tried again. "We just learned that John McCain passed away this morning."

The news hit me like a ton of bricks. My anger and frustration, which had been at record levels, immediately gave way to profound sadness. Excusing myself without explanation, I proceeded back to the residence. I had to tell Denyse.

I walked quickly. As soon as I got to the landing on the staircase between the first and second floor, out of view and earshot of everyone, I stopped and burst into tears. Utterly, utterly despondent, I cried hard for myself, and then I cried even harder for the country.

Chapter Fifty-Nine

Ten months later
Political Limbo

YAHOO! NEWS

June 1, 2019

Now well beyond the midpoint of his presidency, McFadden appears to be stuck in political limbo. Multiple candidates in both major parties are raising money and establishing a national political organization, poised for success in the primaries. McFadden looks and acts at times like a candidate, but he has yet to articulate a path or viable political strategy to reelection. He is getting hit hard on the campaign trail by Democrats and Republicans alike. He is choosing not to return fire and really has no elected officials in his corner to do his dirty work for him. His overall approval rating of 56 percent in the latest Quinnipiac poll shows that there is definite support for him nationally; however, he trails several Republican candidates in a crowded field among Republican voters, and trails a few of the Democrats among Democratic voters by double digits. His best path to reelection may be to run as an Independent again. However, it's not clear that he would do as well as he did in the 2016 election in a field with Donald Trump and Hillary Clinton—two candidates who had negative approval numbers exceeding their positives.

The country remains polarized. McFadden's Supreme Court picks have been blocked. The parties ignored him and passed their own inflated budget, overriding his veto. He has fallen well short of his goals of deficit reduction, entitlement reform, an assault weapons ban, bipartisan immigration law overhaul, and campaign finance reform. Both parties appear to have little or no desire to work with him, adhering instead to a strategy of making him a one-term president and hoping to be able to replace him with one of their own.

Ever since Vice President McCain's death, McFadden seems lost. At this point, he appears destined to join the ranks of one-term presidents, and, absent some miraculous turnaround in his final year, historians will likely not be kind to his administration when opining on his legacy.

Chapter Sixty

June 3, 2019
We're Not Sure We See a Path for You

"The bottom line, Mr. President, is we're not sure we see a path for you."

I stared back at Reggie Karlton, the very pricey political consultant and pollster my campaign organization had retained to craft a strategy to reelection. He and his deputy were giving Murph and I their assessment.

"To be sure," Reggie said, "it's too early to really tell, and things could change dramatically over the course of the next year. You know a year is a lifetime in politics."

"Don't worry—no need to soften it."

"The last time you ran, you faced two candidates who each had negatives exceeding their positives. That had never happened before in our nation's history. It was an extraordinary circumstance. The planets all lined up for you."

"They really did," I agreed, "remarkably so."

"This time, those same planets are colliding with one another."

I laughed instinctively, but there really wasn't anything funny about it.

"If you run as a Democrat, we see a number of candidates who would take you in the primaries," Reggie continued. "Their positions are much more progressive than yours and will be embraced by Democratic voters in the primaries. The party is moving to the left. Medicare for all, decriminalization of illegal immigration, the green new deal, free college tuition. Additionally, there is still lingering resentment among die-hard Democrats about the way you left the party."

"Of course."

"If you ran as a Republican, you'd be torched in the primaries by any number of conservatives. The right-wing media will be merciless to you, and that matters to primary voters."

"I understand."

"And this time around, as an Independent, you almost certainly won't have the benefit of both parties nominating candidates whose negatives exceed their positives. That was a first."

"I get it," I conceded. "I had just hoped that since my approval rating has always exceeded 50 percent, there might be a shot somehow."

"Your presence in the race would likely just seal the deal for one of the other two—likely the Republican."

"I see."

"Don't get me wrong—you could give it a shot," Reggie added. "It's at least possible. You'd have to run a fierce campaign. You've never really campaigned before. Things might change. The economy might pick up. The market might turn around. There may be an international incident that unites the country behind you. The two parties may each nominate imperfect candidates again.

"The problem is you'd take fire from both sides, and no one really has your back to go out and defend you. When Dems get hit, they circle the wagons and hit back. Same with Republicans. You're the only prominent Independent. You'd be out there on your own."

I swallowed hard. This wasn't anything I hadn't anticipated, but it still hurt, nonetheless. I tried to tell myself I didn't want another term anyway, which was true . . . kind of. Reminded me of back in high school when Cindy Cheeseman thought I was about to ask her to the prom, so she made it clear to me that she didn't want to go with me. I wasn't even asking her, but it still hurt as much as any other rejection. I didn't even want to go with her. Although maybe I would have if I thought she wanted to, but that's beside the point.

Chapter Sixty-One

June 3, 2019
What About Your Cause?

Satch and Denyse were both waiting for me when I got back to the residence. "How'd the meeting go?" asked Satch.

"Could have been better," I replied—the understatement of the year.

"They don't . . . ," I paused, "I don't think it's in the cards for me this next time around. They don't see a path to victory. And let me remind you, these are highly paid pollsters and political consultants who are used to telling candidates precisely what they want to hear. This is akin to a surgeon telling a patient he doesn't need surgery or a mechanic saying your car is just fine. How telling is that? If these cats are telling me that, my God, how bad must it be?"

I shook my head. "This is terribly, terribly depressing." I said. "I've never been so distraught." I had never had heart palpitations before, and I didn't even know what they feel like, but I seemed to be having them now.

Denyse jumped up. "What are you talking about? Is this suddenly about you? No, Danny, it's never been about you! Have you forgotten that? This whole thing was never about you, right? Or was it? What about your cause?"

"Well," I responded, "I actually think running could possibly even hurt my whole centrist, anti-party, what's-best-for-the-country cause if I ran on that and lost. Or, worse yet, went down in flames as these political types seem to be suggesting."

"I'm not talking about running. I believe them when they say they don't think you'd win. But does that also mean there's no way for you to continue to further your cause? You tapped into something compelling when you captured the hearts of the country. Are you telling me the only way to forward that agenda is for you to be president?"

I couldn't muster a response.

"I think your girl's onto something here," Satch added. "Tell me this, has anybody ever changed this country from outside that Oval Office? Martin Luther King, Ben Franklin, Susan B. Anthony, Steve Jobs, Thomas Edison, Albert Einstein, Rosa Parks, Ryan White . . . your hero Jackie Robinson. I could go on and on."

"Of course," I responded. "You guys are awesome. Really. Look, I'll pull out of this. I wound easily—that's for sure, But I recover quickly."

A night in the Saloon might just be what the doctor ordered.

Chapter Sixty-Two

June 3, 2019
Put Me in Coach

When I entered the Saloon, Otter spotted me right away. He was at the bar as usual with a bottle of water. He bounced up at the sight of me and quickly walked over to greet me.

I looked out and saw an impressive group of my predecessors assembled at the large oak table in the center of the room—Washington, Lincoln, Jefferson, John Adams, Teddy Roosevelt, Tyler, FDR, Eisenhower, Kennedy, Nixon, Reagan, Clinton, and Obama. *Something's up,* I thought. *I can sense it.* Slowly each of them turned to look at me, which only served to confirm my suspicions.

Otter gave me a bro hug. "There you go, Rook. Have at it."

"What? What do you mean?"

"I believe the brain trust here has developed some answers to the questions you've been struggling with."

"The questions?"

"You asked them to come up with a remedy to fix the political dysfunction in the country, did you not?"

"Oh, yes. Yes I did . . . a while back. Wow!"

I shook my head rather dumbfounded, then suddenly, I became strangely nervous. "Thank you so much for getting them together on this. I owe you something fierce."

"Don't mention it, Rook. It's my role here. I know my role. His unique voice and cadence reminded me so much of Will Ferrell's *Saturday Night Live* impression of him. Before walking away, he added, "Many of the others heard us talking about your request and may swing by as well. Hope you're cool with that."

"Absolutely! That's terrific!" I replied. This was the best news I'd had all day.

He turned back at me again. "Oh, and Big Daddy is really taking this seriously."

"Are you serious?" I never knew with him, but at this moment he seemed it.

"Good luck, kid."

I approached the table and took the empty seat next to Washington. All eyes were on him as the table fell silent. The butterflies in my stomach were multiplying by the second.

The few moments of silence seemed like hours, but Washington finally spoke. "We've been conversing about your dilemma, McFadden. President Bush described it, but please provide us a brief summary as a starting point."

"I would be happy to," I responded. "Thank you so much for your time." After a brief moment to collect my thoughts, I began, "The country appears to be hopelessly and perilously polarized. The government has become completely dysfunctional. The two parties are solely concerned with their own agenda, their own power, and their own sustainability, and place that above all else. No one is acting in the best interests of the country. The art of collegiality and collaboration is dead and has been for quite some time. Compromise is a dirty word and will get you run out of office by your own party in the next primary.

"Some of the most respected men in this room would not be nominated today by their party precisely because of their inclination to work with the other side at times and compromise. And that includes John Kennedy and Ronald Reagan. For God's sakes, Richard Nixon himself might be tossed out by Republicans today for lifting the gold standard and establishing the Environmental Protection Agency."

"I agree," added Clinton. "I am certain I would not be nominated by the Democratic Party today."

"Moreover," I said, "special interests, lobbyists, and big money own legislators and run Washington. The number one job of every legislator is to fundraise in order to create a war chest from which to destroy any challenger in the next election with negative ads. Fundraising constitutes as much as 50 percent of a legislator's working activities."

Teddy Roosevelt, getting agitated, stated emphatically, "Our government—both national and state—must be free from the sinister influence or control of special interests. Exactly as the special interests of cotton and slavery threatened our political integrity before the Civil War, too often special interests control and corrupt the men and methods of government for their own profit." Then standing up, he yelled to us all, "We must drive the special interests out of politics!"

The entire group applauded.

He continued. "To dissolve the unholy alliance between corrupt business and corrupt politics is the first task of the statesmanship of the day." More applause.

I waited for the crowd to settle, then I jumped in again. "A majority of the country identifies with neither party, and therefore has no real influence or impact on the decisions made in Washington. More and more voters abandon the two parties every year, which only serves to make the base of each party more extreme. These extremes now hold all the power in each party and have morphed into intransigent tribes incapable of empathy for the concerns of the other. Worse yet, they exact punishment on members of their own party who would deign to compromise.

"Rightly or wrongly," I continued, "the electorate has lost all faith in so many institutions that have helped to sustain this country for 250 years—the government, the media, organized religion, law enforcement, our financial institutions."

At that point, Thomas Jefferson interrupted, "How did it get to this point?"

Before I could muster an answer, Obama jumped in, "This dynamic has been slowly evolving for decades. Congressional districts are now highly partisan—due to gerrymandering—which consists of legislators redrawing districts specifically to make them partisan and thus 'safe' for one party or the other. It's also due to self-selection, meaning that folks nowadays are moving, in part, to be near others who think and act like them. This contributes to that phenomenon that each district is becoming more and more polarized and willing to inflict punishment on those willing to reach across the aisle. Add to that the cable news and talk radio. Folks these days are likely to get their news from a source that filters it with their own particular partisan lens. They don't get exposed to the views of others, so they have no empathy for the plight of others, and, in many cases may indeed have utter disdain for those who don't hold their views."

"May I add something?" Eisenhower inquired of Washington.

"Please do, General," he answered.

Looking directly at me now, Ike continued, "It was happening in my time. I had no patience for the extreme rightists who call everyone who disagrees with them a Communist, nor with the leftists who shout that the rest of us are all heartless money-grubbers."

Washington spoke up. "I warned the country of the dangers of political factions in my Farewell Address. We need men whose loyalty is to country above all else."

"You may have been the last of those, sir," added Reagan.

Madison, seated next to Washington and listening intently, spoke up. "Please permit me to recount the words of my favorite political philosopher David Hume, who had a profound influence on our Constitutional Convention. 'Factions subvert government, render laws impotent, and beget the fiercest animosities among men of the same government who ought to give mutual assistance to each other.'"

"Our hope was for a republic without parties," added Jefferson. "If I could not go to heaven but with a party, I would not go at all."

"The parties are not going away," I responded. "However, the most puzzling and frustrating part about it is that independents now clearly outnumber each of the two parties, yet have almost no political power."

"And," Washington added, "as I understand it, you do not see a path to the presidency as an Independent or as a member of either of the two parties. Is that correct?"

"I honestly don't, sir. And I've had some of the sharpest political minds in the country analyzing it for me. While I could possibly win the popular vote, I would carry very few states. Most states are heavily Democrat or heavily Republican. The planets really have to be aligned for an independent to win, as they were in the 2016 election. I was up against two of the most unpopular candidates in history, and I had almost no political track record. None of that will be the case this time around."

Washington glanced quickly around the table and said, "We've had the finest minds in this Saloon considering your dilemma." That elicited a few laughs. "We have a solution for you, but I fear it may not be the one you'd like to hear."

"Go ahead," I responded. "I'm eager to hear anything this esteemed group might suggest, and I would have nothing but respect for that opinion."

"We've been discussing this for some time now," Washington resumed, "and several of these gentlemen opined about the impact of having viable candidates in a presidential election from three different factions or, as you refer to them today, three different parties. I can let them describe their experiences directly if you wish."

"Of course," I replied.

Teddy Roosevelt spoke first, "When I lost the Republican nomination in 1912, we started the Bull Moose party, and I ran with them, which merely served to splinter the Republican vote. I handed the election to Wilson. Taft and I combined to receive more votes than Wilson, yet he prevailed."

"I had a rather forgettable experience with a third-party candidate," added George H. W. Bush. "Ross Perot received 20 million votes as an independent candidate in 1992, and I lost by 5 million. Most people believe he cost me that election."

"You know I love you, Papa Bush," responded Bill Clinton, "but all the exit polling at the time showed you and I would have split his votes if he wasn't in the race. But I'll grant you that third-party candidates can throw a monkey wrench into these elections and can potentially be disastrous for the country."

"I ascended to the presidency as a result of a four-way race," said John Quincy Adams. "Jackson won the popular vote, but none of us had a majority of the electoral college vote. I won in the House when Henry Clay, clearly no fan of Jackson, threw his support behind me."

John Tyler, whose voice I had not heard in all my time in the Saloon, spoke next, "My experience, Mr. McFadden, was remarkably like yours. More so, I suspect, than that of any man in this room. No one expected me to ascend to the presidency, least of all me. The Whigs selected me for vice president without even knowing my positions. I was not elected president, but it was thrust upon me when William Henry Harrison died. Like you, I served without allegiance to any party. These positions, while best for the country, left me without a party to gain reelection. Had I run, I surely would have ensured victory for Henry Clay by splitting the vote with Polk. Preferring Polk to Clay, I decided not to run, and Polk, indeed, defeated Clay. I then opted, instead, to focus my energies on annexation of Texas, for which we were successful."

"A more worthy cause I cannot conceive of, Mr. Tyler," answered LBJ, to great laughter throughout the room. "And furthermore," Johnson continued, "I'll tell you something about centrists, McFadden. There's nothin' in the middle of the road but yellow lines and dead armadillos." The room again erupted in laughter.

FDR spoke up. "I should like to summarize for my good colleagues. What we are saying, McFadden, is that we all tend to be in agreement that a third-party candidacy may not be wise or even viable politically. Furthermore, the consensus of the modern fellows, Presidents Obama, George W. Bush, and Clinton, seems to be that with the present condition of the country, they believe the parties are far too extreme to enable a moderate like yourself to earn their nomination."

"I'm afraid I would have to agree with that too," I responded despondently.

Then Lincoln, who had been silently listening to all this, perked up. "There is another option sir, which may indeed be the best thing for the country at this moment in time."

"I would love to hear that, Mr. President!" I proclaimed, at this point on the edge of my chair. My God, how could I not be with Abraham Lincoln addressing me directly with those deep-set eyes, even though I hadn't the slightest inclination where he might be going with this.

"I understand your concern with the division and agitation of the country made manifest by the present state of the two major parties. Multiple parties can be problematic as well of course. When I won in 1860, no less than four different candidates earned electoral votes. The country was perilously divided. I wasn't even on the ballot in eight states! Although I was a moderate Republican, no candidate running was capable of uniting the country."

Lincoln paused and scanned the room. "We'd like to posit a solution, imperfect though it may be, which nonetheless has some merit to address your particular circumstance."

As I looked around, I could see that the other presidents had all entered the Saloon and had begun to fill in around us. This, I could see, was a well-coordinated effort.

Washington saw my reaction and said, "They all wanted to be here. To a man, we are all concerned for you and for the country." He then looked at Lincoln and said, "Carry on, Mr. Lincoln."

A rush came over me as the energy in the room elevated. I felt a sense of support I had never quite experienced before—certainly never in my abbreviated political career.

"Thank you, General Washington," said Lincoln. "We understand, McFadden, that you can boast solid support among what you call independents, and that those may outnumber either major party. We advocate that you harness that support to initiate a new national political party, espousing all those core beliefs for which you contend a majority of Americans in the center hold dear."

"I don't understand," I interrupted, "I thought you all were opposed to a new party splintering the vote."

"Oh, we are," responded Obama. "But this party will be different."

I was intrigued, but quite confused.

Lincoln continued. "This new party will not aim to select and nominate a candidate. Rather, this party endeavors to construct a solid voting block in the center, impervious to corruption by the monied interests and the lobbyists, that will throw its support behind the candidate from either major party most willing to place the interests of the country above all else.'

"Thereby profoundly shaping the political profile of those nominees emerging from the nomination process of the two parties," explained Clinton. "This will be a voting block that has the numbers and the clout to enable a Republican to disavow the NRA and still be elected."

"Or a Democrat to take on entitlement and social security reform," added Reagan.

"Assuming candidates like that even exist," said Nixon, laughing.

"Oh, they will when this concept gains traction," Clinton responded.

Looking at Clinton, Obama added, "This is just the next iteration of your triangulation concept, Bill. This is providing the political cover for folks to do the right thing."

"I would hope we can all get back to the notion of doing the right thing as legislators, regardless of what we feel the politics are," I said, perhaps demonstrating world-class naivete.

"I'm afraid that notion may have left the Capitol in a carriage with President Washington," Lincoln—of all people—said with a smile.

"If I can play even a small role in bringing it back," I replied, "that would be a legacy I'd be thrilled to be a part of."

"Your role in this, sir, will be anything but small," added Washington.

"And success necessitates a true yeoman's effort."

"I'm your man, sir!" I said excitedly, to a rousing round of cheers and encouragement. "Where do I sign up? Put me in coach!"

"You realize, of course," reminded Nixon, "that you'll be opting not to run again, and, for maximum impact, you'll be doing so in the most public manner possible. Not many of us have walked away from the ultimate position of power."

"I understand completely, Mr. President,"

"Now there's a profile in courage!" commended JFK. "You are a fine and admirable man, McFadden!"

The group erupted in applause that lasted much longer than I was comfortable with. I wondered if it could truly be referred to as a profile in courage when half my motivation was coming from the sense that I'd likely lose anyway. But I have to say I really liked this concept. Why not? And who better to lead this cause at this moment than me?

Finally the applause was interrupted by FDR. "Nurse!" he yelled, "We're going to require a whole lot more drinks here."

Tonight, I planned on drinking.

Chapter Sixty-Three

June 8, 2019
A Splendid Addition

The party shifted into high gear immediately—as if a collective weight had been lifted from all of us. I found it tremendously gratifying to see how all these gentlemen seemed just as relieved as I was—both for me and for the country—and optimistic that we may actually have stumbled upon something. And it wasn't lost on me that this was an action plan that most of these folks never would have endorsed during their active political careers.

The drinks were flowing fast and furious while a very versatile band complete with an Elvis impersonator killed it on the stage. *Now this is my kind of party!*

Mary Ann walked around handing out blue cocktails to everyone. "What the heck is this, M.A.?" I asked.

"A blue Hawaiian," she responded.

I must've looked a bit confused. She pointed to the stage. "You know, Elvis . . . *Blue Hawaii* . . . Get it?"

I laughed out loud. "Who's the genius who thought that up? How many of these guys will catch that?" I asked. "Half of them don't even know Hawaii is a state."

"Don't be a hater," she snapped back, but with her patented smile. She handed one to Chester Arthur of all people. Before long, that crazy bushy sideburn mustache thing he had going was bright blue.

Matty was employing a heavy hand with these drinks, and it showed.

"Good luck to you, McFadden," Grant shouted in my ear as he slapped me on the back. He had clearly had a few. "You are a good man. Go travel the world. That's what I did. Have the good ol' U.S. Navy transport you."

"Great idea, sir."

John Quincy Adams approached me. "You remind me of myself,

President McFadden. As I mentioned, I became president in an unusual race with multiple candidates, then I did what I viewed was the best and proper thing for the country. But my unwillingness to cultivate specific lines of patronage left me vulnerable to defeat when I sought reelection. Rest assured, dear friend, you did right by the country—and by yourself."

One after another took me aside with encouraging words. John Tyler, with whom I had a new found kinship, approached me. Tall and thin, with a rather angular face, he sported a pint glass full of champagne. "I see myself in you, McFadden. We are kindred spirits. The road does not stop for you now. I know that great things await you. I expect that great things await our country, too, although it may be hard to see it at the moment. But then, I've had a few too many of these, and frankly, I'm not seeing much of anything at the moment."

I laughed out loud. How priceless was this moment? I only wished I could share it with someone—anyone. Or put it on Instagram…Facebook… anything! Then I thought to myself, *What would John Tyler's Facebook profile page look like?*

Mary Ann came gliding through quickly with another tray full of blue drinks, moving remarkably like a waitress on skates at a 1950s-era drive thru restaurant. "Perfect timing," I said.

"Oh, so it meets with your approval now, your highness?" she said in the most sassy way possible.

"OK," I responded. "I deserved that." I have a rare skill for admitting when I'm wrong, perhaps because I have a lot of experience in that particular department.

Herbert Hoover had been waiting behind Tyler for a chance to speak with me. "Be glad you're leaving on your own terms and won't have an election defeat to recover from and make you bitter, like I did," said Hoover. "My advice to you is to go back to Northern California. We did. Stanford will take you in. So will the Bohemian Club. My camp there—the Cave Man—would love to have you."

"Thank you so much, sir. But I'm not sure I'm welcome there any longer. I gave a lakeside talk recently and told them they needed to admit women."

"Good God, fella, what on earth possessed you to do that?"

"I'm a bit more progressive than you, sir. But I did enjoy the Bohemian

Grove. I stayed with a group of rather colorful characters at a camp called the Pink Onion and thoroughly enjoyed that. And I met Jimmy Buffett."

"Is he a Republican politician?"

"No, more like a philosopher. But I'd love to have him to work with in the House or Senate if he was. He'd be much better than most of the characters currently there. Anyway, I really appreciate your well wishes, sir."

The band continued to play and the drinks flowed for this crowd of men well into the night. Maybe this *was* the Bohemian Grove. The similarities were striking.

I heard Ginger yell, "Last call for presidential spirits!" This was the latest I had ever been in the Saloon. Much of the room bellied up to the bar for another, but I figured enough was enough. I said my goodbyes.

As I was making my way to the exit, someone grabbed me from behind. I whirled around to see who it was. Teddy Roosevelt.

"You are a splendid addition to this illustrious body, McFadden," TR declared.

"That may just be the nicest thing anyone has ever said to me, sir," I replied.

"Choose your next pursuits wisely," he advised. Then with his voice steadily rising, he added, "Remember, a soft, easy life is not worth living. It impairs the fiber of the brain and heart, and muscle. Dare to be great, McFadden. Greatness is the fruit of toil and sacrifice and high courage. Seek a life of action, of strenuous performance of duty. Let us live in the harness, striving mightily. Let us rather run the risk of wearing out than rusting out."

That was priceless. He was a true caricature of himself. Everything I would have imagined. In today's world, he'd be the greatest motivational public speaker we know, with millions of YouTube subscribers.

I looked him right in the eye, seeking to match his passion pound for pound, and roared right back at him, "I vow to live the rest of my life in that harness, sir!" A moment later I added, softly, "I've never been in a harness before, but it will soon become a core part of my being."

God, I love this bar! This experience alone is worth all the headaches of the presidency.

As I walked away, I heard Ginger yell one more time, "Drink 'em up, you presidents! Now or never. And you can't take 'em with you. Don't make me go all Carrie Nation on you!"

That cracked me up. I decided I was gonna miss that staff at least as much as I'd miss those presidents. Maybe even more. But I couldn't help but dwell on my conversation with Teddy Roosevelt. What a beaut he was! Would've made a tremendous coach. The Rough Riders must have loved being led by him—or hated it. What a kick to be able to get to know him! In my mind, he deserves every piece of that rock he occupies up there on Rushmore. And, perhaps best of all, he was speaking my political language. Forget about DiMaggio—where have you gone, Teddy Roosevelt? *A nation turns its lonely eyes to you.* It certainly should. Now more than ever.

The great irony about this all is that for the very first time, I felt I truly belonged in this esteemed club. And it happened to be on the very day I had more or less decided that I would not seek reelection. At least, I think I'd decided that. . . .

Chapter Sixty-Four

June 10, 2019
Live from Mount Vernon

MSNBC

Chris Matthews: You are looking at a live shot of Mount Vernon, George Washington's picturesque plantation on the banks of the Potomac River in Fairfax County, Virginia. This stately manor looks much the same as it did three centuries ago—minus about 300 slaves, of course.

You can see the throngs of cameras and press swarming the back lawn in anticipation of the president's speech here today. Speculation about this speech has been running rampant for days as the country awaits McFadden's decision on the 2020 election. Those around the president have been remarkably tight-lipped—shockingly actually. I'm joined here today by Rachel Maddow and Chuck Todd. Rachel, what do you expect to hear today? The two biggest questions are: Is he running, and, if so, how will he choose to do it? As a Democrat? Republican? Independent? Have you heard anything new from any of your sources?

Rachel Maddow: Chris, this could go many different ways. I have no intelligence of any kind out of the White House, which is mildly shocking, actually. We are not certain who he is consulting about this. However, it is noteworthy to remember that he is still a relative newcomer to politics. His rapid ascent to the White House is almost unparalleled in U.S. history.

We have consulted with numerous sources he has leaned on repeatedly in these past few years for political advice, many of whom we would have expected he would rely on for political advice in this case, but to a person they swear they have been left out of this one. In fact, some of his closest political advisers are wondering aloud who he *is* relying on, fearful that it can't possibly be anyone with any real national political experience.

Rumors emanating from Sidwell Friends, where his son Jack is in school, are that the family may be headed back to Silicon Valley. We have no confirmation of that, but nothing to dispute it, either.

Chuck Todd: We are truly in a unique spot in U.S. political history, Rachel. We have a president who does enjoy some degree of popular support, with respectable favorability ratings, who nonetheless does not necessarily have a path to reelection—certainly not an obvious, traditional one at least. Both parties find him unpalatable, as each seems to be moving toward their polar extremes.

Chris Matthews: I think it's a commentary on the tribalism of our country today. People retreat into their camps. The system no longer seems to allow for a moderate or a person seeking to govern from the center to be successful. Your thoughts, Rachel?

Rachel Maddow: I think conservatives certainly have a set of issues that comprise a litmus test for any candidate—

Chris Matthews: Sorry to interrupt, Rachel, but President McFadden appears to be approaching the podium. Let's go to Mount Vernon. We have no advance text for this speech, as we sometimes get ahead of time. And it looks as though there's no teleprompter set up.

Chapter Sixty-Five

July 10, 2019—6:03 p.m.
We're Better Than This

I walked out the back door of Washington's home at Mount Vernon, crossed the stately white-columned porch, and paused briefly as I peered out upon the Potomac River and the magnificent view the Father of our Country cherished so dearly. That view was every bit as soothing to me as the raucous applause of the very friendly crowd that greeted me. Perhaps those who knew me the very best sensed how much I really needed that support at this moment. There was simply no more appropriate place to deliver these words and this message today in all the world. I was at peace with this decision and energized.

I saw the red lights on the bank of cameras illuminate like a string of Christmas lights. I took a deep breath. Just as I was forming my first word, I noticed a caravan of black SUVs pull up along the side of the estate and head toward the front side of the home. I spent a brief second wondering what that was all about, but then I remembered I had something much bigger in front of me demanding my complete attention. I started rolling . . .

"Friends and fellow citizens. I stand here today in the shadow of Mount Vernon, the home of the Father of our Country, which is clearly one of our national treasures. I come here intentionally and symbolically in an effort to awaken the lost vision George Washington once articulated so prophetically for our country.

I have spent a good deal of time studying our presidents in an effort to learn all I can from their many successes as well as their failures—so much so that, at times, I feel as though I have come to know each of them personally. We are all so familiar with their famous words and speeches. Schoolchildren can recite Lincoln's Gettysburg Address, the famous inaugural quotes from FDR and JFK, and Ronald Reagan's directive to Gorbachev at the Berlin Wall. Today I want to harken back to some largely forgotten words of George Washington, for they are as prescient and compelling now as they were then, 223 years ago.

While sometimes I view myself as a reluctant president, Washington was perhaps our most reluctant president of all. And, glancing at this property behind me, it's not difficult to understand why. But he answered the call to serve his country against his own wishes twice. Had he not done so, the new nation might not have survived its infancy.

While it's certainly self-serving to say this, perhaps reluctant presidents are the ones to whom we should listen most closely. Washington chose to serve a second term largely because he feared the consequences that not doing so would have on the fledgling country. A partisan fight would have developed, as factions had been forming already, and he viewed that political bickering as a great threat to the nation. Little did he know at the time that he would be the only president in our history without a true party. At least, that is, until I came along.

Washington's Farewell Address is perhaps the most important forgotten political dissertation in our nation's history. He started writing it during his first term, believing that he would only serve four years. He dusted it off four years later and, with a little help from Madison and Hamilton, produced his opus to be published in newspapers across the nation as he rode out of town in his carriage.

I am here today in the hopes of reacquainting our country with the grand vision of this flawed yet impressive Founding Father. We need him as desperately now as we did then. He predicted the lion's share of the troubles we now confront in the city that bears his name.

President George Washington had no political base to pander to, no election to raise money for, no party to place above the interests of his country, no fear of not being reelected to cloud his judgment, and no list of donors to pay back. We need more like him. Or even one like him—that would be a great start! We have allowed ourselves, quite slowly over time, to morph into a nation of two peoples or tribes. I would even go so far as to say we have become a house divided against itself, borrowing a phrase made famous by another great President, and we as a country are all too familiar with the consequences of that dysfunctional structure.

In his Farewell Address, Washington warned against the dangers of political parties, believing firmly that parties, by their nature, tended to place their own interests above those of the nation. In his view, the partisan disputes and bickering between parties only served to weaken the government. Washington witnessed the dangers of parties beginning to fester around him—the followers of Hamilton pitted against the followers Jefferson—and he sincerely felt that America would be infinitely better off without strong parties.

In Washington's grand vision, the great American president was a leader for all, utterly devoid of any allegiance to a party or region. Moreover, Washington not only called for civility and mutual respect in the public square, but he struck a powerful example of a strong leader who embodied these noble virtues and employed them effectively to his political advantage. As a result, he earned the admiration of all, even those who fiercely disagreed with his positions.

We would do well to heed his advice, which rings as true today as it ever has. We are, indeed, a house divided. Our politics have devolved, or metastasized to use a more apt description, from the art of noble dealmaking—seeking common ground upon which to forge consensus through creativity and compromise—into a never-ending effort to pander to and rile up one's base, endeavoring to conquer one's political opponents and impose a mandate no matter how slim the margin of victory or how narrow the advantage in Congress.

Our self-serving, party-above-all elected officials are supported by the entire political industrial complex—the lobbyists and special interest groups they serve as a result of the continual gerrymandering of districts—which only fuels our great political divide—and by the ideological cable news, talk radio, and Internet platforms that spew forth not only dramatically politicized opinions twenty-four hours a day but also dramatically politicized versions of the facts. Amidst this landscape there can be no savior.

I'm no George Washington—not by any stretch of the imagination—but I can boast of approval ratings consistently above 50 percent. However, the political buzz saw of gridlock, divisiveness, distrust, dishonesty, and even hate that has infected our politics has proven to be far more formidable than I could contend with. These are now deeply rooted systemic structures much too powerful to budge.

Much speculation has been made of my political future and whether or not it includes another run at the White House—this time an intentional run. I am announcing today that after much careful consideration, thought, and prayer, I have decided that I will not seek reelection in 2020."

An audible groan came over the crowd. I tried to avoid direct eye contact but could not help but see disappointed faces. I felt a tinge of regret. More than a tinge, actually. But I quickly reconvinced myself that this was, indeed, the proper decision for all the right reasons. I continued with my speech:

"That is another reason why I invoke the memory of General Washington and chose this hallowed ground for this announcement— because this is my own farewell address.

While I bid farewell to public office, this is by no means a farewell to this cause. I have consulted with some of the greatest minds I could have ever hoped to assemble to address this political quagmire our country finds itself entangled in and how it can be overcome, and I have decided to attack it from the outside rather than from within.

I firmly believe that this tribal divide stands as a legitimate threat not only to our standing in the world but our future as a republic. We can no longer just keep tacking back and forth with each new administration and Congress—from the far left to the far right and back again—all the while impeding any progress as a nation and yielding further and further ground to our rivals on the world stage.

In its present state, America no longer fits the image of that strong young man about to enter a race that Teddy Roosevelt evoked in 1897. And no matter how hard you strain your eyes, it's difficult to see it as that shining city on a hill that Reagan spoke of. No sir. As America approaches 250 years as a nation, it is indeed showing its age—stiff, rickety joints, no shortage of gray hair and memory loss. My God have we got memory loss as a nation! Worst of all, our political infrastructure is no longer capable of generating the type of leadership necessary to extricate ourselves from this mess, let alone lead the free world.

I am here today to say enough is enough, America. We're better than this!"

The crowd erupted in applause. Their collective disappointment of a few moments earlier had turned back into enthusiasm.

"For God's sake we are better than this!" More and louder applause.

Presidential Spirits

"In fact, we are so much better than this. We are better than all this hate. We are better than these culture wars. We are better than this political divide, this tribalism, this blind allegiance to party over country." I raised my voice considerably as I continued through the applause.

"We are better than all this money and the special interests owning our politicians. And we are certainly better, as a nation, than having nearly half of all registered voters staying home on election day. That perhaps is the ultimate sign that people are losing hope in our democracy.

This cynical, hopelessly divided country is in desperate need of a fresh infusion of life, passion, and energy. I have personally devoted an enormous amount of time and energy in search of a solution to enable us to rise up and rekindle the spirit of Washington. After consulting closely with some of the most successful political minds this country has ever produced, I have arrived at a potential solution. I intend to devote the next chapter of my life to this idea. In fact, I feel so strongly about this plan that I am willing to give up the presidency after one term to see this through. If successful, it would have an impact on every succeeding election—far outweighing any legacy I could fashion by spending another four years presiding over a dysfunctional government that's hopelessly gridlocked.

I hope you'll allow me a few moments to unveil what I hope will be the initial step toward a solution. Registered voters have left the two parties in droves. Independents now far outnumber either party, so what's left of the parties are the extremists. All the independents—again, a voting block that exceeds either party—are permitting the two extremes to choose our candidates in every election. Creating a third party has not proven to be a viable solution. In fact, it only seems to hand elections over to one of the other two parties. Our idea intends to capture and organize this vast middle voting block in a new and different manner—one that I'm not certain has really been tried before in a meaningful way.

First of all, we won't be calling it a party. Washington abhorred parties, or factions as he called them, and so will we. We will be referring to this as an alliance.

Secondly, because we are better than this—we *are* and *should be* and *will be* better than this—*way* better than this—we'll be calling this the We're Better than This Alliance. Or just the We're Better Alliance.

Allow me to set forth the basic tenets of this alliance. It will stand for and promote civility—in the great tradition of George Washington himself. It will stand for the absence of hate. We can hate the policy without hating the person—or a whole group of people. It will stand for collegiality and respect for one another, including—and especially—those on the other side of the aisle.

It will stand for collaboration and bipartisanship, seeking win-win scenarios forged through hard work, listening to one another, and yes compromise. And placing country over party in the spirit of the great John McCain.

Most importantly, this alliance will *not* be running candidates in presidential elections under the We're Better name, nor will it run them in most states and districts. Instead, this will be a voting block comprised of that forgotten middle of the country—that lost and unrepresented block of voters who happen to outnumber both parties. But instead of running candidates of our own from this alliance, it will seek primarily to influence the selection of candidates put forth by the two major parties and move them toward the middle. In the last election, both parties produced candidates whose negatives exceeded their positives. Each of the two major party candidates were disliked by a majority of Americans. That is unacceptable.

The We're Better Alliance will work aggressively to pull both parties away from the extremes. We will operate as a not-so-thinly-veiled threat to each of the parties that they'll risk losing the all-important middle if they continue to nominate from their fringes. We'll examine the candidates throughout the vetting process and make it crystal clear to all where we stand.

In addition to decency, bipartisanship, integrity, and civility, we'll be trumpeting a whole host of other antidotes to the present dysfunction we find ourselves in. We'll be looking to diminish the role of money in politics, as well as lobbyists. Every politician claims that they will do this, but none follow through. Lobbyists should not be drafting legislation. We'll call attention to those who continue to permit them to do so.

We'll work to redress gerrymandering, which only exacerbates our divide. We need to protect the filibuster in the Senate and ensure that no senate majority invokes the 'nuclear option'—seeking to eliminate the filibuster for legislation or judicial appointments. The filibuster preserves a spirit of bipartisanship, even if forced. And we can't allow a Speaker to require that a majority of his or her party favor a bill before bringing it to the floor—otherwise known as the Boehner Rule. That works directly against bipartisanship and places party specifically over country. George Washington would be outraged.

And, perhaps most challenging of all, we need to bring about a ceasefire in the culture wars. We need to figure out a way to hold at bay those who want to stoke the fires of political division for the sake of profit and ratings. These extremists get fat and happy while the country is infinitely worse for it. They're killing our collective spirit. The great irony is that Russia doesn't need to sow division amongst us—as they clearly did in the last election. We're doing an absolute bang-up job of that ourselves.

And there are a whole host of political no-brainers that should not be nearly as elusive as they are. We need fiscal responsibility. Congress has reached a point where it appears physically incapable of the type of give-and-take necessary to agree on anything even remotely resembling a balanced budget. We are better than that.

We'll honor and respect the right to bear arms, but we'll insist upon common sense gun measures. Effective background checks and an assault weapons ban are not an affront to the Second Amendment. And enacting these very measured reforms will not create a slippery slope to eliminating guns.

Roe versus Wade is settled. There we have it. Our system has generated a great American compromise on it. It might not please either side, but let's stop arguing about it, move on, and focus on other areas where we can agree and bring us forward as a society.

We need a better system for choosing presidents. Who can afford to hit the road and campaign every day for two full years, and why would we want to elect anyone who is willing to do that? We have to rid ourselves of these endless campaign cycles. Let's push the parties to condense their primary seasons to entice a bigger field to run. And let's experiment more with 'rank choice voting' in states, which allows third-party candidates to run without the fear of being spoilers—much like Maine does. Australia has had it for a hundred years!

We'll take all comers in this We're Better Alliance—anyone in the middle, anyone fed up with the partisan divide, anyone who has lost hope in our system. And especially the nearly 50 percent of registered voters who don't bother to vote at all and who have effectively ceded elections to the extremes. They constitute fertile ground for us to cultivate. And, perhaps most importantly, we welcome anyone from the two major parties who feels we can and should be better. They are welcome in our alliance as they simultaneously work to influence their party and hold it more accountable in the areas of decency, civility, and bipartisanship.

We'll find candidates to run in either party who fit our values—those willing to put country over party in the spirit of George Washington, those who feel their responsibility extends well beyond just their base, and those unafraid of reaching across the aisle to forge a consensus. We'll enter moderate Republicans in Alabama and Mississippi and moderate Democrats in New York and California. We'll do for candidates what Oprah's book club did for books.

Is this grand vision achievable? Is it feasible? Realistic? Maybe, maybe not. But let me tell you this, I can't afford not to find out. And let me tell you something else – neither can the country. I know this much, it's the best I can do. And I will either make this happen or die trying. But the time to take this country back and summon our better angels starts today, and it starts, ironically, by me giving up this post and committing to serve a cause greater than oneself in the spirit of the late great John McCain.

We welcome one and all to join the We're Better Alliance by signing up on the website today: Democrats, Republicans, Libertarians, Green Party, Independents, you name it—anyone who thinks we can do better as a nation and wants to play a critical role in bringing this about.

We're better than this, America. We start getting better today.

Thank you for your support. I need it now more than ever. God bless you all."

The crowd exploded into applause. Applause that did not stop. And then the most incredible moment of all happened. Soul singer Billy Valentine began belting out "America the Beautiful" accompanied by a blues band as the crowd began swaying back and forth. All eyes then turned to the mansion's porch the as the door opened, and, one by one, out walked Leon Panetta, David Gergen, Colin Powell, Condoleezza Rice, Arnold Schwarzenegger, and several prominent generals, including David Petraeus. The crowd applauded as each proceeded to sign his or her name to a massive poster brought out and displayed next to the podium.

Once each had signed, Leon Panetta took the microphone. "I believe there are a few more back there whom you might recognize."

A collective hush came over the crowd. The band took it down considerably, and out of the house strolled none other than Barack Obama, George W. Bush, Bill Clinton, and Jimmy Carter. The crowd went absolutely crazy. This part was a complete and utter shock to me. The sheer power of the moment nearly knocked me over. With smiles big enough to match the moment, they each strode directly to me. I happily embraced each of them. Then they signed the poster with signatures that would make even John Hancock proud. Each looked much older to me, but never better. No sign of the other forty former presidents, but I think I knew where they stood.

I took a risk with Bush. "Great to have you here, Otter," I said.

"What did you call me?" he asked. At first he looked puzzled, then he immediately smiled and winked at me. "We're all incredibly proud of you. All of us."

OK. That was a clear signal that he knew about the Saloon and perhaps even knew about the all-presidents meeting that gave rise to this new political construct. Or was he just a winker? I've known a few guys like that. But how else would all four of these former presidents have been so moved to take this type of public stand? Granted, the imperative for collaboration and unity had been building since McCain's funeral, for which he'd handpicked Bush and Obama to deliver eulogies—and they did with precisely the sort of country-before-party message McCain had hoped for. Or maybe Panetta, Rice, and Powell had recruited them.

Regardless of how they got here, they were, undeniably, here with me and the alliance. These were not ghosts or spirits or any figment of my imagination. And they'd just added the biggest, loudest, most prominent exclamation point to my call for action that I could've ever wished for.

Maybe we were better. I started to believe it.

Chapter Sixty-Six

July 10, 2019—6:54 p.m.
An Alliance

MSNBC

Chris Matthews: Ladies and gentlemen, I think what you just witnessed is something truly remarkable and extraordinary in the history of American politics. A sitting president with at least a modicum of popular support will not seek reelection—voluntarily walking away from the office and all its trappings of power—that in and of itself is extraordinary—but to then announce a new party . . . or movement—

Rachel Maddow: I believe he is calling it an alliance.

Chris Matthews: Yes, an alliance. He announces this new alliance that is not intending to run candidates and not intending to compete with the two parties, but the sole purpose is to influence the parties and impact the candidates THEY choose and ensure that they produce candidates who appeal to the country as a whole rather than just their base. But then, on top of all that, he manages to trot out all four living presidents as an astounding show of support.

Rachel Maddow: It appeared to me, Chris, as if McFadden might have been surprised by the appearance of the former presidents. I'd love to see the tape of that again.

Chuck Todd: I think you are absolutely right, Rachel.

And I noticed they all showed up after the speech began. I'm sure the backstory on that will come out very soon.

Chris Matthews: But Rachel, what do you make of this grand plan he is proposing? Have you ever heard anything like it, and does it actually stand a chance of leading us out of this partisan quicksand the nation has been stuck in now for years?

Rachel Maddow: I like the bold nature of it. It is new and different, and it helps so much that every living president endorsed it and signed on.

Chris Matthews: We have Tom Brokaw joining us now from his ranch in Montana. Let's bring him in and get his thoughts on the significance of this moment. Did you watch the speech Tom, and perhaps just as importantly, did you watch the aftermath with the presidents joining the cause?

Tom Brokaw: It was great political theater, Chris. I loved his choice of venue for this. McFadden has always seemed to have this fascination with our first president, and his political philosophy and style is so heavily influenced by Washington. And the views Washington expressed in his Farewell Address really provide the framework for this new political alliance McFadden is creating.

Chris Matthews: Only time will tell, but it's just possible that we'll reflect back on this day as the moment in time when our politics did, indeed, start to get better. We'll see if this gains traction and our political leaders answer the call to action.

Chuck Todd: McFadden has the numbers to pull this off, Chris, with heavy support from independents and a decent amount of support from both political parties, He seems to be the perfect poster child for the face of this movement.

Tom Brokaw: And I can't help but think, Chris, that John

McCain is looking down upon this today and smiling. The tone and message today was so reminiscent of what we saw for a solid week in the aftermath of John McCain's death. To the extent that this movement can actually provide a greater degree of unity in the country, McCain certainly deserves some degree of credit for that.

Chris Matthews: Well stated, Tom. And I'll tell you someone else who's smiling down upon this scene here today. George Washington, that's who. Now *there's* someone who'd be very pleased with McFadden's message and his new alliance—not to mention his choice of venue. Washington is one presidential spirit who's very happy today.

Chapter Sixty-Seven

Fifteen Months Later–December 15, 2020
Satch's Date

Our last Christmas in the White House was memorable. We relished every aspect of it—lighting the national Christmas tree, decorating the Blue Room, Denyse hosting her annual holiday celebration for the women and children housed in DC homeless shelters. The parties at the White House were special, particularly the one for the White House staff.

The staff party was the final official White House Christmas function before Christmas Day. Denyse and I spent well over two hours in the Entrance Hall greeting guests, handing out gifts, and posing for photos with staff.

We were still lingering with the late-arriving guests when Rene, our White House party coordinator for the night, began to insist that we join the guests in the East Room. I was wrapping up my conversation with Cathy's husband when I heard Denyse gasp audibly as she pulled at my coat from behind.

"Danny!" she said, motioning toward the front doors, "Look at that!"

I turned around to see Satch walking in with a woman on his arm. They cut quite a striking pair with his impeccable conservative tux and her elegant navy blue evening gown.

"Oh my God!" I exclaimed barely above a whisper.

"Who do you suppose she is?" Denyse asked.

"I have no idea. She's age-appropriate, though," I added, knowing it was one of Denyse's pet peeves to see older men with women half their age.

"Yes, she is, but in his case I don't care how old she is. This wonderful gentleman deserves to be happy. I love her already."

Satch clearly noticed the not-so-subtle commotion caused by his arrival with a date and smiled broadly at us, all the while his lady friend nearby remained unaware of it all. As they approached us, I leaned over to Denyse and begged her, "Please don't embarrass this poor man."

"You have so little faith in me," she shot back.

"There's a very good reason for that."

Marta, the White House staffer who was responsible for somewhat surreptitiously tipping us off to the names of each guest as they arrived, preceded them with her folder in hand. I waved her off.

Denyse hustled over to meet them in her high heels and extended her arms out to Satch's date, who appeared a bit starstruck.

"Welcome!" Denyse blurted out. "Thanks so much for coming! I'm Denyse McFadden."

"Yes, I know, Mrs. McFadden. It's such a pleasure to meet you. I'm honored to be here."

"Mrs. McFadden, meet Christy Manzanetti," said Satch.

"Oh, both of you do me a favor and call me Denyse."

I shook Satch's hand as Denyse momentarily cornered Christy. I leaned in to Satch out of earshot of the ladies.

"So, is this Dom's . . . ," I paused, thinking it best to stop there.

"Grandmother," he said, finishing my thought. "My buddy TJ's widow."

"How's she doing?" I whispered to him.

At that moment, a confident, official-looking woman I didn't recognize began ushering Denyse and me into the party. I reached out my hand to Christy.

"It's so nice to have you with here with us, Christy," I said. "I assure you we will talk later. Promise me you won't leave before we have a chance to visit."

"Of course. I look forward to it," she said, glancing at Satch as we were being pulled away.

Turning around once more I called back to her, "My boys love Dom, by the way."

"Oh, thank you so much," she replied.

As we quickly made our way toward the East Room, Denyse looked over at me with a look that suggested I had been hiding this from her. "So that's Dom's grandma? Satch's Vietnam buddy's wife?"

I smiled and nodded.

"Don't try to tell me you didn't know about this, McFadden." She looked kind of pissed.

I couldn't help but laugh as I looked around at the ushers and Secret Service agents trying hard to pretend they weren't overhearing our conversation.

"I didn't know a thing, babe!" I protested.

Denyse and I each watched Satch and Christy out of the corner of our eye during the remainder of the party, much like parents chaperoning a middle school dance would their children— except in this case we were *hoping* to uncover evidence of something amorous.

Denyse and I both mingled really well with the all the guests. In an effort to ensure we connected with everyone in attendance, we skipped dinner, split up, and took a divide-and-conquer approach.

I always loved seeing who people brought with them. Some brought their mothers, fathers, or other family members. The chance to see the White House and meet so many of the Cabinet and others made that "plus one" quite a valuable commodity. I believe we actually came very close to spending time with every staff member there, which was so important since so many of them I rarely interacted with.

Toward the end of the evening, I caught up again with Satch and Christy. Christy was momentarily alone while Satch held court with a slew of admirers nearby. "It was great having you with us tonight, Christy," I said.

"It was such a pleasure to be here, Mr. President."

"I'm thrilled you stayed 'til the bitter end."

"Oh, I'm exhausted, sir, but Satch enjoys this so much. I just can't pull him out of here—I don't have the heart! But I'm dying to take these shoes off."

"Go ahead!" I encouraged her with a laugh. "These things are far too formal for my taste."

"I wouldn't dream of it, sir. But I appreciate the offer."

"I have been thinking about your family a lot," I said, venturing into territory I was never completely comfortable with but I realized it needed to be said. "Our family has been praying for yours."

"We are much better now, Mr. President. Thanks in no small part to that fella right there." She looked over at Satch, who was busy charming a group of his coworkers but, sensing we were talking about him, turned briefly to smile at us before returning to his conversation.

"He was my husband's dearest friend," she added proudly.

"I have heard so much about TJ," I said. "And not just from Satch, from none other than General Dunford, the Chairman of the Joint Chiefs. After all these years, your husband is still revered."

"You are so nice to say that," she said, tearing up.

"The nation is infinitely grateful for his sacrifice. And yours."

She managed something of a smile through her emotions.

"Please let Denyse and me know if we can do anything for Dom. Our boys love him. I don't think they've seen him much lately."

"He was up here living with Satch for several months until I decided it would be best for him to be back home. I just moved into the house Dom had been living in with my son. I thought it best for him to stay in the same school with his friends and the community he was raised in."

"Good for you. That's very admirable of you. If we can do anything at all, please do not hesitate to ask."

A line had formed of people waiting to say goodbye to me, so I turned away from Christy to thank them one by one for coming. Several minutes later when I turned back around, Satch and Christy were gone.

Chapter Sixty-Eight

January 19, 2021
In the Arena

On my final night in the White House, the emotions were coming fast and furious. In addition to all the family and work-related drama, I knew I had to bid farewell to my favorite saloon. I realized it was a very selfish use of my time. With no future as president, my time with them could no longer be considered "professional development" in terms of a personal justification for this indulgence of mine. That could have been the biggest lie I ever told myself, by the way. But I convinced myself that I deserved to spend one more night with all my drinking buddies. I tended to think this might be my last hurrah there. As much as I wanted to believe it, I could not mentally wrap my arms around how the real me could conceivably continue to experience the Saloon, whether or not my spirit became a permanent patron for all eternity.

I could hear the party clearly from the second floor. It beckoned louder and stronger than ever before. That fired me up like nothing else.

I entered the Saloon and Matty immediately spotted me from behind the bar.

"Danny Mac is in the house!" He yelled it loud and the room burst into an enormous round of applause and cheers, the likes of which would make even Norm Peterson envious.

Tina greeted me with a big hug.

"Am I Danny Mac now?" I asked.

"Otter says you can't be Rook forever. And you know, tomorrow there'll be a new Rook."

Haskell called out to me, "What are you drinking, sir?"

"Please pour me a Guinness."

"Absolutely," he responded, leaning in closer to me. "You know, I've been meaning to tell you how much I admire your decision to pass on another four years in order to reach a more permanent solution for the country."

"I appreciate that very much, Haskell," I replied with a smile.

As Haskell left to pour my drink, Tina shot me a bit of a look. "OK, Tina," I said, returning her gaze. "We both know it was less a decision rooted in courage and more about weighing the practical realities."

"Of course," she said. "I know you really had no choice." Then turning and looking me straight in the eyes, she added, "No man in human history has ever voluntarily walked away from a position of power."

"Wow!" I laughed out loud. "You are absolutely priceless, Tina. And I'm really going to miss you."

"We'll still be seeing you, of course," she replied. "In fact, I'm looking forward to seeing how the post-presidency Danny Mac interacts with these gentlemen. I have high hopes for you, sir."

Before I could even contemplate the thought of that, she offered me a fist bump and returned to the main floor. My mind was racing. Would it be me or some mythical version of me in this Saloon from this point forward? And what on earth would form the basis for my impulses, my words, my actions. And how could they possibly measure up to all I would want them to be? I wanted desperately to ask Tina all these questions. She is sharp as a tack, perceptive, unafraid to speak the truth. I respected the heck out of her. But, for God's sake, how could I possibly seek the answers to such questions from someone who is herself just a part of this alternate reality? My whole train of thought on this perplexing mystery inevitably just led me to a deeper state of mental confusion. I couldn't decide if this was the absolute coolest thing that had ever happened to somebody or, alternatively, the most pathetic coping mechanism ever concocted. I couldn't see how it could possibly be anything but one of those two distinct scenarios.

Whatever the answer, one thing is certain: the Saloon did not disappoint that night. Decked out in all its glory, it had all the appearance of a fine country club set up to host a pretentious wedding reception on the Fourth of July—American flags and patriotic bunting everywhere; bald eagle centerpieces, complete with the arrows and olive branches in the talons; red, white, and blue streamers hanging from the eaves.

A group of musicians warmed up behind the dance floor. Very rarely had I seen food in this place, but tonight was different. The smell of fine barbecue permeated the air. It was quite an upgrade over the usual cigar stench. I had a feeling this was going to be a phenomenal send-off.

Quite a crowd of presidents had gathered near the dance floor. They all appeared to be extremely interested in something there. I walked over to join them. As I drew closer, I noticed they were all surrounding a human-sized replica of the Statue of Liberty that Sheels had wheeled in on a dolly and placed next to the dance floor.

"What, pray tell, might this be?" asked Benjamin Harrison.

Sheels scanned the group and then pointed to Grover Cleveland. "Would you care to do the honors?" he asked.

Cleveland proudly came forward. "This, gentlemen, is a miniature version of a 150-foot copper statue of Liberty Enlightening the World—a colossal figure and lighthouse that adorns New York Harbor on Bedloe's Island."

"It is now called Liberty Island, sir," yelled Eisenhower.

"Is that factual?" responded Cleveland. "Splendid. It well should be. I accepted her as president as a gift from our dear friend and sister republic, France. She is a monument of art and the continued goodwill of that great nation which aided us in our struggle for freedom. They intended her to be a symbol of our commitment to liberty and to our democratic form of government, which France of course fought for alongside of us in the Revolutionary War."

I watched Washington, Adams, and Jefferson chatting with each other, obviously fascinated and pleased with the thought of such a tremendous gift from America's first ally.

Cleveland looked around. "Where is Sheels? He obviously got the coloring wrong. The actual statue, gentlemen, made of copper, is brown, rather than this distasteful shade of green. I must get on him about that."

That elicited chuckles and knowing glances from the more modern presidents. The comment hung in the air, just begging for a smart aleck retort or mean-spirited dig from one of Cleveland's many colleagues, but, to my surprise, no one seemed to have the will to rain on his parade at this moment. The collegiality and civility among this group continued to astound me. I had clearly become far too accustomed to the nastiness of Washington.

Reagan stepped up and took a place next to Cleveland. "As those of you who preceded President Cleveland may not know, this lady has become the most enduring symbol of the hope and promise of America, particularly for all those immigrants who passed her in the harbor, their very first image of this great nation. They came from every land. They were teachers, lumberjacks, seamstresses, factory workers, miners, firemen, and police officers. They built this country, experienced life's great joys and its profound hardships, and passed on to their children their values—values that define civilization and are the prerequisites for human progress. What was it that tied them together? What was it that made them not a gathering of individuals but a nation? The bond that held them together, as it holds us together tonight in this Saloon, has stood every test and travail, is found deep in our national consciousness—an abiding love of liberty. Those of you among us tonight who fought for independence against the world's most powerful empire, those of you among us who braved tremendous hardships to tame the vast wilderness, those of you among us who saved the world from tyranny, which we have now done twice, did so for the love of liberty. And it is for the love of liberty that Americans still champion the cause of freedom and democracy in far-off lands."

The presidents, who had all gathered now around the statue, broke into long applause.

"How precious this gift from our dear friend France," Jefferson said. "Perhaps her greatest gift to us since the Marquis de Lafayette. So appropriate, as the God who gave us life gave us liberty at the same time."

At that moment Sheels and Matty appeared with a larger dolly, this one carrying an impressive miniature replica of Mount Rushmore. *Wow,* I thought. *I'm not sure whether Sheels and his team have planned for any fireworks, but they are about to get their share when this thing gets explained.* Having experienced my share of contentious conversations and disappointed people, I peeled off toward the incredible aroma emanating from the food stations being set up on the other end of the bar. I did spend a few moments wondering who would have the most bruised ego at not being included among the four presidents etched in granite.

While this incredible bar clearly offered the very best array of spirits ever known to man, I was ready to dive into the food. There were multiple stations representing various cuisines native to this great country: lobster and clam chowder from New England, southern barbecue, a Coney Island hot dog stand, Chicago deep-dish pizza, a full turkey dinner with stuffing, Philly cheesesteaks, shrimp gumbo from New Orleans, Tex-Mex,

Dungeness crab from the Northwest, Alaskan halibut, and Hawaiian ahi tuna.

The most versatile band I'd ever seen took the stage with an expertly crafted playlist of iconic American music—jazz, blues, big band, rock, Motown, bluegrass, country, hip-hop, and even a touch of rap. I was impressed. The architect of these musical selections was clearly less interested in pleasing these gentlemen—most of whom had never heard a lot of this music before—and was more focused on doing justice to all that American music had come to embody. I loved every second of it, as did Obama and Clinton, although, on this particular night, they resisted the urge to take the stage.

After a couple hours of the band killing it, they took some well-deserved bows, announced that the next song would be their last of the evening, and then proceeded to play a very stirring rendition of Don McLean's "American Pie" to finish the night. Conspicuously absent in the setlist were any of the traditional Americana songs—those that are played on the Fourth of July every year. However, they had sprinkled in a few protest anthems like "Fortunate Son" and "A Change is Gonna Come."

As they took their final bows, the huge television screen started to emerge slowly across the bar. We hadn't seen it since our memorable baseball tribute night. The presidents all instinctively migrated over to face the big screen.

Matty addressed the crowd. "For this unique celebration of America, we've assembled a collection of some of the most iconic versions of a couple of America's more traditional patriotic songs."

The lights dimmed as the big screen displayed an image of Ray Charles seated in front of a piano at home plate during the World Series in 2001, just a little over a month after the terrorist attacks on September 11. A massive American flag was draped over the outfield at Bank One Ballpark in Arizona. Wearing a dark suit and tie to match his sunglasses, Charles crooned a stirring and emotional rendition of "America the Beautiful," while the camera panned the many uniformed servicepeople in attendance. The crowd joined in toward the end, and a flyover of four Air Force jets punctuated the moment. We all stood and joined in as the Arizona crowd showered Charles with applause. His reaction to this adulation and the emotion of the moment was unlike anything I'd ever seen in a performer. Standing next to his piano, he was so moved by the moment that his body literally shook as he grasped his face with his hands. The applause in the Saloon outlasted the applause in the stadium.

Next up, the screen displayed a twenty-seven-year-old Whitney Houston stride confidently up to a microphone at the 1991 Super Bowl in a pair of Nikes, a white sweat suit, and a white bandana with red and blue trim, just days after a coalition of thirty-five nations, led by the United States, commenced Operation Desert Storm to liberate Kuwait from Iraq. We watched her belt out what is quite possibly the most iconic and emotional version of "The Star Spangled Banner" ever delivered, in front of a live global audience exceeding eighty million people. I recalled being overcome with emotion when watching it live the first time. Now, in this room, given all that had transpired and the present division within the country, it moved me to tears. I looked and saw George H. W. Bush crying as well. It wasn't lost on me that this was a young African American woman, who looked barely older than a teenager, delivering this memorable performance to honor her country. She delivered it with great joy, smiling throughout, finishing with her arms extended triumphantly well above her head just as Air Force F-16s flew overhead. The NFL had initially objected to Whitney's version of the song, complaining that she was slowing it down too much, but she resisted their efforts to get her to change it. Given all that backdrop, I thought this was clearly a version for the ages. While this Jersey girl's struggles at times made her life anything but perfect, she clearly achieved a degree of perfection that evening. I thought that made this all the more apropos for this group. I was so glad to join this collection of iconic American figures watch this wonderful moment of national pride come to life again.

I looked over at Matty, who was managing the videos. *Nothing could possibly top that.* As the people in the room buzzed about what they'd just seen, slowly the lights came back up and the big screen slid out of sight.

I hadn't really planned on saying anything, but now I felt compelled to do so. I stood up, and Matty let out a whistle, as only he can do, which quickly quieted the crowd.

"Gentlemen," I said, then, turning to the bar, "and ladies. I did not think that my affection for this country and those who have labored and sacrificed so tremendously to make it what it is could possibly grow any deeper. However, I have been so moved by my experience these past four years, and, in particular, on nights like tonight. I am so infinitely proud of my association with this country and my opportunity to serve it, no matter how imperfect my service was.

"I never had any grand ambitions for Mount Rushmore or any of the other accolades that so many of you have earned. I merely wanted to play a role in making this divided country one again. I must say that during my time in office, I failed—not just failed but failed famously, failed spectacularly—in that regard. However, thanks to the sage advice and counsel from those of you in this room, I managed to kick-start a process by which, over time, we may be able to unify the political and cultural dynamic that exists in this land. I believe we have taken an important first step toward that, and I have you to thank. The camaraderie that exists in this room of former rivals and political enemies gives me great hope that such a dynamic will one day exist in the halls of Congress and throughout our fifty states. And the clear desire of this group to place the interests of this great nation above all else, most importantly above self and above party, similarly makes me hopeful that someday the country will once again embrace those values. As I say this, it is worth pointing out one more time that these core driving principles of civility and respect for all and of putting country first above party and self are as important today as they were 225 years ago when Washington delivered his prescient warnings to the nation in his Farewell Address.

"I do take tremendous pride in the fact that I did not give in to the powerful temptation to compromise my principles in the name of self-preservation. But, at the same time, I have the luxury of being able to return to a wonderful home and life in Los Gatos. Others, I acknowledge, do not have such an idyllic fallback plan.

"I am eternally grateful to each of you for your acceptance of me, your friendship, and your counsel. My association with you has been the greatest professional honor of my charmed and privileged life.

"I leave Washington with great hope for this wonderful, and wonderfully flawed, great nation of ours, which still thrives after all these years, thanks in no small part to each of you.

"And to Sheels, Tina, Matty, Mary Ann, Ginger, and Haskell, you are each indispensable aspects of this extraordinary establishment. You add life and vitality to this community, which would clearly not be nearly the same without you."

Dan Coonan

One of the most remarkable things about this evening was that, while all of Washington and the country had shifted its focus to the incoming administration, up there in the Saloon, they were all seemingly oblivious to that. In fact, the entire evening took the form of a long goodbye of sorts to me, or at least a graduation, as presumably some form of me would continue on in this Saloon as a former president, although I still didn't know if I would somehow experience that and be conscious of it. As far as I was concerned, this was goodbye. I could only hope the version of me that survived in perpetuity in the Saloon would make me proud. Come to think of it, that's probably as good a moral and decisional compass to guide me in life as any I could think of. Act always in a manner that will cause my Saloon persona to reflect only the very best of me.

The drinks flowed freely, as they are wont to do in this Saloon. I relished every last second with the presidential spirits, whoever they were and whatever this was. Matty, with Washington at his side, let out another ear-piercing whistle, bringing the entire room to a halt.

Washington stepped forward. "Gentlemen," he began, "after much debate and discourse, we have chosen the one of us we believe would be the most appropriate person to deliver the final toast to President McFadden."

"Let's make him guess who we chose!" Otter shouted.

"C'mon, guys," I said. "I'm not the smartest guy in the room—not even near the top half. But I'm sure as heck smart enough not to enter into that no-win trap!"

"In that case," Otter announced, "Will our designated speaker please deliver the sentiments of the room to our friend Danny Mac."

Teddy Roosevelt jumped up and charged toward us from the back of the crowd. Of course it was Teddy. I was very pleased as well as flattered with this selection. I could plainly see that he was too.

"It will come as a surprise to no one here that I cannot allow this moment to pass without offering my thoughts," Roosevelt started. The room seemed to pick up energy by the moment when he had the floor.

"All honor to you, McFadden!" he said raising his glass in toast. "Like all of us, you had your successes, in which you must take immense pride, and inevitably, you had your disappointments which often generated a disproportionate amount of attention. But amidst it all, please remember that it is not the critic who counts; not the man who points out how the strong man stumbles, or where the doer of deeds could have done them better. The credit belongs to the man who is actually in the arena, whose face is marred by dust and sweat and blood; who strives valiantly; who errs, and comes short again and again, because there is no effort without error and shortcoming; but who does actually strive to do the deeds; who knows the great enthusiasms, the great devotions; who spends himself in a worthy cause; who at the best knows in the end the triumph of high achievement, and who at the worst, if he fails, at least fails while daring greatly, so that his place shall never be with those cold and timid souls who know neither victory nor defeat.

"Yes, add my name to those honoring McFadden tonight, for he has performed so valiantly in the arena. And add my name to those honoring this great country of ours, and all she stands for."

The room broke into applause that lasted several minutes before dying down. "But now that we have all so admirably honored this man and this nation and drank many a toast in both their names, allow me to focus on yet another richly deserving subject. I say we've heard quite enough about this fine man and this noble country. Enough of that, dammit! Who joins me in drinking to this Saloon?"

Everyone in the room instinctively jumped to their feet and cheered, as only Teddy can make them do.

He continued. "To the Saloon! We'll always have the Saloon. The country may add scoundrels, frauds, incompetents, and bigots to our group— sometimes all in the same person—but this magical saloon, and indeed, this magical country, endures in spite of us!"

I stood up, toasted, and drank enthusiastically along with all the others. What a concise statement of an absolute truth. Of course I had to stand and applaud for that. That was most certainly a sentiment I fully endorsed. And, looking around the room, there were no dissenters among us. A unified group, to be sure.

Chapter Sixty-Nine

January 20, 2021—6:00 a.m.
The Worst Form of Government,
Except for Every Other Form

I had an incredibly ambitious agenda planned for the few hours we had left in the White House the morning of Inauguration Day. As we had agreed, I met Satch in his office at six o'clock in the morning. There was a palpably different vibe in the air. The White House was deserted, and many offices I passed on the way to his had been cleared out.

Satch broke into a big smile when he saw me. He was seated behind an empty desk with his feet up, his office naked without all the photos and memorabilia blanketing the walls. For the first time, rather than filling my heart with joy, his smile triggered a reflexive sadness deep within me. I had grown incredibly comfortable with him in my life. He had very quickly become not only a great friend to me but part psychiatrist, political adviser, historian, father figure, and life coach. The feeling that came over me was not unlike what I'd experienced my last night of college while saying good-bye to people that I would've given anything to have by my side every day going through the rest of life.

"I have to say, Satch, it is terribly hard to say goodbye to you in particular, my friend."

"I feel the same, sir. And I'll miss Denyse, Kelly, and those boys. You've done a fine job raising them. You should be very proud."

"I can't take any victory laps just yet. We're moving them cross-country again, so I'm fairly certain I won't be getting any Father of the Year awards—at least not from them."

"Oh, I think they have tremendous respect for you, Mr. President."

"I hope I haven't scarred them for life!"

"On the contrary, sir! They have solid character and big hearts. That qualifies you and Denyse for the parenting Hall of Fame."

"You see, that's why I've always loved coming down here these past four years. I walk in here all torn up inside about something and walk out feeling like a million bucks. I'm convinced Drake puts you up to that."

"More likely Denyse than Ms. Drake," Satch said with a laugh.

I had an achy feeling in my heart. I'm certain he sensed it. He senses everything.

"Where do we go from here, sir?" he asked.

"Who? Me or the country?"

"Either." He responded. A moment later he corrected himself. "Both."

I paused in thought. Satch could see I wasn't going to answer that quickly.

"Hold on," he said. "I want to give you a gift." He reached down and grabbed a large frame that was leaning against the side of his desk. "I want you to have this," he said, turning it over. It was a print of the painting of George and Martha Washington at a dinner table with a black servant nearby waiting on them.

"Wow!" I responded. "I don't know what to say. Thank you so much. I've always been intrigued by this."

I looked at it closely. I was more convinced than ever that the slave depicted was, indeed, Christopher Sheels.

"I want you to have it, sir. I know how strongly you admire Washington."

"I have come to identify very closely with him."

"Is he the president you most admire, sir?"

"That's a tough one. Let me think about that for a minute." I thought for a few seconds before continuing, "Washington was such an iconic leader— a towering figure in our early history. Without his military leadership, there's no defeat of the British, no break from England, no new nation. Without his presidential leadership, the new nation likely would not have survived. And I identify so closely with his political philosophy and approach." Then glancing at my new gift, I added. "But it's hard, if not impossible, to get past the slavery issue."

"Yes, there will always be that."

"Let me ask you this," I said. "With what this print clearly depicts, why did you have it up in your office? That always surprised me."

"It's our history," he responded. "We can't hide it or deny it. It's who we are. . . . And let's just say I've come to identify with that gentleman through the years."

I wondered if he was talking in some sort of code.

"Who else do you admire?" he asked. "Do you have other favorites?"

"Well, as an Irish Catholic, I grew up loving and admiring Kennedy until I learned some of the rather disturbing and reckless stories about him. I don't admire that in men. The deeper you look, the more troubling it is. But he certainly had a charisma about him—and what a speaker he was. I love the great orators. And a thousand days is not nearly enough to allow for a fair grade on his presidency. He's a very interesting gentleman . . . um, at least he seems like he was.

"Lincoln seems to get everyone's vote. He confronted the most challenging set of circumstances imaginable and achieved success, righting a terrible wrong in the process. But he wasn't perfect, either. He ran roughshod over the Constitution at times, including jailing newspaper editors, suspending habeas corpus, and deporting some critics, just to name a few abuses of power. It all worked then, but presidents shouldn't be able to do that.

"FDR presided over a war that saved the world and was a progressive hero domestically. But he paved the way for the Cold War and appeasement of Stalin, sought too much power at home, and had his own share of race issues, like the internment of Japanese Americans. He also nominated a former Klansman to the Supreme Court and refused to invite black Olympians like Jesse Owens to the White House. And he could've done more for the plight of Jews during the Holocaust.

"I do like Reagan—his personality, his strength on the world stage, his speeches. Such a great speaker. He was too conservative for my taste, even though he was nothing like the conservatives we have today. By today's Republican standards, Reagan would be considered a moderate. He'd be primaried.

"I like Obama too. Maybe I'm the rare person who would like both Obama and Reagan. Obama is such an inspirational and charismatic speaker—and a likable person. You want that in a president. And classy. However, I didn't think he fully delivered on his promise of bipartisanship. Not that achieving that is a picnic—I know that all too well. And he wasn't as strong perhaps internationally as I would've liked—particularly with Syria.

"Jefferson is a study in contradictions. Fascinating character. Brilliant.

Deep thinker. The Louisiana Purchase was the greatest deal in American history."

"Or at least until the Yankees bought Babe Ruth from the Red Sox for the rights to *No, No Nannette*," replied Satch.

"Yes, of course," I laughed. "And Jefferson so eloquently and perfectly captured the core mission of the new country in prose, which provided the inspiration for America's lofty ideals. But that just makes his own inability to embrace equality for all men—both throughout the country and at home at Monticello—all the more puzzling . . . and disturbing."

"Yes," agreed Satch. "He may have been the most brilliant of them all, but he had such deep internal contradictions."

"Maybe it's Teddy I like the best. How can you not absolutely love him, for God's sake? A bundle of energy and passion. But I'm sure he was certainly a handful to deal with in his time. Had a bit of an ego too. At least that's what I gather."

"All these guys had big egos, sir."

"Ha! You're right about that, Satch."

"They all had issues, too. None of them were perfect," added Satch. "Washington got a bunch of the really big things right, but he and his contemporaries certainly got a few of the really big things wrong. These men were all deeply flawed. And why shouldn't they be? After all, humans are deeply flawed—particularly those with large egos, grand ambitions, and self-interest. But you know what? They all supplied pieces to the puzzle. The founders created a tremendous system of government based on a set of lofty principles, but at the time, had they attempted to rid the new country of the scourge of slavery, they may have never gotten off the ground in the first place."

It was astonishing to hear that statement come from Satch. I was relishing all of this.

"Humans are unquestionably the best thing about this world," he continued, "and just as assuredly, they are the absolute worst thing about this world."

"No question," I wholeheartedly agreed.

"Could we have done better?" he asked rhetorically. "Sure. But just as humans are deeply flawed, democracy itself is deeply flawed. As a nation, we get some things right, but others we get horribly wrong. Tragically wrong. Always will. But this country endures. In spite of democracy, and because of democracy, it endures. Like Churchill said, 'democracy is the worst form of government, except for every other form ever created.'"

"Yes, and that is certainly true. But we can be so much better. That's the most frustrating part."

"Yes we can, Mr. President. And you know what? You got us closer to that. You moved the dial, as you like to say, in that direction more than any other recent politician. You were right to channel Washington. Like him, you set aside your comfortable life and private ambition for the good of this deeply flawed but incredible country.

"And democracy doesn't act quickly. As Dr. King said, 'The arc of the moral universe is long, but it bends toward justice.' It works slowly but eventually gets it right."

"I'm well aware of that quote, Satch. I'm just not sure I buy it. It seems to be bending back lately. And to the degree it suggests we should just be patient, that's bullshit. We need an urgency on a lot of these issues."

"Well, that's where your new initiative comes in, Mr. President. That's another piece of the puzzle in this country—a very valuable piece that you have supplied. This country is far from perfect, but your efforts are getting us closer. Making us better. And whoever thought this experiment would last 250 years in the first place? It's OK to demand the best of our presidents and our country, but we need to realize we'll never completely attain it. And, at the end of the day, we need to be satisfied with the knowledge that we gave it our all and focus on that rather than lamenting the failure to achieve perfection."

"I'm gonna miss the heck out of you, Satch."

"I've never heard anybody put it quite like that before, sir, but I think I know what you mean." He smiled. "You realize you are now immortal, my friend. You know that, right?"

I smiled back. "How do you figure that?"

"You all live forever."

My first thought was the Saloon, which had been on my mind so much today, wondering if somehow I would continue to experience that.

"You presidents are like the celluloid heroes in that classic Kinks song. You never really die. People will always know you. Kids will always memorize your name and presidential sequence number and learn all about you.

Presidential Spirits

Grad students will study your administration. People will misappropriate your quotes. Biographers will dig up all the dirt on your affairs."

"Ha!" That made me laugh out loud. "I don't suppose anyone will find my personal life all that compelling. It is absolutely idyllic for the five of us in our family, but it's not noteworthy or remarkable in any manner."

"In all seriousness, sir, I expect your idyllic family life could be a part of a new narrative—a wave of committed family men in the White House, like George W. Bush and Barack Obama. That's quite admirable and refreshing in light of the rather colorful history of this place."

"Not sure the books about me will sell like Kennedy's."

"That speaks well of you, Mr. President."

"I've gotta get upstairs," I said. "Hey, I know Denyse would really like to say goodbye. Can you meet us up in the Oval Office in about a half an hour? We can say our final farewells in the Oval Office. Somehow that seems appropriate."

"I would love nothing more, sir."

I got up to leave. Before I got to the door, I turned back toward him. "One question that's been kind of bothering me, Satch."

"What's that?"

"If Washington gave the gold coin directly to Adams, and Adams passed it on to Jefferson, and so on, then why is it that you gave it to me? Shouldn't it have come directly from Obama?"

"That is a great question, sir. You know how sacrosanct traditions are around this place. As I understand it, the coin was passed down personally from president to president for roughly the first eighty years of the country, until Grant took over for Johnson. To say they didn't care for one another would be putting it mildly. Grant was highly critical of Johnson. Grant refused to ride in the carriage with him to the inauguration, and Johnson could not bring himself to pass along the gold coin to him, leaving it instead with the White House valet, who had been the one to pass it to Johnson after the assassination of Lincoln. That valet then took it upon himself to continue this fine tradition. And since that time, following that tradition, the presidents have largely left it to the valet to handle. I suspect that helps in times where there is bad blood between the men or their parties. And, of course, all too often the transition of our presidents has come about by assassination or death."

345

"That makes sense," I responded. "In my case, however, I think it is important that I pass it along myself—given everything I've been preaching about national unity and bringing the country together. Does that make sense?"

"Makes perfect sense, sir."

"Great. Then I will do so."

Gold coin in hand, I made tracks all the way up to the third floor. I looked at my watch and noticed I was running a few minutes late. I paused outside Saloon door. I heard what I thought were feint sounds of music. The big heavy door slowly opened. The Saloon was uncharacteristically empty. I could hear a single violin playing. The place was mostly dark, with the only light coming from the dimly lit backbar. The lighting and music combined to create quite a mystical vibe – even more than usual for this mysterious place.

When my eyes adjusted to the light, I could see him sitting on a stool by the stage, music stand before him and a violin wedged below his chin. He was waiting for me, just as I had requested.

"President Jefferson," I called to him. "I am so sorry to have kept you waiting all alone for me."

"Rubbish," he responded. "My music is a most suitable companion. It is the favorite passion of my soul. It sweetens all the days of my life."

"In that case, I hate to interrupt, sir." I always felt so terribly inferior in his company. "But I'm running a bit late, so please follow me," I said, quickly walking toward my entrance to the Saloon. "I really appreciate you doing this for me."

"Happy to do so," he responded.

Thomas Jefferson wore the same outfit I had become so familiar seeing him in: a light brown coat, red waistcoat, and breeches. His hair was powdered. He was clearly treating my request as a very formal occasion.

I watched him follow me out my exit onto the third floor of the White House. Until he made it through that door, I wasn't entirely sure the presidential spirits could actually walk through that exit onto the third floor. That got my mind wondering. If I had Obama or Clinton or Otter exit the Saloon, then potentially there could be a younger version of themselves walking around. That blew my mind—like everything else around this place. After four years, I really wasn't any closer to figuring this whole thing out than I

346

was on that first night with the thirteen toasts.

I slowed our pace and turned to Jefferson. "If you can just walk out that door into the White House anytime, then why don't any of you do it?" I asked.

"McFadden," he said stopping momentarily, "do you not realize the purpose of the Saloon? And the purpose of each presidents' very existence in the Saloon? Did you think it was all for our own benefit?"

I let his words hang in the air, contemplating precisely what he was getting at. Of course. How could I not see that? Unfortunately, I didn't have time to fully think it through.

I led him quickly down the stairs to the first floor. As we walked, I could see the wheels spinning within his brain. He took everything in. I wished I had the time to let him download his thoughts to me. He took particular interest in every painting and portrait we passed. He smiled broadly at the nearly life-size portrait of Dolley Madison.

"Gregarious woman," he said. "Quite lovely. I should like to tell James about this portrait."

Jefferson drew many double takes as we passed quite a few White House staffers and security on our way to the Blue Room. Some waved or gave a thumbs-up, which seemed strange to me. One staffer went even further. "That looks spot on!" he exclaimed, stopping and looking right at Jefferson. "I love it! So well done."

Then it occurred to me: people must be assuming he's just part of the inaugural festivities. This was perhaps the perfect day to pull this off.

When we arrived at the Blue Room, Professor Harris was waiting for me. I had not prepped him in any way for this. How could I, really? I merely told him he needed to be there. He came without question—one of the reasons I love the guy.

The thought that I was introducing my college government and history professor to Thomas Jefferson was yet another one of those epic moments. I'd never messed with any mushrooms or LSD in my life, but I imagined that this feeling must be pretty similar to what that was all about.

"Professor," I said, not knowing really where to start, "it is my great honor to be able to introduce you to none other than Thomas Jefferson—the president you once told me you'd most like to meet."

The professor laughed out loud. "This is priceless!"

"Professor, I wish I had the time to fully explain, but I have to leave you two alone now. It may take you five minutes or forty-five minutes, but I'm pretty sure you will eventually come to realize that this really is Thomas Jefferson."

"Of course it is," Professor Harris replied with a wink.

"Go ahead," I said. "Ask him anything."

"So," the professor began with a wry smile, "you're Thomas Jefferson. Tell me, where did you attend college."

"The College of William and Mary, sir."

"OK, you've done a little homework, I see."

"Professor," I said, "trust me. The sooner you believe me, the more you'll be able to relish this moment in time—"

"Who was your vice president?"

"Is that a trick question? For I had two—Aaron Burr and George Clinton."

I had to go. Denyse had been texting me from the Oval Office. I should have scheduled this for a day when I could have devoted more time to both of them to make it a more productive experience.

As I prepared to leave, I walked over to the professor, looked him square in the eyes, and said, "Please, do me this one favor."

"Sure," he replied.

"For the next hour or so, pretend that this is really Thomas Jefferson. Just go with it. Do your damnedest to convince yourself that it's the truth, and then just sit back and thoroughly enjoy the conversation. Trust me when I tell you that you'll be glad you did. I'll be back in an hour."

With that, I proceeded to leave, but not before I heard the professor ask a question that desperately made me want to stay: "Of all your contemporaries in the time of the Revolution and the formation of the new country, who did you admire the most?"

That question stopped me dead in my tracks. *What a great question! How could I conceivably leave now?* I had been with Jefferson in the Saloon many times over the past four years and never thought to ask him that.

I slowed my pace to ensure that I could hear the answer, but Jefferson paused, deep in thought. I stopped, my ears peeled for his words.

"Of course, there were scores of admirable fellows," Jefferson replied. "But my answer must begin with Benjamin Franklin."

Presidential Spirits

Of course, I thought. *I might have predicted that answer if I had thought about it some more.* I was actually surprised Franklin's name hadn't come up more often in the Saloon. It kind of made me wish he'd been a president, even if for no other reason than to have met him. He clearly had a strong enough personality to make a discernible impact on that crowd in the Saloon. And think of the humor he would've added! It's a pity Hamilton isn't in there as well, although he's landed his own version of eternal life now on Broadway.

As much as I wanted to hear the rest of Jefferson's answer and all the other questions this brilliant professor was about to ask, I had to hustle back to the Oval Office. I hoped my professor friend would at some point come to realize that this really was Thomas Jefferson, so he could enjoy the experience as much as I do.

When I got to the Oval Office, Satch was just walking in. Inside we found Denyse and Christy waiting for us, in addition to two unexpected guests: Montana and another very rambunctious dog.

"Well what do we have here?" Satch asked, looking right at Christy.

"Denyse invited me here so they could bid farewell to the two of us together."

"Who the heck is this?" I asked, watching a crazy dog antagonize Montana. "He looks familiar."

"Yes," responded Satch. "I've been meaning to tell you about that. I kept one of Tipsy's pups. I didn't think there'd be any harm in that. When Jackie died, I didn't think I'd ever be able to have another dog. But having Tipsy at home with me and seeing her pups kind of stirred something inside of me. When we had difficulty finding a home for the last one, I took that as a sign from God, or from someone, that I needed another and this was the one."

"That is priceless!" I exclaimed with genuine enthusiasm. "Looks like the one in the painting over there, doesn't it?" I added, pointing up at the shot of Washington on the hunt."

"Why, yes, it does sir! Now that you mention it, it does. Perhaps Rosa is a descendant of a Mount Vernon hunting dog. Wouldn't that be something."

"That would be something, alright," I replied, staring right at Satch, who seemed suddenly unable or unwilling to make eye contact. I was becoming more and more convinced that he knew a heck of a lot more than he was letting on.

After a few awkward moments of silence, he uttered, "Yes indeed."

Denyse jumped in, "Satch, we are all going to miss you so much it hurts! I can't tell you how much you have meant to all of us. You became a part of our family, and I don't want to say goodbye."

"I couldn't agree more," I added. "When you were pointing out downstairs that all humans are necessarily flawed, I think I would beg to differ on that contention. I have yet to see yours."

"Trust me, they are there, sir. We're all going through life just trying our best to figure this whole thing out. I would regret a lot in my life if I stopped to think about it. But I choose to focus instead on what's in front of me. If you resolve to try to be the best version of yourself possible every day, you'll end up throwing a heck of a lot more strikes in life than balls."

"And the boys will miss you possibly even more than us," Denyse said. "They'll miss Hank a ton too."

"And Dom," I added.

"Speaking of Dom, Mr. President . . . ," Satch paused, with the room seeming to hang on his every word, "I've figured out my last chapter." Then he placed his arm around Christy and gave her a kiss.

I looked at Denyse and could see she was starting to cry. Her mind worked a heck of a lot faster than mine, particularly when it came to love and happy endings.

Christy proudly lifted her left hand, which displayed an engagement ring. Denyse leapt up and sprinted over to give Christy a hug. Taking my lead from her, I gave Satch a bit of a bro hug.

"Dom is going to be raised from this point forward by his grandmother and her new husband," said Satch, his voice noticeably cracking. Denyse and Christy were in full crying mode at this point.

"I'm moving to Virginia, and we're in contract on a new home for the three of us in Dom's neighborhood."

"One question," I said. "Does it have a pitcher's mound in the backyard?"

"It will very soon, sir."

"That Dom is a lucky kid."

"No, I'm the lucky one, Mr. President."

I teared up as I thought of Satch and TJ meeting as young men in Vietnam and forming a bond that not only survived but endured long after TJ's death. With all the hell that war put them through and the way it forever shattered not only TJ's life but that of his wife and, even more so, his son, a few rays of happiness stemming from all the chaos I'm sure seemed just too good to be true. Obviously I never knew TJ, but if he was anything like Satch, I'm certain he would have been nothing short of thrilled with this result as well.

Just then, Cathy opened the door and motioned to me. "It's time, Mr. President."

I turned to Satch. "Do you have twenty minutes for me?" I asked. "Come with us."

"What's going on, sir?" Satch asked.

"Just follow us," I said.

Chapter Seventy

January 20, 2021—8:02 a.m.
One Sweet Ride

Denyse and I got up and led Satch and Christy out the door to the West Wing colonnade walkway outside. The dogs followed along behind us. It was unseasonably warm on this winter day in DC.

"Did you tell her?" I asked Denyse.

She nodded.

"Tell her what?" Satch asked. I'm not sure I had ever seen Satch mildly annoyed before. Now he looked quizzically at Christy, too, who was all too tickled just to smile back at him.

As we approached the back driveway of the White House below the Truman Balcony, we could see that the entire White House staff had gathered.

Satch looked at Denyse and said, "They all came out to say goodbye to you, Mrs. McFadden."

"Actually," responded Denyse, "I think they're here for you."

A podium had been set up, and one by one, longtime White House staffers offered this great man the most genuine, heartfelt goodbyes I had ever witnessed. When the last one had finished, I took the microphone, knowing I could not add anything meaningful in the way of words to all that had just been uttered. "Satch," I began, "these folks have said it all in the most heartwarming manner imaginable. You clearly know how deeply you are loved and how sorely you will be missed. So I think all that is left for me to do is ensure that we send you off in style."

At that moment, Brett pulled up alongside us in a classic Riverside Red '63 Corvette Stingray convertible with Dom in the passenger seat. Satch looked at me and just shook his head with a huge smile. The dozens of staff that had assembled erupted in applause.

"I don't suppose this is your new car, is it Brett?" Satch asked, appearing a bit overwhelmed.

"No, sir," Brett replied as he jumped out of the car and tossed Satch the keys. "I wish!"

"There you go, buddy," I said, slapping Satch on the back. "That dream set of wheels is all yours, my friend, on behalf of a grateful nation, as Abraham Lincoln would say."

"This is from Uncle Sam?" Satch asked.

"Well, actually it's from Denyse and me, but the nation is indeed grateful, as are we."

I could tell he was profoundly moved by it all.

"I love you, Satch," I said, tearing up as I gave him a final fist bump just before he started the engine. Christy hopped in along with Rosa, making for a very crowded vehicle. I would have been concerned if I thought they were driving anywhere other than the White House lot to get Satch's other car. Brett did his best to hold Montana back, but it took all he had.

"You'll remember to take care of the coin transfer to our new president?" Satch shouted at me.

I walked closer to him and lowered my voice, "That's a really stupid question . . . Of course I will. I'll hand it to her in the limo on the way over to the Capitol today."

"Perfect."

"Who takes over for you as the keeper of this legacy of the gold coin?" I asked.

"They have all that worked out, Mr. President." He began to pull away.

"Wait!" I called out. "Who has all of that worked out?"

"You know who, sir," Satch said, pulling away further.

Now I was the one starting to get a little angry. I jogged alongside the car to remain within earshot.

"No. No, I don't. I don't know who! Tell me!" I shouted.

"Big Daddy, Otter, and Sheels."

"Wait!" I yelled. "How do you know about . . ." I stopped dead in my tracks, dumbfounded.

Satch slowed for a second, turned, and looked back at me. Amidst the noise from the engine, he yelled, "You're going to enjoy meeting my replacement," he said with a grin as he pointed back toward the White

House.

What? Big Daddy, Otter, and Sheels? He's known about those guys the whole time? How could I be so blind? And he has a replacement? Someone who also knows about all this as well?

Then he sped away in his dream car with his new fiancée at his side, his new grandson sitting up on the back right behind them, and his dog—a descendant of George Washington's own carefully bred hunting dogs—between them. It was a crowded, but happy, vintage ride. *Now that,* I thought, *is a pretty good start on that last chapter of his.* If he hadn't just sent my head into a tailspin, I would have certainly paused for a moment to be really, really, happy for him.

I thanked all the staff who had shown up to help me send Satch off in style. That meant so much to me that they came out to make this special. Many of them now had to get to work transitioning the entire White House for the new administration in just a few hours.

With Denyse, Kelly and the boys by my side, I addressed the staff to say my own goodbyes. It was terribly emotional for us and for them, but there was much left to do. In two hours, Denyse and I were expected to greet the new first couple at the front entrance for a photo op, then we'd all have coffee on the Truman Balcony before heading off to the inauguration. But in the meantime, I still had a few things planned.

When we got back inside, we stopped in front of a bank of televisions tuned to preinaugural coverage.

FOX News

Neil Cavuto: Despite all his shortcomings as a president, Danny McFadden undeniably impacted this election. The fact that he was the first person ever to speak at both conventions and that he, indeed, seemed to pull both parties toward the center suggests his legacy will lie more in the impact he had on our political climate and discourse in this country than anything he actually accomplished as president.

Denyse looked over at me to see how I took that. "That's OK, right?" she asked.

"I'll accept that. The truth is he's both giving me props and slamming me in the same sentence. But that's the truth."

Then she pulled at my arm and said, "Let's go, Danny. Just focus on the compliment and move on. No need to listen to any more of this."

But I wasn't ready to move on just yet.

> **Bret Baier:** What do you think is next for McFadden?
> **Cavuto:** Given the initial success of his new party—
> **Baier:** Alliance.
> **Cavuto** (rolling his eyes): Yes, given the initial success of his new *alliance,* let me make a bold prediction right now: I'm not convinced we won't see another McFadden inauguration at some point in the future.

Denyse shrieked with glee and whirled around to face me. "You hear that?" she shouted. "I'd say that's a powerful legacy for you. I love their prediction of another McFadden inauguration."

"Ha ha!" I laughed. "Unfortunately, I'm not quite sure I have it in me."

"Who said they were talking about you?" Denyse said with a smile as she shot me a look and then quickly walked ahead of me, humbling me as she does so well.

Moments later Drake caught up to me. "Hey, Boss. I noticed you haven't touched those pardons Brian prepared for you. I don't mean to bother you, but I wanted to make sure you were intentionally passing on them rather than merely forgetting to do so."

"I didn't forget."

"Alright. Just checking. You know, of course, that signing the ones in the black folder could provide the key to funding a pretty spectacular presidential library in your name."

That made me laugh. "I know you are kidding me now," I said, even though I was fairly certain she wasn't. "You seem to be confusing me with some of my esteemed predecessors. I don't think that's exactly what James Madison had in mind when he argued for the pardon power.

"And I think you know me better than to think I'd erect a monument all

355

for the glorification of me!"

"OK. Cathy guessed right. We'll place those in the rejection file."

"Please do."

I then proceeded up to the second-floor residence where several people were moving about on the Truman Balcony, obviously setting up for our ceremonial powwow. Denyse was out there deeply engaged in conversation with one of the staff members, whose back was turned to me. Her silhouette looked very familiar. I walked outside to see them, and everyone turned in my direction to say hello. When I saw the familiar-looking lady with Denyse, I froze.

"Danny, have you met Tina? She's the new Head of Hospitality and will also be taking over for Satch overseeing the entire custodial staff."

It was Tina—Tina from the Saloon. That Tina. *Oh my God!*

Tina smiled wide. It was startling to see her in a pantsuit with her hair down and not in her usual waitress attire. "It's such a pleasure to meet you, Mr. President." She couldn't stop grinning, enjoying this moment perhaps a little too much.

"You've got big shoes to fill, as I'm sure you know," I replied, shaking her hand.

"From what I gather, I think she's up to the task, Danny," Denyse added.

"Where do you come from, Tina?" I asked, dying to hear how she'd answer that.

"I've been working in government hospitality for quite some time now."

"Your former employer must be devastated to lose you." For some reason, I felt the need to push her buttons.

"Oh, I don't know about that. I'm not sure how much they actually appreciated me, to be honest."

As much as I enjoyed messing with her a bit, I was racking my brain attempting to figure out how exactly this appointment could possibly have come about.

Pressed for time, I needed to move on. "Thanks for your help with our coffee meeting today," I said. "And good luck to you with the new administration. If you need any advice on how to handle working for presidents, I'd be happy to provide you with some helpful tips."

"Oh, I'm pretty sure I know the drill," she said, laughing. "Just stroke their enormous ego as much as possible."

Presidential Spirits

"You're gonna do just fine. Good luck to you."

I looked at my watch and noticed time was getting short, and I still had a few things to do before I needed to greet the new first couple.

"Are you OK here?" I asked Denyse. "I've got a few things to take care of, and besides, I trust your instincts on this setup here anyway."

"What's going on, Danny?" Denyse asked.

"I'll explain tonight on our deck in Los Gatos over a bottle of wine. Maybe two."

For some reason that I couldn't really explain, I needed a few more final moments in the Saloon. Maybe a little closure and a proper goodbye. I have always romanticized the great bars in my life—and there were many—but none even remotely like this one.

***

In the dim light, the empty bar looked surreal as I stood there reflecting upon it all. What an exhilarating spot this had been for me during the past four years. I wondered what this place would be like ten, twenty, or fifty years from now, assuming that the Saloon and this country made it that long. What kind of personalities would be added to this distinguished group? What issues would emerge? Would the country ever get past this fundamental divide? I hoped that the Alliance, which seemed to have genuinely started to make a real difference, could help heal this hopelessly broken country over the long run.

I knew well the value of this Saloon. It was so much more than just a drinking establishment. It hadn't taken me long to figure that out. What a godsend it was. It not only helped me find my bearings as president, it provided me with an unmistakable sense of what this country is—and should be—all about. Whatever its supernatural or mystical origin, maybe this Saloon was the reason this country had not only survived but thrived for nearly 250 years in the face of some considerable global challenges and in spite of some distinguished but deeply, deeply flawed leaders.

Amidst this powerful moment, my trance was broken by the door opening behind me. In the past four years, no one had used that entrance except me. And McCain. . . and, well, the dogs.

I whirled around to see Tina peering in. "I had a feeling I might find you here, Danny Mac."

"My how quickly we shed our formalities," I joked. "I'm still president

357

until noon, you know."

She approached me carrying a cardboard box. She set it down then gave me a big hug.

"What have you got there?" I asked.

"A box of hats for all the patrons of the Saloon." She opened it up and pulled out a couple dozen green baseball caps with the words, "WE'RE BETTER THAN THIS" embroidered across the front.

I laughed out loud. "This thing has taken on a life all its own!"

"That's a very good thing. Your buddies in this bar are quite proud of your new alliance," she said. "They feel some share in the ownership of it."

"Are you kidding me? They should. . . . It was all their idea!" I replied then paused for a moment before continuing. "Let me ask you this. . . . How on earth did you manage to pull off Satch's position?"

"Let's just say I have friends in high places."

"But who actually hired you?"

"If I told you, I'd have to kill you, sir." I could tell she was enjoying this. "You've heard of the deep state?" she asked with a smile. "Well, it's hard at work behind the scenes pulling all the levers of power." She laughed.

"So you'll be replacing Satch as the keeper of the legacy of the coin as well?"

"That's me."

"So that's what Satch was referring to. What happens if the next president doesn't stumble upon the Saloon like I did?"

"That's where I come in. We have ways to control such things."

"Fascinating. That blows my mind. Do you think you'll be happy in that role?"

"I may try to parlay it into a West Wing job eventually. I've certainly studied presidents enough to know a thing or two."

"If anyone can make that transition, Tina, I'm sure you can. I'm a believer. Aren't you worried though that your unique voice and viewpoint will be missed in the Saloon?"

"Not at all," she answered. "That angle is covered now."

"Oh, yes, of course. Our new president should fill that void."

"I wasn't referring to her."

I gave her a blank stare. Then it hit me. "Oh, you're referring to me? Ha ha! I'm afraid I'm not nearly worthy of that. You may recall that time and again I was a few steps slow out of the box in advocating for those causes."

"But you've learned a lot from me," Tina said with a smile, "and without me being there, I have every expectation that you will rise to the occasion."

"I appreciate your faith in me, as misplaced as it might be," I said.

I think this was yet another effort on her part to influence my positions without me realizing she was doing so. She was a master at that.

"There's something else I'm dying to know, Tina. With Bush, Carter, Obama, and Clinton all showing up and surprising me for my speech at Mount Vernon . . ." I paused for a second, trying to decide how to phrase the question, "it's almost like they knew about the night in the Saloon when the presidents sprung that plan on me. But the present-day versions of them were in attendance at Mount Vernon, not the Saloon versions."

"Yeah . . . so?"

"How does that all work? Will I be conscious of what's going on in the Saloon in addition to my own reality?"

"I guess you're about to find that out now, aren't you?"

"Really? That's all you're gonna give me? I must say I'm really not a fan of this deep state stuff." I looked at my watch. "I've gotta go. Have to ensure another peaceful transition of power and all. But oh my God, Tina, they will miss you so much here in the Saloon."

"I appreciate that very much. Not all of them will, but thank you for the kind words." Then she added, "And you'll get a kick out of what they did to replace me in here."

"What's that? Or are you going to make me wait to figure that out on my own too?"

"Sheels hired a gay waiter."

"Get out! That's awesome!" I exclaimed. "That ought to rock their world a bit. You could sell tickets to that. Broadcast it on pay-per-view. This Saloon seems to lag the country culturally by several generations. That ought to be as educational for some of those old farts as it is entertaining."

"Yeah, right? I kind of wish I was there to watch. I think it will have an impact on the old timers."

Then she paused and looked me straight in the eyes as if to signal a big reveal. "He won't be the only one in the Saloon, however."

"What?" I asked. It really wasn't all that surprising to me—the startling part was that I really had no idea who.

A president?" I asked. All I saw looking back at me was a poker face.

"Who, Buchanan? I know he was single and quite close, shall we say, with a senator from Alabama."

A blank stare.

"A staff member?" I asked. "Haskell?" I thought longer. "You...is it you?"

She smiled back. "It makes no difference, as you well know. In time you may learn, but I'm not here to out anyone—myself or anyone else."

"OK. As much as I'm dying to know I respect that."

"I've really gotta run," she said, "but I wanted to find you and say a proper goodbye. Couldn't exactly do that downstairs." Then she added, "I want you to know I really admire the path you've taken."

"I appreciate that," I replied.

"You know, of course, that your alliance is already having an impact?"

"I certainly hope so. But I'm smart enough to know that can turn on a dime."

As I turned to walk away, she looked back at me. "And one more thing, Danny Mac."

"What's that?"

"Because of you, sir," she seemed a bit choked up. "Because of you. . . we are better." With that, she tossed me a green hat and walked away.

I promptly put it on, looked up at the sign above the exit, which said, "THE PRESIDENTIAL SPIRITS SALOON, SERVING PRESIDENTIAL SPIRITS SINCE 1792," and strode out of this enchanted bar for the final time.

Well, maybe for the final time . . .

Chapter Seventy-One

January 21, 2021
A New Beginning

Following the inauguration, we said our goodbyes to the new first couple in the shadow of the Capitol building, well aware that the entire world was watching. We wished them luck, turned, waved to the cameras, and boarded the helicopter. I thought of Nixon famously flashing the victory sign as he boarded Marine One to return to California almost fifty years ago. I wasn't leaving in disgrace like he did, but I couldn't really claim victory, either. I think I landed somewhere in that expansive gray middle ground, like so many presidents these days.

Denyse and I settled in, put on our headphones so we could communicate during the brief trip to Andrews Air Force Base, and exhaled. I had so many emotions running through my head. The past four years had flown by in the blink of an eye.

We had arrived in Washington with very little expectations but so much hope. And it's hard to say we'd gotten close to achieving our goals. However, this new alliance had a chance to become the foundation for real political change in this country. But it was way too early to tell if that dynamic had real staying power. I sat back and pictured the family enjoying a California winter for the first time in four years. Those are my kind of winters. I could get in shape again. Maybe coach one of Jack's teams. Write. No more fundraising, lobbyists, elections, or gridlock. I had an overwhelming feeling of relief, but clearly I was mixing in plenty of regret at the same time.

We circled the DC area a couple of times on the way out, as I had requested. Washington is always impressive, but this view whipped up my emotions even beyond that first night in the limo coming home from the balls.

I looked down upon all the larger-than-life symbols of our nation and all it stands for: the majesty of the Capitol—the people's branch. The Supreme

Court just down the road. We are, after all, a nation of laws. As impressive
and powerful as the other two branches are, this branch can and does over-
rule each of them. The ultimate arbiter of the Constitution. And, of course,
the White House, which from now on for me will evoke memories of all my
ghostly predecessors—and their dogs. I cannot think of it without smiling; I
hope that is always the case. And the thought that somehow, someway, some
version of myself might live on in that Saloon for the remainder of our years
as a nation is both exhilarating and daunting.

As I saw Arlington, I thought of Lincoln wanting a federal cemetery
within his view so that he would always be reminded of the consequences of
war. I could see the Washington Monument, the Jefferson Memorial, and the
Lincoln Memorial. Lincoln earned his place there by cleaning up
Washington and Jefferson's unfinished business.

I spotted the Pentagon and thought of 9/11, and how the heroes of Flight
93 likely spared the White House or the Capitol. Seeing the Potomac made
me think of John Quincy Adams's morning swims—not exactly a great visual. Viewing the World War II Memorial conjured up images of D-Day and
the sheer audacity of that invasion and all it meant for the world. I will forever treasure the memory of Eisenhower detailing that operation to General
Washington.

How appropriate, I thought, to have this town named for Washington—
not so much because he was perfect, but because, like America, he was not.
Larger-than-life and ambitious beyond belief, both clearly represent and
project the very highest and best ideals; but no, neither can be considered
perfect by any stretch of the imagination.

I realized I had not turned my phone back on. But failing to do so had
allowed me this priceless final moment of reflection. *Perhaps I should try
that more often.*

I turned it back on, and it immediately lit up like a Christmas tree, displaying dozens of texts and missed calls.

"Turn that off, babe," scolded Denyse.

Ignoring that directive, I glanced at the messages. Several were from
Professor Harris:

"When are you coming back?"

*"This guy really thinks he's Jefferson. And he almost has me believing
it too! Fascinating gentleman. I'm not convinced his accent is believable,*

though."

"Are you coming back?"

Then from the Head of the White House Secret Service detail: *"What do we do with the Jefferson impersonator? Was he somehow with you?"*
"There's no record of him entering the grounds today."

"He doesn't seem to want to break character."

"There's no video of him coming on the property. He may be a security threat. What do you know about him? Unless we hear from you soon, we're going to have to take him into custody."

Then one more from Professor Harris:

"I'm still at the White House with your Mr. Jefferson. Scary as this may sound, I'm starting to believe he actually is Thomas Jefferson. They want to arrest him. I need to talk to you as soon as possible. Either you or a psychologist. Perhaps both. Many of our phone calls make more sense now."

I stopped reading. Denyse saw the worried look on my face.

I looked down and just shook my head. "I completely forgot to make sure Jefferson got back in the Saloon."

"What? You let Thomas Jefferson out of the Saloon?"

Denyse laughed out loud, reached over, and grabbed my phone. "Let it go, babe. All these problems, Danny, big and small, will work themselves out. They always do for this country, and they always do for you. There is something uncanny about the constitution of each of you that seems to enable you both to triumph in spite of your flaws. And let me tell you, both you and the country have considerable flaws."

"OK, you've made your point—"

"By the way, that next wife of yours you are always talking about might not be as forgiving of some of those flaws of yours as I am."

"Actually, you're the one that's always talking about—"

"But this will work itself out. Let it go."

I smiled, exhaled, and turned off my phone. Surely, Tina would step in and straighten it all out.

And Denyse was right, at least with respect to the country. The nation would right itself, as it eventually always does. And we have some of my drinking buddies to thank for that. They undoubtedly got some things right when they put this whole experiment together nearly 250 years ago. Really, remarkably right. For all its failings, imagine a world without America and all it stands for leading the way. I shudder to think what that world might look like. Yes, indeed, they got some things right.

Another one of those things is the Saloon. The Presidential Spirits Saloon. That magical, mystical, supernatural saloon. It is impossible for me to think of it without smiling. The presidents, the toasts, the cocktails, the dogs, the music, the yoga, the staff, everyone up there constantly busting each other's chops for all eternity—or at least for as long as this nation survives. God, I will miss that camaraderie. However, more than anything else, I will miss the burning desire of all of them to see the country they love so much succeed above all else.

I sat back and decided I had an awful lot to smile about. I was excited to be getting home to California. I missed it dearly. The thought of Satch made me smile all the more. Satch now had his dream car, his new love, and a new pup—clearly all he needed for his last chapter, which would now also include making good on a lingering indebtedness to his long-deceased best friend. And for the first time in a long time, thinking of this country also brought about the makings of a smile—how perhaps there was finally a ray of hope to get at bridging this debilitating political divide. Maybe, just maybe, we at long last have a viable political solution to this national political dysfunction. That's a start, and one well worth smiling about. And with that, I felt I had fulfilled my promise to McCain at the Up the Creek Bistro. And while I could never really tell anyone precisely where the idea for the We're Better Alliance was hatched, knowing its true origin was immensely satisfying, and one secret well worth keeping.

Oh, and Jefferson did eventually make it back into the Saloon safely, but not before causing quite a national stir. I could tell you all about that, but that's really another story entirely. . .

SOURCES

While this is obviously a work of fiction, much of the dialogue is taken directly from actual words of the presidents that appeared in their speeches, letters, interviews, memoirs or other papers, and is adapted to fit the context of the novel. References are provided in such instances to allow for examination of the original quote and context. Additionally, dozens of other citations are provided to many other historical references that were relied upon to write this novel that might be of interest to some reading this. I thank all of those who did the work referenced in these sources and thus made a novel of this style possible.

Chapter One

Some of the baseball related history comes from William Mead and Paul Dickson, *Baseball: The President's Game* (Washington D.C.: Farragut Publishing 1993).

On the Bushes hosting T-ball games on the South Lawn: Edwin Chen, "Bush to Bring T-Ball Games to White House Lawn," *Los Angeles Times,* Mar 31, 2001.

On Reagan hosting Pony League Games on White House Lawn: Norman D. Sandler, "Baseball on White House Lawn," UPI May 11, 1983.

On Reagan insisting on wearing a coat in Oval Office: Edmund Morris, "The Unknowable, Ronald Reagan's Amazing, Mysterious Life," *The New Yorker,* June 20, 2004.

Chapter Four

The Michael Smerconish Program is a national radio show broadcast by SiriusXM on the POTUS channel, hosted by author, lawyer and journalist Michael Smerconish. The transcript which appears in this chapter is a completely fictional interview for this story.

On 45 percent of the country now considering themselves independent, exceeding both Republican and Democrat numbers: Party Affiliation, Gallup News, https://news.gallup.com/poll/15370/party-affiliation.aspx. Gallup has been tracking party affiliation monthly since 2004. Independents typically fluctuate between 36% and 46%, exceeding either of the two major parties.

On Hamilton and Jefferson wanting Washington to serve another term: John Avlon, *Washington's Farewell: The Founding Father's Warning to Future Generations,* (New York: Simon & Schuster 2017), 50.

In 1884 Civil War General William Tecumseh Sherman, addressing the possibility that he might be considered as a potential Republican candidate for president, stated, "I will not accept if nominated and will not serve if elected." Through the years that has evolved into, "If nominated, I will not run. If elected, I will not serve." That version is more commonly known and used today. Rich Galen, "If Nominated I Will Not Run..." CSN News, May 18, 2011, https://www.cnsnews.com/blog/rich-galen/if-nominated-i-will-not-run.

On whether Ross Perot took votes from Bush or Clinton: *The Ross Perot Myth,* a film by FiveThirtyEight, argues that, contrary to popular opinion, Perot did not actually take votes away from Bush.

Chapter Five

Anderson Cooper 360 is a national nightly cable television news broadcast on CNN, hosted by news anchor and journalist Anderson Cooper. The transcript of the broadcast which appears in this chapter uses some language from the actual broadcast on October 8, 2016, to create a fictional broadcast for this story.

Chapter Six

On the history of "faithless electors": Nina Agrawal, "All the Times in U.S. history that Members of the Electoral College Voted Their Own Way," *Los Angeles Times*, Dec. 20, 2016.

Chapter Eight

The procedure for election of the vice president is spelled out in the Twelfth Amendment to the U.S. Constitution. If no one has a majority of the electoral college vote, then the Senate votes between the top two candidates receiving votes in the electoral college.

The procedure for appointment of a new vice president to fill a vacancy is contained in Section 2 of the Twenty-fifth Amendment to the U.S. Constitution. The appointment is made by the president and needs a majority approval of both houses. "25th Amendment - Presidential Disability and Succession," National Constitution Center.

The Incompatible Offices Clause appears in Article I Section 6 Clause 2 of the U.S. Constitution. Some scholars argue that the clause does not restrict a congressman from simultaneously serving as vice president: Michael Stern, "Can Joe Biden Be Senator and Vice President at the Same Time?" *Point of Order,* Dec 20, 2008.

Chapter Nine

Portions of O'Reilly's "Memo" are taken, adapted, or fashioned from statements made in various airings of *The O'Reilly Factor,* which ran on FOX News between October 1996 and April 2017, hosted by Bill O'Reilly, to create a purely fictional transcript of a show for this novel.

Chapter Twelve

On Washington's gold coin: Washington did in fact keep with him a gold coin produced by a group hoping to get a contract to mint U.S. currency. He turned down the request but accepted the coin as a gift: Jill Serjeant, "Unique George Washington Gold Coin at Auction in First Since 1890." *Reuters,* June 13, 2018. ⸲ The same coin was recently sold at auction: "George Washington Gold Coin Sells for $1.7 Million," *Reuters,* August 16, 2018. https://www.reuters.com/article/us-auction-washingtoncoin/george-washington-gold-coin-sells-for-1-7-million-dUSKBN1L207W

Chapter Fifteen

The drinking preferences of presidents appearing in this book are taken from many sources, including: Mark Will-Weber, *Mint Juleps with Teddy Roosevelt: The Complete History of Presidential Drinking,* (Washington D.C.: Regnery Publishing 2014).

Eisenhower quotes taken, adapted or fashioned from many sources, including: Dwight D. Eisenhower, *Crusade in Europe,* (Easton Press, 1948); Kristine Phillips, "D-Day's Heavy Toll on Eisenhower, One of America's Greatest Generals," *Washington Post*, June 6, 2017; Interview with Eisenhower by Walter Cronkite on the twentieth anniversary of D-Day June 6, 1964, CBS News. https://www.cbsnews.com/video/eisenhower-recalls-sacrifices-of-d-day-20-years-later/

The letter to the troops that Eisenhower never delivered can be viewed at: Dwight D. Eisenhower Presidential Library & Museum, (Accessed November 30, 2019).

In Eisenhower's Memoirs he describes Washington as his hero: Dwight D. Eisenhower, *At Ease: Stories I Tell My Friends,* (New York: Doubleday, 1967), 40-41.

Chapter Sixteen

On the Adams–Jefferson rivalry over credit for the creation of the new country and system of government: Gordon S. Wood, *Friends Divided: John Adams and Thomas Jefferson,* (Penguin Press 2017), 390-405.

On the thirteen toasts: It was customary at some gatherings in the years following the American Revolution, particularly on the Fourth of July, to offer thirteen toasts in pubs, parties, and other celebrations—one for each state in the union. Sometimes the toasts would be published in newspapers. Many cites, including "Toasts Proposed During Revolutionary War," *Colonial Quills,* December 30, 2011; Lorillard S. Spencer, *The Illustrated American,* Volume 18, 1895, Page 53; Andrew Smith, *The Oxford Encyclopedia of Food and Drink in America,* (Oxford University Press 2013).

Adams's toast describing the Constitution as *"the sacred palladium of political safety"* uses language from George Washington's Farewell Address, September 17, 1796. Avalon Project, Yale Law School. https://avalon.law.yale.edu/18th_century/washing.asp

A portion of Reagan's toast and quote about George Washington is taken in part from Reagan's first State of the Union Address before Congress, January 26, 1982. Reagan is referencing and paraphrasing Washington's 1790 State of the Union Address. Miller Center, University of Virginia. https://millercenter.org/the-presidency/presidential-speeches/january-26-1982-state-union-address

A portion of Nixon's toast is taken from Richard Nixon's final remarks at the White House to his Cabinet and staff, August 9, 1974. Transcript of Nixon's Farewell Speech to Cabinet and Staff Members in the Capital, *New York Times*, August 10, 1974. https://www.nytimes.com/1974/08/10/archives/-transcript-of-nixons-farewell-speech-to-cabinet-and-staff-members.html

A portion of Bill Clinton's toast is taken from a June 13, 1998 commencement speech given by Clinton at Portland State University. Presidential Libraries, Master Tape 08558 08560. https://www.youtube.com/watch?v=2VOi1R0ylDs

On Teddy Roosevelt claiming to have more fun being president than any other president: David Rubel, *Mr. President: The Human Side of America's Chief Executives,* (Agincourt Press, 1998), 154.

On Teddy Roosevelt being shot and then delivering a speech before seeking medical attention: "The Speech That Saved Teddy Roosevelt's Life," Patricia O'Toole, *Smithsonian*, November 2012.

A portion of Teddy Roosevelt's toast is also taken from the speech he delivered that day in Milwaukee, Wisconsin October 14, 1912: Theodore Roosevelt Association.

Chapter Seventeen

References to the third floor of the White House and Zachary Taylor's slaves, Woodrow Wilson's daughters, and FDR assistant, Missy LeHand: "White House Residence Third Floor," The White House Museum.

Chapter Twenty

Portions of Rush Limbaugh's comments are taken, adapted, or fashioned from statements made in various airings of *The Rush Limbaugh Show,* a radio program hosted by Rush Limbaugh on Premier Networks, including episodes which ran February 15, 2016, November 10, 2016, and July 26, 2017, to create a purely fictional transcript of a show for this novel.

Chapter Twenty-Two

On Justice David Souter living with his Mom: Bill Hewitt, "A Retiring Yankee Judge Aims to Hang His Shingle at a New Address: The Supreme Court," *People*, August 6, 1990.

Truman quote, *"...dumb son of a bitch"* adapted from quote appearing in Merle Miller, *Plain Speaking: An Oral Biography of Harry S. Truman* (New York: G.P. Putnam's Sons 1974).

Teddy Roosevelt quote, "*I could have carved out of a banana...*" adapted from: Todd S. Purdum, "Presidents, Picking Justices Can Have Backfires" *New York Times,* July 5, 2005.

Eisenhower quote, *"biggest damn fool thing"* adapted from quote appearing in: Michael O'Donnell, "Commander v. Chief," *The Atlantic,* April 15, 2018.

Ford quote about Justice Stevens and his legacy adapted from a quote appearing in: Amy Davidson Sorkin, "Gerald Ford's Justice," *The New Yorker,* April 12, 2010.

Additional background for this chapter taken from Ed Lazarus, "Four Enduring Myths," *Time,* May 26, 2009.

TR quote, *"It is dreadful misfortune..."* taken from: Teddy Roosevelt, *Theodore Roosevelt, An Autobiography* (New York: Charles Scribner's Sons, 1913).

On Andrew Johnson appointing a judge and Congress abolishing the seat: Erick Trickey, "The History of 'Stolen' Supreme Court Seats," *Smithsonian,* March 20, 2017.

Chapter Twenty-Three

The later editions of Joseph J. Ellis, *American Sphinx* (New York: Vintage Books 1998) provide the details on the Jefferson and Sally Hemings affair, the coverage of the matter in the press at the time and through history, and the latest on the DNA evidence.

On Jackson having killed a man in a duel, and having bullets in his body from duels: Jon Meacham, *American Lion, Andrew Jackson in the White House,* (Random House, 2008), 26. Jackson killed Charles Dickinson in a duel in Nashville following an argument over a horse race and a slur about Jackson's wife, Rachel.

On Samuel Tilden being called a "drunken, syphilitic swindler:" Kevin C. Swint, *Mudlingers; the Top 25 Negative Political Campaigns of All Time,*

(Westport: Praeger, 2006), 82.

On Woodrow Wilson's racist tendencies: Dick Lehr, "The Racist Legacy of Woodrow Wilson." *The Atlantic,* November 27, 2015.

Chapter Twenty-Four

Obama has taken the stage to sing a portion of "Sweet Home Chicago" and "Let's Stay Together" more than once. Chris Cillizza, "When Barack Obama Sang 'Sweet Home Chicago' with B.B King," *Washington Post,* May 15, 2015; President Obama Sings "Sweet Home Chicago" (February 22, 2012); President Barack Obama sings Al Green "Let's Stay Together" at Apollo Theatre, New York (January 20, 2012), https://www.youtube.com/watch?v=WUl_jf9aWZI;

For a discussion of musical instruments that U.S. presidents played: Chris Gray, "The Most Musical United States Presidents," *National Association for Musical Education*, Feb 13, 2015.

On John Quincy Adams believing Jefferson tells "large stories" and Jefferson learning Spanish: Joseph J. Ellis, *American Sphinx, the Character of Thomas Jefferson* (New York: Vintage Books, 1998), 82.

Chapter Twenty-Five

Some background for this chapter found in "Why we always find excuses for cops who kill," Issac Bailey, *CNN,* July 7, 2016.

Portions of Sean Hannity's comments are taken, adapted, or fashioned from statements made in various airings of *Hannity,* a television program hosted by Sean Hannity on the FOX News channel, including episodes which ran on September 26, 2017, April 17, 2018, April 25, 2018, and April 30, 2018, to create a purely fictional transcript of a show for this novel.

Chapter Twenty-Six

On LBJ scaring visitors at his ranch: Joseph A. Califano, *The Triumph and Tragedy of Lyndon Johnson: The White House Years,* (Simon & Schuster 2014), 8.

Bobby Kennedy deer hunt story: Robert Caro, *The Passage of Power, The Years of Lyndon Johnson,* (Penguin Random House Books, 2012).

Lincoln quote, *"One of the most meritorious men in America…"* from: John Eaton *Grant, Lincoln, and the Freedmen* (Longman's Green & Co., 1907), 176.

On Douglass' criticism of Lincoln for talk of colonization, holding racist views and four years of war: Frederick Douglass, "The President and His Speeches." *Douglass' Monthly. (*Rochester, NY) September 1862.

On Hamlin and his son's role in the decision to enlist black troops: David Herbert Donald, *Lincoln,* (New York: Simon & Schuster, 1995), 430.

The White House in the early days was typically referred to as the executive mansion, and not formally called the White House until the Teddy Roosevelt Administration: "The White House Building," The White House, (Accessed November 30, 2019).

Lincoln quote, *"I will keep my faith to friends and enemies…"* from: Roy P. Basler, editor, *Collected Works of Abraham Lincoln Volume 7 (*New Brunswick, N.J: Rutgers University Press, 1953), 507.

On Lincoln and Douglass having tea at Lincoln's Summer Cottage and Douglass initially not supporting Lincoln's reelection: James Oakes, *The Radical and the Republican: Frederick Douglass, Abraham Lincoln ant the Triumph of Antislavery Politics* (W.W. Norton & Company, 2007).

On the reluctance of African American leaders to support Lincoln for a second term: David Herbert Donald, *Lincoln,* (New York: Simon & Schuster, 1995), 541.

Some background for the Fredrick Douglass conversation: Michael Shank,

Dan Coonan

"'Lincoln': Where Was Frederick Douglass?" *Washington Post*, Nov 28, 2012.

John Quincy Adams quote, *"Slavery is a great and foul stain…"* taken from: *The Memoirs of John Quincy Adams, Comprising Portions of His Diary from 1795-1848.* New York: Scribner, 1951, quoting a diary entry from February 24, 1820.

John Quincy Adams quote, *"The inconsistency of the institution of slavery …"* comes from his Oration on the Declaration of Independence, at Newburyport, 4 July, 1837, printed in: Stedman and Hutchinson, *A Library of American Literature: An Anthology in Eleven Volumes,* 1891, Vol. IV: Literature of the Republic, Part I., Constitutional period, 1788–1820, The Crime of Slavery.
Other John Quincy Adams background: David Waldstreicher and Matthew Mason, *John Quincy Adams and the Politics of Slavery* (Oxford University Press, 2016).

On Jefferson's earlier version of the Declaration of Independence ("the original rough draught") blaming "the Christian King of Great Britain,": "Declaring Independence: Drafting the Documents," Library of Congress. https://www.loc.gov/exhibits/declara/ruffdrft.html.

A portion of John Adams's quote *"evil of colossal magnitude…"* adapted from his letter to William Tudor: "From John Adams to William Tudor, Jr., 20 November 1819", Founders Online National Archives.

Lincoln quote, *"All honor to Jefferson…"* adapted from a Lincoln letter to Henry L.Pierce and others April 6 1859: Roy P. Basler, editor, *Collected Works of Abraham Lincoln Volume 7* (New Brunswick, N.J: Rutgers University Press, 1953).

On Jackson clearing the Cherokee: Deneen L. Brown, "Trump Called Andrew Jackson 'a swashbuckler.' The Cherokee called him 'Indian killer.'" *Washington Post,* May 3, 2017.

Jefferson quote, *"God is just…"* from: Thomas Jefferson, *Notes on the State of Virginia,* Query VIII: Manners (London: John Stockdale, 1787).

Presidential Spirits

https://docsouth.unc.edu/southlit/jefferson/jefferson.html

The *Richmond Recorder* reported in September 1802 on Thomas Jefferson's alleged relationship with a slave woman, Sally Hemings, which was then reported nationwide: Joseph J. Ellis, *American Sphinx, the Character of Thomas Jefferson* (New York: Vintage Books, 1998), 258.

Madison Hemings, Sally's second-to-last child, claimed in an interview in 1873 that his mother told him that Thomas Jefferson was not only his father but the father of all of her seven children. Madison Hemmings and S.F. Wetmore, . *Pike County Republican* (Ohio) March 13, 1873. This account was confirmed in an interview with former slave Israel Jefferson. Israel Jefferson and S.F. Wetmore, *Pike County Republican* (Ohio) December 25, 1873. In 1998 *Nature* magazine reported that scientific evidence demonstrates that DNA sequences in the Y chromosome in the Jefferson family matches DNA present in the Hemings family. Henry Gee, "The Sex Life of President Thomas Jefferson," *Nature,* November 12, 1998. While all of this certainly makes it likely that Jefferson is the father of one and possibly more of her children, some still argue that it is not by itself conclusive because other Jefferson males, including his brother Randolph and his sons, were also present at Monticello often during those years. Eliot Marshall, "Thomas Jefferson Off the Hook?" *Science,* January 6, 1999.

On Grant refusing to ride to his inauguration in a carriage with Johnson: Joseph Cummins: "From Drunken VPs to Dead Canaries: The Long History of Inauguration Drama," *Politico,* January 19, 2017. wwwpolitico.com/magazine/story/2017/01/inauguration-trump-history-drama-disasters-214663

John Adams quote *"...not a planter in all of Virginia..."* taken from John Adams letter to Colonel Joseph Ward, January 8, 1810, Microfilm Edition of John Adam Papers, Massachusetts Historical Society, Reel 118. Joseph J. Ellis, *American Sphinx, the Character of Thomas Jefferson* (New York: Vintage Books, 1998), 259.

On Nixon viewing abortion being "necessary" in the case of "a black and white:" in the White House tapes: Charlie Savage, "On Nixon Tapes, Ambivalence Over Abortion, Not Watergate," *New York Times* (June 23,

2009).

On Sally Hemings likely being the daughter of Jefferson's father-in-law, and, thus, a half-sister of his wife Martha: Joseph J. Ellis, *American Sphinx, the Character of Thomas Jefferson* (New York: Vintage Books, 1998), 179.

On Van Buren being born in a tavern in Kinderhook, New York: Bill Harris, *Homes of the Presidents,* (CLB International, 1997), 37.

On Abigail Adams counseling John Adams to "remember the ladies:" from a letter, "Abigail Adams to John Adams 31 March 1776," Founders Online (National Archives).

On Reagan's relationship with and respect for Margaret Thatcher, "Reagan and Thatcher: 'Political Soulmates'," Halimah Abdullah, CNN.com, April 9, 2013.

Chapter Twenty-Seven

Lincoln is known to have written five copies of the Gettysburg address, two contemporaneously and three later. All were given away to staff and others as gifts. He delivered the speech reading from papers he pulled from his coat pocket. It is unknown if these were one of the five known originals or another. Nathan Raab, "5 Unanswered Questions about the Gettysburg Address," *Forbes,* November 19, 2013.

Chapter Twenty-Eight

On whether Babe Ruth actually called his shot, the contemporaneous reporting on the game and Ruth's own conflicting statements about it through the years: Ed Sherman, "Unraveling the mystery of Babe Ruth's Called Shot" *Sporting News*, April 7, 2014. www.sportingnews.com/us/mlb/news/babe-ruth-called-shot-charlie-root-yankees-cubs-book-ed-sherman/1w29vd8i39z0x1iho1uj8ciqdt

On George H.W. Bush meeting Babe Ruth, and Babe Ruth's quote: William Mead and Paul Dickson, *Baseball, The President's Game,* (Washington

D.C.: Farragut Publishing 1993), 178.

On Reagan calling the re-creation of Babe Ruth called shot game: Lyle Spencer, "Baseball, Presidents Go Back A Long Way," MLB.com, Feb 15, 2016.

On FDR throwing out the first pitch at the Ruth "called shot" game: "Who saw Babe Ruth's 'called shot?' FDR," David Jackson, *USA Today,* April 23, 2014.

Nixon quote about the Angels: "Love of the Game: RN and Baseball." Richard Nixon Foundation, April 23, 2014. https://www.nixonfoundation.org/2014/04/love-game-rn-baseball/.

On Nixon saying that if he did it over again, he would "end up a sportswriter," "President Richard Nixon Baseball Related Quotations," Baseball Almanac.

On Eisenhower's biggest regret being that he was unable to play baseball at Army: "President Dwight D. Eisenhower Baseball Related Quotations," Baseball Almanac. https://www.baseball-almanac.com/prz_qde.shtml

On Hoover playing baseball briefly for Stanford: Earl Odell, "Hoover Holds Place In Stanford Athletics," *The Stanford Daily,* Volume 117. Issue 7, February 14. 1950.

Hoover quote, *". . . next to religion, baseball . . ."* taken from "President Hoover Baseball Related Quotations," Baseball Almanac. . https://www.baseball-almanac.com/prz_qde

On Ruth endorsing Hoover's opponent, Al Smith: "Presidents Who Knew the Babe" *New York Times,* April 11, 2015.

For FDR's letter to Landis from January 15, 1942: "Keep Baseball Going," National Baseball Hall of Fame.

Background for the account and quote regarding George W. Bush's first pitch at the World Series following 9/11 based upon: "Yankees Helped New York Heal Post 9/11," *ABC News.* https://abcnews.go.com/US/fullpage/-

baseball-yankees-helped-york -heal-post-911-president-33663881

On Teddy Roosevelt's disdain for baseball: William Mead and Paul Dickson, *Baseball, The President's Game,* (Washington D.C.: Farragut Publishing 1993), 17-20.

Teddy Roosevelt quote, *"...bully fight..."* is often quoted, including: Caryn James, "A Roosevelt Who Exulted in Bully War," *New York Times,* July 19, 1997.

Lou Gehrig's farewell speech found at: http://www.lougehrig.com/farewell.

On Truman at various times throwing out first pitches with both his right hand and his left: William Mead and Paul Dickson, *Baseball, The President's Game,* (Washington D.C.: Farragut Publishing 1993), 83-84.

On the crowd chanting "We want beer" at Hoover at the 1931 World Series: Matt Bonesteel, "A history of booing the president at MLB games, from 'we want beer' to 'lock him up,'" *Washington Post,* October 28, 2019.

The Jackie Robinson/Pee Wee Reese moment in this novel reflects how it is depicted in the movie 42. The book Jackie Robinson, A Biography contains a good discussion of the various versions of this incident. There are conflicting accounts of the time, place and extent of the gesture. Arnold Rampersad, *Jackie Robinson, A Biography,* (New York, Alfred A Knopf, Inc. 1997), 182-3.

Chapter Twenty-Nine

On Jefferson and Sally Hemings: Joseph J. Ellis, *American Sphinx, The Character of Thomas Jefferson* (New York: Vintage Books, 1998) 363-367; Eliot Marshall, "Thomas Jefferson Off the Hook?" *Science,* January 6, 1999.

Chapter Thirty

For background on Washington's slave Christopher Sheels: Erica Armstrong Dunbar, *Never Caught, the Washingtons' relentless pursuit of their runaway slave, Ona Judge,* (New York: Atria Books, 2017).

More background on Christopher Sheels and slavery: Marie Jenkins Schwartz, *Ties That Bound: Founding First Ladies and Slaves* (University of Chicago Press, 2017).

Chapter Thirty-One

Photos of Evelyn Lincoln in her office at the White House show framed pictures of John Kennedy on the walls. "President Kennedy, Presidential Secretary Evelyn Lincoln," John F. Kennedy Presidential Library & Museum, Archives. www.jfklibrary.org.

On Washington and Jackson distilling whiskey at Mount Vernon and The Hermitage: Mark Will-Weber, *Mint Juleps with Teddy Roosevelt: The Complete History of Presidential Drinking,* (Washington D.C.: Regnery Publishing 2014), 1, 56.

In a Playboy Magazine interview November 1976, Jimmy Carter is quoted as saying, "I've looked on a lot of women with lust. I've committed adultery in my heart many times:" Robert Scheer, "A candid conversation with the democratic candidate for the presidency," *Playboy,* November 1, 1976.

The Nixons added a one-lane bowling alley under the North Portico of the White House in 1969. "White House Bowling Alley," The White House Museum. www.whitehousemuseum.org.

Chapter Thirty-Six

On Rutherford B. Hayes' battlefield conversation with a Confederate soldier as they both lay injured: David Rubel, *Mr. President: The Human Side of America's Chief Executives,* (Agincourt Press, 1998) 118.

Rutherford B. Hayes' wife Lucy did not want him drinking and they banned alcohol at official White House functions—but it was more her convictions about it than his: Mark Will-Weber, *Mint Juleps with Teddy Roosevelt: The Complete History of Presidential Drinking,* (Washington D.C.: Regnery Publishing 2014), 156.

On Millard Fillmore opening up trade with Japan for the first time: David Rubel, *Mr. President: The Human Side of America's Chief Executives,* (Agincourt Press, 1998), 83.

On Zachary Taylor having no formal education: David Rubel, *Mr. President: The Human Side of America's Chief Executives,* (Agincourt Press, 1998), 75.

On Zachary Taylor's preference for whiskey: Mark Will-Weber, *Mint Juleps with Teddy Roosevelt: The Complete History of Presidential Drinking,* (Washington D.C.: Regnery Publishing 2014), 100-101.

On Madison assisting along with others in drafting Washington's Farewell Address: John Avlon, *Washington's Farewell: The Founding Father's Warning to Future Generations,* (New York: Simon & Schuster 2017), 225.

Washington quote, *"Rely upon the goodness of the cause…"* adapted from: "General Orders, 2 July 1776," Founders Online, National Archives, https://founders.archives.gov/documents/Washington/03-05-02-0117. [Original source: *The Papers of George Washington*, Revolutionary War Series, vol. 5, *16 June 1776–12 August 1776*, ed. Philander D. Chase. Charlottesville: University Press of Virginia, 1993, pp. 179–182.]

Chapter Thirty-Eight

For background on Washington's slave Christopher Sheels: Erica Armstrong Dunbar, *Never Caught, the Washingtons' relentless pursuit of their runaway slave, Ona Judge,* (New York: Atria Books, 2017).

More background on Christopher Sheels and slavery: Marie Jenkins Schwartz, *Ties That Bound: Founding First Ladies and Slaves* (University of Chicago Press, 2017).

On Hoover speaking Mandarin: Sally Hyroad, "The Only U.S. President That Spoke Mandarin Chinese," Odyssey, July 3, 2016.

The Gradual Abolition Act, enacted in Pennsylvania in 1780, freed any slave who lived in the commonwealth for more than six continuous months. Erin Blakemore, "George Washington Used Legal Loopholes to Avoid Freeing His Slaves, *Smithsonian Magazine,* February 15, 2016. www.smithsonian-mag.com/smart-news/george-washington-used-legal-loopholes-avoid-free-ing-slaves

Chapter Thirty-Nine

On Lincoln being Obama's favorite president: *"Public Papers of the Presidents of the United States – Barack Obama, 2013 Book One, January 1 to June 30, 2013* (Washington D.C.: United States Government Publishing Office, 2018) 572.

On 6 presidents together being the record at the opening of the Reagan Library: Craig Hlavaty, "Five Presidents Together is a Lot, But Once There Were Six" *Houston Chronicle,* April 25, 2013.

Chapter Forty-Two

On Pres limo details: Paul Eisenstein, "Trump's New Limo Costs 1.5 million and comes with a fridge full of his blood type," *NBC News,* September 25, 2018; "9 Mind-blowing facts about President Trump motorcade." *Dazzling News.* March 7, 2017.

On McCain wanting to preserve the filibuster: Jennifer Calfas, "'A Stupid Idiot.' John McCain Doesn't Think Much of the Nuclear Option," *Time,* April 4, 2017.

McCain quote *"I've made a lot of errors..."* adapted from a response McCain gave during an interview with CNN's Jake Tapper, reprinted in: Dan Nowicki, "From Jokester to "Maverick," John McCain is a Study in Contradictions," *USA Today,* April 3, 2018.

Chapter Forty-Four

On the presidents' dogs, names and breeds: Roy Rowan and Brooke Janis, *First Dogs: American Presidents and Their Best Friends,* (Algonquin Books of Chapel Hill, 2009); "List of U.S. Presidents and their Dogs," Dogtime. https://dogtime.com/dog-health/general/5668-list-of-us-presidents-and-their-dogs

On LBJ picking up his beagles by the ears: Roy Rowan and Brooke Janis, *First Dogs: American Presidents and Their Best Friends,* (Algonquin Books of Chapel Hill, 2009), 5.

On Teddy Roosevelt's bull terrier, Pete, tearing the pants of French Ambassador: Stanley Coren, *"The Pawprints of History: Dogs in the Course of Human Events."* (New York: Free Press 2002).

Truman quote, *"If you want a friend in Washington…"* is widely attributed to him, but some question whether he ever actually ever said it. Nadia Pflaum, *"John Kasich misquotes Truman on dogs, wins Ohio anyway,"* Politifact, March 17, 2016. www.politifact.com.

Coolidge quote *"Any man who does not like dogs…"* adapted from quote appearing in: Roy Rowan and Brooke Janis, *First Dogs: American Presidents and Their Best Friends,* (Algonquin Books of Chapel Hill, 2009), 3.

On Obama promising Sasha and Malia a dog in his acceptance speech: Stacy St. Claire, "Obama Promises His Daughters a Puppy in the White House," *Chicago Tribune,* November 5, 2008.

Chapter Forty-Six

On John Quincy Adams swimming naked in the Potomac every morning: David Rubel, *Mr. President: The Human Side of America's Chief Executives,* (Agincourt Press, 1998), 41.

On James Monroe being part of the operation that crossed the Delaware on

Christmas Eve 1776, and being personally injured in the Battle of Trenton, taking a musket ball to the shoulder: Joseph J. Ellis, *His Excellency, George Washington,* (Vintage Books, 2004) 98.

Chapter Forty-Seven

George H.W. Bush's dog Millie's book, which reached #1 on the New York Times Best Seller List: Barbara Bush, *Millie's Book, as Dictated to Barbara Bush,* (Harper Perennial, 1992).

George H.W. Bush quote *". . . these two bozos."* found in: Leslie H. Gelb, "George, Bill and Millie, *New York Times,* November 1, 1992.

On Washington receiving staghounds as a gift from Lafayette and breeding them with his coonhounds: Lesley Kennedy. "George Washington: Founding Father—And Passionate Dog Breeder, *History,* December 23, 2019. www.history.com/news/george-washington-dogs

On Washington caring for General Howe's dog: Carolyn Tiger, *General Howe's Dog: George Washington, the Battle for Germantown and the Dog Who Crossed Enemy Lines,* (Chamberlain Brothers 2005).

Chapter Forty-Eight

On the use of the 25th Amendment in history: Michael Kranz, "The 25th Amendment has been used 3 times to relieve presidents deemed unfit to govern—each case involving physical health," *Business Insider,* October 12, 2017.

Chapter Fifty-Three

Some gun statistics taken from "America's Gun Culture in 10 Charts," *BBC News,* March 21, 2018.

Obama quote on Sandy Hook taken from: Nicole Gallucci, "Barack Obama emotionally reflects on highs and lows of his presidency," *Marshable,* Jan 14, 2017.

Obama quotes, *"Every time I think of those kids..."* and *"This has to be a catalyst..."* adapted from Lester Holt interview with Barack Obama, *NBC News,* January 14, 2017, which includes clips from Obama speeches.

Obama quote, *"The one advanced nation on earth..."* adapted from: Nikita Vladimirov, "Obama reflects on legacy as presidency comes to an end," *The Hill,* December 7, 2016.

"List of Obama Gun Control Measures," Tom Murse, *ThoughtCo,* Feb 21, 2018. www.thoughtco.com/obama-gun-laws-passed-by-congress

Reagan quote, *"I was lucky,"* taken from Ronald Reagan Op-Ed: "Why I'm for the Brady Bill," *New York Times,* March 29, 1991.

Ronald Reagan quotes adapted from: Janel Davis, "Did Reagan Support an Assault Weapons Ban?" PolitiFact, February 5, 2013. https://www.politifact.com/georgia/statements/2013/feb/05/barack-obama/did-reagan-support-assault-weapons-ban/ and: Clare Kim, "A Look Back at Gun Control History," MSNBC, January 23, 2013.

More on Reagan and guns: Ian Shapira, "Before Trump's Wild Shifts on the NRA, Ronald Reagan took on the gun lobby," *The Washington Post,* March 2, 2018; "Ronald Reagan, the NRA and the 1984 Assault Weapons Ban," *Washington Post*, March 2, 2018. Reagan, Ford and Carter sent a joint letter on May 3, 1994 to members of the House of Representatives urging support for a bill barring semiautomatic weapons sale and further manufacture.

Clinton quotes adapted from: Marc Lacey, "Clinton Recalls Columbine and Pushes for Gun Control," *New York Times,* April 13, 2000.

George W. Bush quote, *"I did think..."* adapted from his words in Presidential Debate, October 13, 2004, stating his support for an assault rifle ban & closing the gun show loophole. "October 13, 2004 Presidential Debate Transcript," Commission on Presidential Debates. www.debates.org/voter-education/debate-transcripts/october-13-2004-

debate-transcript/James

Some background for George W. Bush position on gun issues: "George W. Bush on Gun Control," On The Issues. https://www.ontheissues.org/celeb/-george_w_bush_gun_control.htm

James Madison quote, *"The great mass of respectable people…"* adapted from "Speech on Amendments to Constitution, James Madison, June 8, 1789," Teaching American History. https://teachingamericanhistory.org-resources/bor/madison_17890608/

Madison's quote, *"unlike some countries we are not afraid of putting guns in the hands of our people,"* adapted from James Madison's writings in *Federalist Paper* No. 46, "The Influence of the State and Federal Governments Compared," January 29, 1788. Avalon Project, Yale Law School. https://avalon.law.yale.edu/18th_century/fed46.asp.

Madison quote, *"A well regulated militia was the best security…"* adapted from Madison's original draft of the amendment which would become the Second Amendment. "Five Items Congress Deleted from Madison's Original Bill Of Rights," Constitution Daily, National Constitution Center. https://constitutioncenter.org/blog/five-items-congress-deleted-from-madisons-original-bill-of-rights.

Madison quote, *"Those best acquainted…"* adapted from Madison's writings in *Federalist Paper* No. 46, "The Influence of the State and Federal Governments Compared," January 29, 1788.

Jefferson's quote, *"The tree of liberty…"* adapted from "Thomas Jefferson letter to William Smith, Paris, November 13, 1787," Library of Congress, Exhibitions Thomas Jefferson.

Jefferson quote, *"I hold that a little rebellion…"* adapted from "Thomas Jefferson letter to James Madison, Paris, January 30, 1787," The Thomas Jefferson Foundation, Thomas Jefferson Encyclopedia. https://www.monti-cello.org/site/research-and-collections/tje.

Additional background for this chapter found in: David W. Brown, "How Alexander Hamilton Solved America's Gun Problem—228 Years Ago," *The*

Week, June 15, 2016.

The John Adams quote, *"To suppose arms in the hands of citizens..."* adapted from: *The Works of John Adams, second President of the United States, with a Life of the Author,* Notes and Illustrations by his grandson Charles Francis Adams, (Boston, Little, Brown & Co., 1856), Volume 6, 438.

The Jefferson quote, *"...disarm only those who are neither inclined nor determined..."* adapted from a passage Thomas Jefferson translated and included in his *Legal Commonplace Book,* 1776, originating from Cesare Beccaria's Essay on Crimes and Punishments, published in Italian 1764. The Thomas Jefferson Foundation, Thomas Jefferson Encyclopedia. https://www.monticello.org/site/research-and-collections/laws-forbid-carry-ing-armsspurious-quotation

The Reagan quote, *"...not a sporting weapon or needed for the defense of the home,"* adapted from Reagan response to an audience member's question on gun control at a town hall-type event held on the campus of The University of Southern California on February 12, 1989. USC News Service. Video: https://www.c-span.org/video/?c4462648/user-clip-1989-reagan-condemns-assault-weapons

George H.W. Bush quote, *"This is a human problem..."* from a Mar 10, 1980 letter written by George H.W. Bush to Olga Jonasson, M.D., reprinted in: George H.W. Bush, *All the Best, George Bush* (Simon & Schuster 2014), 291.

On Clinton's warning of the political price of passing gun control legislation: Russell Riley, "Bill Clinton's Costly Assault Weapons Ban," *The Atlantic,* June 25, 2016.

Kennedy quote, *"Sometimes history produces the vindication..."* taken from John F. Kennedy, *Profiles in Courage,* (Harper & Brothers, 1957).

The quote *"...we must have licensing..."* adapted from Lyndon B. Johnson "Remarks Upon Signing the Gun Control Act of 1968," Lyndon B. Johnson, *Public Papers of the Presidents of the United States, Lyndon B. Johnson – 1968-69* (Best Books, 1970).

Chapter Fifty-Five

Ronald Reagan quote, *"I was the Errol Flynn of B movies,"* has been attributed to him many times, including: Jim Denney and Michael Reagan, *"Common Sense of an Uncommon Man"* (Thomas Nelson, publisher, 2014).

The Irish Brigade was a group of Irish immigrants from New York who fought with distinction for the North in the Civil War, (the 88th New York Infantry Brigade) particularly at Gettysburg. Father William Corby was the unit's chaplain. He was an ND graduate and Holy Cross priest who later became ND's president. A statue depicting Fr. Corby blessing the troops before battle stands on the battlefield at Gettysburg, with a duplicate statue on the campus of Notre Dame. I do not believe this brigade is the official reason ND is called the Fighting Irish - but perhaps it should be!

Chapter Fifty-Six

Jefferson quote *"...nature intended me for the tranquil pursuits of science ..."* taken from Thomas Jefferson letter to P. S. Dupont de Nemours, Washington, March 2, 1809. "Sanctum Sanctorum," The Thomas Jefferson Foundation. https://www.monticello.org/thomas-jefferson/a-day-in-the-life-of-jefferson/sanctum-sanctorum/

On Jefferson's interest in paleontology: Thomas O. Jewett, "Thomas Jefferson: Paleontologist," Varsity Tutors. https://www.varsitytutors.com/-earlyamerica/jefferson-primer/thomas-jefferson-paleontologist

For a discussion of how the French tried to impact the election of 1796 in favor of Jefferson: Sarah Pruitt, "That Time a Foreign Government Interfered in a U.S. Presidential Election—in 1796" History Stories, History, March 6, 2017. https://www.history.com/news/that-time-a-foreign-govern-ment-interfered-in-a-u-s-presidential-election-in-1796

Washington quote *"...unwise to implicate ourselves in the ordinary vicissitudes..."* adapted from Washington's Farewell Address, the "nut paragraph". September 17, 1796. Avalon Project, Yale Law School. https://avalon.law.yale.edu/18th_century/washing.asp.

Reagan quote *"...run against the tide of history by denying human free-dom..."* adapted from Ronald Reagan speech to the House of Commons June 8, 1982. William Safire, *"Lend Me Your Ears: Great Speeches In History,"* (W. W. Norton & Company 1992), 863-864.

"Peace through strength" is a common quote of Reagan and many others through the years, including Roman Emperor Hadrian in the first Century AD.

On Teddy Roosevelt walking Eleanor Roosevelt down the aisle, "President Roosevelt Gives the Bride Away," *New York Times,* March 18, 1905. The Eleanor Roosevelt Papers Project. https://www2.gwu.edu/~erpapers/teach-inger/q-and-a/q8-newsarticle.cfmb

Truman quote *"The atom bomb was no great decision..."* adapted from Harry S Truman's response to a questioner in a symposium at Columbia University, April 28, 1959. Reprinted in Harry S Truman, *Truman Speaks,* (Columbia University Press 1960).

Thomas Jefferson quotes: *"... an empire for liberty as she has never sur-veyed since the creation...,"* and *"...make barbarism disappear from the earth,"* adapted from the letter written by Jefferson to Madison on April 27, 1809. Founders Online, National Archives. https://founders.archives.gov/-documents/Jefferson/03-01-02-0140

John Kennedy quote regarding John Winthrop and Percicles adapted from Kennedy's Farewell Speech to Massachusetts. Historic Speeches, John F. Kennedy Presidential Library. https://www.jfklibrary.org/learn/about-jfk/historic-speeches/the-city-upon-a-hill-speech

Ronald Reagan often invoked the vision of America as a "shining city on a hill," notably in his State of the Union speech in 1988 and his Farewell Address in 1989. "Transcript of Reagan's Farewell Address to the American People." *New York Times,* January 12, 1989: https://www.c-span.org/video/?c4746361/shining-city-hill-ronald-reagan-1988-state-union-address.

Monroe quote, *"...the American continents, by the free and independent condition which they had assumed and maintained..."* adapted from James Monroe's Seventh Address to Congress December 2, 1823, traditionally viewed as the source of the Monroe Doctrine. "Monroe Doctrine, December 2, 1823." Avalon Project, Yale Law School. https://avalon.law.yale.edu/18th_century/washing.asp

Teddy Roosevelt quote, *"I took the Isthmus, started the canal, and then left Congress not to debate..."* adapted from a speech given by Teddy Roosevelt in Berkeley, California in 1911. "After a century, the Panama Canal still symbolizes executive power," National Constitution Center, August 15, 2019. https://constitutioncenter.org/blog/after-100-years-the-panama-canal-still-symbolizes-executive-power

Teddy Roosevelt quote: *"...the young giant of a nation..."* adapted from letter from Teddy Roosevelt to John Hay, American Ambassador to the Court of Saint James, London, June 7, 1897.

Woodrow Wilson quote: *"...to make the world safe for democracy..."* adapted from Woodrow Wilson address to Congress on the State of War with Germany, April 2, 1917. "Making the World 'Safe for Democracy': Woodrow Wilson Asks for War," History Matters. http://historymatters.gmu.edu/d/4943/.

Woodrow Wilson quote: *"...the cause of humanity and mankind..."* adapted from Woodrow Wilson speech visiting American gravesites at Suresnes Cemetery, May 30, 1919. Woodrow Wilson, "Memorial Day Address at Suresnes," Library of America. https://loa.org/news-and-views/1524-woodrow-wilson-memorial-day-address-at-suresnes.

Woodrow Wilson quote, *"...determined to teach South American republics to elect good men..."* adapted from Woodrow Wilson quote November, 1913, "Woodrow Wilson," Matthew Yglesias, The Atlantic, January 4, 2007.

Franklin Roosevelt quote, *"...political conditions thousands of miles away could no longer be avoided by this great Nation...,"* adapted from Franklin Roosevelt's address to Congress on the Yalta Conference. March 1, 1945. University of Virginia, The Miller Center. https://millercenter.org/the-pres-

Dan Coonan

idency/presidential-speeches/march-1-1945-address-congress-yalta

Franklin Roosevelt quote, *"...rendezvous with destiny..."* adapted from Franklin Roosevelt's June 27, 1936 Acceptance Speech for the Democratic Nomination in Philadelphia. University of Virginia, The Miller Center. https://millercenter.org/the-presidency/presidential-speeches/june-27-1936-democratic-national-convention.

Dwight Eisenhower quote, *"...must learn how to compose differences not with arms, but with intellect..."* adapted from Dwight Eisenhower farewell address to the nation, January 17, 1961. "Transcript of President Dwight D. Eisenhower's Farewell Address (1961)," https://www.ourdocuments.gov/-doc.php?flash=false&doc=90&page=transcript.

Harry Truman quote, *"...to establish freedom from aggression and from the use of force in the North Atlantic community...,"* taken from: "Address on the occasion of the Signing of the North Atlantic Treaty: August 24, 1949," Truman Library & Museum. https://www.trumanlibraryinstitute.org/this-day-in-history-4/.

Obama quote, *"Our alliance with our NATO partners..."* adapted from "Remarks by President Obama and Chancellor Merkel in Joint Press Conference," White House Archives. https://obamawhitehouse.archives.-gov/the-press-office/2016/11/17/remarks-president-obama-and-chancellor-merkel-germany-joint-press

Obama quote, *"Standing together, shoulder to shoulder, we rebuilt Europe from the ruins of war, prevailed in a long Cold War..."* adapted from: " Obama welcome speech to NATO at the outset of the NATO Summit in Chicago: "Message from President Obama," NATO Review, May 7, 2012. https://www.nato.int/docu/review/articles/2012/05/07/message-from-president-obama/index.html.

Obama quote, *"...guiding this ship of state towards a peaceful resolution..."* crafted from the sentiments expressed by Obama in a speech at American University, August 5, 2015. "Remarks by the President on the Iran Nuclear Deal," Obama White House Archives. https://obamawhitehouse.-

archives.gov/the-press-office/2015/08/05/remarks-president-iran-nuclear-deal.

LBJ quote, *"To begin with, Kennedy should have had more than 18,000 military advisors…"* adapted from LBJ quote given in an interview with writers from the New York Times and The Atlantic: Leo Jangs, "The Last Days of the President—LBJ in Retirement," *The Atlantic*, July 1, 1973.

Kennedy quote, *"…they were the ones who would have to win it, the people of Vietnam themselves, against the communists,"* adapted from a John Kennedy quote in a . "Transcript of CBS Broadcast with Walter Cronkite, 2 September 1963." John F. Kennedy Library. https://www.jfklibrary.org/-asset-viewer/archives/JFKPOF/046/JFKPOF-046-025.

Richard Nixon quote, *"It left the United States so crippled psychologically that it was unable to defend its interests ,,,"* adapted from Nixon' words appearing in his book: Richard Nixon, *No More Viet Nams,*(Simon & Schuster 1985).

Nixon quote, *"…Neither of these two great nations wanted to dominate…"* adapted from Nixon statements in a discussion with Chairman Mao and Henry Kissinger: "Mao Zedong meets Richard Nixon, February 21, 1972," USC US-China Institute, USC Annenberg School. https://china.usc.edu/mao-zedong-meets-richard-nixon-february-21-1972.

Nixon quote, *"The only time in the history of the world that we have had any extended periods of peace is when there has been balance of power…"* adapted from Nixon quote appearing in January 3, 1972 issue of Time Magazine, which awarded him Man of the Year. "Man of the Year: Nixon Determined to Make a Difference," *Time,* January 3, 1972.

On trust developed between Reagan and Gorbachev through four meetings and 40 letters: Jason Saltoun-Ebin, "Recently Released Letters Between Reagan and Gorbachev Shed Light on the End of the Cold War," *Huffington Post,* February 27, 2013.

Chapter Fifty-Seven

For background on McCain and the Up the Creek Bistro Wine Bar: Alice Li, "At McCain's favorite restaurant, the owner plays one last farewell song," *Washington Post,* August 29, 2018; Alden Woods, "On a quiet creek in a peaceful valley, John McCain made Cornville, Arizona, home," *Arizona Republic,* August 26, 2018; Tamar Lapin, "This sleepy Arizona refuge was McCain's Camelot," *New York Post,* August 26, 2018.

Chapter Fifty-Eight

Senator McConnell's quote "I'm not going to bring this up for debate..." crafted from: Leah Ann Caldwell, "McConnell won't commit to Senate debate on guns," *NBC News,* March 1, 2018. https://www.nbcnews.com/politics/congress/mcconnell-won-t-commit-senate-debate-guns-n852511

Senator John Thune quote *". . . don't know why we'd need to have that vote again . . ."* adapted from his statements reported in: Alexander Bolton, "Republicans waiting out Trump on gun control," *The Hill,* March 4, 2018.

Senator Marco Rubio quotes adapted from statements he made to students who survived the Parkland, Florida shooting, at a Town Hall on gun rights February 21, 2018 which was televised live on CNN. Transcript: "Stoneman students' questions to lawmakers and the NRA at the CNN town hall," CNN, February 22, 2018.

Senator Mitch Rudnik is a purely fictional character.

Chapter Sixty-Two

Teddy Roosevelt's quote, *"...we must drive the special interests out of politics."* adapted from Teddy Roosevelt's "New Nationalism" speech in Oswatamie, Kansas, August 31, 1910. "Theodore Roosevelt's Osawatomie Speech," Kansas Historical Society. https://www.kshs.org/p/kansas-historical-quarterly-theodore-roosevelt-s-osawatomie-speech/13176.

Presidential Spirits

Teddy Roosevelt's quote, *"To dissolve the unholy alliance between corrupt business…"* adapted from Teddy Roosevelt speech August 1912, reprinted in Theodore Roosevelt, *Theodore Roosevelt, an Autobiography,* (Charles Scribner's Sons, 1913). This language was also included in Roosevelt's Progressive Party Platform in 1912, and similar language was used in many of his campaign speeches.

Eisenhower quote about "rightists" and "leftists" adapted from quote appearing in Dwight D. Eisenhower, "Ike Takes a Look at the GOP," *Saturday Evening Post,* April 21, 1962, 19.

James Madison quote referencing David Hume taken from: David Hume, *Political Writings,* ed. Stuart D. Warner, (Indianapolis: Hackett, 1994), 58.

Thomas Jefferson's quote, *"If I could not go to Heaven but with a party…,"* adapted from: "From Thomas Jefferson to Francis Hopkinson, 13 March 1789," Founders Online. National Archives. https://founders.archives.gov/documents/Jefferson/01-14-02-0402.

Most founders feared what would happen if "factions" developed and they hoped there would be no political parties: *Thomas Jefferson, an Intimate History,* Fawn M. Brodie, (W. W. Norton & Company, 1974), 260.

On Hume being Madison's favorite philosopher: John Avlon, *Washington's Farewell: The Founding Father's Warning to Future Generations,* (New York: Simon & Schuster 2017), 114.

John Tyler's thought on how running as an independent would only throw the election away from Polk and in favor of Henry Clay, and on working for a larger goal—annexation of Texas: David Rubel, *Mr. President: The Human Side of America's Chief Executives,* (Agincourt Press, 1998), 65.

LBJ quote, *"There's nothing in the middle of the road,,,"* taken from a quote appearing in: Jim Hightower, *There's Nothing in the Middle of the Road but Yellow Lines and Dead Armadillos: a Work of Political Subversion,* (Harper Collins, 1997). This was a comment Hightower had heard from an unnamed farmer and former Texas Agricultural Commissioner.

Chapter Sixty-Three

On Tyler's preference for champagne: Mark Will-Weber, *Mint Juleps with Teddy Roosevelt: The Complete History of Presidential Drinking,* (Washington D.C.: Regnery Publishing 2014), 82.

On Herbert Hoover being a member of the Bohemian Grove and belonging to the "Cave Man" camp: Aine Cain, "A shadowy and controversial secret club meets in the California woods every year—and at least 5 US presidents were members," *Business Insider,* March 11, 2018.

Teddy Roosevelt quote, *"...a soft, easy life is not worth living..."* adapted from a speech given by Teddy Roosevelt on October 5, 1898 at the opening of his gubernatorial campaign. Drake Baer, "Teddy Roosevelt Quotes on Courage, Leadership and Success," *Patriot Ledger,* February 14, 2016.

Chapter Sixty-Eight

Grover Cleveland quote on Statue of Liberty adapted from a speech he gave on May 11, 1886: *"May 11, 1886 Message on the Statue of Liberty,"* University of Virginia, Miller Center, Presidential Speeches, Grover Cleveland Presidency.

Reagan quote on the Statue of Liberty crafted largely from a speech he gave on Governor's Island at the lighting of the torch following restoration of the statue. "Remarks on the Lighting of the Torch of the Statue of Liberty in New York, New York," Ronald Reagan Presidential Library, July 3, 1986. https://www.reaganlibrary.gov/research/speeches/70386e

Thomas Jefferson quote, *"the God who gave us life..."* adapted from Jefferson quote appearing in Jefferson's book: Thomas Jefferson, *Notes on the State of Virginia*, Published by John Stockdale, 1785, Query XVII.

Teddy Roosevelt quote, *"...in the arena..."* crafted largely from Roosevelt's speech delivered at The Sorbonne, in Paris, France, April 23, 1910. "The Man in the Arena," Theodore Roosevelt Center, Dickinson State University. https://www.theodorerooseveltcenter.org/Blog/Item/The%20Man%20in%2 0the%20Arena

Some of the background on Whitney Houston delivering the National Anthem at the Super Bowl in 1991 following the commencement of Operation Desert Storm.: Daniel Smith, "When Whitney Hit the High Note," *ESPN The Magazine,* February 1, 2016.

Chapter Sixty-Nine

The popular impression that Babe Ruth was sold by Red Sox owner Harry Frazee to the Yankees to enable him to finance the Broadway show No, No Nannette is apparently myth. George Vecsey, *"A Myth That Should Not Be Perpetuated,"* New York Times, September 24, 2004.

Churchill uttered his *"democracy is the worst form of government..."* line in a speech to the House of Commons on November 11, 1947, and this quote is widely attributed to him. However, at the time he said these words Churchill stated that others had said this before him - this according to Churchill scholar, writer and historian Richard M. Langworth Senior Fellow, Hillsdale College Churchill Project. Winston Churchill and Richard M. Langworth (editor), *Churchill By Himself* (Rosetta Books, 2013).

Jefferson quote, *"the favorite passion of my soul..."* based on quotes of Jefferson, including: "Jefferson and Music." Thomas Jefferson, Montecello.org. https://www.monticello.org/thomas-jefferson/a-day-in-the-life-of-jefferson/a-delightful-recreation/jefferson-and-music/

On Jefferson's tremendous respect and admiration for Benjamin Franklin among all those Americans in the Revolutionary era: Joseph J. Ellis, *American Sphinx, The Character of Thomas Jefferson* (New York: Vintage Books, 1998), 91.

Chapter-Seventy

On the debate between James Madison and George Mason regarding the president's pardon power in the proposed Constitution: D W Buffa, "The pardon power and original intent," Brookings, July 25, 2018.

ACKNOWLEDGEMENTS

For over thirty years I've kept a folder of notes outlining potential plotlines for that novel I was going to write someday. Thirty years. My desire to do it was real, but I always convinced myself I didn't have the time to pull it off. The folder sat there year after year oozing potential but collecting dust. Then one day in August of '17 I finally sat down and started to write. I didn't choose one of the many in that folder. This one just kind of poured out of me. I got some great advice to write the novel that I would most like to read. This is it.

There are so many people to thank. That has to begin with my parents. They are both educators at heart and are the children of great educators. What a gift for us to be raised in that environment. With my Dad's lifetime of read-ing about history he surely has the equivalent of several doctoral degrees. And I'm certain my mom, the former English teacher, is correcting my grammar as she reads this—and Lord knows she's terribly disappointed in my use of a few "inappropriate" words. She's from Springfield, Illinois, so I learned all about Lincoln from her at a very early age. I hope I did your guy justice here, Mom.

Paul Giannini was a gem of a grade school teacher and principal at St. Anthony's in El Segundo. His unique approach to teaching Creative Writing with my 6th grade class made me want to be a writer. I am so appreciative of that, and I love that I had a chance to tell him that and thank him when I saw him last year.

I learned U.S. Government from the very best possible instructors in Ron Harris at St. Bernard High in Playa del Rey and Peri Arnold, Ph.D at Notre

Dame. Both of them were born to do what they did for generations of students fortunate enough to have them.

I have to thank two phenomenal authors who happen to be friends of mine: Julie Finigan Morris (*Exit Strategy*), who provided the spark for me to actually attempt to write this and continued to counsel and inspire me the whole way; and Julie Clark (*The Ones We Choose, The Last Flight*), who advised me to "treat this project like a job - and show up at your job!"

I need to thank all the first readers for taking the time to complete this and provide meaningful feedback, beginning with Brendan Owen and Kevin Appleby, with whom I visited many presidential libraries and a few Civil War battlefields through the years. Thanks also to Tom Preston, Mary Alice Whalen, Jim Pinkelman, Kathy Kale, Jim Garza, my brother Dennis, my best man, John Elliott, and Dr. Peri Arnold at Notre Dame.

I need to thank Constitutional Law scholar and University of Illinois Law Dean Vikram Amar for his expertise, particularly with respect to the electoral college and the complicated election scenario presented here. Additionally, my brother Terry lent a bit of expertise regarding American military history.

I want to thank Goose River for taking this on, James Slate for a cover design I love, and Jennifer Huston for being much more a partner on this than an editor.

As a guy who clearly loves a saloon as much as anyone, the great irony of this book is that writing about a saloon caused me to stop drinking. With this project I didn't have time! Unlike many of these gentlemen I've written about, I find I just can't be productive after a few pops (Some may say I'm not so much even before a few...), and I needed to be efficient and productive with my time. That enormous time commitment brings me to the final thank you—to my wife, Donna, who sacrificed so many nights while I sat on the couch writing away. She was a great sounding board on so much of this. When she first read a few chapters and felt the protagonist mildly resembled me (I cannot quite imagine how she came to that conclusion), she said to me, "All I can say is that guy better well love his wife!" He does.

More than she could ever know.

In the end I wanted this to be both a love letter to America as well as a wake-up call. I know it qualifies as the former. If it can play even the tiniest role as the latter as well, I'll be thrilled.

Thanks for spending a little time in the saloon. Hope you enjoyed it nearly as much as I did.

Cheers!

ABOUT THE AUTHOR

In addition to being a history lover and political junkie, Dan Coonan has been a leader within the field of intercollegiate athletics for twenty years. He presently runs The Eastern College Athletic Conference (ECAC). He has also practiced law, co-managed a congressional campaign, and served as Chairman of the Board of LifeMoves, the largest homeless shelter network in the San Francisco Bay Area. He resides in Connecticut with his wife and three children.

DanCoonanAuthor.com

Facebook @DanCoonanAuthor

CPSIA information can be obtained
at www.ICGtesting.com
Printed in the USA
LVHW090737190520
655735LV00008B/53